A People's History of SFO

The publisher and the University of California Press
Foundation gratefully acknowledge the generous support
of the Peter Booth Wiley Endowment Fund in History.

A People's History of SFO

*The Making of the Bay Area and
an Airport*

Eric Porter

UNIVERSITY OF CALIFORNIA PRESS

University of California Press
Oakland, California

© 2023 by Eric Porter

This project was supported in part by funding from the
University of California Presidential Faculty Research
Fellowships in the Humanities, MR15328710.

This research was also supported by Faculty Research
Grants awarded by the Committee on Research from the
University of California, Santa Cruz.

An earlier version of chapter 4 was published as
"A Black Future in the Air Industry? Liberation and
Complicity at San Francisco International Airport,"
California History 97, no. 2 (Summer 2020): 88–111.

First Paperback Printing 2024

Library of Congress Cataloging-in-Publication Data

Names: Porter, Eric (Eric C.), author.
Title: A people's history of SFO : the making of the Bay
    Area and an airport / Eric Porter.
Description: Oakland, California : University of
    California Press, [2023] | Includes bibliographical
references and index.
Identifiers: LCCN 2022012703 (print) | LCCN 2022012704
    (ebook) | ISBN 9780520380035 (hardback) |
    9780520402331 (paperback) | 9780520977075
    (ebook)

Subjects: LCSH: San Francisco International Airport
    (Calif.)—History. | San Francisco Bay Area (Calif.)
Classification: LCC HE9797.5.U52 S267 2023 (print) |
    LCC HE9797.5.U52 (ebook) | DDC 387.7/36097946—
    dc23/eng/20220609
LC record available at https://lccn.loc.gov/2022012703
LC ebook record available at https://lccn.loc
    .gov/2022012704

Manufactured in the United States of America

32 31 30 29 28 27 26 25 24
10 9 8 7 6 5 4 3 2 1

Dedicated to the memory of Scipio Porter Jr.,
Mary Ruffin, Arlene Jackson, and John Sherry

Contents

Introduction

Three Views of SFO

If you have ever flown into San Francisco International Airport (SFO) on a clear night—the often-foggy ones provide a different experience—you were likely confronted by a spectacular, perhaps disorienting tapestry of lights as you approached the Bay Area or banked over it. With sufficient knowledge of the region and the right vector of approach and seat assignment, those lights may have offered up to you a metropolitan map drawn by illuminated landmarks: bridges, freeways, ports, oil refineries, airports, and urban downtowns, as well as less easily identifiable suburban enclaves sprawling across flatlands, dotting hills, and snaking into canyons. The picture may have been completed by the black space of the Pacific Ocean and San Francisco Bay waters and of the various open lands not yet or perhaps never to be electrified.

The networks of lights perhaps said something to you about power: a subject you may already have considered in flight in relation to your seat assignment and the skin color, dress, words, or seatback video viewing choices of fellow travelers. Indeed, gazing down at the ground from aircraft has long opened up a perspective on power, albeit often in ways that serve it. Almost from the beginning, as scholars such as Chandra Bhimull and Jenifer Van Vleck make clear, aviation attended the projects of colonialism and empire across the globe by accelerating access to and mapping of territories and markets yet to be exploited while simultaneously producing vertical and hierarchical distance

FIGURE I. Night shot of the Bay Area, looking west from the East Bay toward San Francisco. The lights of, among other things, the Port of Oakland, the Bay and Golden Gate Bridges, Treasure Island, and downtown and residential San Francisco are prominently distributed across "the cloth of black velvet" of San Francisco Bay and the Pacific Ocean. iStock.com/Gfed.

between those who engineered, controlled, and accessed flight and those (often the racially exploited and the colonized) who did not.[1]

There is, in fact, a thread of boosterism that has used the view on approach to SFO to illuminate and celebrate the metropolitan growth that followed conquest, settlement, environmental transformation, and urban development (in other words, settler colonialism) in the Bay Area as well as the region's expanding, imperial reach. Take Bay Area Reuters correspondent William Flynn's *Men, Money and Mud,* a 1954 booklet published as part of the celebration of SFO's new international terminal. A passenger flying into a recently modernized SFO at night, Flynn effuses, perceives it as a collection of gems. "The sheath of shimmering platinum against the cloth of black velvet is the hundreds of acres of land that has risen from the mud and muck of the Bay to be formed into the firm foundation of your destination, San Francisco International Airport. The rubies are the runway lights, the flickering signals on the buildings that sprawl over the western edge of the vast expanse of land." These precious lights help to illuminate SFO's status as a "metropolitan concentration of industry, of travel, of service" that connects the larger metropolitan Bay Area to Southern California, cities across the nation, Europe, and the "continents of the great Pacific Basin, already identified as the arena where will develop the next Era of Man."[2]

Flynn's account of SFO's development from muddy landing field to major international airport over the course of just three decades centers the heroic individualism of white men, assumes a hubristic certainty about the region's progress, and revels in a triumph over nature. The realization of SFO is, in his view, the product of the expansive vision, rational planning, technical know-how, and political persuasion of an evolving cast of engineers, municipal officials, airline executives and other businessmen, military officers, pilots, and, ultimately, a citizenry that over time developed the good sense to follow the lead of these men and lend their financial support to the airport by means of bond measures.

This is all a little hard to take in the political and analytical present. But the account from above in *Men, Money and Mud* still raises the question of how a differently oriented story of colonialism and empire, and how Bay Area residents supported, survived, and otherwise lived it, might be told with SFO at its illuminated and illuminating center. What happens when we let those lights seen on approach help us analyze critically rather than celebrate things like the proliferation of business parks fertilized with technology and finance capital, the relative proximity of neighborhoods to industrial sites, the amount of earth moved and the number of rivers dammed to light up this largely hydroelectrically powered region? What do we learn from tracing brightly lit networks of roadways, railways, transmission lines, and concentrations of commercial development? And what do we perceive in their arrangement across a "cloth of black velvet"?

A People's History of SFO takes up this challenge by using the history of the airport to tell a multifaceted story of power, development, and encounter in what is now a nine-county region with one hundred cities located on the left coast of North America, at the eastern edge of the Pacific Rim, around the large, shallow estuary of San Francisco Bay.[3] Situated about a dozen miles south of downtown San Francisco upon former tidelands and open bay water in San Mateo County, SFO was, for many years, the Bay Area's only international airport and is still its largest. As such, SFO is a manifestation of and has helped to shape multiple instantiations of accumulated and protean power in the region, conjunctures that I will often refer to as the Bay Area's colonial present or its regional colonial present.[4]

Built upon land and lifeways dispossessed from Indigenous peoples who had been in the area for millennia before being subjugated, expelled, or killed, what became the Bay Area was next defined by its development as a settler society of Spanish and US empire with a brief stint as a hinterland of the Mexican republic in between. Within just a few decades of California statehood, as Gray Brechin and others have shown, San Francisco and, eventually, the Bay Area as a region, had established imperial relationships with other places in California, the United States, and the world beyond, while operating as a key node of US empire as a continental and global project. The Bay Area became, among other things, a financial and planning center for various extractive, agricultural, industrial, and technological enterprises; a locus of military development in times of war and peace; and a site of state- and capital-serving knowledge production.[5] What the Bay Area's colonial present looked like at any given moment was a product of the accumulated effects of colonial and imperial relationships of the past as they were extended into the present and imagined into the future. From the beginning, these relationships were shaped by the waves of human beings who conquered, occupied, settled, survived, were brought to, traveled through, worked in, sought opportunity in, found refuge in, and otherwise lived and died in the area.

Like other major airports, as scholars like Mark Salter, Gillian Fuller, and Ross Harley describe them, SFO has operated as a kind of assemblage. It is a complexly networked infrastructure whose operations have drawn together and been constituted by the interactions among various groups of humans (e.g., travelers, workers, and government officials); municipal, state, and federal laws and regulations; economic flows of different scales; built urban, suburban, and exurban environments; and natural phenomena such as the wind patterns that determine the orientation of runways.[6] Not only have such actants made the airport an assemblage; SFO has, as an assemblage, drawn together and facilitated interactions among an even wider range of assemblages within the Bay Area and beyond. A focus on SFO, then, provides a particularly useful lens for viewing the shifting, often-unexpected entanglements and interfaces of multiple systems, relations, and structures—at once locally focused and, given the nature of air commerce, far reaching—that have shaped the Bay Area in the twentieth and twenty-first centuries.

SFO has also been a symbolic point of regional reference. Some observers have viewed it as an engine of economic growth and metropolitan ascendancy, and more generally as a site representing progress, cosmopolitanism, and freedom. But SFO has also been seen as a manifestation of inequality, poor planning, and ecological catastrophe.[7]

Attending to conversations about SFO first brings into focus how political and business elites envisioned the Bay Area. Tracing these conversations over time also shows how people across the social spectrum viewed their region (and its constituent cities and neighborhoods). Collective understandings of the Bay Area as Anglo-Saxon imperial outpost, center of commerce, immigrant and queer sanctuary, environmentally friendly utopia, refuge from the Jim Crow South, and cosmopolitan technology hub, among other things, are all evident in commentary about SFO.

A People's History of SFO thus offers a new perspective on how the Bay Area, through its emergence and expansion as a metropolis, has been made in both material and symbolic ways, at the interface of small human acts and political activity as shaped by and responsive to overlapping, constantly evolving networks of colonial and imperial power.[8] Such networks are instantiations of a broader history of racial capitalism, as conceptualized by political theorist Cedric Robinson: that is, the global economic and political system predicated on and productive of hierarchical notions of racial and, by definition, gendered human difference that emerged in early modern Europe as a mechanism for reproducing wealth and the social groups that create it.[9] Over time, racial capitalism's manifestations in various colonial and imperial enterprises, state-building projects, financial transactions, and so on have led to an ever-growing proliferation of human differences and asymmetrical social relationships particular to time and place while significantly altering nature along the way.[10] Although some of the most horrific manifestations of racial capitalism and its constituent regimes have been consigned to the past, we continue to live through their afterlives as well as through related, emergent formations that produce and destroy life for individuals and groups.[11] We do this as their victims, as their beneficiaries, as the people who try to fix the problems caused by them, and sometimes as all three at the same time.

A People's History of SFO, then, proceeds from the assumption that telling the story of the airport as infrastructural manifestation of accumulated power from the past and as nodal point in the production of new forms of it in the present opens up a window to some of this complexity that has defined the Bay Area and the lives lived there. As they have manifested within and around SFO, the interactions examined across this book shed light on some of the ways differently positioned Bay Area people have invested in, defied, remained ambivalent about, but ultimately been incorporated into the networked power that has defined the region. But this is also a study that exceeds both region and

FIGURE 2. Jet ascending over SFO's current (as of late 2021) cell phone waiting lot. Located to the north of the previous cell phone lot, and farther from the end of runway 28, this one does not quite provide the sonic experience of its predecessor. But it is still a good place to watch jets fly into the sunset. Photo by author.

airport, even as it uses them as focal points, by offering a more broadly relevant account of colonialism's and empire's legacies, emergences, and futures as lived within its North American, metropolitan laboratories. While acknowledging and contending to some degree with some of the most brutal, exclusionary, and targeted manifestations of these phenomena as brought to bear on the most vulnerable residents of the region—Indigenous dispossession, racial discrimination in employment, and exclusionary and punitive immigration policies, for example—it considers as well how they have been prosaically lived by a wide range of people connected with one another, with institutions and infrastructures, with social organizations and movements, and so on in often-contingent, unexpected ways.[12]

So, with that in mind, I will suggest that another productive visual (and aural) perspective could be found at SFO's old cell phone waiting lot, located at the northwestern edge of the airport, not far beyond the end of runway 28, underneath the flight paths of ascending jets. Dusk here was often stunning, with illuminated aircraft flying into the orange glow over the hills to the west. One could be awed by the still-marvelous technology, by the idea that a half-million-pound metal tube full of jet fuel, people, and their stuff can propel itself into the lower stratosphere and back. But the encounter could be unnerving, too. The sonic vibrations from ascending larger jets were sometimes felt in the chest; their jet wash perceptibly shook the waiting automobiles. As the jets wounded the earth and sky with noise and vaporized kerosene, they reminded us, if we let them, that we humans are immensely creative, destructive, and fragile.

The multisensory spectacle of the noisy, ascending jets is an apt metaphor for this book's approach to ongoing projects of domination, displacement, and production in the San Francisco Bay Area. As they help to connect the Bay Area—socially, financially, imaginatively—with other regions, these jets leave behind a kind of wake: trailing vortices formed by air flowing from the bottom of the wings, around the wing tips, to the tops of the wings. These rotating vortices are invisible but still powerful as they dissipate slowly, falling to earth or remaining airborne, moving horizontally or not by the wind to the extent that it is blowing. Vortices from larger aircraft, known as wake turbulence, can knock smaller ones out of the sky and must be avoided.

The swirling, falling, shifting, decaying vortices are like the afterlives of key events in the colonial and imperial history of the Bay Area: structuring the production of difference and the political and social possibilities that follow, always unstable, contingent and unpredictable in their movement, often not apparent to those without insights into their existence, but with the potential to disrupt, terribly. And then more jets ascend, avoiding the turbulence from other jets by delaying takeoff, becoming airborne closer to or farther from the runway end, or executing their turns toward eventual flight paths at different coordinates, but leaving their own wakes nonetheless: different trajectories of ascent, different sonic vibrations, different trailing vortices, different instabilities, different contingencies, different possibilities layered across regional colonial presents.[13]

There is one more view to consider: that from inside SFO's concourses. Some observers emphasize the homogeneity of airport terminal spaces across the globe, at least once you get past the locally oriented design elements, views of surrounding landscapes, and nods to regional culture in the restaurants and gift shops. Airport spaces have been described as alienating "non-places," to use the anthropologist Marc Augé's well-known description, that are products of the growing circulation of people, information, architectural styles, and so on in a

FIGURE 3. SFO's International Terminal departure hall, late 2021, at a moment of reduced, pandemic-era concourse. James Carpenter's installation *Four Sculptural Light Reflectors* helps to throw light and shadow across the space. Photo by author.

globalizing world.[14] But contrary to some writing about airports, *A People's History of SFO* proceeds from the position that airport terminals and other buildings can still tell us much about the places where they are situated and the populations that they serve. The concourse space is after all the site where locally specific concourses (i.e., gatherings, per another definition of the term) of multiple human actors engage in concourse (i.e., cooperative or combined actions, per yet another definition) with one another and with nonhuman things.[15]

Indeed, complex stories of regional race, gender, class, and citizenship dynamics have unfolded inside metropolitan airport terminals that have served as transportation hubs, ports of entry, dining destinations, and, more recently, high-end shopping malls and museums. Once the province of elite travelers, airports used to sort people largely by who flew and who did not. Now they do so by the paid work people do there, the scrutiny paid to them at the security gates, the passports they hold and the questions asked of them at customs, where they shop and eat, their access or not to airline lounges, and whom they queue up before and after as they board their flights.[16] I can recall vividly some of the lessons about local social dynamics offered by the scene of service work at airports. The proliferation of white people working the fast-food counters at Sea-Tac in the early 1990s brought home the fact of that working class's declining fortunes in the region. A decade later a white woman purposefully tossing trash at the feet of a veiled, Somali custodial worker at Phoenix Sky Harbor suggested the rising Islamophobia, the changing face of anti-Blackness, and the challenges facing East African immigrants in the region after 9/11.

But I had already learned similar lessons from my own family's history. I actually do come from a line of porters in the occupational sense. The family surname preceded the occupation, set in motion, as it was, by a Mississippi slave owner bestowing his name on his human property, including my great-great-grandmother and her young daughter. "Porter" was later passed along through a generation of matrilineal naming because interracial marriages were illegal and quite possibly fatal in East Texas in the late nineteenth century. But in 1942, a product of such an unsanctioned union, my grandfather, then living in Shreveport, Louisiana, found employment as a porter (or skycap, as the job would later be called) at San Francisco's airport. This event initiated the Black side of my family's participation in what is known as the Second Great Migration from the southern United States to points north and west. Carrying white people's luggage into and out of the terminal was servile but good-paying work, and my grandfather used it to secure geographic and social mobility for himself and his family, who joined him in the Bay Area the following year. My father earned extra cash working summers and weekends as a skycap at SFO during the 1950s, before graduating from college and embarking on a career in social work, civil rights activism, and eventually law.

In other words, exclusions and complicities, resonant with past events, proliferate in and around airport concourses (and terminals more generally), including SFO's. The concourse is, after all, the scene of the whirling dance of contingent encounters where human actions and networks are brought together *in medias res* in ways that simultaneously define and transcend that regionally specific space. It is also where we observe one another engaged in such encounters, under and exceeding the surveilling eye of the state. The concourse is simultaneously exhilarating and terrifying, spectacular and banal, a site of movement and stasis, of aspiration and ennui.[17] The view from it, then, suggests that we avoid thinking through Bay Area power and struggles against it (as well as those beyond the region) in simple terms; we might instead approach regional colonial presents as scenes of asymmetrical and often contradictory connection.

. . .

A People's History of SFO offers a series of chapters that trace the development of SFO as a nexus of networked power while examining important airport-related phenomena that have shaped the Bay Area. The book first shows how relationships among widening arrays of people transformed the salt marsh, mud flats, and open water in northern San Mateo County upon which the airport was eventually built, all the while establishing some of the future facility's economic, social, and political foundations. As a kind of prehistory of the facility, then, chapter 1 begins by describing the relationships established on and near this site by its original Ramaytush Ohlone stewards and then moves on to account for some of those orchestrated by the various settlers who lived and labored there under Spanish, Mexican, and then United States control.

As it describes some of the ways the airport became an assemblage itself, the book next examines how SFO reflected and produced emergent, multifaceted, and asymmetrical relationships across different spheres of human activity within changing colonial presents. Chapters 2 and 3 examine the development of the airport itself, from its opening as Mills Field in 1927 through its official designation as San Francisco International Airport in 1954. Chapter 2 takes the story through World War II. It emphasizes how the establishment and early growth of San Francisco's airport were in significant part products of early commercial aviation's ties to militarism, airport officials' and boosters' dreams of economic expansion and regional imperial destiny, and US government subsidy. In other words, it shows how the airport during its formative years was part and parcel of the racial capitalist restructuring of the Bay Area and the revamping of its modern settler state formations. Focusing on a multiday festival held in 1954 to celebrate the airport's new terminal and "international" status, chapter 3 continues the story laid out in chapter 2 while addressing how SFO was, by the 1950s, in more dramatic ways than before, an assemblage that connected multiple actors—albeit in exclusionary ways—across the region and beyond.

The following three chapters shift the focus away from infrastructural developments—although those remain part of the story—in order to address how members of increasingly visible and vocal Bay Area constituencies engaged with the airport as workers, businesspeople, neighbors, and travelers. All three chapters center airport-focused protests, as they offer perspectives on how struggles for dignity, rights, comfort, safety, and remuneration in the Bay Area have often been fraught, contradictory affairs. As they address the kinds of political struggles that often figure prominently in histories of the region, these chapters contend with some of the ways that liberal and even progressive efforts to gain access to and justice in a region known for its hospitality and cosmopolitanism could reproduce the inequalities and exclusions of the colonial present in complicated ways.

Chapter 4 examines Black labor and antidiscrimination activism at SFO from the late 1950s into the 1980s. It shows how Black work, business, and struggles to make them better at SFO were complex, entangled processes of liberation and complicity. These struggles were representative of how broader efforts to overcome Black social and spatial confinement in the Bay Area were uneven, incomplete, and, when successful, often only temporarily so. Chapter 5 addresses efforts by primarily white neighborhood and environmental activists (many of them women) to mitigate jet noise at and around SFO during the same period. By tracing their struggles, as well as the actions and words of those who lined up to oppose them, the chapter illustrates some of the ways that power in the region was challenged and reproduced at the nexus of environmental activism and governmental infrastructure development and resource stewardship. Chapter 6 explores how airport-focused activism around immigration from the late 1970s to the present often upheld the Bay Area as an enlightened social and political space. Yet such efforts—ranging from protests against the banning of "homosexual" travelers from entering the United States to those against President Donald J. Trump's 2017 "Muslim ban"—included their own elements of exclusion and subordination, whether intentional or not.

Chapter 7 returns to SFO's infrastructure by examining the development of its public art and museum programs from the late 1970s through the opening of the new International Terminal in 2000. The chapter attends to some of the ways SFO's cultural works have articulated important critiques of persistent, asymmetrical social relationships in the Bay Area while contributing to a multicultural display that, as situated at the airport, smooths over some of the inequalities and exclusions defining the Bay Area in the twenty-first century. Finally, chapter 8 examines SFO's sustainability programs and nascent efforts to address rising sea levels. Like other local entities, SFO has incorporated elements of progressive environmental and social struggles into its operations over the past few decades. But such efforts to develop a putatively more equitable ecology of humans and things in and around the airport speak just as loudly of the limits of such moves. Although I try to end on a hopeful note, I also suggest that the future of accumulated, protean regional colonial presents may well be the spread of human hardship and the reclamation of the former salt marsh, mud flats, and open water upon which SFO sits by a rising San Francisco Bay.

CHAPTER I

Out of the Mud

SFO's own histories often begin with the mud upon which the airport was built. While perhaps unexpected, given the verticality of flight, attention to the ground makes sense for practical and political reasons. The airport, after all, opened in 1927 as Mills Field on reclaimed bayside salt marsh that was leased and eventually purchased from the descendants of wealthy California banker Darius Ogden Mills. Its subsequent expansions involved dumping huge amounts of dry earth onto a muddy expanse of San Francisco Bay tidelands and the adjacent estuary floor. Descriptions of the airport's rise from its earthly origins—as well as from early follies, including aviator Charles Lindbergh getting his airplane stuck in the muddy airfield two years after its opening—buttress the boosterish orientation of such histories. Such evolutionary narratives also appear designed to prevent the names of city and airport officials from becoming, or at least remaining, mud in the court of public opinion given the immense public expenditures necessary to grow and maintain a not-always-appreciated facility that served some constituencies better than others.

This approach is evident in William Flynn's aforementioned 1954 booklet *Men, Money and Mud,* with its account of SFO's development as an outgrowth of, as then San Francisco mayor Elmer Robinson put it in his prefatory remarks, "the conquest of the deficiency of Nature's handiwork."[1] Flynn describes, with great ideological flourish, the engineering and political triumphs required for the airport's transformation over a few decades from simple, muddy landing field to major international airport. But even the measured 2000 publication *SFO: A Pictorial History*, by SFO Museum curator John Hill, foregrounds flight attendant Irene Simon's description of the early airport as "a mud hole." It then dutifully describes a series of sound governmental actions, technological developments, and engineering feats that defined the history of "one of the Bay Area's most valuable and visible resources."[2]

Following the lead of SFO's own histories, this one also begins with the mud. Rather than starting in the 1920s, however, with contemporaneous people and their institutions acting upon a rather inert, albeit difficult-to-work, substance, it digs deeper to explore a history that was already embedded in a more dynamic and dispersed mud by the time construction began on the original airport. Indeed, by 1927 the future SFO site (and the Bay Area more generally) had already been shaped by millennia of Indigenous practices of land stewardship and the changes brought by a succession of colonizing powers. Over the course of these collisions, the Bay Area moved from the peripheries of Spain, Mexico, and eventually the United States—all the while being defined by centers and peripheries of its own—to become an integral core of a settler colonial, continental empire and a tentacular US empire stretching far overseas. Relationships with and upon this land constituted a shifting array of assemblages that were defined by residual and emergent projects of social differentiation that racial capitalism, more foundationally, had always depended upon for its existence.

By presenting a necessarily incomplete but hopefully illuminating account of interactions upon, near, and in relation to the salt marsh, mudflats, and open water upon which SFO was eventually built, this chapter sets the stage for subsequent discussions that focus on the airport as built upon its environs. Contending with this prehistory of the airport, so to speak, helps us understand how the resonances of earlier asymmetrical and sometimes devasting encounters among people and the land persisted in the twentieth- and twenty-first-century political-economic, social, environmental, and imaginative entanglements that made SFO and the Bay Area as metropolis more generally.

. . .

The human-made dry land on which the airport currently sits forms a small peninsula on the western side of San Francisco Bay, adjacent to the present-day San Mateo County cities of, moving from north to south, South San Francisco, San Bruno, and Millbrae. At various times in the past this land has been dry of nature's own accord. Fifteen to twenty thousand years ago, at the peak of the last Pleistocene ice age, much of what is now San Francisco Bay was a wide, flat valley defined by a major river flowing from the northeast and draining California's interior valley as it was joined by a smaller river bringing water from hills and valleys to the south. The conjoined rivers met the ocean around thirty miles west of the current Golden Gate. What we now know as San Francisco Bay was largely formed around five thousand years ago, after melting glaciers and ice sheets eventually caused a sea-level rise that inundated the river valley.[3]

For millennia, Ramaytush Ohlone people organized themselves into communities on what is now known as San Francisco and the San Francisco Peninsula.[4] The precapitalist Indigenous economy benefited from a geographically specific "wealth of nature." Guided by an ethos of respectful coexistence with other living things, local people drew sustenance from the bay and its tidelands: focal points, as they were, of solar energy, atmospheric elements, nutrients carried into the bay by rivers and streams, and carbon fixed by bulrushes and other vegetation. They harvested wild plants and cultivated others; hunted waterfowl, shorebirds, and sea mammals; fished and gathered shellfish; and built evaporating ponds to collect salt. Farther from shore they burned brush to create beneficial habitats for edible flora and fauna and for medicinal plants.[5] In other words, Indigenous inhabitants of the Peninsula were shaped by their environment, at the most fundamental level of their existence, even as they managed it and drew it into the complex assemblages of material, social, and spiritual relations that defined their world.

When Spaniard Gaspar de Portolá's expedition arrived in the region in 1769, the Ramaytush Ohlone living closest to the future airport were the Urebure, a small group whose territory is thought to have run from the bay to the eastern slopes of the Santa Cruz Mountains, moving east to west, and from San Bruno Mountain in the north into the present-day city of Millbrae to the south. Their primary village was in the foothills of what is now San Bruno, near the eponymous San Bruno Creek. Their neighbors to the south, the Ssalson, resided primarily in what is now the city of San Mateo, but their territory stretched north into Millbrae. Shell mounds that once sat by the bay in what are now Millbrae, San Bruno, and South San Francisco may also have been sites of habitation for one or both groups. Memory of these sites and some signage mark the historical presence of Indigenous people and their cosmologies (some shell mounds were ceremonial and burial sites) as well as their symbiotic relationships with the mud over which the airport now sits.[6]

Ramaytush Ohlone lives and imaginaries, as well as the land, water, flora, and fauna that they were bound up with, would be violently and irrevocably transformed by the Spaniards. Although first encounters were sometimes cordial, they were still part of Spain's conquest and occupation of the Bay Area, designed to secure its western North American territory in the face of increasing British and Russian activity in the region. As had been the case elsewhere in the Americas, the military-economic colonial project was yoked to a mission system—developed in California under the direction of the Franciscan padre Junípero Serra—designed to conquer and, if not always successfully, convert Indigenous peoples. The military garrison Él Presidio Real de San Francisco, with a strategic view from elevation of the bay's entrance and an expanse of the Pacific Ocean beyond, and Mission San Francisco de Asís (Dolores) were both established in 1776. So was the settlement of Yerba Buena, situated between them, which became the secular foundation for the future city of San Francisco.

The future airport lands were peripheral to these settlements, but colonialism's impact was still devastating for their inhabitants. Some local Indigenous people died in armed conflicts with Spaniards or in those among neighboring groups that followed the Europeans' arrival. Most were incorporated into the Mission Dolores community. Some were taken by force, but others went of their own accord. The new god and saints had their appeal, and communities were collapsing as a result of Spanish violence (sexual and other), environmental degradation, and disease. The removal of the entirety of the surviving Urebure into the mission community by 1785 came closely behind that of most of the Yelamu to the north. The missionization of the majority of the Ssalson quickly followed. By the end of 1793, there were no Indigenous villages remaining on the upper and mid-Peninsula.[7]

At Mission Dolores, Ramaytush Ohlone people, along with Indigenous peoples from across the region, gave up existing relationships with land, community, and other living things and entered into others. They were proselytized, enculturated, and incorporated into a system of servitude combining enslavement and peonage following the debt incurred for religious instruction. Salvation may have been part of the equation, but the friars also needed household and agricultural labor as well as money to keep their facilities operational and themselves and their neophytes fed. Indigenous people at the mission also produced agriculture- and handicraft-based surplus for local consumption and trade with local Spanish authorities, Russian merchants passing through the Bay Area, and others farther afield.[8]

Many Ramaytush Ohlone did not survive the missionization process. Over the following decades, women and children especially experienced a high mortality rate, with waves of disease exacerbated by cramped, dirty living conditions and malnutrition. Others resisted by running away or, in a few instances, engaging in raids on Spanish settlements. But those who did survive within the mission system became part of complex new assemblages composed in part of gods, saints, peninsular Spaniards, mestizos, mulattoes, Hispanicized Indigenous peoples from the south, and local Indians from multiple tribes and linguistic groups. They were, on the one hand, part of an emergent, locally inflected version of the racial order of the Spanish hinterlands, which was rooted in a hierarchical religiosity and constructs of *gente de razón* (people of reason) and *gente sin razón* (people without reason) that generally corresponded to those of *español* (even as multiracial category) and *Indio*. Yet mission society was also defined by fluid and shifting social identities, with overlapping hierarchies and factions within the Spanish and Indigenous constituencies. Despite the traumatizing conditions, some Native people survived and remade themselves. They married and procreated across tribal lines more extensively than before the establishment of the mission system and incorporated certain elements of precontact Indigenous beliefs and social roles into an evolving colonial society. Ultimately, demographic decline, relocation, a resultant increase in intermarriage across tribal and linguistic groups, and new political affinities led to the emergence of "mission Indians" as a social and cultural group.[9]

Spanish colonialism's transformation of Urebure and Ssalson territory went beyond its human depopulation. The dispossession and removal of Ramaytush Ohlone stewards, as happened elsewhere in what became Spanish Nueva California, likely led to a local population increase of deer, shorebirds, sea mammals, shellfish, tubers, fungi, and other species that had been hunted or foraged near the bay.[10] But many of these plants and animals would soon be displaced from what would be called Buriburi (later, Buri Buri), a large expanse of mission-held lands running from San Bruno Mountain to present-day San Mateo. When they arrived in 1776, the Franciscans and the Spanish garrison brought three hundred head of cattle, which they initially grazed in the hills near the Presidio while growing crops nearby. The mission soon expanded its farming and grazing operations into its southern periphery via several small ranchos meant to provide food and crafts for sustenance as well as surplus through trade. Early on, before the local

Danse des habitans de Californie à la mission de S.ᵗ Francisco.

FIGURE 4. Native Californians dancing at Mission Dolores in San Francisco.
Lithograph by Ludwig Choris, 1816. Depiction illustrates how Bay Area Indigenous
peoples maintained some of their cultural and spiritual practices while being assimilated
into mission society. Courtesy of the California History Room, California State Library,
Sacramento, California.

Indigenous villages were eliminated, this economic project—which
depended upon villagers' labor in fields, pastures, and corrals—was
intertwined with a proselytizing one.[11]

Meanwhile, the Presidio, whose growing herd could not be accom-
modated locally either, drove its cattle to Monterey. But in 1797 the
Presidio gained control of (although not title to) much of Buri Buri to
graze its own herd closer to home, consume what it needed, and use the
profits from the sale of surplus beef, hides, and tallow to fund its activities. The mission resumed control of the land in 1815 before relinquishing it again to the military shortly after Mexican independence. In the
1810s, Buri Buri was home to roughly ten thousand cattle and ten thousand sheep (the latter grazing on its southern end), almost one thousand
horses, smaller numbers of mules, goats, and pigs, and a handful of private farming operations that produced grains and legumes. Mission Indians continued to be the primary source of labor for these operations.[12]

All of these agricultural enterprises reshaped the future airport lands
and surrounding areas, but the impact of cattle was most profound. As
large mammals bred to grow quickly, in need of significant stores of

energy to regulate their body temperature, cattle trampled and ate up the plants that the Ramaytush Ohlone had nurtured and those that grew wild. Among them were native perennial bunchgrasses. These grasses were often replaced by non-native grasses or invasive weeds brought to California in adobe bricks and animal feed and bedding, and as seeds and burrs embedded in cattle hides. Or they were not replaced at all, which led to erosion during the rainy season that began to silt areas of the bay. Although the salt marshes remained somewhat on the periphery of this grazing economy, they were transformed when cattle, some of which had become wild, wandered into them to feed during drier periods and when postgrazing runoff made them boggier during wetter months.[13]

Colonial processes reshaping land and people were extended during the Mexican period, with significant changes coming with the secularization of the missions. Secularization had been anticipated in an 1813 Spanish decree promising the eventual return of mission lands to Indigenous people and in a series of policies instituted by the newly independent Mexican state (as of 1821), which included the granting of citizenship rights to Indians in 1826 and the abolishment of slavery in 1829. Secularization and the closing of the California missions was put into motion by an 1833 congressional decree and an 1834 provisional ordinance. Following the spirit of other Mexican reforms, the decree called for the transformation of mission communities into autonomous, self-governing Indian pueblos. The provisional ordinance called for the redistribution of some mission lands, livestock, and supplies to individual Indigenous families and created common areas for grazing. Yet the ordinance also gave license to other claims to the land and the perpetuation of asymmetrical relations by, among other things, requiring Indigenous people to devote their labor to projects related to the "public good" and giving the government significant leeway in redistributing the land as they saw fit. As a sense of regional exceptionalism in what was now known as Alta California grew—fueled by a burgeoning Californio political identity that connected this group's supposed racial and class superiority, their assumed purity of (Spanish) blood, to their geographic circumstance— commitments to substantive land and labor reform quickly diminished. Only a handful of Indigenous people received any land; elite *gente de razón* were able to gain title to the vast majority of it.[14]

Mission Dolores was secularized in 1835. None of its lands were transferred to native hands. Rancho Buri Buri was the first large parcel to be sold off, purchased that same year by José António Sánchez, a fifty-two-year-old officer recently reassigned to the Monterey Presidio from

San Francisco's. Sánchez had made a name for himself leading military expeditions against Indigenous people in the Bay Area and California's interior valley. He had received "temporary possession" of Buri Buri in 1827, after the military herd had fallen on hard times, and had begun raising his own cattle and growing crops. In 1835, after two years of negotiation, Sánchez received title to the roughly fifteen-thousand-acre tract running north to south from San Bruno Mountain to the San Mateo rancho—one of the mission's agricultural outposts located in the present-day city of Burlingame—and east to west from the edge of the salt marsh of the bay to the San Andreas Valley. Sánchez and a crew of surveyors and witnesses began their official mapping of the tract from a Ramaytush Ohlone shell mound at Point San Bruno along the bay shore. Although the adjacent salt marsh was not technically part of the grant, it was symbolically attached by virtue of proximity.[15]

Sánchez's estate was part of a rancho system that expanded across the state as military and church-focused accumulation gave way to that of private interests. The hide and tallow trade became increasingly international in scope after the Mexican government ended Spain's monopolistic trade practices and gave greater access to California ports to ships from England, New England, Russia, Peru, and elsewhere. Growing numbers of immigrant merchants, trappers, sailors, mercenaries, and the like established themselves in California as well. Increased cattle production enabled the Californios to purchase—sometimes using the hides themselves as a form of money—the consumer goods that marked their ascendant wealth. These shifts were symbolized by Sánchez's decision to move the rancho's base of operations from the existing Casa de Buri Buri in the northwest foothills of the property to a larger family home located in the flatlands of what is now Millbrae. The new home lay close to El Camino Real, the road that provided access to the anchorage and supply houses in San Francisco, as well as to a minor estuary where small supply boats could dock at high tide.[16]

Sánchez incorporated missionized Indigenous people with Ohlone roots into the Buri Buri project as servants, laborers, and vaqueros. They were likely joined by Miwoks and others from the greater Bay Area who had more recently joined mission society and, possibly, even by victims of the postsecularization slave trade in Indigenous children from the Sierra Nevada and North Coast. Some lived on the property itself. An 1852 census placed fifty-six Indigenous people at Rancho Buri Buri, at that point under the control of Sánchez's descendants, and twenty-seven more living on San Pedro Rancho, on the coast, which

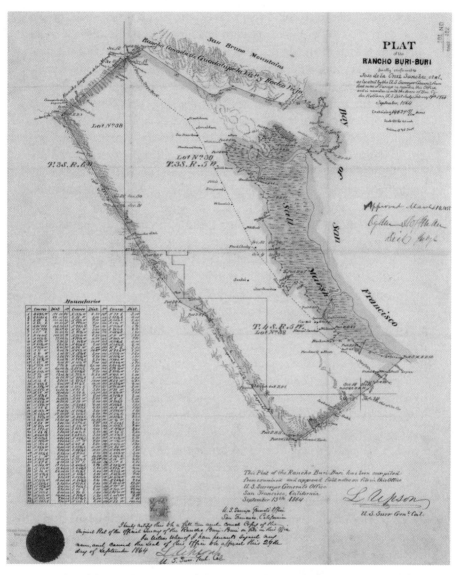

FIGURE 5. Plat of the Rancho Buri-Buri, finally confirmed to José de la Cruz Sánchez et al., 1864. Land Case Map E-232, The Bancroft Library, University of California, Berkeley. This map was created during litigation over the title of the property, as most of it passed from José António Sánchez's heirs to Anglo purchasers. The salt marsh, while technically outside of the rancho boundary, would be the future home of SFO.

was owned by Jose António's son Francisco. For a time, some Indigenous workers at Buri Buri appear to have lived to the south in a small village at Rancho San Mateo, which remained the property of the mission in San Francisco until it was sold off in 1846 to Cayetano Arenas. When the subsequent Anglo owner, William D. Howard, took possession of San Mateo and dispossessed its Indigenous residents in the early 1850s, some went to live and work on the Sánchez property.[17]

In this unfolding set of colonial relationships developing across California, some Indigenous workers were paid and free to come and go, while others (often women and children) were unpaid and coercively bound to the ranchos through debt bondage and physical intimidation. These subordinated, racialized people were tied to a patriarchal, social arrangement that facilitated, for their Californio overlords, the simultaneous extraction of value from Indigenous labor and an opportunistic self-conception drawn from their putatively paternalistic guidance (through work and proximity) of those who had once been the charges of the missions.[18] José António Sánchez's 1842 will, for example, honored each of "the Indians who attend the corral" on his estate with a "heifer." Yet the fact that he could not or did not bother to honor them by name—"My sons know who they are," Sánchez explained—indicates the limits of the paternalistic relationship at Buri Buri.[19]

The Indigenous people who labored at the ranchos maintained family and social networks as best they could. Some may also have been able to rekindle old practices of hunting, foraging, and otherwise tending the lands that continued to be radically transformed, now by the Sánchez family's growing herds of cattle and horses.[20] As they did so, however, these people, many of whom had already been remade as "mission Indians," were in the process of being erased as a people, at least in the eyes of the Anglo settlers already arriving in the area and the anthropologists who would follow them. Even after the missions closed, people were still dying from disease, while others left the area. Those who stayed carried to a lesser and lesser degree the signs—language, clothing, rituals, foodways, connection to specific geographic locales, and so on—that marked them as Indians to outsiders. While some Indigenous rancho workers remained *Indio* to themselves and to their Californio employers and landlords, many would become differently legible in the emerging, colonial order, either by passing as white or by becoming Mexican.[21]

Indeed, dramatic transformations would come with the US conquest of California at the end of the US-Mexico War in 1848, the subsequent rush of people seeking gold the following year, and statehood in 1850. Although Californio property rights were putatively protected by the Treaty of Guadalupe-Hidalgo, Anglo squatter claims, and an Anglo-friendly US Board of Land Commission (established by the Land Law of 1851) and judiciary, scam artists and unscrupulous attorneys, rising family debt (often from land-claim litigation costs), and the appeal of cash in hand conspired to transfer land ownership across the state to the recently arrived settlers.[22] Rancho Buri Buri was a case in point. José António Sánchez died in 1843. Plans for the division of the property among his children and grandchildren were finalized by 1851. But as a result of his descendants taking on usurious mortgages, having the land seized by the state to satisfy their debts, falling victim to fraudulent business practices, dying intestate, or simply selling at a fair market price, Sánchez family members lost most of their only recently appropriated land in the 1850s. By the time the legal wrangling over the subdivided estate concluded in 1869, the Sánchez heirs retained only 4 percent of the original rancho, and most of the fifty or so owners of the former Rancho Buri Buri were of English or Irish extraction.[23]

Thus, the nascent settler colonial project of the Spanish missionaries and Californios that shaped the future airport lands was replaced by a more systematic one under the Anglos that dovetailed with the United States' expanding industrial economy and imperial reach. As US whites came to the area in growing numbers, the economy began to diversify in San Mateo County (carved from a previously larger San Francisco County in 1856) as it developed as a closely situated hinterland of the rapidly growing City *and* County of San Francisco. The grazing economy went into decline as lumbering, dairying, and an expanded array of crop growing emerged. So did a different kind of cattle business that Charles Lux and Henry Miller established on a large tract of formerly Buri Buri land (in what is now South San Francisco) that Lux had purchased from one of the Sánchez heirs. Lux and Miller assembled and fed cattle on this property that they had reared elsewhere in the state before sending them to market in San Francisco.[24]

These changes marked the end of Indian labor qua Indian labor in the county and an even greater decline in the Indigenous presence. The removal of Indigenous workers from the San Mateo Rancho in the early 1850s is instructive. Although these refugees were able to find work with the Sánchez family at Rancho Buri Buri, the arrangement was only temporary. As new agricultural practices, businesses, and residences were built atop the previous rancho lands in the 1850s and 1860s, many property owners and businesspeople opted for surplus white labor, which flowed to the area when individuals' search for riches in the Sierra foothills gold fields did not pan out. Others looked to Chinese workers, who had been arriving in the Bay Area in growing numbers since the Gold Rush and finding work through family and social networks and district associations located in the region's Chinatowns. Census data indicates that Chinese labor was displacing Indigenous labor on big estates in San Mateo County between 1860 and 1870.[25]

Economic and demographic transformations in San Mateo County and elsewhere in California were carried forward by a virulent racial ideology. The patronage system of the ranchos, defined by racial subordination but also mutual obligation, was displaced by a more explicit white supremacy and firmer racial divisions. This system served most of all an ascendant elite, but it also produced cross-class affinities among whites of varying social status, who received both material and psychological compensation, to invoke the perspective of W. E. B. Du Bois, for their investments in whiteness.[26] Members of other groups were incorporated in exclusionary fashion into the social order or simply deemed disposable depending on the needs of free and unfree local labor markets (extractive, agricultural, domestic, sexual, and so on) and broader social dynamics. Native Americans were generally positioned at the bottom of a social system that in asymmetrical ways incorporated the Mexican inhabitants of the newly conquered lands (racialized differently depending on their proximity to whiteness) and, soon, later-to-be-excluded Asians; initially unwelcome, disenfranchised, and, until the 1860s, occasionally enslaved Blacks; and not-quite-white Europeans. Facilitating the abject status of Indigenous people were a series of state and local laws that seized their land, limited their rights as citizens, facilitated their indenture and enslavement as laborers and sexual partners, and sanctioned US and California state-sponsored genocide, especially in the northern reaches of the state.[27] With no land to expropriate in San Mateo County and growing pools of otherwise differentiated labor available for exploitation, Indigenous people—with the exception of a few survivors, such as members of the extended Evencio family, who were among those driven from Howard's estate—were becoming even less visible in the area's racial order. Each US census between 1870 and 1920 counted fewer than ten identifiable Indigenous people in San Mateo County.[28]

One of the major Anglo purchasers of Rancho Buri Buri land, and the one most central to the story of SFO, was Darius Ogden Mills, at one point said to be the richest man in California. Mills relocated to

Sacramento from Buffalo, New York, arriving in 1849 after a six-month journey that, given the crush of others en route to the gold mines, left him stranded in Panama and eventually required a detour through Peru to secure passage to California. Settling in Sacramento, Mills made a small fortune trading merchandise, buying gold dust, and selling it on the New York market. Shortly thereafter he made an even bigger fortune by taking deposits of gold and lending capital to finance California's meteoric economic growth through his bank, D. O. Mills and Company, and then by managing his bank's and his own personal investments in mining operations and associated businesses like sawmills and canal companies. Contemplating retirement in 1862, he sold two-thirds of his shares in the bank and turned over management to his partners, his brother, Edgar, and (a different) Henry Miller. But he reimmersed himself in the profession in 1864, when William Chapman Ralston recruited him to join the founding board of the Bank of California in San Francisco and become its first president. He became even wealthier.[29]

Mills is important to this story because his family leased and then sold the tract of drained salt marsh that eventually became the airport but also because he and others of his professional circles and social set helped set into motion—as bankers, investors, property owners, developers, and so on—an array of relationships that would reshape the region. Under Mills's control and influence, the salt marsh and submerged land that became the airport, as well as surrounding Buri Buri lands, would eventually be swept up in racialized processes of capital accumulation that radically transformed the Bay Area socially and environmentally while linking it to broader colonial and imperial projects.

Mills purchased approximately 1,500 acres of Rancho Buri Buri land in the 1850s. By 1868 he owned close to 1,600 acres of former Sánchez family holdings in two parcels and co-owned with his brother-in-law, Ansel I. Easton, approximately 1,800 acres more. He had also acquired 335 acres of adjoining salt marsh.[30] The wetlands were available because following the Treaty of Guadalupe Hidalgo, submerged lands, tidelands, and swamp and overflow lands in California were held in trust by the US government until the new state could be admitted to the union. California then took title to all such land not designated by Mexican or Spanish land grants or held in reserve by the federal government. In 1855 California encouraged settler development within its borders by passing legislation that facilitated the sale of state-owned swamp and overflowed lands to private parties so long as they were, or were composed of, citizens of the state or those entitled to become citizens.[31] By

1909, the year before his death, Mills owned close to 2,300 acres of former Buri Buri land and the roughly 1,200 acres of salt marsh that would eventually be sold to San Francisco for its airport.[32]

It took some time for Mills to develop his property fully, in part because of uncertainties about the ownership and boundaries of Buri Buri parcels originally held by individual Sánchez family members as well as the legitimacy of Anglo squatter homesteads in the area. A lawsuit pertaining these issues—*Ansel I. Easton and D. Ogden Mills v. Charles Lux et al.*—finally clarified most title claims in 1869.[33] But Mills was still party to some infrastructural improvements before that happened. In the late 1850s and early 1860s, he invested in the construction company that built a toll road connecting San Francisco to San Bruno and then points south via El Camino Real.[34] Then he and other local elites supported the construction of the San Francisco and San Jose Railroad. With financing by private interests and public monies obtained through bonds approved by voters in San Francisco, Santa Clara, and San Mateo Counties, ground was broken for the railroad in 1861 and it was completed in 1864. Roughly one mile of track ran through Mills's Buri Buri property, and he served as both director and treasurer of the railroad beginning in August of 1865.[35]

The completion of the railroad, which supplanted stagecoach and steamship, made living in San Mateo County and doing business in San Francisco more convenient while increasing the value of land held by Mills and others along the line. It also linked the agricultural areas of San Mateo and Santa Clara Counties to the city, helping to facilitate the emergence of industrial agriculture that was a significant driver of the Bay Area economy from the later 1800s until the 1940s. The railroad promoted regional trade at first and then, when taken over by the Southern Pacific and linked to other railroad lines in California and the transcontinental network, connected the fast-developing agricultural hinterlands across the state to consumers and processers in the Bay Area and East Coast markets. Mills played his own small part in the region's agricultural development by establishing with a business partner a dairy business on his Buri Buri holdings in 1865.[36]

Mills played a larger role in the region's future as a banker and investor who helped reshape the political economy of the Bay Area and its hinterlands by helping to produce expanding networks of finance, trade, extraction, and transportation. Mills, Ralston, and other members of the Bank Crowd, as they were known, generated astronomical amounts of finance capital by tapping into the mineral wealth of nature in California and Nevada. Mills profited particularly well from Nevada silver-mining operations through the Bank of California, the founding of which in 1864 occurred the year Nevada became a state, the closely related San Francisco Stock and Exchange Board, established in 1862, and his own personal investments.

Initially, the Bank of California, with its local representative William Sharon taking the lead role, generated a significant amount of its profits on the Comstock Lode by financing others' mining operations. But Mills, Ralston, and Sharon and others eventually conducted much of their Comstock business through their Union Mill and Mining Company, which allowed them to funnel profits to themselves directly rather than to Bank of California shareholders. The company acquired existing mines and ore-processing mills, some by foreclosure for nonpayment of loans, and subsequently developed new ones. By 1869, Union Mill and Mining owned seventeen mills on the Comstock. Sharon, Ralston, Mills, and other investors also earned huge profits from allied, often monopolistic Comstock businesses. Their Carson and Tahoe Lumber and Fluming Company extracted timber from the Lake Tahoe basin and brought lumber to the Comstock. Their Virginia and Gold Hill Water Company supplied water to mining operations and the surrounding community. And their Virginia and Truckee Railroad carried materials into and silver out of the Comstock. The railroad began operations in late 1869, and its offshoot, the Carson and Colorado Railway, started up in 1880.[37]

The Virginia and Truckee Railroad principals extended their operation to Reno in order to connect with the Central Pacific Railroad, which the Bank of California, as well as Mills and other bankers as individuals, helped to finance.[38] The Central Pacific, of course, made up the western portion of the Transcontinental Railroad, the completion of which in 1869 was facilitated by, among other things, the expropriation of Indigenous lands in California, Nevada, and Utah; massive federal land grants for the railroads for sale and bond collateral; and labor supplied by Chinese workers. This infrastructural endeavor, as Manu Karuka argues, helped to consolidate a continental empire and economy—by hastening the military campaign to dispossess Indigenous people across the West and connecting multiple urban cores and rural peripheries—and integrated California into it. In other words, Mills, Sharon, Ralston, and their cronies used capital generated from mining on loan, as well as their various transportation and extractive operations, to help make previously peripheral settler colonial projects in California and Nevada more integral to those of the nation as a whole.[39]

Such imperial projects benefited from blurred lines between corporations and the state. Leland Stanford, for example, served simultaneously as governor of California and president of the Central Pacific and was later a US senator. As governor, he appointed Edwin Bryant Crocker, an initial director of the Central Pacific and the older brother of current company principal Charles Crocker, to the California Supreme Court. Judge Crocker, after serving seven months on the court, returned to the railroad as its chief counsel.[40] Sharon, described by the Virginia City newspaper *Territorial Enterprise* as "a hyena in human form," served as a famously absent and ineffective US senator from Nevada from 1875 to 1881.[41] And Mills endowed a professorship of philosophy, was a trustee of the Lick Observatory, and served overlapping terms as a regent (1874–81) and treasurer (1868–80) of the new University of California, at a moment when harsh critiques of regents abounded for profiting from their appointments.[42]

Beyond mining and railroads, late nineteenth-century settler colonialism in the Golden State was driven by a dizzying circulation of capital among corporate and personal bank accounts and an expanding array of business ventures. These financial entanglements helped to transform radically the Bay Area's natural environment and that of its hinterlands while catalyzing metropolitan expansion and the attendant growth of labor markets, infrastructures, populations, and the relationships among them. Mills, for example, personally and through his banks, redirected profits from Sierra foothill and Comstock investments into ventures across California, the western states and territories, and beyond. These included still more mining, railroad, timber, and banking operations; oil production; agriculture and ranching; sugar refining; wetlands reclamation and irrigation projects; quicksilver (mercury) mines; water companies; real estate development, including San Francisco's first steel-framed skyscraper; and Lux and Miller's cattle operation. Mills helped to extend the region's rapidly expanding imperial reach overseas through the Bank of California's financing of Pacific Rim and inter-American trade and transportation as well as British colonial operations. And his personal investments included those in various business ventures in Mexico and the Cerro de Pasco Mining Company in Peru.[43]

These ventures were all, of course, founded upon and reproductive of the racial differentiation of those who inhabited or worked the landscapes where value was accumulated, and they sometimes resulted in horrific acts of violence. The opening up of the gold and silver mines was genocidal for some Indigenous communities in the Sierras and on their western and eastern slopes. The mining and railroad industries in California employed racially divided workforces, with Mexicans, Chinese, and a handful of African Americans and surviving Indigenous people generally relegated to menial forms of labor and exposed to state-sanctioned and vigilante violence. Wetland reclamation projects in the Central Valley relied heavily on Chinese labor for this dirty and dangerous work. Farther from home, Bay Area capitalists' investments in Mexican timbering, mining, ranching, and the like worked hand in hand with Porfirio Díaz's land privatization efforts to displace peasant farmers and Indigenous people from the lands they had worked and lived on. The Cerro de Pasco venture in Peru consigned Indigenous miners to a system of debt peonage.[44]

Even those marked as white paid a price, albeit a different one. A significant amount of the wealth obtained by the San Francisco Bank Crowd in the 1860s and 1870s percolated up from small investors engaged in a frenzied, often fraudulent, trade in stocks and futures.[45] Meanwhile, many local Anglo and ethnic white industrial, extractive, and agricultural workers sold their labor under exploitative conditions. During the depression roiling California in 1869 and 1870, there simply was not enough work in these sectors to meet the needs of the growing numbers of migrants entering the state to take advantage of its supposed abundance. With railroad and mining work drying up, and opportunities for small farmers limited with growing emphasis in the hinterlands on large-scale wheat production, people flocked to San Francisco and smaller cities and towns, where job opportunities were not much better. And with greater integration into the national economy facilitated by the transcontinental railroad came greater exposure to the Depression of 1873 and its lingering effects, which had a more profound impact on working people.[46]

Moreover, as the contemporary political economist and journalist Henry George theorized in 1871, the scarcity produced by the monopolization of land by large holders in and around San Francisco furthered the exploitation of labor and the production of great wealth for elites. As settlers poured into the area following the completion of the transcontinental railroad, the growing demand for land permitted property owners to raise prices and, by extension, take a higher percentage of workers' wages. As George put it, "The value of land is the power which its ownership gives to appropriate for clarity the product of labour, and, as a sequence, where rents (the share of the landowner) are high, wages (the share of the labourer) are low."[47]

George was no critic of settler colonialism. In fact, he championed white settlement as a potentially democratizing phenomenon that could break the backs of the oligarchs who controlled the political and economic systems. He advocated a policy that redistributed land from large to small owners by shifting taxation from production to the land itself, with exemptions for small holdings. He thought forty acres would be a reasonable holding for those settlers interested in working the land, but the racially exclusionary aspect of his vision was laid bare by the lack of reference to "a mule" and, by extension, to the recent, ill-fated plan for the redistribution of southern lands in that increment to recently emancipated Black people.[48] But George's work still sheds light on how Mills's and other Anglo Californians' wealth was magnified by the ongoing project of settler colonialism when they obtained land cheaply through the legal and extralegal expropriations of Californio holdings, railroad land grants, and other acts; when that produced a scarcity; and then when that scarcity, alongside the ongoing rush of white settlers and other arrivals to the region, increased the value of land.

George was invested in showing how such increase happened irrespective of "improvements" made by the land's owners. But improvements certainly did not hurt, especially when many of them were undertaken by low-wage Chinese workers, recently arrived from the railroad work gangs or from their home country. George wrote about Chinese labor, too, before he had fully developed his thesis on land valuation, in a May Day 1869 *New York Tribune* article. The piece was, on one level, a racist, anti-immigrant tract warning of the "utter subversion of Republicanism" and civilizational "destruction" should the "dragon's teeth" of Chinese immigrants be allowed to "germinate." It was also an insightful analysis of the economics of Chinese labor and an attendant and growing racism. George noted the inroads that Chinese workers, laboring at depressed and, for white workers, depressing wages, had made over the decades in manufacturing, railroads, agriculture, personal service, and other endeavors in California and elsewhere in the West. Such labor, he argued, produced much wealth for employers, ranging from "great corporations" to small businesses to households with a single servant, and a "correspondingly intense" "anti-Chinese feeling" among white workers.[49]

One notable local employer of the mostly male population of Chinese immigrants mentioned by George was the San Francisco and San Jose Railroad. With construction starting in 1861, Chinese workers labored there before any were hired by the Central Pacific three years later. They constituted an inexpensive, tractable labor force, whose status as such was being defined by the 1862 Anti-Coolie Act. By levying a tax on Chinese business owners and those working gold mines, the act hastened Chinese workers' retreat from an enterprise (mining) that Mills profited from and facilitated their entry into another one (railroad construction) that benefited him by improving his property even before their labor on the transcontinental railroad or the Virginia Truckee began to pay off.[50]

The Anti-Coolie Act also contributed to Chinese immigrants being defined as threatening racial others, though the San Francisco and San Jose Railroad's employment of Chinese workers seems to have been relatively uncontroversial in San Mateo County given the absence of the hostile white unionism developing in San Francisco. Yet Chinese workers were building an infrastructure that eventually hastened their local exclusion, symbolically and legally, if not entirely materially. At the urging of Mills and others, the San Francisco and San Jose Railroad was incorporated into the transcontinental railroad system after being purchased in 1868 by the Southern Pacific Railroad, which in turn merged with the Central Pacific in 1870.[51] Chinese low-wage labor became less desired, and their racialized cultural difference became even less welcome as the railroad facilitated both white working-class resentment and mass white migration to the region from the eastern United States.[52] The following decade saw an array of local and state ordinances designed to limit immigration and disrupt community formations. In 1882, the federal Chinese Exclusion Act effectively ended Chinese immigration to the United States.

Mills played a small part in the development of anti-Chinese sentiment, ironically while trying to ameliorate it. After a mob of whites murdered people and set fires in San Francisco's Chinatown amid the national labor unrest of July 1877, San Francisco's mayor A. J. Bryant made clear that the city's police force was incapable of maintaining order. Mills proposed a Committee of Safety to do so through extralegal means. The brigade, several thousand strong and armed with rifles, carbines, and pick-handles, patrolled the streets for several days before disbanding. Shortly thereafter, one of its members, Denis Kearney, drew upon his experiences as a vigilante agent of San Francisco's elite as he mobilized twinned, collective resentments against Chinese workers and the capitalists (especially railroad interests) who employed them at a moment of ongoing economic crisis and, as exemplified by the railroad strikes in the East, rising militancy among workers across the nation more generally. Kearney helped to found the Workingmen's Party of California, a force in San Francisco politics over the next several years that played a major role in fomenting anti-Chinese sentiment.[53] Mills remained supportive of Chinese workers in the United States, in no small part because of their low cost. Later in 1877 he described them as "temperate, exceedingly industrious, and economical" and, in the wake of growing violence, suggested that the government take measures to protect them from "the rougher element of society." But as a practical matter, given recent events, he admitted it might be best "for Congress to check temporarily the flow of Chinese immigration, by levying a tax upon each immigrant."[54]

It is no surprise that Mills had a favorable view of Chinese labor but warmed to the idea of scaling back its supply. He had, after all, recently reaped its benefits. Clear title to his property and the completion of the local railroad inspired him, like other elite San Franciscans with San Mateo County holdings, to develop it lavishly. He completed his forty-two-room mansion on his southernmost holding in 1870 and named his estate—which now included gardens, a conservatory, three artificial lakes, a dairy, and a five-hundred-head herd of dairy cows—Millbrae. Chinese laborers planted thousands of shrubs and trees on his grounds over the years, including rare species from other continents. They also built levees to enclose four hundred acres of the future-airport salt marsh that he had acquired to provide additional pasturage for his dairy cows.[55] Mills may well have been inspired to take on this project (and to bring in experienced Chinese workers) by his investments in contemporaneous efforts to reclaim Sacramento River Delta and Central Valley wetlands for agricultural purposes.[56]

Mills, who was already spending significant time in New York, moved his family and much of the focus of his business there in 1880. But he continued to winter at his San Mateo County estate (he died there in 1910), where he looked after his California business affairs, gardens, and dairy.[57] Mills's move came more or less at the moment when the California and Nevada mining industries' decline was a foregone conclusion and when heavily capitalized agricultural production was of growing primacy to the California economy. It also followed what some see as a signal event in this transition: a major scandal, involving his Bank of California partner William Chapman Ralston, who had succeeded Mills as president in 1873, that was closely related to still more transformations of the local environment.

Just as San Francisco elites had looked to San Mateo County's abundant streams to water their new estates, city officials and financiers sought to colonize the county as a source of drinking water when San

Francisco's own supplies proved inadequate to serve its growing population. San Francisco, primarily through the privately held, increasingly monopolistic Spring Valley Water Company, had engaged in a number of damming, diversion, and pumping projects to collect and transport water from San Mateo County watersheds in the 1860s and 1870s. Chinese laborers played a significant role in these projects as well.[58]

Ralston leveraged a takeover of the profitable Spring Valley, as well as the rights to coveted sources of water in Alameda County across the bay that would help to meet San Francisco's growing needs. He profited handsomely from selling the water rights to his new company, but his plan to peddle the company itself to San Francisco for a healthy profit fell apart amid public outcry over what seemed to be an extortionist scheme. Ralston had raised the funds to purchase Spring Valley through a risky and unauthorized sale of Bank of California certificates. Thanks to this episode and other shady dealings, Ralston was financially ruined, and he almost took down the Bank of California with him during the financial crisis of the summer of 1875. Yet Mills, Sharon, and other principals saved the bank. Ralston was forced to resign for mismanaging the bank's affairs and died the same day during a San Francisco Bay swim. Mills resumed the presidency and served in that capacity until 1878. Sharon, in turn, would take on the controlling interest in Spring Valley, with Mills and other local elites heavily invested in it as well.[59]

Spring Valley's watering of large estates and early suburban developments transformed San Mateo County ecologies with the introduction of thirstier non-native plants, like those on Mills's estate. Such processes accelerated after the 1906 San Francisco Earthquake, which sent many of the city's denizens south to rebuild their lives. Subsequently, many large San Mateo County land holders subdivided their land, initiating a boom in home construction and the significant population growth that, over the course of the twentieth century, would radically reshape the bayside of the county into a heavily populated suburban landscape. Mills participated in this process to a small extent during his lifetime, selling off in 1906 a roughly one-hundred-acre plot of land straddling the Southern Pacific railroad line that he had acquired in the 1870s. The land was developed into the San Bruno Park neighborhood in what would eight years later become part of the city of San Bruno.[60]

Meanwhile, the open waters east of the salt marshes that would eventually be filled to accommodate an expanding airport were also being transformed. After the United States took possession of the area, a multiracial cast of foragers, hunters, fisher folk, and commercial enterprises extended to species-depredating excess the millennia-old Indigenous practices of harvesting salt, marine life, and waterfowl and their eggs at the western edges of the bay. Entrepreneurs quickly created a productive and financially lucrative fishery in the decades after statehood along San Mateo County's bayshore. Oysters were the primary commodity. Initially, oysterers tried their hand at harvesting native Olympia oysters (*Ostrea lurida*), but these were not entirely appealing to the Anglo arrivals because of their small size and metallic taste. Before 1869 the Bay Area oyster business was based primarily on transplanted Shoalwater Bay oysters (a larger version of *lurida*) from the Pacific Northwest, which were transported to and stored briefly in northern areas of the bay before sale. The opening of the transcontinental railroad that year enabled the importation of more desirable Atlantic oysters (*Crassostrea virginica*) to the region. Although these oysters could not successfully spawn in western waters with colder year-round temperatures, a steady supply of oyster larvae from the East Coast kept the business going.[61]

This shift in species occurred just as the industry's bases of operation were, as a general rule, moving from the northern and eastern portions of the bay to its southern reaches, in no small part because of the local environmental effects of the Bank Crowd's far-flung business ventures. As Sierra gold mining shifted from surface placer to hydraulic operations, San Francisco capital funded the construction of gigantic wooden flumes that rerouted rivers so access could be gained to their beds. It bought the hoses and water cannons for hydraulic mining operations that blasted into hillsides to expose deeply buried gold, and it built the dams and artificial waterways that created the necessary water pressure. San Francisco capital also bought up and then sold off for lumber much of the Sierra Nevada's old-growth forests to build the wooden flumes. Mining and deforestation channeled massive amounts of soil into Sierra Nevada streams and rivers, which eventually filled the Sacramento River and then San Francisco Bay. Clogged and overflowing rivers caused frequent and massive flooding in the Central Valley and a dramatic increase of sediment in the bay.[62]

Oysters had difficulties adjusting to the heavy influx of cold water and silt into the bay during the winter rainy season, which proved a particular challenge for oyster companies in the North and East Bay regions, closer to the inputs of the Sacramento and San Joaquin Rivers. Obstructed waterways, combined with extraordinary rainfall during the winter of 1861 to 1862, produced massive flooding in the interior of California and a deluge of river water that temporarily turned San Francisco Bay into an almost entirely fresh water body of water. This, in turn, led to a massive die-off of many estuarine species, including almost the entire Bay Area oyster crop. As hydraulic mining debris continued to enter the bay through the 1860s and 1870s, the industry shifted to the South Bay, the area farthest from the major sources of fresh water and mining runoff, with the west side of the body of the water along the San Mateo County shore providing the best habitat given its gentle currents and protection from storms. Several oyster companies operated there, but the tremendously profitable business, primarily employing Scandinavian and Scandinavian American labor, was ultimately dominated by the Morgan Oyster Company.[63]

San Mateo County oyster companies, the primary suppliers of the mollusks to the western United States in the late nineteenth century, prospered in part from their ability to make "oyster claims" on publicly held submerged land and from the state's willingness to sell off the submerged land at low rates pursuant to the 1855 legislation. The Morgan Oyster Company eventually obtained approximately three thousand acres of underwater land to use for oyster beds in the area. But then the oyster business declined early in the twentieth century. Oysters themselves suffered from the cumulative effects of human, agricultural, and industrial waste on bay water quality as well as from the loss of oxygenating vegetation when marshlands were reclaimed. The oyster business never overcame decreasing yields and the bad press after word got out about the possibility of contracting serious illness, including typhoid, from the sewage-fed bivalves.[64]

A different labor force and a geographically broader market for marine creatures shaped life in the waters above the San Mateo County oyster beds, where seafood harvesting was significantly undertaken by Chinese fishermen, some of whom traveled downstream after their work on the transcontinental railroad was complete. Chinese fishermen were, generally speaking, kept out of established Bay Area fisheries, but they were able to make inroads in shrimping, outcompeting a small Italian fleet in the process, by using methods and equipment brought from their own home country. Operating out of camps in Marin, San Francisco, and San Mateo Counties, Chinese fishermen used large, conically shaped bag (or trap) nets to catch the crustaceans. Some of their efforts were focused on the shallows under and near what is now SFO. Some shrimp camps were constituted as companies in and of themselves, while others were owned by larger enterprises based in San Francisco's Chinatown. A portion of the catch was sold fresh locally, while the rest was dried and for the most part exported to China, where the meat was sold for human consumption and the shells for fertilizer. At the peak of the San Mateo County shrimp fishery in the 1890s, close to two hundred Chinese fishermen were settled there in a half-dozen camps, including at Point San Bruno, where a shell mound once marked the Ramaytush Ohlone historical presence and the northeast corner of Rancho Buri Buri.[65]

As with other dimensions of the airport's prehistory, environmental transformations developed hand in hand with those of racial differentiation and exclusion. White fishermen had been pushing the state to police Chinese fishermen since the 1860s. Beginning in 1880, the California State Legislature passed a series of laws banning particular methods of fishing, like those used by Chinese shrimpers, that decimated their intended catch as well as other species caught accidentally. The laws were passed at this moment when there were growing concerns about declining fisheries globally, nationally, and locally, but this legal infrastructure, as well as its selective enforcement, was also motivated by the rising tide of anti-Chinese sentiment. A 1901 state ban on commercial shrimp fishing during the summer months, unsuccessfully opposed by Chinese fishermen all the way to the 1903 US Supreme Court decision *Ah King v. Superior Court of San Francisco,* made things more difficult. Although a seasonal restriction was lifted a few years later, that ruling came with a state ban on the exportation of dried shrimp. The effective end of the San Mateo County shrimp camps came in 1910, when the legislature banned bag nets.[66]

Still, like Indigenous people, displaced Mexican workers, and others, Chinese shrimpers survived their regional colonial present as best they could, reshaping their environment in the process. Operating out of San Francisco's Hunter's Point, a group of shrimpers resumed operations in San Mateo County waters after the state reversed the bag net ban decision in 1915. With the shrimp population recovered somewhat following the hiatus, they maintained their operation until the United States seized the land on which the camp sat in 1939 in order to build the San Francisco Naval Shipyard, although by that time harvests had fallen because the crustaceans had become less fashionable as a food source.[67]

Darius Ogden Mills died in 1910. He left his sizable fortune of roughly $35 million, including his Bay Area properties, to his children Ogden Mills and Elisabeth Reid. As with their father over the final thirty years of his life, the Mills children's social lives, philanthropic endeavors, and business interests were largely focused in the eastern United States, but they continued to tend to the family's California

FIGURE 6. Larkin Goldsmith Mead statue of Christopher Columbus receiving Queen Isabella's commitment to finance his initial voyages to the Americas. Gifted by Darius Ogden Mills to the State of California and installed in the Capitol rotunda in 1883. It remained there until its removal in the summer of 2020 following protests against police violence and structural racism. Courtesy of the California History Room, California State Library, Sacramento, California.

properties and investments with the assistance of the corporation, Mills Estate, Inc. Although the family sold off a few parcels of the former Rancho Buri Buri to suburban developers, they clearly were not short on cash. The Mills siblings held onto the mansion, the gardens, the dairy, and much of the grazing land. They continued the winter visits, bringing their servants with them to California.[68] Ultimately, Mills's family-owned salt marsh that had been reclaimed by Chinese workers was available for lease to build a municipal airport in early 1927, and then for purchase the following decade to permit the facility's first expansion, because great wealth inspired preservation. That 1930s expansion also occasioned the city's appropriation of state-owned underwater land previously used for oyster cultivation, but no longer profitable as such, and its purchase of such land still in private hands.[69]

In 1883, shortly after he moved to New York, the senior Mills gifted the State of California a statue of Christopher Columbus kneeling at the feet of Queen Isabella of Spain while receiving her commitment to finance his initial voyages to the Americas. The statue sat in the Capitol's rotunda until it was removed in the summer of 2020 in the wake of nationwide protests against police murders and structural racism. It was a fitting parting gift from Mills given his role in extending the colonial processes initiated in the Americas by Columbus's voyages. As Mills's brother and banking partner Edgar put it at the dedication of the statue: "California, more than any other state in the American Union, fulfills [Columbus's] visions of marvelous lands beyond the setting sun."[70]

Of the many peoples who, up until 1883, had lived, worked, traveled on, or otherwise shaped the land that became the Mills estate, the Ure-bure and Ssalson experienced Columbus's "visions" most directly and tragically. But their brutal encounter with Spanish colonizers was just the first of many entanglements that happened at that place. Soon, the more locally situated settler colonial processes of grazing, shrimping, oystering, and recreating that had defined this land—shaped as they were by the imperialistic reach of Mills's and others' transnational business practices—would be superseded by others. These processes were still local, but they reached farther and more consistently "beyond the setting sun" as they drew Bay Area residents and others into ever-growing and farther-reaching assemblages. The relationships that defined them were products of a denser integration of local capital, governmental, military, and social networks that were eventually facilitated and imagined through a new kind of infrastructure—San Francisco's airport.

CHAPTER 2

Making San Francisco Airport

On January 15, 1911, as part of an airshow based at Selfridge Aviation Field in San Bruno, Lieutenant Myron S. Crissy dropped a six-pound bomb into the nearby marshland from a biplane piloted by Philip Parmalee. What was purported to be the first successful demonstration of aerial bombardment with live ammunition "from a heavier than air machine" left a hole the "size of a washtub" in the bayside mud. The long-term implications of this experiment were not lost on a reporter, who averred that Crissy had "assumed the fatal power of Jove" and prophesied that "at the next battle between civilized nations . . . yesterday's mimicry of war will have its vital, or deadly, repetition." The prediction would soon be realized. That November, an Italian pilot dropped several small bombs on Turkish forces in Libya during the Italo-Turkish war. The rest, as we know from the hundreds of thousands dead in Hiroshima, Nagasaki, Tokyo, Dresden, London, Cambodia, and other decimated places, is history in some of its most brutal articulations.[1]

Crissy's escapade was yet another chapter in the story of military activity on Ramaytush Ohlone land, and it would not be the last. Selfridge Field, located just to the northwest of the present-day SFO, was at Tanforan Racetrack, named after Jose Antonio Sánchez's grandson-in-law Toribio Tanforan. The US Army used the racetrack as a training center during World War I. Over several months in 1942, eight thousand Japanese Americans were processed at Tanforan before being sent to concentration camps. But the militaristic elements of early aviation in the

FIGURE 7. Lt. Myron Crissy, along with pilot Philip Parmalee, preparing for what, in 1911, was purported to be the first successful demonstration of a live bomb dropped from an airplane. The bomb exploded in the bayside marsh at or near what is now SFO. Courtesy Golden Gate National Recreation Area, Park Archives, PAM Photograph Collection, GOGA-1766.

Bay Area that Crissy's bomb emphasized upon that mud—which, if not part of the current SFO property, is certainly close by—are particularly relevant to the story of SFO's emergence and early development told in this chapter.

SFO opened as Mills Field in 1927 as a civilian airport, but, from the beginning, the US military shaped its operations. Military departments had since the war in Europe encouraged the proliferation of civilian airports across the country to help support their own operations. In turn, civilian aviation relied heavily on the aviation technologies, airways, and individual know-how developed for and within the armed services. Mills Field, like other early airports, also benefited from the military's direct financial subsidy of its infrastructure. More generally, the military bases and defense plants that supported the United States' participation in World War I, as well as its military operations in its western states and Mexico during that country's revolution, helped to feed the Bay Area's growing industrial economy. And that growth created both demand and justification for the development of civilian aviation in the region.

Aviation, then, supported at both the symbolic and material levels local government officials' and businesspeople's pursuit of a regional, imperial destiny during Mills Field's initially small-scale operations. This quest continued to be part of the story at what was soon renamed San Francisco Airport as it (like the commercial aviation industry more generally) expanded operations during the 1930s and 1940s. Civilian aviation was a kind of tributary of what historian Roger Lotchin calls the "metropolitan-military complex," composed of defense bases and plants, allied industries, and associated, large-scale public works projects, that reshaped the region across these decades.[2] But it was a tributary that nonetheless played a key role in the Bay Area's racial capitalist restructuring at the interface of military purpose and public works. Aviation helped to revamp the region's settler colonial formations, its growing imperial reach (especially as oriented toward the Pacific Rim), the concomitant individual and collective aspirations of its inhabitants, and the increasingly complex networks and relationships that defined their lives.

. . .

Commercial aviation in the United States was primarily an airmail business before it was a passenger business, and that enterprise benefited from aeronautical advances developed during World War I. When the US Post Office established airmail service in May 1918, it did so with the cooperation of the US Army, which provided the planes and pilots. Even after the Post Office took over flying operations several months later, it still received assistance from the military. A portion of the Post Office's aircraft fleet was purchased from the Army, Navy, and War Department, and its pilots, many of whom had been trained by the military, relied on Navy Department radio stations for navigation. Many civilian flights followed military airways that originally had been charted by the army. And, because they could not afford to build a sufficient number of airports themselves, both the Post Office and the military departments encouraged and provided guidance for the construction of civilian airports by municipalities and private entities. Such efforts dovetailed with those of urban boosters and aviation enthusiasts who thought the economic interests of their communities could be advanced through flight.[3]

US military personnel also played a role in fostering civilian interest in aviation and airport construction. In October 1919, Lieutenant-Colonel R. S. Hartz of the US Army's Air Service landed at the Presidio's airfield to great fanfare as part of a "round-the-rim of the United States flight," designed both to prepare for a planned round-the-world flight and to map out potential airmail routes in the United States. When Colonel Hartz spoke to the Bay Area press after his arrival, he linked the development of transcontinental airmail routes to the growth of domestic passenger traffic and to future "transpacific" flights of humans and mail. He said there was great potential in a nearby civilian airfield on the former grounds of the 1915 Panama-Pacific International Exposition that celebrated the construction and opening of the Panama Canal. With proper development of this site, he noted, San Francisco could be home to "the main airport in the West."[4]

Beginning the following year, the US Air Mail Service did use this nearby airfield, alternatively known as Montgomery Field or Marina Field, as the terminus of the transcontinental airmail route and the hub for mail flights to other destinations in the western United States. Leased by the city from private landowners, the short-lived airport had a rather tenuous existence, however, as the city wrangled with its insurers and its landlords over the state of the facility and its financial viability. Limited by the Presidio's hills and the width of the reclaimed land upon which the airport sat, it had room for only one runway for takeoffs into the prevailing winds. Eventually, that runway proved too short as airplanes grew in size. Another problem was consistently foggy conditions during the summer months. Still another was that local developers and district residents complained about the noise of increased air traffic and its potential effects on real estate prices. Given these problems, and with civilian flights prohibited at the neighboring US Army facility—now named Crissy Field after Major Dana (not Lieutenant Myron) Crissy, a victim of a 1919 aircraft crash—the US Air Mail Service moved its base of operations to the East Bay city of Concord, thirty miles to the east, in early 1925.[5]

Airmail operations returned to the west side of the bay a few years later, thanks in part to two pieces of federal legislation. The Air Mail Act of 1925 (also known as the Kelly Act) transformed the nation's airmail service from a government operation to one run by private carriers working under contracts awarded by the US Postal Service. The Air Commerce Act of 1926 gave the Department of Commerce's Aeronautics Branch responsibility for promoting air commerce by implementing and enforcing regulations for aircraft, air traffic, and pilots and by developing and maintaining airways and navigation aids between them. Although the act technically prohibited direct government funding for the construction of airports, it provided regulatory, professional, and infrastructural guidance for local municipalities. San Francisco now had financial and administrative incentive to build a new airport and take back the transcontinental airmail terminus from the inconveniently placed Concord without losing it to Los Angeles in the process.[6] Racial and imperialist ideologies would help too.

The search for San Francisco's new airport site involved a good deal of technological fetishism and utopian, futuristic imagining common in early airport planning in the United States and Europe. Some proposals sought to elevate the city's aeronautical infrastructure. One called for the airport to be built atop piers on San Francisco's waterfront. Another suggested it be located on a platform over the Southern Pacific train sheds at Third and Townsend Streets. A third recommended it be built over the Exposition Auditorium, a component of the complex of Civic Center buildings west of downtown, which were built in time for the city's 1915 Panama-Pacific Exposition.[7]

The first two proposals spoke to how planners often imagined that the commercial air industry would be established upon existing rail lines and shipping corridors and their terminuses—that is, over the transportation infrastructure that had facilitated the original violence of settlement in the Bay Area, the growth of the industries (mining, timber, petroleum, agriculture, and so on) that had enriched the region, and the development of overseas markets and extractive relationships that developed the region further. Moreover, boosters across the country commonly likened airports to harbors to justify public ownership of facilities that would connect their communities to other places.[8] The third proposal, with a raised airfield above a functional monument to the United States' growing imperial reach in Central and South America, spoke to how some aviation boosters' prosaic designs on the airmail industry were intertwined with an investment in the region's imperial (and racial) destiny.

Such expansionist sentiments had more generally been growing among white Bay Area elites and more centrist elements of organized labor since the Spanish-American War brought home even more than before the rewards of finding profitable outlets for their accumulated capital in overseas ventures supported by US government and military power. Japanese victory over Russia in 1905 made clear there was competition in such endeavors around the Pacific Rim.[9] Aviation promised more spoils. By the mid-1920s, European colonial powers were using aircraft to extend the work of empire by diminishing time and space separating metropoles and peripheries from one another.[10] Meanwhile, the US Army's 1924 round-the-world flight, in which three out of the original four pairs of military pilots circumnavigated the globe over the course of 175 days, provided new evidence to observers that commercial aviation could be an expression of the United States' power and ingenuity and a potential vehicle for expanding its political, military, and economic influence.[11] What better way, in some local boosters' minds, for San Francisco to realize its imperial ambitions than to build a new airport?

With the vertically oriented airport designs and potential ground-level locations inside the city deemed impractical because of engineering, geographical, or meteorological challenges, a committee appointed by the San Francisco Board of Supervisors began looking outside of the city. Conversation focused on six sites near the bay in San Mateo County. Second-closest to San Francisco was one on reclaimed Mills estate marshland. As San Francisco evaluated these sites, it received and took seriously a proposal from the owners of Bay Farm Island near Oakland that the airport should be located there. On November 2, 1926, San Francisco voters approved a charter amendment granting the city permission to purchase land for an airport outside the city limits.[12]

As debates over possible airport sites developed before and after the voters green-lighted the project, they were shaped by competing visions of Bay Area regionalism. One thing to work out was whether San Francisco's new airport would be an outgrowth of intraregional cooperation or the city's regional hegemony. The waterfront airport platform proposal had been pushed by Fred Dohrmann Jr., president of the Regional Plan Association of San Francisco Bay Counties. The association had been one of several major players promoting regional integration and shared public financing for infrastructure (roads, bridges, water supply, sewage treatment plants, and so on) and economic development across the ever-expanding Bay Area over the preceding decades. Although such proposals promised conveniences and cost savings from integration, they invariably raised concerns outside San Francisco that the city's political and economic interests would dominate and that the various participants would be unfairly subsidizing one another. This happened, for example, when San Francisco officials failed in the early 1910s in their linked efforts to achieve intramunicipal support for the tremendously expensive Hetch Hetchy water project and to incorporate cities of southern Marin County, the East Bay, and northern San Mateo County as boroughs of a New York City–like "Greater San Francisco."[13]

The Bay Farm site presented fewer obstacles to avoid during takeoffs and landings and was said to have less fog. Yet an East Bay location would require an additional leg of water transport to get mail, passengers, and goods to and from San Francisco, and it might pose a threat to San Francisco's regional centrality. As the debate over location proceeded, Mayor James Rolph Jr. criticized the more cooperative vision of Bay Area regionalism that a Bay Farm airport represented. Decrying the Bay Farm proposal as "a real estate scheme," Rolph argued against the "putting of San Francisco's money in any other place than bears the name of San Francisco." The implication was that the East Bay, whose voters and politicians had played key roles in defeating the earlier Greater San Francisco plan, was more competitor than collaborator when it came to San Francisco's hegemonic future. Instead, Rolph proposed placing the airport in San Mateo County, which "is today knocking at our door asking for permission to join San Francisco in a greater San Francisco."[14]

Rolph had a point about some San Mateo County residents' collective interest in becoming part of San Francisco. In 1912, it was one of the few counties to approve the proposed state constitutional amendment to create a Greater San Francisco. More recently, members of the Three Cities Chamber of Commerce of San Mateo, Burlingame, and Hillsborough, seeking to improve local infrastructure and business development, had been pushing a more limited version of the idea that would include only San Mateo County cities in Greater San Francisco. Yet other San Mateo County residents opposed such planning on the grounds it would diminish political power in San Mateo County and ultimately serve San Francisco.[15] Although San Mateo County remained independent in the end, local boosters soon got some of the hoped-for infrastructure in the form of an airport. The City and County of San Francisco, in return, was able to maintain what was in a sense a colonial relationship with its southern neighbor.

Initially, the frontrunning San Mateo County site was an underwater and marshland parcel in South San Francisco owned by the South San Francisco Land and Improvement Company. Midwestern meatpacking magnate Gustavas Swift had organized this stock corporation to purchase Miller & Lux land holdings and cattle operations as part of his efforts to establish a West Coast base of operations. As a potential airport location, Swift's holding appealed because it was closest to San Francisco and because South San Francisco offered initially free use of the land with an option to buy later. However, San Francisco began

FIGURE 8. Mills Field site in February 1927, shortly before construction of the airport began. As discussed in chapter 1, this marshland was surrounded by a levee built by Chinese workers in the nineteenth century and drained to provide pasturage for D. O. Mills's dairy cows. Collection of SFO Museum.

looking at other sites given concerns about some speculative aspects of the proposed land deal and pilots' and aviation companies' complaints about potentially unsafe conditions at the site because of fog, wind, and the presence of nearby San Bruno Mountain.[16]

Boeing Air Transport was awarded the contract for the Chicago–San Francisco leg of the transcontinental air mail route on January 27, 1927. As the debates over airport location continued into February, Boeing threatened to base its operations at the Bay Farm Island airport, which was now being developed by the City of Oakland with the assistance of the military. With renewed impetus to make a decision about a Peninsula site, San Francisco's supervisors turned their attention to the Mills estate, which, while slightly farther away from the city than the South San Francisco site, appeared to have better fog and wind conditions and did not reek of corruption. Indeed, the Mills family was initially lukewarm to the idea of the airport being based on its land and did not push the idea, but as negotiations proceeded, D. O. Mills's son Ogden eventually became more amenable.[17]

Although the Mills family's pursuit of wealth had propelled San Francisco's imperial development in the late nineteenth century, now in the twentieth century their relative comfort and their ambivalence about accruing more wealth enabled them to cut the city a reasonable deal, thereby helping to push the city in a new imperial direction. San Francisco signed a three-year lease with the Mills estate for the use of approximately 150 acres of drained, leveed pastureland at the cost of $10 per acre per year ($1,500). The city would also be required to pay the estate $25 per acre ($3,750) at the end of the lease period to cover reconditioning back to pasturage. For its part, the estate promised to maintain the levees separating the reclaimed marshland from the bay as well as the pumping station used to keep it as dry as possible. The San Francisco Board of Supervisors approved appropriations of $50,000 to develop the land and build aircraft hangars. In April, the site was officially named Mills Field Municipal Airport of San Francisco, and construction, undertaken by San Francisco's Department of Public Works, commenced. With its first runway completed, the city dedicated its new airport in San Mateo County on May 7, 1927.[18]

Symbolism abounded that spring and summer about how the still-fledging commercial aviation industry could develop hand in hand with US global expansion and the linked project of national defense. The airport opening was designed to coincide with a California Development Association–sponsored aeronautical conference in San Francisco and an associated "air tour" of fifty planes that traveled the state of California to promote commercial aviation. In his greetings to the conference—delivered via airmail, he was obliged to say—President Calvin Coolidge made one of these connections as he articulated the federal government's support for the development of the industry: "The existence of a large number of aircraft engaged in the peaceful pursuits of commerce will assure the instant use of one of the most important weapons of modern defense in case we should be called upon to repel an enemy invasion."[19]

Between the May 7 dedication and the facility's opening on June 7, Charles Lindbergh made his historic transatlantic flight between New York and Paris in *The Spirit of St. Louis*. Lindbergh quickly became a national hero, often represented by the press as a rugged, masculine individual who symbolically linked the fortunes of the white imperial nations of the North America and Europe while confirming the United States' ascendant role as a technologically advanced, modern nation. Lindbergh's flight, as well as his own commentary linking success in aviation to white and Western superiority, helped reproduce the distinctly inegalitarian phenomenon of early civilian aviation by distinguishing those putatively advanced peoples who flew from those who did not.[20] Closer to home, the imperialist aspirations associated with early Bay Area aviation were evident in efforts to complete a new packed-earth runway at Mills Field by early August so it could be used for the high-profile Bay Area-to-Oahu air race that month sponsored by "pineapple king" James Dole. Inspired by Lindbergh, the colonial planter held the competition to generate publicity for his canned, Hawaiian-grown pineapple products.[21]

The aviation industry was contributing to US imperial projects in material ways as well, especially in Latin America and the Caribbean. The United States used airplanes in its invasion and occupation of Nicaragua in 1927 and 1928, but aircraft also played a role in the expansion of "soft power" across the region. Pan American Airlines began flying airmail from Key West to Havana in October 1927 and passengers on the route the following January. It soon expanded its transport of not only mail and tourists but also corporate agents, military officers, and government officials representing US economic power and political hegemony across Mexico, the Caribbean, Central America, and South America. Lindbergh, who began consulting for Pan Am on its Latin American operations in 1929, had earlier served as agent of US empire when, during late 1927 and early 1928, at the behest of the US government, he took the *Spirit of St. Louis* on a goodwill tour of the region that in practice was also a demonstration of US power and technological expertise. His tour, after all, coincided with the appearance of a US delegation, led by President Calvin Coolidge, at the Pan American Congress meeting in Havana, where the future application of the Monroe Doctrine was on the table. Lindbergh was also tasked with surveying and assessing future commercial aviation routes.[22]

Yet it would be a while before Mills Field adequately served such imperial ambitions. Indeed, the first few years of its operations were decidedly mixed. The airport took a public relations hit when contestants in the ultimately ill-fated Dole race (only two planes finished the race, with three others lost at sea and five more crashing before or at the beginning of the race) opted to use Oakland's airport for takeoffs because it had a better runway. San Francisco lost out to Oakland again when Boeing, after beginning its Mills Field airmail operations in October, moved to the Bay Farm Island site in December because of poor field conditions and inconsistent weather across the bay. Other carriers would follow. Then a $1 million San Francisco bond measure designed to secure additional funding for the airport was narrowly defeated in November

1928. Adding insult to injury was the so-called Lindbergh incident. The iconic pilot visited the Bay Area in March 1929 as part of a cross-country trip in which he was testing a prototype, Keystone Patrician K-78, then the largest, fastest, and, unfortunately, heaviest commercial airplane built in the United States. While preparing to take off from Mills Field for an air tour with fifteen well-heeled passengers aboard, his plane became stuck in the mud to the side of the runway. Despite Lindbergh's protestations that Mills Field was still a perfectly fine facility, the incident generated a good deal of negative press and public commentary.[23]

With Mills Field now reduced to being a home for flying schools, private pilots, air shows, and a few short-lived commercial passenger ventures, airport and city officials redoubled their efforts to improve the facility and bring back business. But, as was the case with municipal airports elsewhere during the early Great Depression years, officials and boosters were faced with the daunting prospect of improving the facility to keep up with larger, faster planes and increased air traffic amid diminishing enthusiasm among voters for large public expenditures that did not obviously serve their interests.[24]

Officials commissioned a new meteorological study of fog conditions purporting to show that "nature favored San Francisco Airport" over its East Bay rival, and they emphasized Mills Field's proximity to the larger population of potential air travelers in San Francisco. They publicized as well the infrastructural projects they already could afford to undertake—including improvements to the drainage system to get rid of "dangerous soft spots." They also secured permanent control of the land upon which the airport sat. Following the stock market crash, the Mills family became more amenable to selling rather than renting their property, and San Francisco was able to come up with the agreed-upon purchase price of $1.05 million for the entire 1,112.5 acres of Mills estate, located between San Bruno and the "deep water of the Bay," upon which the airport's original 150 acres were located. Airport and city officials subsequently developed an ambitious plan for updating and expanding the airport's infrastructure.[25]

To finance these improvements, San Francisco placed a $4 million bond measure before San Francisco voters in November 1930. "Already with the world's greatest sea port," a flyer supporting the measure crowed, "San Francisco now plans the world's greatest airport." It added a quote from Lindbergh about the quality of the facility in an effort to put the previous year's mishap behind.[26] In the run-up to the vote. Supervisor E. Jack Spaulding held a hearing of San Francisco's Airport Committee, in which he trotted out for the press and other observers a host of aviation experts, businessmen, and others to make the case for expansion. Developing Mills Field, various speakers argued, could help the Bay Area, with San Francisco at its center, realize its imperial economic destiny. The opportunity would be lost, however, if the city and its voters did not act quickly with a public subsidy to take advantage of aviation's ascendancy.[27]

At the hearing, William Marvin, representative of San Francisco's Downtown Association, described aviation as a mechanism for extending the city's economic power and international reputation that had been established via "sea-borne commerce." Yet the railroad also provided a relevant model, in part because its success had depended on public support. "When the railroads pioneered the West," he argued, "the Central and Union Pacific, they had to depend upon government grants of land in order to make their railroads pay because they had to develop and pioneer and explore a new country. And that is what we are doing with the San Francisco Airport; we are pioneering a new commerce. We want a great port here that will take care of our air traffic." Captain Edison E. Mouton, head of the Western Division of the US Department of Commerce, made the imperial reach of this pioneer vision more explicit when waxing on about how municipally financed aeronautics in San Francisco would develop hand in hand with federally subsidized military and commercial aviation across the region. "San Francisco is destined to become one of the biggest aviation centers in the world. Can you picture a bombing base in Marin County, a tremendous army depot at Alameda, the Alameda Airport on the Alameda Mole, the San Francisco Bay Airdrome on the other side, Oakland Airport and a tremendous airport in San Francisco? There will be nothing like it in the world." Indeed, the Downtown Association, along with various Bay Area chambers of commerce, successfully lobbied the US government and contributed funds for the establishment of military air bases in Santa Clara, Marin, and Alameda Counties over the next few years.[28]

As a means both of centering San Francisco's role in this regional imperial destiny and of escaping Mills Field's "boggy" reputation, Marvin suggested renaming the facility "San Francisco Airport." Marvin would get his wish when the city's supervisors officially did so on June 9, 1931, though the redesignation came not as a triumphant articulation of ascendant regional power but as a desperate attempt at public relations for a facility that still appeared, in the eyes of some detractors, to be a failing boondoggle. The $4 million bond measure was approved by the majority of San Francisco voters that November, but it did not receive the two-thirds majority necessary for passage.[29] Escape from the muddy past through public subsidy, as envisioned by Marvin and Mouton, would have to wait for another, more effective round of public relations and some strategic leveraging of New Deal funds.

A key figure in catalyzing the emergent set of relationships leading to San Francisco Airport's stabilization and growth was Bernard Doolin, a veteran World War I fighter pilot and engineer in the Aviation Division of Standard Oil. Doolin was appointed as airport superintendent in June 1932 by San Francisco's Public Utilities Commission (SFPUC), which had taken on responsibility for airport operations that January. Doolin drew upon his "war tempered" connections with powerful figures associated with commercial and military aviation. First, he convinced a few small carriers and then larger airlines (United Air Lines and Transcontinental and Western Air, Inc., which later became TWA) to initiate service at San Francisco Airport or move operations from Oakland. Doolin also engaged in significant public relations activities in an effort to garner public support for the facility. These efforts bore fruit in November 1933 when a more modest $260,000 San Francisco bond measure passed by the requisite two-thirds margin. Subsequently, Doolin parlayed the citizenry's capital expenditure into a more significant investment when he used his position as airport supervisor for the California Civil Works Administration (CWA) and, subsequently, the Federal Emergency Relief Administration for California (SERA, as a branch of FERA), to secure agency funds for San Francisco Airport.[30]

Doolin's successful lobbying initiated San Francisco Airport's participation in a process that supported the growth of commercial aviation across the country. State and then federal New Deal relief and recovery programs dramatically expanded the nation's system of airports across the 1930s and helped to transform thinking about the role the federal government should play in financing them. Although the 1926 Air Commerce Act technically limited direct federal expenditures on airports, the exceptional circumstances of the economic crisis permitted New Deal programs to devote substantial funds to airport construction and renovation. Prior to 1933, airport operators, whether municipalities or private entities, had borne almost the entire cost of airport development in the United States, with the federal government contributing only 0.7 percent of the total cost. By 1938 the federal share had risen to 76.7 percent.[31]

The CWA, FERA, and the Works Progress Administration (WPA) were primarily relief programs. FERA, established in 1933, made grants to state relief agencies, which, among other things, distributed payments directly to families in need and instituted work programs. The short-lived CWA, largely run by FERA personnel, was a federal work program that ran from November 1933 to March 1934. The WPA, established in 1935, was a public employment program that superseded FERA. While very much a federal program, it coordinated efforts with state and local relief agencies. All three agencies supplied labor and materials for airport projects pursuant to proposals based on local need or in response to government initiatives designed to improve commercial aviation across the country. The WPA often took over projects started under earlier federal programs before undertaking its own, more extensive nationwide program. Initially, there was little expectation of local government contribution to such projects other than the land upon which airports were situated, although eventually community investments of around 30 percent of total project costs were the norm.[32]

Communities could also apply for Public Works Administration (PWA) grants and loans, alone or in tandem with relief projects, which provided funds for hiring private contractors for public works construction. Not technically a relief program, the PWA, also launched in 1933, was designed to stimulate the economy by regrowing the construction industry and creating demand for building materials. Although the percentage of federal subsidy (i.e., the "grant" portion) for PWA projects was typically smaller than for WPA proposals, PWA awards came with a fair amount of federal oversight at the engineering, planning, and fiscal levels while providing a form of welfare to local businesses and workers who were not necessarily drawn from the ranks of the unemployed and could be paid prevailing wages. Unions were given "first call" for positions on PWA projects. Given the relatively built-up nature of the core Bay Area, and the resultant need for skilled labor on construction jobs there, local sponsors frequently drew simultaneously from both WPA and PWA support for large infrastructural projects. These federal programs were sometimes supplemented with state funds, in some cases through programs where state agencies were conduits for federal funds.[33]

Doolin helped to coordinate a first wave of San Francisco Airport improvements financed by a combination of funds from the 1933 bond measure, CWA and FERA relief funds, PWA grants and loans, and other municipal sources. The major aspect of this expansion of the facility involved reclaiming and filling thirty-eight acres of tideland to permit the building of two longer, paved, intersecting runways, better oriented to take advantage of prevailing wind conditions. Earth for the fill was pulled from neighboring hillsides and supplemented with discarded oyster shells dredged from the bay floor. Other improvements included a lighting system, a sewage treatment plant, and additions to hangars. This expansion both facilitated and was encouraged by the growth of the air traffic at SFO, which was in part the result of larger, faster, and more comfortable airplanes that helped airlines—most notably, United—expand passenger operations and turn a profit by transporting people rather than relying on airmail as the foundation of their business model.[34]

Yet even before construction on this first wave of projects broke ground, Doolin was developing greater ambitions for the airport as the key node in a statewide aviation system. Operating both as San Francisco Airport superintendent and as airport supervisor for SERA, Doolin helped to devise a 1934 plan for improving ninety-eight airports across the state, which he subsequently presented to the Federal Aviation Commission. He proposed that San Francisco, described as the "main air terminus of the Pacific Coast," undergo a "complete modernization" at a cost of $1.6 million. Total project expenditures across the state would be $6.9 million, with local communities, federal relief programs, and the airline industry ideally sharing the cost. Once again, the argument for subsidizing the development of commercial aviation (and, now, relief and employment in a depressed economy) included claims that such growth would be good for national defense. Included with the plan was a letter from Brigadier General Seth E. Howard of the State of California, Division of Military Affairs, who argued that the improvement of the state's airport facilities was an "urgent necessity . . . not only from the military standpoint but from that of commercial aviation as well."[35]

Doolin's vision for a federally funded modernization of San Francisco Airport and improvements for airports across the state was more fully realized with the establishment of the WPA. Given the intensive labor required for ground improvements—digging, grading, paving, and so on—airports were ideal sites for rapidly deploying large numbers of unskilled workers. The WPA-financed expansion of the nation's airport system initially outstripped the nation's commercial aviation capacity, but the massive influx of public funding into airports—combined with new aviation technologies, consumer desire, and the needs of capital to extend and enhance markets—would enable the industry to catch up with its infrastructure.[36]

By December 1935, WPA funds of close to $1 million had been secured for major improvements to San Francisco Airport of the scope envisioned by Doolin the previous year.[37] These and other San Francisco Airport improvements during the second half of the 1930s, largely carried out under the auspices of the WPA and PWA, were part of a broader set of massive, federally subsidized public works projects—such as the Golden Gate and Bay Bridges, the Caldecott Tunnel, and, as will be discussed later, Treasure Island—that facilitated a growing sense of metropolitan coherence in the Bay Area. Such a vision infused the political rhetoric of local officials, boosters, and labor leaders, in tune as it was with contemporary writers' and artists' celebrations of Bay Area regionalism. Back of the vision was a growing sense that San Francisco and its neighboring cities needed further infrastructural development to compete with Los Angeles and other cities for control of West Coast and transpacific trade. The vision was also supported by an array of governmental, corporate, and military entanglements.[38]

San Francisco Airport improvements begun in the second half of the decade included the construction of a new, Spanish Revival–style terminal and administration building, various infrastructural enhancements (water, gas, electricity, telephone, sewage, pavement, etc.), and the expansion of the facility through the reclaiming and filling of approximately four hundred acres of open water and tidelands. The expansion enabled the completion, early the following decade, of a seaplane port, a small US Coast Guard base, and longer runways (two at five thousand feet, one at six thousand feet) that could accommodate the twenty-one passenger Douglas DC-3s and even larger four-engine planes being developed.[39] The majority of the funding for the expansion came from the federal government, with much of the work coordinated by WPA and PWA officials. Federal funds primarily paid for labor—largely through the WPA's expenditure on relief work, with a lesser amount funneled to workers through the PWA's payments to private contractors—although both entities funded the purchase of construction materials and purchase and rental of equipment. The city's contribution was smaller than the federal government's, but it was still significant, aided as it was by a $2.85 million bond measure approved by San Francisco voters in November 1937. The city obtained necessary underwater acreage for the expansion by purchasing it, at relatively low cost, from San Mateo County oyster companies.[40]

The Spanish Revival–style terminal building, a project undertaken by a San Francisco–based contractor and subcontractors under the auspices of the PWA, was consistent with one of the trends of WPA- and PWA-funded airport buildings, which was to align them with regional architectural aesthetics.[41] As such, designers matched it with a cultural and architectural movement across the state (especially in Southern California) over the preceding few decades. In the Bay Area, this recuperation of the Spanish past, encouraged by preservationists, scholars, educators, journalists, and the tourist industry, included the refurbishing of local missions and the installation of "mission bells" along El Camino Real.[42]

As scholar-activist Carey McWilliams long ago observed, this movement helped to produce a "fantasy heritage" of a genteel Spanish and Californio past that masked both the foundational colonial violence in California and the ongoing systems of racial and class domination in the state, especially vis-à-vis its Mexican and Mexican American populations.[43] While doing so, this romanticized vision, built into the environment, as historian Phoebe Kropp argues, positioned present-day, Anglo-dominated California as the leading edge of a national imperial project that had succeeded Spain's.[44] The new terminal, then, was a fitting element of self-representational architecture for the newly revamped San Francisco Airport, as it referenced a longer history of colonial relations in the region while putting a benign face on them and their imperial afterlives. Moreover, as with other contemporaneous programs that promoted economic recovery, social welfare, and public works, the New Deal's support for aviation was a putatively race-neutral project that built racial exclusions into infrastructures that would play an ever-growing role in catalyzing asymmetrical relationships in the Bay Area and elsewhere.[45]

The SFPUC confidently stated, in its early 1937 report on airport operations, that "the status of San Francisco Airport has passed from that of national to international renown." Such renown, according to the report, was in part a function of the airport's recent negotiation of an agreement with Pan American to make the facility, with its seaport under construction, the base of the airline's transpacific operations.[46] Indeed, as Jenifer Van Vleck documents, Pan Am had done well during the Depression years. It expanded its operations across the Caribbean and Latin America in ways that preceded and then developed hand in hand with the United States' "Good Neighbor" approach to maintaining hegemony in the region as announced by President Franklin D. Roosevelt in 1933. More recently, the airline had established mail and passenger service between California and China as a means of expanding trade to the country and other Asian nations. Pan Am's president Juan Trippe won the political and financial support of the Roosevelt administration—which allowed him to build the necessary landing facilities on Guam, Midway, and Wake Islands and to use the US Naval facilities at Pearl Harbor, Alameda, and Manilla—because of growing fears of Japanese militarism and influence in the Pacific. Trippe helped his case by promising to be a naval "surrogate" in the Pacific, maintaining a US presence, monitoring Japanese activities via aircraft radio equipment, and establishing airfields and attendant facilities that the United States could use if war broke out. The inaugural airmail flight of Pan Am's China Clipper from Alameda to Manilla occurred on November 22, 1935—a date California's governor proclaimed as Pan American Airways Day—with one hundred thousand watching the Martin M-130 fly through the Golden Gate.[47]

When airport officials announced the following month that Pan Am's base of operations would be moved to the Peninsula airport rather than staying put in Oakland or going to Los Angeles or another West Coast port, San Francisco and San Mateo County officials celebrated it as a major coup. San Mateo officials also breathed a sigh of relief given the uncertainty at the moment, as will be discussed later, about the role the San Mateo County facility would play in the future given plans for a second San Francisco airport on Treasure Island.[48] Regardless, local officials recognized that government subsidy for this prestige-making, imperial endeavor would be an important boon for the depressed local economy by providing assistance for unemployed workers and business interests alike. Although the airport was at this point run by a skeleton crew of permanent employees, city and airport officials were beginning to promote the facility as an economic engine for the region that would be anchored by large airlines as tenants while drawing in a variety of associated businesses. In addition to United and Pan Am, TWA had recently worked out an arrangement to reestablish operations at the facility. "Scheduled air transport operation," the SFPUC argued, would be the key to the airport's success as a public utility, in terms of both generating revenue for the city and stimulating associated economic growth through expanding regular employment.[49]

The late 1930s was a moment when moderate Bay Area labor and business interests increasingly found common ground, in part through cooperative efforts to secure New Deal–subsidized urban development in the region, after a period of intense conflict culminating in the 1934 West Coast–wide walkout by the International Association of Longshoreman (ILA), the subsequent San Francisco General Strike after the murder of two workers outside of ILA headquarters on Steuart Street, and the vigilante and police violence that brought the strike to an end. Unions cut agreements to guarantee their access to jobs on New Deal–

sponsored construction projects in the Bay Area, including signing no-strike pledges on occasion. Although WPA relief workers on the airport job in March 1936 briefly protested after their pay was late to arrive, activism by union construction workers was not a factor beyond that being done behind the scene by leadership to secure a portion of the federally subsidized employment.[50]

The incorporation of labor into this project was, however, exclusionary along the lines of race and gender in ways that anticipated the airport's future role as an incubator of opportunity and exclusion. New Deal public works projects were, after all, subsidizing a construction industry and building trades that, in the Bay Area and elsewhere in the United States, had long developed as the province of white men and, for the most part, were still actively discriminating against women and nonwhite men.[51] Although contracts for federally subsidized San Francisco Airport expansion projects had nondiscrimination clauses, going back to the first wave of projects negotiated by Doolin, in practice these could do little to rectify existing inequalities, even if they were intended to do anything about them in the first place.[52]

Generally speaking, people of color were more successful in finding work on projects on which the WPA was the primarily supplier of unskilled labor, such as grading and paving projects. Black and Chinese American workers from San Francisco were among those transported to the San Mateo County facility for construction projects. Yet such work was generally temporary for those pulled from relief rolls and seldom led to more consistent employment with local construction contractors that routinely practiced racial discrimination. Such was no doubt the case with the new administration building job undertaken by an established, San Francisco–based contractor and similarly-placed subcontractors. Although the contract specified a preference for WPA workers pulled from the relief rolls, there was an exception that gave the contractor and subcontractors the right to employ the union (read white) labor that they typically used on their projects. Unlike with contracts for jobs elsewhere in the United States, the nondiscrimination clause for this particular PWA project did not specify that it must include a percentage of minority workers based on their distribution in the local construction trades. Not that it would have made much difference in San Francisco and San Mateo Counties, whose racial minority populations were tiny in the 1930s and whose unions routinely practiced racial discrimination. Moreover, the citizenship requirement in contracts specifying WPA-supplied labor for construction projects by definition excluded some

FIGURE 9. Works Progress Administration (WPA) workers on 1936 San Francisco Airport paving project. The WPA provided significant labor and materials for the expansion of the airport during the New Deal, as it did for major infrastructural projects in the Bay Area and airport construction and expansion across the United States. Collection of SFO Museum.

Asian American and Latinx people from even temporary, low-skilled relief work.[53] In other words, the future airport-as-employment engine gestured to by the SFPUC, as will be discussed later, would be an explicitly racially exclusionary institution for the next few decades and a contradictory and limited site of opportunity after that.

Even as the San Mateo County facility grew, airport and city officials and members of the local business community developed plans for a second San Francisco airport on human-made Treasure Island, to be built over the shoals north of Yerba Buena Island, in the middle of the bay between San Francisco and Oakland. Although the second airport project was never fully realized, it helped to extend, along with the Golden Gate International Exhibitions of 1939 and 1940, the imperialistic vision associated with Bay Area aviation. And it was precisely through Treasure Island's unexpected future as a military facility that the original San Francisco Airport would obtain even more government spending, as the New Deal welfare state morphed into the warfare state that was consolidated during the run-up to World War II. This funding, in turn, helped propel San Francisco's airport toward its eventual "international" status and more complex function as a locus of networked power.

Given the early uncertainties about the condition of Mills Field, lingering concerns about its distance from San Francisco, and the failure of the city to pass the 1930 bond measure, San Francisco's Junior Chamber of Commerce (Jaycees) began pushing the idea for the island airport in late 1931 as one several alternatives for replacing it. The Chamber's Aeronautics Committee solicited the assistance of various experts and officials, including Superintendent Doolin, even as he was working hard to revive Mills Field. By December 1932 the SFPUC had formal plans for the island in hand, and in June 1933 now–California governor James Rolph granted the necessary underwater land to the city.[54] The pursuit of this large, visionary public works project was dependent on the completion of the Bay Bridge, which Congress approved in May 1931, as well as on the broader public's investments in San Francisco's metropolitan, imperial vision and the idea that it could reassert its dominance over Los Angeles as the premier West Coast city. But the idea of building an "island airport," oriented toward the islands of the Pacific and serving the needs of local business elites with financial interests across the Pacific Rim, really took off, so to speak, when plans began to emerge to hold an international exposition there prior to its dedication to full-time use for airport operations.[55]

San Francisco voters approved the development of the site in May 1935, and the city subsequently embarked on what would become a $4.7 million project, with the majority of funding, labor, and expertise supplied by the WPA, the Army Corps of Engineers, and the PWA. The arrangement was mapped out in part at a meeting at the Bohemian Grove, the exclusive Sonoma County retreat grounds of the powerful Bohemian Club, whose members included some of the most powerful corporate and political leaders in the United States. The US Army Corps began work in February 1936 with the construction of a seawall that defined the island perimeter. This created a lagoon that workers filled with sand, mud, and assorted living and dead plant and animal life dredged from the bottom of the bay. The WPA did much of the architectural and engineering design work for the island, and its laborers graded, landscaped, paved, and otherwise worked the new land while also contributing to PWA-funded building projects, including hangars and a new administration building for the future airport. The San Francisco

Building Trades Council supported the endeavor and the metropolitan vision behind it by agreeing not to disrupt construction with a strike so long as union labor was used on the project.[56]

As Treasure Island was being built, there was significant uncertainty about the roles San Francisco's two airports would play. News of San Francisco's plans to reclaim the Yerba Buena shoals for the exposition and a future airport caused San Mateo County officials to worry in the summer of 1935 that the city would simply move the airport to the new facility rather than maintaining two sites. But the San Mateo contingent was somewhat mollified that December when Doolin announced the plans for the future Pan-Am seaplane terminal at the original site and said San Francisco would, for the time being, continue to operate both facilities.[57] Although the SFPUC hinted a few years later that Treasure Island would become the city's primary terminal, such talk was, by this point, likely just the hedging of bets. The planned six-thousand-foot runway at the San Mateo County site would be able to accommodate the high-altitude airplanes that were to be put into operation within a few years, while the once-ballyhooed four-thousand-foot runways at Treasure Island would soon be obsolete.[58] Still, the two-airport vision was celebrated at the 1939 exhibition, where visitors at the San Francisco Airport exhibit could listen to radio transmissions from the San Mateo County facility's tower from the site of the city's "second airport of the future."[59]

San Francisco's two-pronged airport development project benefited significantly from more centralized national defense– and economic recovery–linked federal airport planning and funding at the end of the decade. Municipalities had been pushing for such support for a few years given their collective difficulties, despite New Deal assistance, in coming up with the money to maintain and grow facilities that could keep up with expanding aircraft size and flight operations. In late 1936, the American Municipal Association proposed that "the Federal Government should prescribe a system of National Civil Airways and Airports, just as it prescribed and plotted a system of Federal Highways," based in part on the idea that aviation had become critical to both national defense and interstate commerce. The following year a US Bureau of Air Commerce committee followed up with its own proposal for a "national system of public airports" with costs shared by state, local, and federal government, adding as a necessary corollary that restrictions on direct federal funding for airports be deleted from the Air Commerce Act of 1926.[60]

The Civil Aeronautics Act of 1938 created a new, independent agency, the Civil Aeronautics Authority (CAA), and expanded government regulation and support of the industry, including the regularizing of airmail service, increasing oversight of air traffic, accident investigation, and safety inspection and certification. In March 1939 the CAA determined that airports were a "proper object of Federal expenditure" and not just in exceptional times of high unemployment and economic depression. Funding preference was to be given to airports that were "important to the maintenance of safe and efficient operation of air transportation along the major trade routes of the Nation" as well as to those "rendering special service to the national defense." The CAA's recommendations were not fully implemented until the Federal Airport Act of 1946, but the creation of the Authority and its recommendations shaped the planning and funding climate at the end of the 1930s. After its creation, the CAA worked with the PWA and WPA—and the Federal Works Agency (FWAS), under which the PWA and WPA were consolidated in 1939—to certify the adequate completion of federally funded projects and the approval of new ones.[61]

The San Francisco Airport and Treasure Island projects both received additional funding in those years, enabling the planned Coast Guard base at San Francisco Airport to be commissioned in November 1940.[62] Another significant development at the former Mills Field was the October 1940 agreement between United Airlines and the city to establish its Western Division operation, maintenance, and overhaul base at the airport, following a competition with other cities in the West. The city provided the land and the buildings, while United contributed construction costs as well as a rather nominal amount in landing fees and rent. Airport and city officials stressed that the real economic benefit came in the form of local purchasing of materials for its operations and the local spending by the estimated five hundred new employees with a payroll of $1.3 million a year. As the SFPUC put it, the project was "the greatest single industrial development in the history of San Francisco Airport and it will be an ever-expanding addition to the commercial life of the city and the community."[63] In other words, this agreement illustrated how militarily inflected federal largesse helped to underwrite the civic/corporate agreements that facilitated growth of the air transport industry in the Bay Area, as they did elsewhere, and made aviation a more significant component of its economy.

The imperial aspirations of such growth were, at least for the moment, more apparent at Treasure Island. Northern California WPA official William R. Lawson predicted that once the Golden Gate International Exhibition closed, "the island will become one of the world's most important airports—useful to civilian and commercial aviation in time of peace and a tower of strength in the defense of the Nation in time of war."[64] The exhibition itself, which opened in February 1939, offered imperial visions of various vintages. The reenactments of frontier conquest in the production at the 1939 fair "Cavalcade of the Golden West," as well as in the proliferation of costumed Indians, cowgirls, cowboys, and Mexican campesina/os among performers and patrons alike, referenced local colonial pasts while presenting the Bay Area as a regionally specific site of American progress. Evoking one such past was the fact that small traces of gold were found in Treasure Island's soil, which was a factor in it being named as such. The gold presumably made it to the bay floor amid the sediment washed from the Sierra Nevada foothills during nineteenth-century hydraulic mining operations—likely with Bank Crowd capital behind it.[65]

The exhibition theme, "Pageant of the Pacific," looked to the future, however, by promoting Pacific Rim trade and cultural exchange at a moment when East Asia was the fastest-growing market for US investments—in significant part because US militarism had helped to provide access to it in previous decades—and there were increasing fears of competition from Japan for such spoils. Granted, the exhibition grounds were a site of contradictory meanings. Diego Rivera's *Unión de la Expresión Artistica del Norte y Sur de Este Continente* (The marriage of the artistic expression of the North and of the South on this continent), a mural painted and displayed at the 1940 exhibition, offered up a radical vision of international relations in the spheres of cultural expression, labor, and knowledge production. Distancing themselves somewhat, though not completely, at a moment of ascendant New Deal liberalism, from previous displays of colonial and imperialist impulses at such exhibitions, the fair's courts, pavilions, and exhibits presented a putatively enlightened and egalitarian, albeit exotic, vision of the peoples in Latin America and Asia whose societies surrounded the Pacific Rim. Still, a hegemonic US and, by extension, white American role in a Pacific Rim future was a key part of the story. According to exhibition organizers, "The course of empire moves West, and the future greatness of San Francisco and her neighboring communities in the Bay Area is bound up in a great measure with growth and development of our trade and commerce with the nations of the Pacific."[66]

Pan Am played a significant role in crafting this vision. Even as construction of the seaplane base in San Mateo County proceeded, the airline signed a ten-year contract with the city to relocate its operations from Alameda to Treasure Island in time for the exhibition and put into service five new Boeing B-314s for the occasion that would ferry their elite passengers to Asia for extravagant fares. Pan Am water takeoffs and landings at the "Port of the Tradewinds" became a popular attraction, and tourists could also watch the clippers being serviced inside a hangar dubbed the Hall of Air Transportation.[67] During the second iteration of the fair in 1940, Pan Am opened up a new route out of Treasure Island to New Zealand, with city officials bragging that it would give the Bay Area access to the $2 billion in trade running through the "Antipodes."[68]

Conflict with Japan indeed made Treasure Island a "tower of strength in the defense of the Nation in time of war," although not in the way envisioned by Lawson and others in 1939. The civilian airport serving national defense purposes never materialized at the manmade island, which instead became a naval facility. And in significant part because of the failure of the civilian island project as originally conceived, San Francisco's San Mateo County airport expanded dramatically during World War II—in terms of operations, infrastructure, and generation of capital—as a hybrid civilian and warfare facility.

Indeed, World War II was a period of tremendous growth for the aviation industry across the United States. With war in Europe ramping up, and in the wake of the 1939 CAA decision on federal aviation expenditures, New Deal agencies boosted airport construction and improvement spending, with increasing reliance on private contractors, as they shifted their orientation from job creation and welfare for business to national defense preparation under the direction of military agencies. Much of the funding went to strategically located East Coast, West Coast, and southern airports. Once the United States entered the war, its military took direct or partial control of or made financial investments in civilian aviation facilities across the nation that they used for transportation, training, staging, or other purposes.[69] Although the attack on Pearl Harbor, air raids on the home front, and knowledge of destructive bombing on other continents created anxieties about aviation among members of the US public, during World War II many Americans became more acclimated to it and its growing role in the economic and social life of the nation. This was in no small part the result of various propaganda campaigns on the part of government officials, the airline industry, and other business and leaders to link the growth of aviation to the United States' domestic economic development, ascendancy in an international order, and pursuit of "national security."[70]

As the second version of the Golden Gate International Exhibition wound down in September of 1940, San Francisco officials began planning to transform Treasure Island from fairgrounds to airport and applied for additional WPA funds to complete the work. Shortly thereafter, with the entry of the United States into World War II appearing more likely, the US Navy entered into negotiations with the city to take over the island temporarily as a training facility. In February 1941 the parties agreed to a year-to-year lease, giving the navy control of the entire island except for the Pan Am facility, two-thirds of the administration building, and a small area of land adjacent to it. In exchange, the navy agreed to sponsor a $1.68 million WPA job (subsequently run by the FWA) to build the runways and make other improvements to the island. On April 1, the facility, along with parts of neighboring Yerba Buena Island, were commissioned as Naval Station Treasure Island, the headquarters of the Twelfth Naval District. Groundbreaking on the construction commenced soon thereafter.[71]

After Pearl Harbor, however, the navy began increasingly heated discussions with the city about securing permanent control of the facility. They used as justification federal rules preventing it from building permanent military structures on leased land. With discussions at an impasse, the navy instituted condemnation proceedings, following the Second War Powers Act of March 1942, granting the executive branch the power to acquire land for military purposes, and took ownership of the island on April 17 of that year.[72] Negotiations then proceeded over the compensation the city might receive from the US government for a facility that federal funds had essentially built. Thanks in part to the well-connected Bernard Doolin's lobbying efforts in Washington, San Francisco received as compensation for relinquishing its title to Treasure Island separate $5 million contracts from the US Navy and US Army for improvements to its San Mateo County airport. The army agreed to add approximately one hundred acres of bay fill to the facility and use it as a basis for doubling the width of the prevailing-wind runway and extending its length to eight thousand feet. It also added forty thousand square yards of taxiways and airplane parking. The navy, again using condemnation proceedings to justify the construction of permanent facilities, took control of ninety-three acres of land north and northwest of the Seaplane Harbor and built upon it a naval air transport base and associated buildings.[73]

This work was done with the understanding that Pan Am would, as previously planned, move its transpacific operations base and air terminal from Treasure Island to San Francisco Airport when construction was complete. The transition ran all the more smoothly given that Pan Am was serving as contractor to the Naval Air Transport Service during the conflict. This was part of the broader agreement that the entire set of infrastructural improvements undertaken by the army and navy, as well as the land upon which they were built, would be turned over to the city "in fee simple" shortly after the end of hostilities. Although the military ostensibly was granted priority use of the airport, this agreement came with the understanding that the city would continue to use portions of the facility not dedicated to military use for civilian purposes.[74]

These military contracts were major boons to the construction industry, benefiting large national infrastructural construction firm Morrison-Knudsen as well as local contractors. Even before the future Pan-Am base was complete, San Francisco officials saw the finally realized arrival of a third major airline to the city as an economic and job creation engine for the region. Now, according to the SFPUC in 1943, it was not the United base but the navy- and army-funded expansion of the airport that "represents the greatest single industrial development in the history of the San Francisco Airport, and will be an ever-expanding addition to the commercial life of the city and community." And it was a commercial life that would benefit from the presence of both explicitly military and military-subsidized civilian projects in the region in the years to come.[75]

Indeed, the army- and navy-financed infrastructural transformations—dramatically supplementing already-underway projects funded by the WPA, the CAA, municipal bonds, and United Airlines—helped to expand commercial operations at the airport during the war years. Although the number of civilian flights declined during the middle of the war, the number of paying passengers using the airport increased at least slightly each year, thanks to more efficient use of planes, with major increases in passenger numbers at the end of the war. In fiscal year 1939–40, 126,546 passengers used the airport. By fiscal year 1944–45 that number had climbed to 414,392. Airmail and air cargo tonnage increased consistently and substantially as well.[76]

United Airlines, the primary commercial airline presence at the airport, expanded its operations dramatically once its new facilities opened in 1942. Its passenger numbers were enhanced both by growing civilian consumer demand and by its contracts with the US Army Air Transport Command to move military personnel among bases and points of embarkation in the United States as well as to and from the Pacific theater. TWA's operations increased dramatically after it signed a new, twenty-year lease on its facilities in the fall of 1942; Western Airlines returned to San Francisco Airport in May 1944 with a focus on the highly popular San Francisco / Los Angeles route; and Pan American moved its civilian operations to the facility that November.[77]

As the war wound down, San Francisco Airport and city officials sought to leverage the airport's wartime expansion for even-greater civilian operations. In December 1944, Doolin, Cahill, and SFPUC officials requested that the San Francisco Board of Supervisors put before the voters a $20 million bond measure to further expand and modernize the airport, relocate the Bayshore Highway, just completed in 1937, to the west to increase usable airport acreage and improve access, and make other improvements in order to accommodate the anticipated growth of civilian air transportation after the war. They emphasized the tremendous growth in both employment and airport operations over the previous several years, and they anticipated that such trends would continue as current carriers using the airport announced plans for expansion, other carriers proposed to begin using the facility, and industry and government entities prognosticated an increase in foreign and domestic airline travel after the war.[78]

Drawing on a recent study, the SFPUC argued that by 1953, San Francisco Airport would see on-site employment of sixteen thousand persons, who would earn a payroll of $43 million while processing 2.7 million passengers, 222 million pounds of airmail, and twenty-four million pounds of cargo annually. They recognized the role that military funding had played in the development of San Francisco Airport, but they argued that reconversion and expansion of the facility for civilian purposes would require different kinds of public investment as catalysts for private investments by airlines and allied businesses. Ultimately it would be the combination of municipal funding and corporate capital that would enable San Francisco Airport to keep its air industry tenants in place while recruiting others. Thus would San Francisco's airport maintain its favorable position vis-à-vis other Bay Area and farther-flung West Coast airports as both local generator of local wealth and jobs and access point to the Pacific Basin, the "greatest yet undeveloped

FIGURE 10. San Francisco Airport looking south, 1950. Illustrates the development of the airport over its two decades of existence. This work involved significant facilities construction and a major incursion into the bay to accommodate the airport's intersecting runways. Collection of SFO Museum.

trade area in the world."[79] San Francisco officials, airline executives, journalists, and Mayor Roger Lapham's Citizens' Postwar Planning Committee—which included increasingly centrist local labor leaders invested in cooperating with government and business to secure publicly funded infrastructural growth—made similar arguments over the next year, often with particular emphasis on competition with Los Angeles over control of the air transport business. The bond measure passed in November 1945.[80]

Less than two decades after its opening, then, San Francisco Airport was firmly established as a publicly subsidized infrastructural assemblage that facilitated an ever-widening array of relationships among Bay Area residents, networks of various kinds, and elements of the natural world while helping to put them in relationship with entities elsewhere. These relationships were fundamentally structured by residual inequalities and exclusions from the past that had accumulated at that site and in the world beyond as well as by emergent ones that the airport helped to facilitate. These phenomena were manifest in the airport's increasingly important role in the region's expanding imperial portfolio and in the social positions and deeds of the growing numbers of people who traveled through, worked at, and did business at the facility. And San Francisco Airport was set to grow in ever more complicated ways.

CHAPTER 3

Of Fighting Planes and Flowers

The expansion of SFO envisioned by its supporters at the end of World War II was at least partially realized a decade later. Improvements completed by then included a new, modernist terminal building and concourses, extended runways requiring additional bay fill, new airmail and air cargo facilities, and upgrades to airport utilities. SFO had even met some of the rosy prognostications of airport operations and employment used to sell the 1945 bond measure. True, the nine thousand people working at the airport in 1954 paled in comparison to earlier estimates of sixteen thousand by 1953. But the 2.5 million passengers who used the airport in fiscal year 1953–54 almost met the earlier estimate of 2.7 million, and the 46.7 million pounds of air express and air freight almost doubled what had been imagined a decade earlier.[1]

SFO's expansion was part of an early Cold War airport construction boom across the United States. New suburban facilities came on line, and others expanded to accommodate an industry (and the metropolitan development of which it was part and parcel) that was expected to (and would indeed) grow even more once commercial jet travel became viable in the United States. These projects included the opening of Greater Pittsburgh International Airport in 1952; the inauguration of international terminals at New York's Idlewild and Chicago's O'Hare airports in 1957 and 1958 respectively, with further expansion soon to follow; the completion of Los Angeles International Airport's terminal complex in 1961; and the dedication of Dulles International Airport outside of Washington, D.C., in 1962.[2] Indeed, the volume of people and things moving through SFO had grown as civilian air travel and commerce expanded dramatically during a postwar economic boom, with lower-cost commuter flights to Southern California and domestic and international tourist fares now widely available to consumers and air freight an increasingly affordable option for businesses.[3]

In other words, SFO was ever more integral to economic and social relations in what was now a more fully realized Bay Area metropolitan region in terms of population growth, the dispersion of industry and professional operations, suburban sprawl and infill, expanding transportation and infrastructure networks, the incorporation of new municipalities, large-scale regional planning efforts, and other phenomena.[4] By extension, SFO had become an increasingly significant vehicle for regional identification. The airport had for several decades been celebrated by local elites as a symbol of civilian militarism and imperialistic reach that they perceived as, or at least argued was, serving the common good. But now, more than ever, SFO was an infrastructure to which members of a wider public could link their individual mobility and progress—whether expressed through air travel or not—as well as to that of the fast-growing region in which they lived.

This was all on display in late August 1954 when SFO celebrated its expansion and recent redesignation as San Francisco International Airport with a Flight Festival and terminal dedication. Five hundred thousand people from across the Bay Area descended on SFO over the three-day celebration sponsored primarily by the San Francisco Public Utilities Commission and the city's chamber of commerce and Jaycees. For some visitors, it was a chance to take their first look inside an aircraft: forty-three of them were on display. Others spent significant time among the throngs at the new terminal's state-of-the-art cocktail lounge. The festival also afforded visitors the opportunity to invest in regional pride and various visions of internationalism presented to them by airport officials, airlines, local business and community service groups, government officials, the military, and entertainers. There were clowns and acrobats; wandering folk artists; US Air Force, Army, Coast Guard, and Marine bands; and beauty queens. Festival-goers could watch airline-sponsored films promoting travel to Hawaii, Mexico, Japan, Tahiti, and US destinations at the "See the World" exhibit and pick up travel brochures; participate in drawings for prizes brought from Europe by TWA; join the crowd hoping to catch one of the packets of imported Irish shamrocks (also courtesy of TWA) dropped from a Hiller

FIGURE 11. New terminal, planes, and crowd at what was now officially San Francisco International Airport at its 1954 Flight Festival and terminal dedication. A major theme of the celebration was internationalism, as exemplified by the distribution of prizes from overseas, diverse entertainments, and exhibits promoting foreign travel. Collection of SFO Museum.

helicopter hovering overhead; or inspect a Pan Am Boeing 377 Stratocruiser, which the airline used for flights to Honolulu and Oceanic and Asian destinations beyond.[5]

The festival was also a performance of the gendered whiteness of the airport as workplace, travel hub, and economic engine, which made perfect sense given the demographics of California and Bay Area power and wealth at this moment—outgrowths of the long history of colonial and imperial development that was back of SFO's own expansion into its current, early Cold War–era form. Written descriptions and photographs of the weekend's festivities show uniformly white and male groups of elected officials (including local mayors and California governor Goodwin Knight), union leaders, and airport officials presiding over the dedication and other events. Their wives were there, too, but very much as wives, offstage in their finery. The beauty queens on display also enhanced the whiteness and the heteronormativity of the

festival. Even most of the cosmopolitan array of folk artists—
Yugoslavian dancers and Spanish troubadours, for example—had European roots.[6]

The festival crowd was remarkably white too. Again, this was not
surprising given that the Bay Area population was still over 90 percent
white in 1950, despite recent migrations of African Americans, Mexican Americans, Native Americans, and others to the area to work in the
defense industry.[7] But photographs of the event show a crowd even
whiter than that.[8] This site-specific demographic seems, in part, a product of the asymmetrical distribution of spending power among the
region's inhabitants. Civilian air travel in the United States was, in
1954, despite its recent democratization, still largely the provenance of
reasonably well-off white consumers. The largely monochromatic
crowd was also likely a function of what sociologist Wilson Record
called the "basic racial provincialism" (i.e., social and residential segregation) that underlay "the Bay Area's surface cosmopolitanism" during
the postwar period.[9] Moreover, given that the crowds likely included a
high representation of people with an economic relationship to the airport, as well as their family members, the whiteness of the festival-goers
would have stemmed from, as will be discussed in subsequent chapters,
the systematic racial discrimination in airport employment, in the local
building trades whose members worked on airport construction
projects, and among local vendors and other businesses that provided
services to the facility. It spoke more generally to how massive postwar
infrastructure projects in San Francisco and the Bay Area more generally, as Destin Jenkins discusses in great detail, publicly funded by federal aid and low-interest municipal bonds, primarily benefited white
consumers and workers, even though current and future Black and
Brown residents remained on the hook for paying for them with their
tax dollars and through the lack of investments in projects that would
have benefited them more directly.[10]

There were, to be sure, some cracks in this monochromatic facade
that anticipated the challenges to those racial configurations of social
space as well as the demographic shifts the Bay Area would witness over
the coming decades. A few Black folk are evident in at least one of the
extant photographs of the crowd.[11] The St. Mary's Chinese Girls' Drum
Corps diversified the waves of marching bands and drill teams parading
around the festival, and a Japanese employee of Japan Airlines was a
member of the flight attendant subset of "flight festival queens."[12]
Although it would still be a few years before US airlines hired nonwhite

FIGURE 12. Planes and visitors at the 1954 festivities. Approximately five hundred thousand people visited SFO over the course of the three-day event. The couple on the right-hand side of photograph are among the few Black (or other BIPOC) visitors who appear in extant photographs or descriptions of this event. Collection of SFO Museum.

women to work on domestic flights, they could be encountered in 1954 working for foreign carriers or on US carrier flights to the Caribbean or Hawaii.[13] Yet even as these forms of display anticipated future shifts in sociability and access in the region, they also betrayed the exclusionary foundations of what was to come.

Two particularly notable signifiers of the air industry's expanding infrastructure and international reach proliferated at the festival: fighting planes and flowers. Both were signifiers of the Bay Area's development as metropolitan region. Emphasizing their roles in the festival and the ways they were discussed in the press offers insights into the airport's growing operations and their broader significance in the colonial present of the early Cold War period. For at this moment, when SFO's role as economic engine and transportation hub was more fully realized, it also became more significant and symbolically visible as an assemblage with both local and global reach, and with an intensifying capacity to draw people and things together in differentiating relationships.

• • •

Bombers, fighter jets, and other military aircraft arrived at the facility on the first morning of the celebration. Prominent among them was an air

FIGURE 13. Spectators viewing fighter jets at the 1954 event. Military planes were prominent among those exhibited on the ground at and participating in flight demonstrations above the festivities. Most of the commercial aircraft on display had martial origins too. The Pan Am Stratocruiser in figure 11 was a civilian version of the C-97 Stratofreighter military transport plane, an offshoot of the B-29 Superfortress bomber used to, among other things, drop atomic bombs on Hiroshima and Nagasaki. Collection of SFO Museum.

force B-47 Stratojet long-range strategic bomber, with the designed capability to drop nuclear weapons on the Soviet Union. Thereafter, visitors could take in "spectacular exhibition[s] of precision flying" by the US Air Force Thunderbirds and US Navy Blue Angels and view their planes parked on the tarmac, observe three B-47s being refueled in flight, and witness demonstrations of US Coast Guard helicopter rescues.[14]

The Coast Guard helicopter demonstration signaled that SFO continued to be home to its air station, as is still the case today, and therefore to direct military operations.[15] The festival occurred not long after plans were put into place at the beginning of the Korean War to ready the airport for civilian defense. Flights carrying cargo, airmail, and troops during the conflict contributed significantly to the subsequent growth of its operations.[16] The air force and navy acrobatic flight teams, although based out of state, visually and sonically signified the growing presence of air military operations elsewhere in the Bay Area. The Alameda Naval Air Station across the bay, Naval Air Station Moffett Field in the South Bay, Travis Air Force Base in Solano County, and Hamilton Air Force Base in Marin County were all sites of West Coast military air power in 1954.

Many of the commercial aircraft on display in 1954 had military origins as well. Some commercial aircraft put into operation after World War II were civilian versions of planes used for bombing runs and troop transport during the conflict. Others were simply reconverted military planes. The postwar US aviation industry had benefited greatly from the Arnold-Powers Agreement of 1942, which assigned Great Britain's more limited resources to the building of fighters and bombers, while the United States built more transport planes. This gave the United States an advantage when it came to postwar civilian reconversions and redesigns.[17] The B-377 Stratocruiser, put into operation in 1947, was a civilian version of the C-97 Stratofreighter military transport plane, which was itself an offshoot of the B-29 Superfortress bomber used to, among other things, drop atomic bombs on Hiroshima and Nagasaki.[18] The festival also featured United Airlines' "public acceptance" of a new DC-7, a civilian version of a Douglas Aircraft C-47 Globemaster military transport plane.[19]

As noted in chapter 2, the facility itself had benefited from being put into service to World War II and from the federal government subsidies and promotion of aviation that followed. Moreover, the war revived the national economy and led to a sustained, albeit inconsistent, period of economic growth that was part and parcel of private and governmental investments in commercial aviation. Once travel restrictions were lifted at the end of the war, demand for airline travel increased dramatically. This was in part a function of airlines introducing cheaper fares and developing marketing campaigns to stimulate consumer desire as well as civic boosters' and federal officials' own promotion of air travel and airport development as engines for economic prosperity and personal fulfillment.[20]

Government subsidy also played a large role in the postwar air travel and air commerce booms. Construction on the SFO expansion project financed by the $20 million bond measure that passed in November 1945 began the following May with a massive bay fill project to accommodate longer runways. But airport officials soon began making noise about needing more money to finish the job because of cost overruns and inflation, and they argued that even further expansion and improvements, including a new and improved terminal building, were necessary to keep up with the facility's ever-growing operations and passenger load. San Francisco voters failed to pass a follow-up bond measure in 1948, but in November 1949 they approved the expenditure of $10 million to complete the project for what local officials now described as the future San Francisco *International* Airport.[21]

One mechanism used to generate enthusiasm for this additional public expenditure was a series of one-day Air Fairs at the facility in the late 1940s, put on by the airport and the San Francisco Jaycees. Beginning in 1947, these events were geared to connect the interest in military aviation developed during World War II and the early Cold War with support for a civilian aviation infrastructure. At the October 30, 1949, fair, for example, a kind of prelude to the 1954 festivities, the one hundred thousand attendees, including California governor Earl Warren, were able to witness the arrival by helicopter of beauty queen Joan Leslie, the "Fairest of the Fair"; view US Air Force, Coast Guard, and Navy flight exhibitions; and inspect United's and Pan Am's airport facilities as well as the New Deal–era passenger terminal. The printed event program urged attendees to vote yes on what would be a successful bond measure in the upcoming November election.[22]

The program also featured a letter from the Jaycee president that distilled some of the arguments used to sell growth and related public expenditure to the local population during the postwar period. One of these was to emphasize San Francisco's and the airport's roles in an expanding network of global production, distribution, and finance that accompanied the United States' growing imperial reach as it emerged from the war as a global superpower. The ongoing construction, the Jaycee argued, would "make the air terminal facilities of San Francisco second to none in the world of Pacific trade and travel." "Standing as it does with great production centers on one hand and the vast markets of the Pacific basin on the other," he continued, "San Francisco is the port through which great air commerce of the future will pass."[23]

SFO's expanding internationalism would also benefit from a new phase of federal expenditure and oversight of the nation's system of airports. The Federal Airport Act of May 1946 was justified in part by the idea that a healthy civilian aviation system would ultimately support national defense. The act called for the creation of a National Airport Plan under which the CAA identified infrastructural projects necessary to maintain this system, and it established an appropriation of $500 million (with an additional $20 million for Alaska, Hawaii, and

Puerto Rico) to fund the work, with the assumption that local agencies would match such expenditures. Grants were administered by the CAA, with coordination by its regional offices. Although these funds were not sufficient given the scope of the National Airport Plan, the act played a significant role in developing commercial aviation nationwide when they supplemented local investments.[24] San Francisco drew upon these funds to complete its postwar expansion, receiving $6 million in postwar federal airport aid by the end of fiscal year 1954–55.[25]

The internationalism espoused by local businesspeople and officials, as well as commercial aviation more generally, benefited from US government efforts to expand overseas aviation routes and US carriers' access to them. During and after World War II the US government sought through negotiation and treaty, and with varying degrees of success, to develop "open sky" policies geared to gaining access to skyways and airports controlled by other imperial nations. After the war, following unsuccessful attempts to develop multilateral agreements for air trade access, the United States secured most of the access it desired through bilateral agreements.[26]

This imperial reach was pursued locally with a renewed sense of municipal and regional destiny, albeit one that was complicated by the shifting relationships among stakeholders within and outside the Bay Area. Competition for primacy among West Coast airports defined many early postwar calls for funding and development, but these sometimes gave way to more cooperative approaches. At certain moments SFO officials became less focused on diverting operations from Los Angeles and other West Coast airports as they struggled to keep up with the growth already under way and the concomitant complexity of operations. Even as they competed for Federal Airport Act funds, they recognized that the prosperity of their own operations depended in part on the success of other big airports. San Francisco officials ultimately wanted more air traffic than Los Angeles—the two airports at this time alternated between being fourth- and fifth-busiest in the nation—but they also needed their southern competitor to do well. At the more cooperative moments there seemed to be plenty of international flights to go around, and low-cost flights to and from Los Angeles had become a mainstay of the facility's growing operations.[27]

San Francisco city and airport officials were not nearly as concerned with competition from across the bay in the late 1940s as they had been in previous decades. SFO's wartime expansion had significantly advantaged the facility over Oakland's. Not only did the military grow San

Francisco Airport, but it took over Oakland Airport in 1943, with all scheduled civilian flights shifted to San Francisco. Airlines only slowly returned to Oakland after the war. Given the challenges of postwar conversion more generally, this was also a moment witnessing efforts to promote greater cooperation among county and municipal governments across the Bay Area, with significant impetus coming from business interests and labor leaders. One reflection of this was the formation, in 1944, of the Bay Region Council (subsequently called the San Francisco Bay Area Council), an organization that identified the need for economic development to be based upon coordinated buildout of the region's infrastructure.[28]

In June 1948 San Francisco mayor Elmer E. Robinson commissioned the San Francisco Bay Area Council and the Bay Area Aviation Committee to create an "Airport Plan for the San Francisco Bay Area." Authored by a "technical advisory committee" drawn from the two groups, with input from the California Aeronautics Commission, various counties, and airport operators, the 1949 report surveyed Bay Area aviation needs through 1960. It assumed the primacy of San Francisco Airport but argued that other existing airports would have to grow and new airports would have to be built in order to accommodate both current growth in commercial and private aviation and that which would come later with the introduction of civilian jet aircraft. Ultimately, the report argued, better regional planning would enable the Bay Area, as a group of communities paradoxically connected to as well as isolated from one another by San Francisco Bay, to take better advantage of its "strategic situation in the network of national and international trade routes."[29]

Thus, circa 1950, airport officials and supporters were, in ever more granular ways, emphasizing the role of airport growth in the economies of local communities as they justified its sometimes-disruptive operations and high costs. The internationally oriented infrastructure, they argued, should be understood as one that would help individual households and businesses through its growing payroll and contracts with local construction firms and other vendors of goods and services. The airport supported grocery stores, the housing industry, automobile sales and servicing, and schools by increasing the local tax base. The capital generated by the airport, they added, "filters down to every walk of life, making everybody a little more prosperous. When the new passenger terminal is put into service, the airport no doubt will attract even more allied aviation industry, so that the value of the San Francisco Airport to its owners, the San Francisco taxpayers, will continue to grow each year."[30]

The operators were not simply trying to keep San Francisco taxpayers happy; they were also trying to convince a primarily white cadre of San Francisco workers, at a moment when the city was losing jobs to the suburbs, to finance a facility that, while distant, might still serve them. San Mateo County workers and residents, some of whom were concerned with the disruptive, growing operation in their midst, also required some convincing. It was precisely the nature of the airport as an "industrial" facility, airport officials argued, with unspoken admission of all it brought in terms of noise, odor, and congestion, that enabled it to contribute to the local economy. And at a moment when San Francisco was fighting San Mateo County over the latter's ongoing efforts to impose property taxes on the facility, the airport operators were compelled to make an argument that the county was otherwise receiving an economic benefit from it.[31]

The aspirations and tensions that defined these ongoing and intersecting geographical imaginaries, modes of development, and local political machinations were performed in various ways at the 1954 festival. San Mateo County's board of supervisors took out a full-page advertisement in the "International Airport Souvenir Edition" of the *San Mateo Times,* published just before the festival, congratulating the City and County of San Francisco on the dedication of the new terminal. The county was already recognized as "*the* place" for industry, professional and business offices, and suburban living, and they invited further investment in it from their neighbors to the north.[32] SFO and San Francisco officials reciprocated with a full-page advertisement of their own, welcoming San Mateo residents to the festival to view what should be considered "San Mateo County's Pride."[33] When labor officials from San Francisco and San Mateo Counties assisted with the planning of the event, organized an exhibit there, and then appeared at the festival, they performed their investments in the growth of the facility as well as a reconciliation of sorts given ongoing debates, and sometimes conflicts, over which county's union members would be employed on airport construction and maintenance jobs.[34]

As indicated earlier, such relationships continued to be built upon military foundations, as signified at the festival by the presence of bombers, fighter jets, and civilian aircraft with martial origins. But airport-related entanglements and desires, as they were imagined into the future, were somewhat differently expressed through the multiplicity of flowers on display over the course of the three-day event. Visitors to the festival were greeted at the airport entrance by an array of blooms spelling out

FIGURE 14. Flowers, as symbol of soft imperial power and local economic growth, figured prominently at the 1954 Flight Festival and terminal dedication. Here, American Airlines flight attendant Jean Bailey, California governor Goodwin J. Knight, Virginia Knight, Queen of Flowers Jacqueline Lower, and American Airlines flight attendant Ann Roland prepare to send flowers (by air) to President Eisenhower and other dignitaries. Collection of SFO Museum.

"California industry salutes the California flower industry for its major contribution to the development of the air freight commerce of the nation."[35] Those in attendance on the first day had the opportunity to witness Jacqueline Lower, "Flight Festival Queen of Flowers," arrive by motorcade. The festival quickly put Ms. Lower to work. She and her court of nineteen princesses "drawn from every major industry in the state" were tasked with greeting dignitaries that Friday as they mounted the stage for the main dedication ceremony. Shortly thereafter, Lower joined California governor Goodwin Knight, Mrs. Knight, flight attendants, and others in a ceremony that sent off air express shipments of San Mateo County–grown bouquets of "floral greetings" to high-profile political figures and their wives. The list included President Eisenhower and Vice President Nixon, Chief Justice (and recent California governor) Earl Warren, California's US senators William Knowland and Thomas Kuchel, and the mayors of major cities in the eastern United States.

The mayors were also to receive a follow-up letter extolling the "delights of Peninsula living and the desirable industrial land available" for development. Lower and her court were then tasked with greeting regular festival visitors in the new terminal and presenting them with flowers for the remainder of the three-day festival. On the final day, the flower-distributing queen and her princesses were joined in their duties by San Francisco–raised Miss California (and future Miss America and television Catwoman) Lee Meriwether and Miss San Mateo, Darlene Williams, who arrived at SFO in two separate helicopters in a ceremony of their own.[36]

As the welcoming floral display, princess sponsorship, and correspondence with East Coast mayors all make clear, flowers were, in the minds of festival organizers, a spectacular and fragrant signifier of local economic growth with increasingly international reach. And for good reason. As festival promotional materials and local reportage made clear in their celebratory account of the economic benefits of expanding airport operations, the Peninsula's flower business was both beneficiary of and catalyst for the rapidly growing air freight business. Flowers, at the time, constituted roughly one-half of the air freight departing SFO.[37]

The Peninsula had been a significant producer of cut flowers since the nineteenth century. Most of the distribution, however, was regional, by truck or train, until after the war, when larger, faster, and more frequently flown planes permitted wider and more cost-effective distribution of these perishable commodities. Emergent cargo carriers transported flowers between airports, as did the larger passenger carriers in their available cargo space. The first cargo carrier in the United States, Flying Tiger Line, began operations in 1945; it was joined the following year by Slick Airways, founded in 1946. Both airlines were operating out of SFO in 1954. Like air travel by humans, the air cargo business drew from military subsidy. Cargo airlines used surplus military planes and new aircraft based on military design while benefiting from Defense Department contracts to transport service personnel and equipment. Also necessary to the expansion of the air cargo industry was the development of a shipping, distribution, and delivery infrastructure created by freight forwarders. The incentive to build cargo infrastructure at SFO for goods requiring rapid delivery was in part an outgrowth of the Port of San Francisco's declining throughput in the wake of competition from Los Angeles, Long Beach, and Oakland. Further regularizing this side of commercial aviation and facilitating its expansion was a 1948 decision by the Civil Aeronautics Board to put air freight forwarding under its jurisdiction. Airborne Flower and Freight, Inc., which began operations in 1946, could brag in 1954 that flowers had helped them become the largest freight forwarder in the United States and that they had helped the flower business become the fourth-largest industry in the Bay Area. San Mateo growers and boosters, in turn, crowed about their flowers being distributed across the United States and beyond. Their product had, after all, found its way to England for the 1947 nuptials of the future Queen Elizabeth and the Duke of Edinburgh.[38]

The proliferation of flowers, and the women who distributed them, also symbolized a transition, as the militaristic power on display—in both its explicit (B-47) and covert (B-377) forms—was being connected to the expanding enterprise of commercial aviation. As during the war, when military planes bore women's names and images of pinups graced their hulls, women's bodies were frequently used in the 1950s to represent progress in aviation and sell the experience of air travel to businessmen and tourists alike. Blossom-offering beauty queens and princesses at the SFO festival helped to domesticate the experience of flight, making even international travel seem more normative in gender-specific ways. At the festival and beyond, less well-to-do, would-be travelers were invited to buy vacation travel on credit to the United States' Hawaiian colonies, its Cold War–allied countries in Europe, and other areas of the globe that fell under its hegemonic reach, where they would ideally be able to offer favorable impressions of their society.[39]

Visitors were also invited, through flowers, to see the airport as an economic engine for an emergent affluent society and as a potential workplace for its participants. It was not just the flower growers that benefited from the ramping up of the air freight business; the $3 million "spent each year to ship this delicate commodity to every city in the United States" also went to wages for airline, air-forwarding, trucking, and other workers involved in their transportation and by extension to the businesses where those wages were spent. And with that came the prosperity of individuals and surrounding communities in the form of automobile and home ownership.[40]

The white glamour girls' welcome, of course, was not fully extended, even if polite pleasantries and flowers were offered to all who visited. Whites across class lines entered a festival space and a set of relations that they could, without much work, see as their own, while others would have to take a leap of faith that participation in that space and such relations, however alienating it might be, would offer its benefits. The warmth of greetings, the cultivated smiles and fragrant blossoms, helped to put a benign gloss on a fast-developing aviation infrastructure that reproduced exclusionary social formations rooted in the past even as it beckoned a wider array of people to benefit from an emergent set of relations with growing imperial reach. United Airlines could boast at the moment of the festival that its Bay Area employees owned 5,223 cars and 2,679 homes and had 12,982 retail charge accounts.[41] Yet the Bay Area's housing market was still significantly defined by segregationist practices, including racially restrictive covenants and discriminatory Federal Housing Administration loan policies, and many of the businesses where charge accounts were held practiced systematic credit service and employment discrimination. Moreover, airport work and travel were still riven by profound racial and gender exclusions that compounded the class distinctions among different kinds of airport workers (white pilots and flight attendants, Black skycaps) and travelers (first class and tourist class).

The flower business had its own elements of exclusionary inclusion. Although it was not apparent from the demographics of the local flower queen and princesses, or from press accounts of flower production and transportation in the region, Chinese American and Japanese American growers were key players in the San Mateo County flower business.[42] After long and more recent—in the case of Japanese American growers who had been interned during World War II—struggles against racist treatment and ethnic prejudice and concomitant threats to their livelihoods, these growers were now reaping the benefits from a rapidly expanding air freight economy. Yet they were still largely erased from representations of the region's growing imperial reach that assumed whiteness as a symbolic metropolitan anchor.

Beyond blossoms, there were other referents through which festival visitors were invited to think about SFO as a nexus where networks of people and things came together and to imagine themselves as participating in the exchanges that the airport facilitated. The themes of "gateway" and "crossroads" were prominent in descriptions of the renovated and expanded facility and its operations. For example, a San Francisco Public Utilities Commission pamphlet issued on the occasion of the festival described the new terminal as both the "crossroads of the West Coast" and the "gateway to the Orient." It hailed Bay Area travelers (and those transferring at SFO) with descriptions of convenient access to the facility, accessible ticket counters, a comfortable waiting area, and an array of amenities—shops, a flower stand, a cocktail lounge, hair stylists, a telegraph office, a post office, even a children's carousel—to entertain them before or between flights. Those arriving in the Bay Area would also have convenient access to ground transportation to their final destination.[43]

Some visitors may have been drawn to the rhetoric about how the airport connected the Bay Area to other cities both near and far via runways and flight paths; movements of people, commodities, and capital; government regulations and personnel; and roadways, utility lines, and other infrastructures of varying scales. A feature on Pan Am airlines in the *San Mateo Times* special issue described its SFO base of operations for its foreign trade and transportation efforts as "a small 'city' in itself." The airline had its own police and fire departments, steam plant, medical department, credit union, garage, photography studio, cafeteria, and newspaper.[44] Anyone picking up a copy of William Flynn's brief history of the airport, *Men, Money and Mud,* which was sold at the festival, had access to a similar description of SFO. Flynn described SFO as a "metropolitan concentration of industry, of travel, of service" that linked the Bay Area to Southern California as well as to cities across the United States, Europe, and the Pacific Rim.[45]

Those so inclined had opportunities to examine the infrastructural bases of these connections. Festival-goers had the run of much of the terminal. The *San Mateo Times*'s "floor-by-floor" tour of the building described in detail those areas geared toward getting people and their luggage into and out of the terminal and onto and off airplanes, and toward making them comfortable while they waited to do one of these things. But it also made clear that the terminal building was home to corporate as well as federal and municipal offices that facilitated airport operations and linked them to broader networks of governance and capital accumulation and distribution. Airlines had offices in the building, as did the CAA, the US Weather Bureau, and the US Post Office. The US Customs Service, the US Immigration and Naturalization Service, and the US Public Health Service had offices in the attached concourse. During the planning for the new terminal, representatives from these agencies had offered their input on the building design and their own space allocations. A facility for processing airmail and air freight was located nearby. Visitors could tour it during the festival, along with a heating plant and an electrical substation.[46]

Men, Money and Mud, along with other publicity sources, offered additional perspective on the entangled physical infrastructures, both public and private, that linked airport operations to other places via transportation and energy networks. These infrastructures had grown dramatically during and after the war to support industrial growth and the region's expanding population. They were also environmentally destructive outgrowths of long histories of colonial extraction on current and former indigenous lands in the United States and places overseas. New airport roadways connected SFO to the relocated and reconfigured Bayshore Freeway (US 101), funded in part by 1945 bond measure funds, and, by extension, to the expanding system of high-speed (theoretically) and high-volume roads that tied it to sites across the Bay Area, California, and the United States. Two hundred miles of freeways were built in the Bay Area between the end of World War II and early 1957, with further expansion occurring after that date as federal funds became available through the Federal Aid Highway Act of 1956.[47] Standard Oil and Shell Oil both built, at their own cost on leased SFO land, fuel storage tanks, pipelines, and aircraft refueling systems in an effort to take advantage of the airline industry's rapidly growing demand for aircraft fuel. These facilities were connected to their East Bay refineries, to refining and oil extraction facilities in the United States, the Middle East, and elsewhere, and to the railways and shipping routes among them.[48] A revamped, city-owned electrical distribution system at SFO connected the airport, via transmission lines, to Hetch Hetchy project hydroelectric plants operated by the city and to the privately held Pacific Gas and Electric Company (PG&E), which had recently become the primary supplier of power to the Bay Area as it operated under the supervision of the California Public Utilities Commission. PG&E generated power in its rapidly expanding system of hydroelectric power plants situated on rivers across the state, and it piped in natural gas from the US Southwest to supply consumers with the substance and to run its steam-electric generating plants.[49]

Glimpses could also be had of a still-nascent, yet growing, security apparatus at the airport that was tied to increasing passenger operations, higher values of infrastructure and commodities on-site, and the growth of policing more generally in the Bay Area during the post–World War II period. The late forties had already seen the creation of what was initially a seven-member Airport Security Detail, composed of San Mateo County deputy sheriffs, whose duties focused on traffic control and the "protection of life and property." A company of the San Francisco Fire Department was also first stationed at the airport during this period.[50] The INS's and PHS's feedback on terminal space needs was tied to assumptions about their growing role, after the passage of the Immigration and Nationality Act of 1952, in monitoring and policing people in transit at the airport amid increasing international travel and immigration by air.[51]

Likely evident to some festival-goers were some of the costs to the surrounding natural and human environments that stemmed from the expansion of the airport and its infrastructure. Visitors looking west as they arrived at SFO might have seen the scar from the approximately 12.5 million cubic yards of earth taken from the hills above Millbrae for the bay fill upon which recent runway extensions and parts of the rerouted Bayshore Freeway were built.[52] And some would have had plenty of time to take in this view given the heavy traffic at the airport entrance at various points over the weekend—a reminder of the congestion that plagued even the now-widened highway, especially during shift changes at the airport and commute hours.[53] Suburban airports like SFO were designed to be accessible by automobile, but despite the millions spent on adjacent highway and roadway upgrades, planning for such infrastructural integration often did not keep up with the volume of operations. Frequent traffic jams around airports (Idlewild/JFK was particularly infamous) were one particularly frustrating expression of these limits of vision.[54]

Those gathered on the tarmac to inspect the parked planes and view the aerial displays would have smelled aircraft fuel, burned and unburned, a clue to the ways the facility was poisoning the surrounding air and water. And they would have experienced the noise of aircraft engines, which, among other things, interrupted the festival speechifying.[55] Airport noise was not yet the object of public outcry that it would be after the introduction of jet engines on commercial aircraft a few years later, but it was still a nuisance for some SFO neighbors, whose complaints the government was starting to notice. The Truman administration had commissioned a study designed to improve safety and noise conditions near airports. The commission visited the Bay Area, where they heard complaints from a group of disgruntled San Bruno residents and surveyed officials from affected local communities. But their 1952 report, *The Airport and Its Neighbors,* relying heavily on feedback from airport and industry officials, downplayed the problem and emphasized the limits of what could be done to mitigate it.[56]

Some first-day festival attendees would have been drawn to the arrival of the noisy, jet-engine powered B-47 Stratojet, whether they welcomed it or not. Regardless, its presence signified that the US aviation industry would continue to benefit from the ramping up of aeronautical militarism during the early Cold War. There was still incentive to develop new military technologies that eventually would have civilian applications—most notably, improved jet engines, which would have large-scale commercial applications by the late 1950s. Capital from military contracts enabled aircraft manufacturers to mass-produce more modern passenger planes.[57] The B-47, which the air force put into regular service in 1951, was a prime example. Boeing built over two thousand of the jets and incorporated some of the design elements into its 707, which went into regular commercial operations in late 1958 and is largely seen as ushering in the "jet age."[58]

In 1956 San Francisco voters expressed their support for the jet age by passing a $25 million bond measure for the additional SFO expansion seen as necessary to accommodate the jets and the additional passengers they would bring with them. This expansion included extending runways even farther into the bay and building the new South Terminal, which was completed in 1963.[59] The airport got a lot noisier, too, over those next several years, as it drew growing numbers of people, the things they built, and the land and sky into expanding sets of relationships of which the facility was both catalyst and product. As earlier, these relationships reflected and reproduced residual and emergent colonial and imperial power, even as they offered an increasing array of rewards for Bay Area residents. The gifting of flowers at the 1954 festival had indeed welcomed an ever-growing Bay Area population to participate in the enterprise as workers, businesspeople, and travelers, although the relationships that followed would be complicated, uneven, and quite often exploitative.

CHAPTER 4

A Black Future in the Air Industry?

On a July morning in 1970, three Black skycaps, Theodore Traylor, John Hatch, and Edward Anderson, performed a "friendly" citizen's arrest on United Airlines' SFO operations manager Kenneth Wardle. The men escorted Wardle into a Volkswagen and drove him from SFO to San Francisco's Hall of Justice, where they treated him to coffee and pastry while waiting for the courts to open. The action came several months into protests and legal actions against United by skycaps and Local 3051 of the Brotherhood of Railway, Airline, and Steamship Clerks, Freight Handlers, Express and Station Employees (BRAC) that represented them. The issue was the announcement that the airline would terminate a contract with Allied Aviation for the supply of skycap labor and hire its own skycaps through its nationwide, in-house employment system. As a result, twenty-three of thirty-five Allied workers skycapping for United, including Traylor, Hatch, and Anderson, were released or transferred to other airlines. The men wanted Wardle charged with violating California Labor Code sections 970 and 973 (requiring employers to inform potential employees about ongoing labor disputes) for not educating the newly recruited skycaps about the conflict. The skycaps' case was heard that afternoon by a judge who, despite the circumstances of the arrest and the circus atmosphere in his courtroom, took the matter seriously enough to transfer the case to a colleague before leaving for vacation.[1]

Although the case against Wardle was ultimately thrown out, and most Allied skycaps were not rehired by United, this episode provides a useful entry point into the story of Black labor and antidiscrimination activism at SFO.[2] The particulars of the skycaps' struggles—as unionized employees of a private contractor providing services to an airline, at a municipal airport, with the conditions under which they labored shaped by corporate restructuring and recent efforts to transform the racial logics of airport employment—call attention to the ways that Black work at the airport was a complex web of possibility and exclusion.

The figure of the Black skycap more generally provides useful perspective as well. Skycaps were, as one contemporaneous observer put it, "a special situation." They engaged in servile labor, yet they generally earned high wages from tips and tended to hold onto their jobs tenaciously.[3] They were often visible, well-connected members of Black communities in the Bay Area and elsewhere, who maintained something of the cosmopolitan aura held by Pullman porters before the rise of commercial aviation and the associated decline in long-distance railroad travel led to their professional and political decline. Skycaps secured geographic and social mobility by carrying white people's luggage and the racialized baggage that came with it. I know this, as noted in the Introduction, from my own family history. As a symbol of Black servility and accomplishment, then, the figure of the skycap gestures to an array of contradictory meanings associated with Black airport labor and entrepreneurialism, whether situated in earlier, exclusionary material and symbolic economies or in subsequent, more equitable formations that refracted general trends in commercial aviation as well as the changing contours of the Bay Area's networked and layered colonial formations.

Well-known episodes from the civil rights movement such as the Montgomery bus boycott and the Freedom Rides, as well as research on these and less visible struggles by historians like Robin D. G. Kelley, Mia Bay, and Anke Ortlepp, tell us that racist treatment on public transportation and employment discrimination in transportation industries were important targets of African American protest going back to the nineteenth century. Steamships, stagecoaches, trains, and streetcars, and then buses, automobiles, and planes, as well as the places where they stopped and nearby accommodations, had been highly charged spaces of racial conflict where whites tried to enforced Black immobility, sometimes with violence. Gaining more dignified access to using transportation and working in transportation were means by which working- and middle-class Black people, through individual acts and collective action, were able to achieve some measure of mobility and attendant civil and economic rights. A long history of activism that sought to achieve such access picked up steam

FIGURE 15. The author's grandparents, Scipio and Laura Porter, at a 1951 "Skycappers Ball." Scipio Porter landed a skycap job at San Francisco Airport in 1942, initiating the family's participation in the Second Great Migration (from Shreveport, Louisiana) and securing for them some measure of social and geographical mobility. Photograph courtesy of the Porter family.

amid an array of struggles for racial justice during and after World War II.[4] Yet cultural theorist Paul Gilroy's discussion of African American automobility cautions us to consider how workers' and travelers' struggles for freedom in the sphere of transportation sometimes could draw Black people into and, depending on their relative social status and various contingencies, implicate them in exploitative relationships—for example, as participants in consumer capitalism and in the imperialist, neocolonialist, and environmentally destructive oil economy.[5]

By charting a history of Black liberation and complicity at SFO, this chapter facilitates a pivot in this book's narrative, as it shifts some focus away from the powerful and toward those less powerful actors who nonetheless sought to make more reasonable lives for themselves by entangling themselves in expanding sets of relationships manifest at the airport. Indeed, individual and group efforts by Black people to secure jobs and economic advancement at SFO were shaped by the interfaces of heterogeneous actors and systems that redistributed power at the airport and beyond: shifts in the national and global economy; public and private capital investment; government and corporate antidiscrimination and affirmative action programs; the work of local and national networks of business elites, labor organizers, and activists; and a concomitant symbolic economy regarding the Black presence in the Bay Area.[6] The sum of these entanglements challenged the way power composed the Bay Area in the mid-twentieth century while reproducing elements of its future asymmetries.

This chapter begins in the 1950s, as SFO's metropolitan vision and function were being more fully realized along with the region's imperial reach. It concludes in the 1980s, when the recently deregulated air industry was an exemplar of post-Fordist transformations of the economy and emergent neoliberal government policies, and the post-Bakke affirmative action rollback was symbolic of a wider anti-Black backlash that was then picking up steam. Labor activism by SFO skycaps and janitors at this moment demonstrated the extent to which Black antidiscrimination struggles and related programs had advanced only as far as producing a precarious and patchy inclusion in the Bay Area's colonial present: a kind of holding pattern defined by piecemeal professional integration and the more widespread consignment of Black men and women to low-wage, low-skilled work, intermittent employment, and unemployment. This story thus provides a glimpse into a subsequent decline of the collective Black presence and status in the Bay Area that followed, among other things, deindustrialization, urban redevelopment and gentrification, military base closures and containerization, the rise of finance and technology economies, mass incarceration, out-migration, and the growing presence, visibility, and political clout of other minority groups.

. . .

Black workers had entwined themselves in the Bay Area's economic expansion during World War II. In 1941, in response to A. Philip Randolph and Bayard Rustin's threatened march on Washington, D.C., President Franklin D. Roosevelt issued Executive Order 8802, which outlawed discrimination in defense work and established the federal Fair Employment Practice Committee. The order initially had little effect locally, but thanks in part to pressure from Bay Area resident and Brotherhood of Sleeping Car Porters vice president and NAACP official C.L. Dellums, who was active in the March on Washington movement, Black men and women secured work in local shipyards and other defense facilities. Civil rights activists and Black unionists opened up additional opportunities as well. The local Black population grew accordingly, as migrants, primarily southern, moved to the area in search of newfound opportunities.[7]

Yet wartime employment at San Francisco's airport remained largely restricted to the handful of established residents and migrants (like my grandfather) who worked as skycaps or in lower-wage service occupations. Black labor in commercial aviation had been significantly structured by railroad industry practice. Congress incorporated provisions of the 1926 Railway Labor Act into commercial aviation through the 1938 Civil Aeronautics Act. This arrangement brought into the industry vehemently discriminatory railway unions; generally restricted bargaining to "craft and class" unions, which limited intraworksite mobility; and placed the industry under a national mediation board that generally ignored and sometimes perpetuated workplace discrimination. Adding to the problem was the lack of training and educational opportunity available to Black workers for positions like pilot and aircraft mechanic, often a result of discrimination within a segregated military. Moreover, the airlines themselves were reluctant to hire qualified Black workers, like veteran Tuskegee Airmen, who had managed to secure the necessary job skills. All told, the aviation industry privileged white workers and concentrated the limited number of Black workers in unskilled or service positions with little chance of advancement.[8]

Black people were initially excluded from participating significantly in the imperial project of the postwar airport as well. Although they were able to secure employment in various public and private employment sectors in the Bay Area during the late 1940s and 1950s, airport employment was part of the parallel and brutal story of Black employment discrimination and displacement in the putatively liberal region. Postwar reconversion, industrial plant closures and relocations to other areas, the automation of skilled and unskilled jobs, and employers' and unions' commitments to protecting white workers' interests led to significant Black job loss in the shipyards, on the docks, and in the manufacturing sector. Layered on top of that was the active discrimination by employers and unions in construction, retail, and other growth areas of the local economy. The result, not surprisingly, was economic hardship, rising crime, punitive policing, and other social ills in Black working-class neighborhoods in San Francisco, Oakland, Richmond, and elsewhere.[9]

Airline craft unions continued to discriminate against Black workers, as did construction firms and concessionaires operating under contract at the airport. Although airlines were theoretically subject to federal fair employment legislation because of their contracts for carrying mail, military personnel, and military cargo, they routinely ignored nondiscrimination clauses, and the government did next to nothing during the 1940s and much of the 1950s to enforce them. Presumptions about the offense that customers would take when encountering nonwhite pilots or personnel in sales and other nonservile, public-facing occupations was part of the justificatory framework for the lack of minority hiring. Even as SFO's workforce grew dramatically in the late 1940s and early 1950s, along with Cold War–era commercial travel, Black workers and activists focused their efforts on employment—like military-based and public sector jobs—where articulated government policy and word-of-mouth stories suggested there were actual possibilities for finding work.[10]

Different job opportunities eventually began opening up for Black workers at SFO and other West Coast airports in the late 1950s, and a handful broke occupational barriers by securing work as mechanics or reservation clerks. Locally, these changes appear to have been, in part, the result of cultural shifts wrought by the civil rights movement, press coverage of protests against air industry discrimination in other regions, and, most important, Bay Area activists' efforts to establish state and local fair-employment practices commissions and programs. San Francisco's largely ineffectual, voluntary fair-employment program (begun in 1950), its somewhat more effective Commission on Equal Employment Opportunity (established in July 1957), and California's Fair Employment Practices Committee (established following the 1959 Fair Employment Practices Act, which barred employment discrimination in the state based on race, color, religion, natural origin, or ancestry) appear not to have had a large influence on airport hiring at this point. Yet the existence of these entities and the increasingly vocal local activism behind them—Dellums, for example, played a prominent role in getting the state legislation passed and was the first committee chairman—appear to have convinced some airport employers and unions to take a closer look at Black applicants, albeit in piecemeal fashion.[11]

Eventually, knowledge about job growth in general at the facility, the foreclosure of employment opportunities elsewhere because of deindustrialization, automation, and discrimination, and the concomitant recognition among residents of Black neighborhoods in San Francisco and other Bay Area communities that a longer commute might be required to achieve occupational success caused more African Americans to view the airport as a potential site of employment.[12] Moreover, at a moment when people across social divisions perceived air travel to be thoroughly cosmopolitan and sophisticated, airport employment held aspirational appeal to some Black workers seeking social mobility, even if the work, for most, was mundane or demeaning, and employers still generally saw Black labor at the airport as servile.[13]

Black people's efforts to secure SFO employment were assisted by local activists as the civil rights movement was ramping up at the beginning of the 1960s, with increasing attention to segregation and discrimination in local and interstate transportation. In the US South, activists focused on airport terminals; in the Bay Area, the emphasis was on airport employment.[14] Explicitly segregated passenger facilities were not the issue in the Bay Area as they were elsewhere, and this was also the moment of renewed focus on workplace and union discrimination by local activists. The Negro American Labor Council (NALC), founded by A. Philip Randolph in 1960 in response to the AFL-CIO's inadequate response to racial discrimination among its constituents, established Bay Area chapters that sought to pressure union locals to change their ways. The early 1960s also witnessed renewed militancy within local NAACP branches and their coalition building with the Congress of Racial Equality (CORE) and other organizations that gave growing attention to employment discrimination.[15]

The West Coast branch of the NAACP asked California's FEPC to investigate the discriminatory hiring practices of Interstate HOSTS' restaurants and bars at SFO.[16] Subsequently, the *Sun Reporter,* San Francisco's African American newspaper run by physician and longtime activist Dr. Carlton B. Goodlett, called upon the FEPC to investigate the discriminatory actions of the airlines and other "leaseholders."[17] In May 1961, UC Berkeley activists, led by Black graduate student J. Herman Blake, protested United Airlines' participation in a campus job fair to interview potential flight attendants because of its discriminatory practices.[18] In the summer of 1963, a group of Black workers at United Airlines' SFO maintenance base secured the assistance of the NALC as well as local civil rights and religious groups, in lodging complaints with the airline and picketing their downtown San Francisco ticket office in response to systematic discrimination in hiring, upgrading, and promotions at the facility.[19]

As activists undertook this work, the federal government finally began to take some action to alter the terrain of Black employment at SFO and other airports. President John F. Kennedy's Executive Order 10925 of March 6, 1961, established the Equal Employment Opportunity Commission (EEOC) and required that government contractors "take affirmative action" to prevent discrimination based on race, creed, color, or national origin within their ranks. It gave the EEOC the authority to persuade labor unions and other entities representing workers on projects under government contract "to cooperate with, and to comply in the implementation of, the purposes of this order."[20]

Subsequently, the Kennedy administration, as part of its face-saving, moderate civil rights agenda—which also included efforts to end segregation in southern airport terminals—pressured the commercial aviation industry (and airlines in particular) to adhere to the requirements of fair-employment legislation in light of the government contracts that subsidized the industry. Between 1961 and 1964, Vice President (and subsequently President) Lyndon Baines Johnson secured "Plans for Progress" agreements to improve minority employment from well over one hundred large companies, including six major airlines: American, Eastern, Northwest, Pan American, United, and TWA. As the parties worked out these agreements, the US Supreme Court opened up legal avenues for opposing industry discrimination through its 1963 decision in *Colorado Anti-Discrimination Commission v. Continental Airlines,* ruling that the airline had unfairly denied Black pilot Marlon Green a job several years earlier.[21]

The effects of these limited interventions were slow to materialize. United Airlines, for example, did not sign its Plans for Progress agreement until June 17, 1964, only days after it became clear that the 1964 Civil Rights Bill would pass in the US Senate.[22] Some smaller airlines did not sign agreements at all. Neither the airlines that signed them nor the unions representing their employees were particularly proactive in reversing decades of discriminatory hiring practices, and few Black applicants held qualifications for skilled positions such as mechanic or pilot. Moreover, the gains eventually made through the airlines' affirmative action programs looked reasonable in terms of absolute numbers but appeared less so when it came to what they represented in terms of percentage of the workforce. Airlines were hiring more Blacks, other people of color, and women but more white men as well. In 1966, Blacks still made up only 4.3 percent of the total commercial aviation labor force and remained concentrated in the low-wage, low-skill positions that represented 51 percent of the total Black labor force. Only about 1 percent of Black workers occupied "white-collar" positions. While Black women were better represented in white-collar work (flight attendant positions counted), they represented only 2 percent of a female labor force that in the aggregate constituted just one-quarter of the industry total. Still, Plans for Progress opened up some measure of employment opportunity and established, along with the 1964 Civil Rights Act, a context of possibility for job seekers and activists alike.[23]

These shifts were most visible locally in efforts—by the women themselves, the activists who supported them, the federal government, and the airlines—to secure work for Black women as flight attendants. Black female flight attendants had played a central role in efforts to desegregate airline employment in the Midwest and on the East Coast in the late 1950s and early 1960s.[24] In so doing, they tapped into the activist role of the Brotherhood of Sleeping Car Porters as they tried to gain access to the job category (i.e., flight attendant) that, ironically, was superseding that of the porters as air travel was displacing long-distance railroad travel during the early jet age.[25] As Black flight attendants and their allies continued such efforts in the mid-1960s, they made clear how struggles for Black inclusion in the air transport industry would be facilitated not only by activism in the legal and political spheres but also by shifts in the cosmopolitan aura facilitating the marketing and consumption of commercial aviation.

As Johnson negotiated Plans for Progress agreements, he betrayed their public relations function by emphasizing the need to hire Black flight attendants, given their visibility. As a result, the major airlines increased efforts to do so through recruitment efforts at "Negro schools," advertisements in African American newspapers, federal jobs programs, and outreach to local NAACP and Urban League branches.[26] United Airlines began running flight attendant recruitment advertisements in the *Sun Reporter* in early 1964.[27] After such efforts failed to produce a successful Black recruit based at SFO—United claimed there had been "no qualified applicants"—the airline announced to the Bay Area's Black community in February 1965 that flight attendant positions were open and it was "particularly interested in hiring Negro stewardesses." In case there was any doubt, a subsequent recruitment advertisement in the *Sun Reporter* featured a photograph of a Black flight attendant in uniform.[28]

Bay Area Black women pushed for these jobs as well. The Western Region of the NAACP fielded discrimination reports from potential flight attendants, and in April 1966 the organization filed complaints against TWA with both the EEOC and the state FEPC because of its failure to hire a Berkeley woman as a flight attendant under suspicious circumstances.[29] News of these complaints may well have prompted United Airlines to redouble its recruitment efforts, as it informed the San Francisco NAACP later that month that it adhered to antidiscrimination law and "would be glad to consider for employment any individual that your organization might wish to refer."[30]

There were other pressures on United to put on a good public face. Airlines were beholden to "community mores" that shifted in complex ways, with the major carriers in particular needing to maintain a reasonable national reputation for purposes of marketing their product to Black and liberal non-Black consumers and to cultivate favorable local relations for legislative purposes so that they could maintain the public expenditures and subsidies for airports upon which they relied.[31] As civil rights activism and uprisings refocused attention on Black job discrimination and poverty in urban areas, some major corporations wanted to appear sympathetic and helpful. They were often also worried that urban unrest would hurt their bottom line.[32] Indeed, from 1964 forward, the major airlines made Black and other in-house minority advancement, as well as commitments to community service and civil rights, a growing component of their self-representation in advertisements, employee communications, and messaging to shareholders.[33] Black servility and exclusion were also increasingly difficult to reconcile with liberal self-perception of the Bay Area as a putatively progressive region, as Black people became more symbolically central to a regional cosmopolitanism and Black consumers were being recognized as well.

Employing Black women as glamorous flight attendants was one component of the airlines' growing efforts to incorporate Black people into their self-representation, and Black women and their allies seized the opportunity. Flight attendants' glamour, however, defined the limits of this activism. During this period, they had to adhere to strict age, height, and weight limits and could not be married. The airlines also preferred light-skinned Black women, and women with darker complexions received the brunt of racist hostility from coworkers and passengers alike.[34] Black flight attendants may have diversified a white, heteronormative, servile labor force, but general conformity to Eurocentric (and sexist) standards of femininity continued to be reproduced and legitimized in the face of shifting, liberal sensibilities.

All the while, flight attendants participated in the display of feminine bodies in flight that aestheticized while legitimating US power, prestige, and imperial reach.[35] This was, after all, work tied to a facility and an industry that were to varying degrees dependent upon the development of military technologies, the transportation of cargo and troops to the imperial war ramping up in Southeast Asia, widening circles of international trade and tourism, and oil production and attendant social and environmental devastation. Moreover, this was a moment when the United States as a global power benefited from displays of liberal integration given the slow pace of racial reform within its borders and the widely disseminated images of the violence being perpetuated against those trying to achieve it.

In other words, Black flight attendants, who were essentially a temporary labor force by virtue of employment criteria based on age, appearance, and marital status, operated as largely disposable, feminized units of exchange in the economy of good deeds, visible accomplishments, and cost-benefit analyses that shaped the implementation of corporate affirmative action policies under government mandate. Still, their efforts to secure work were a struggle, at both the material and symbolic levels, that advanced the cause of antidiscrimination in the industry and helped make it clearer that a different kind of airport work was possible for Black workers across class and gender lines.

Black employment opportunities at SFO expanded somewhat with the implementation of an airport affirmative action program instituted at the municipal level by the San Francisco Human Rights Commission (SFHRC). A series of demonstrations by local civil rights activists, community organizations, and student allies against the discriminatory employment practices of local businesses pushed Mayor John Shelley to establish an Interim Committee on Human Relations in early 1964. Following activist demands that a permanent commission be created, the San Francisco Board of Supervisors gave the SFHRC its "essential mandate" that July: to "prepare, encourage and coordinate programs of voluntary affirmative action to reduce or eliminate existing inequalities and disadvantages in the City and County resulting from past discriminatory practices." Much of the SFHRC's early focus was on Black employment discrimination given the bleak statistics it was collecting on the matter and a growing fear of uprisings in the city. Toward that end, it publicized employment opportunities, intervened in employment disputes, and pressured unions and employers to improve minority hiring efforts. When these efforts proved largely ineffectual, and following more pressure from activists, the SFHRC shifted its emphasis to developing municipal nondiscrimination ordinances and city-run affirmative action programs.[36]

The SFHRC focused much of its early efforts on SFO, in part because of local activist pushback against using public funds to pay for the expansion of a facility that demonstrably discriminated against Black people. In the summer and fall of 1966, Goodlett and other prominent African American leaders called on voters in their community to vote "No" on upcoming general obligation bond measures A and B to fund expansions of SFO and MUNI, the city's public transportation system, respectively. Although advocates promoted the measures as engines for minority job growth, Goodlett and his allies countered that the airport was better understood, despite Black voters' long record of supporting municipal bond measures for infrastructure, as the place "where Negroes are discriminated against in employment by airlines, concessionaires, and the San Francisco Public Utilities Commission."[37]

The SFHRC had actually been trying to do something about jobs at the airport. It had, since it was an interim body, been assisting the West Coast branch of the NAACP and the state FEPC in their efforts to get Interstate HOSTS to hire more Black workers.[38] The SFHRC had also been trying to get the board of supervisors to approve a nondiscrimination ordinance for city-funded contracts, which it finally did in October 1966. This followed the feared urban uprising that materialized over three days in late September in the Bayview and Hunters Point neighborhoods after the police killing of an unarmed sixteen-year-old, Matthew "Peanut" Johnson, as he fled from an incident involving a stolen car.[39] Yet the ordinance, with its implications for contracts at SFO, would not be enforced in any substantial way until 1970, as city officials, civil rights and labor organizations, and businesses wrangled over the details. At the time of the November 1966 election, then, San Francisco had not significantly increased Black employment at the airport.[40] Both bond measures failed, with some claiming they were doomed by a lower-than-usual level of support from African American voters.[41]

Airport backers tried again to secure funding with a fall 1967 ballot measure. The new Measure A would authorize $98 million in general obligation bonds to expand passenger and cargo facilities and make other improvements. Supporters again emphasized the airport as a job creation engine, an assessment that Goodlett, the NAACP, and others again rejected as they vowed to continue to oppose the measure unless substantial changes to Black employment practices at SFO were made. This time around, however, with a set of demands from the NAACP in hand, city officials took what appeared to some to be visible steps in that regard. In June, the San Francisco Public Utilities Commission (SFPUC) agreed to hire a fair employment practices employment officer, and then the San Francisco Board of Supervisors authorized the SFHRC to apply for funds from the EEOC for a "special and intensive affirmative action program" at the airport. By the end of the month, the SFHRC had negotiated a $20,000 grant for the project. With funds secured in mid-August, the SFHRC hired an "employment representative" and a "special consultant" to begin implementing the program in early September.[42]

Goodlett, who was increasingly invested in Black Power, developing a sense that local Black economic advancement would come only with significant representation on municipal boards and commissions, and doubtful that the extant system of municipal contracts flowing to white contractors and their racially exclusionary unions would change, announced he would continue to withhold his support for the bond measure until employment gains and the diversification of the relevant commissions and boards were actually realized. But other prominent Black San Franciscans—including Assemblyman Willie Brown and City Supervisor Terry Francois—who were more invested in the local Democratic Party machine, dependent as it was, on union backing, gave the measure eleventh-hour support, helping it pass.[43]

The SFHRC initially described its airport initiative as a comprehensive assessment, training, and community-outreach program developed with the cooperation of employers, unions and union councils, the local Urban League, and other entities. But efforts to establish a working committee with airline representatives broke down, and relations with local labor organizations soured as the commission challenged their authority and autonomy. Instead, the SFHRC worked out agreements with individual airlines, which involved three types of activities: altering employment criteria and engaging in "more affirmative recruitment" in minority communities; offering preselection and tutoring to minority candidates for positions requiring additional qualifications; and targeting "the hard-core unemployed" for lower-level positions through job training and "radical changes in the selection requirements." The latter effort, influenced by a Manpower Training Act program at United's Chicago O'Hare base and then presented back to the airline at SFO, became the basis for a nationwide program run by United and other airlines.[44]

The SFHRC programs, combined with ad hoc efforts by the airlines and civil rights organizations to encourage in-house promotions and transfers, facilitated some improvements in minority hiring at SFO through the end of the decade. The SFHRC reported at the beginning of 1970 that between December 1966 and June 1969, minority employment at SFO-based airlines increased by two-thirds (from 1,400 to 3,488 jobs), bringing that workforce up to 15.2 percent of the total employment of 23,244. Blacks represented the largest group of minority hires. Moreover, positions opened up in more prestigious occupations like reservation agent, flight attendant, and mechanic. Minority hiring rates were especially good in the first half of 1969, representing 28.3 percent of new hires.[45]

Still, some international carriers and regional airlines, like Western Airlines, refused to cooperate with the SFHRC. Agreements with the more cooperative airlines went only so far in addressing the vexing combination of discrimination and harassment from racist coworkers and supervisors or structural impediments—like the craft-based organization of airport jobs—even as some airlines implemented their own, revamped national affirmative action programs, as United did in 1969. Moreover, the recession at the end of the decade began to affect the airline industry by the middle of that year, resulting in a decrease in hiring and some layoffs. Ultimately, there was a 60 percent drop in the overall hiring rate at SFO between 1968 and 1970, with a significant impact on minority hiring, and while minority hiring numbers at SFO increased during this period for United and Pan Am, they declined for other airlines.[46]

The first few years of the program also exposed its limits along class lines. The "hard-core unemployed" jobs program, however well-intentioned, was, from the beginning, limited in its scope, resulting only in the hiring of perhaps a few hundred workers in this category at SFO during the late 1960s. The program thus betrayed the shortcomings of federal and local government as well as airline commitments to reallocating resources and opportunities to poor people. As the Bay Area's Black population endured discrimination, plant closures and relocation, and automation across the job sites more likely to hire semiskilled or unskilled workers, the municipal affirmative action program at SFO, notwithstanding its problems, was better at improving the employment mobility for those who were established in the workforce, whether at SFO or elsewhere, than it was for those who were long displaced from it or disadvantaged when it came to entering it in the first place. The limits of such commitments were further defined when the "hard-core" program was terminated at the end of the decade amid the economic downturn in commercial aviation and the broader dismantling of Great Society–era employment and social welfare programs.[47]

As antidiscrimination policies and affirmative action programs were being put into place in the late 1960s and early 1970s, Black SFO workers developed a variety of approaches to addressing the opportunities and limits of airport employment, as befitted their wide range of political orientations, occupations, and employment situations. They organized as Black workers, but they did so via different organizational structures and political modalities, some long-standing, some emergent, and via alliances with a fluctuating complex of actors from business, local government, activist organizations, and personal networks.

United's Allied skycaps, as noted earlier, organized primarily through their union and, in the one case, took radical action. They had been under collective bargaining agreements since 1963, when Allied took over much of the skycap operations at SFO, including those provided by Johnson's Porter Service, a nonunion, Black-owned concession for whom my grandfather and father worked.[48] But since at least 1967, United had been considering hiring its own skycaps at SFO as a means of cutting costs and providing better service. The 1970 decision to bring the skycaps in house, as the current contract with Allied expired, by relocating United-employed skycaps from other airports may well have been influenced by the airline's recent policy, following airline industry downturn and its own financial overextension, of giving priority to furloughed United employees for open positions across the system. Another likely factor was its contemporaneous effort to generate greater company identification among public-facing workers as the airline promoted its "friendly skies" image.[49]

The Allied skycaps were, for the moment, decidedly unfriendly. They organized pickets at SFO and then at San Francisco's City Hall while the board of supervisors discussed the creation of an airport commission that would take over the running of SFO from the SFPUC. In response, the supervisors passed a resolution supporting their cause. Shortly thereafter, the skycaps called for a nationwide boycott of United.[50] The skycaps also drew upon support from established local Black political and social networks. They were relatively high-earning,

FIGURE 16. Allied Aviation skycaps Edward Anderson, Theodore Traylor, and John Hatch at 1970 protest against United Airlines. These men were among the Allied workers who learned they would lose their jobs after the airline terminated its contract with their employer for skycap labor and hired its own skycaps. Courtesy Labor Archives and Research Center, San Francisco State University, and *People's World.*

high-status individuals, described in the local Black press as good "family men" whose job loss would "create long range economic problems within the Black community." The fact that Allied had taken over the concession from a local, Black-owned business had been an ongoing point of contention; one of the NAACP's demands during the politicking over the 1967 bond measure was that the concession be returned to a Black-owned business. A few years later, the Black-business roots of the corporately held concession gave Allied skycaps some historically grounded rhetorical clout as they sought to keep their jobs.[51] When the skycaps picketed United Airlines' downtown San Francisco office, they were joined by activist religious leaders, including the Reverend Cecil Williams of Glide Memorial Church. Local civil rights leaders and city officials publicly supported their struggle as well.[52]

The support helped, up to a point. Relatively early on, United changed its plan to replace all thirty-five Allied skycaps and instead kept twelve on as United employees. Yet despite continued protests, the airline went ahead and dismissed the other twenty-three while keeping the new employment arrangement in place. Subsequent efforts to reverse the decision through a civil lawsuit, petitions to the State Labor Commission and the National Labor Relations Board, and the citizen's arrest of the United Airlines executive were not successful.[53] Ultimately, the Allied skycaps' "special situation" located them outside of the parameters of municipally instituted affirmation action protections and thus vulnerable, despite their relative privilege among semiskilled workers. United's new skycaps, ironically, whether transferred from Allied or from other United facilities, were counted by the airline as evidence of their improved Black employment numbers as SFO.[54]

Other African American airline workers organized as employees of major airlines. Black employees of TWA and United established local Black Caucuses in the late 1960s. Employees of these and other airlines also organized locally as members of the primarily Black Airlines Minority Employees Association (AMEA), which viewed its efforts as an extension of the work done by single-airline caucuses.[55] The emergence of these groups reflected a growing sense among Bay Area Black workers, across occupational and class lines, that autonomous, race-based, collective action as company employees, independently or allied with civil rights organizations, might protect their rights better than working with unions.[56] Their activism was also shaped by the airlines' piecemeal responses to the Nixon administration's pressure on businesses receiving federal money to implement affirmative action programs.

United's Black Caucus described its mission as one of "eradicat[ing] all racial barriers that have been employed by United Airlines to systematically exclude Blacks from achieving upward mobility in all job classifications." It presented itself as part of a larger movement for Black liberation, as evidenced by the name of its newsletter, *The Black Caucus Speaks*, likely a reference to the Nation of Islam's newspaper, *Muhammad Speaks*, Philip Foner's 1970 volume, *The Black Panthers Speak*, or both.[57] The San Francisco–based Black Caucus of TWA Employees sought to "advance and promote the interest and welfare of Black and minority workers" at the airline by "promot[ing] racial equality and fairness" and "combatting racism throughout TWA's corporate structure."[58]

In November 1968, TWA's Black Caucus presented their grievances to airline executives, the press, and local civil rights organizations. They acknowledged the recent implementation of antidiscrimination laws and affirmative action programs but insisted that these did not significantly change supervisors' racist behaviors and unions' unwillingness or inability to challenge individual-behavioral or structural impediments

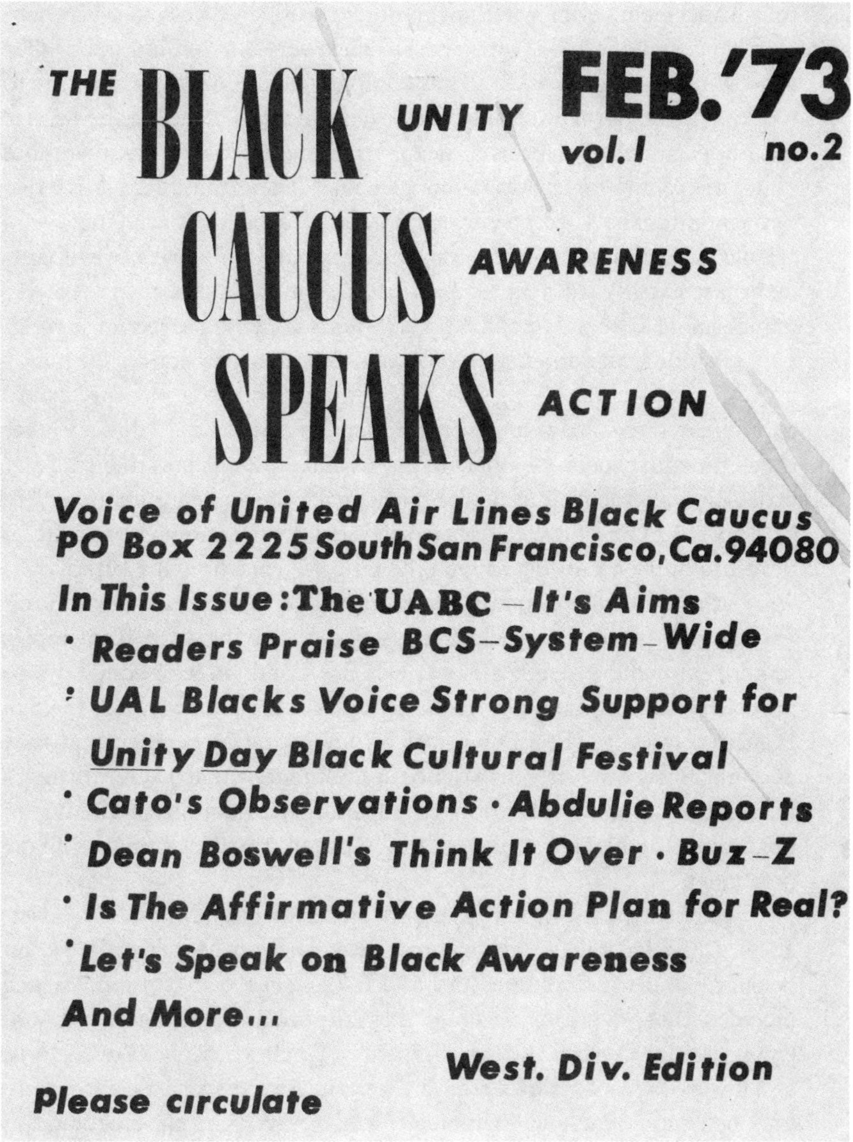

THE **BLACK** UNITY **FEB.'73**
vol. I   no. 2

CAUCUS AWARENESS

SPEAKS ACTION

Voice of United Air Lines Black Caucus
PO Box 2225 South San Francisco, Ca. 94080

In This Issue: The UABC – It's Aims
* **Readers Praise BCS–System–Wide**
* **UAL Blacks Voice Strong Support for**
  Unity Day Black Cultural Festival
* **Cato's Observations · Abdulie Reports**
* **Dean Boswell's Think It Over · Buz–Z**
* **Is The Affirmative Action Plan for Real?**
* **Let's Speak on Black Awareness**
And More...

               West. Div. Edition
Please circulate

FIGURE 17. Cover page of the February 1973 issue of *The Black Caucus Speaks,* newsletter of the SFO-based Black Caucus of United Airlines employees. The article, casting a suspicious eye on the airline's recently implemented affirmative action program, reflects the dissatisfaction that led local United employees and civil rights activists to support a US Justice Department lawsuit against the airline for discriminatory workplace policies and inadequate affirmative action policies. From Materials Relating to the TWA Black Caucus, [ca. 1960–ca. 1980], BANC MSS 85/138 c, The Bancroft Library, University of California, Berkeley.

to advancement, even when sympathetic to their Black members' circumstances. Black TWA workers said they were not antiunion, but they vowed to organize across crafts as company "employees" in addition to working through their unions. They even sought to associate themselves with upper management as a means of addressing the harassment and abuse of "White lower level management." The group offered five recommendations to TWA to address problems facing its Black employees: regular meetings between the Black Caucus and "all levels of management"; sensitivity training for "all employees"; a reassessment of lower management's "social qualifications"; more Black employees in supervisory positions; and an examination of promotion procedures for bias.[59]

TWA received the group's list of grievances and took measured steps to address them, including running sensitivity trainings and meeting regularly with caucus members to discuss possible changes to hiring and promotion protocols. But by February 1970, caucus representative Willie Thompson had publicly labeled the sensitivity trainings "a waste of time and money," noting as well the intransigence of white supervisors when it came to fair promotion practices and disciplinary procedures. Shortly thereafter, the Black Caucus began meeting with local representatives of the NAACP's Legal Defense Fund (LDF) about how to proceed.[60] Caucus members filed a series of complaints through the San Francisco office of the EEOC, which found, that November, that they and others were unfairly disciplined and ultimately that TWA, "through its discriminatory application of rules and regulations and lack of upgrading for Black people, creates a disparate effect upon its Black personnel."[61]

The next step, with the EEOC's encouragement and the LDF's assistance, was a federal lawsuit against TWA filed on March 8, 1971, on behalf of all Black employees at the "TWA San Francisco station," which included those working at Oakland's airport as well. The complaint emphasized the systematic consignment of Black workers to lower-status and lower-wage jobs, the dearth of Blacks in management, the unscrupulous behavior of whites in management, the lack of clear promotion guidelines, and the fact that Thompson and fellow caucus member Henry Spencer had been unfairly disciplined after speaking out about his group's activities in the *Sun Reporter*.[62] LDF attorney William J. Turner described the Black Caucus as "a new kind of plaintiff for a federal discrimination suit and a new and alternative kind of organization for blacks employed by large companies. In industries where discrimination may be practiced and unions do not vigorously take up the cause of the black employees, . . . the black employees should get themselves together to represent their own special interests."[63]

As the lawsuit proceeded, members of the Black Caucus continued to meet with TWA officials, sometimes amicably and sometimes contentiously, and succeeded in getting the airline to put additional hiring and promotion policies in place.[64] TWA and some of the plaintiffs settled the case in March 1974 and agreed to a consent decree that remained in place until 1990—under which the airline agreed to maintain and extend recent programs to improve minority hiring and promotion at its San Francisco operation and report regularly on its efforts—although other plaintiffs refused the settlement and continued (largely unsuccessfully) to have the particulars of their grievances addressed by the court.[65]

The LDF filed the TWA case on the same day that the US Supreme Court issued its decision in *Griggs v. Duke Power Co.*, another case brought by the LDF, which held that discriminatory intent in hiring and promotion practices did not have to be proved for employers to be liable for discrimination under Title VII of the 1964 Civil Rights Act. They could instead have "disparate impact liability." The *Griggs* decision inspired a new wave of antidiscrimination lawsuits and compelled employers to create or revamp affirmative action programs to avoid Title VII liability, with "numeric goals and targets" becoming a more significant part of corporations' approaches to hiring. Also compelling was the US Labor Department's February 1970 Order No. 4 (rereleased in December 1971), which expanded the reach of the Nixon administration's Philadelphia Plan, geared toward the construction industry, by requiring all businesses under federal contract to develop written affirmative action and compliance programs with attention to local demographics.[66] TWA counsel's willingness to settle the Black Caucus case was based in part on a recognition of the company's vulnerability in this climate without a comprehensive affirmative action plan in place and with hiring decisions still left largely to the whims of white lower-level management.[67]

Local Black airline employee organizations were also party to *United States of America v. United Airlines et al.*, a case with broader implications. United's 1969 affirmative action policy was hampered by the recent industry downturn that limited hiring and mobility within the company. A 1971 federal edict, pursuant to Order No. 4, to "develop and implement" additional affirmative action plans impelled the airline to do more. The SFO "supplement" to United's national program consisted of stepped-up outreach and recruitment efforts in local communities, changes in promotion policies, internal reporting on minority and women's advancement, and efforts to promote similar policies among labor unions and contractors. Notably, in the wake of both Order No. 4 and *Griggs,* the plan also included an analysis of deficiencies in minority and female employment across job categories, as well as targets for success, given the percentages of each in the Bay Area workforce (30.9 percent and 36.2 percent, respectively).[68]

Many of United's Black employees were unimpressed with the revamped plan. For much of the spring and summer of 1972, Leonard Carter, director of the Western Region of the NAACP, was in dialogue with local and national United management to communicate their Black employees' grievances, lobby on behalf of individual workers seeking redress, and collect information about the deficiencies in United's employment practices and affirmative action programs.[69] In October, United's Black Caucus ramped up its organizing after learning the details of the airline's newest affirmative action plan, which it described as "an ineffectual watered down equal opportunity proposal that glosses over the real need for equal opportunity and progress for all, but maintains the status quo!"[70] The following spring, United employee and AMEA member Pat James said recent figures showing some improvement in job placements at United had more to do with "reshuffling and reorganization (rather than promotions)."[71] This interpretation was in line with a 1972 AMEA statement, referencing a contemporary term for token hires, that "affirmative action programs are akin to the spook sitting by the door—a highly visible showpiece at mid-management level while the majority of black workers compose the traditional 'black bottom.'"[72]

The NAACP's and AMEA's analyses and activism were informed, in part, by their recognition of the political implications of the growing purchasing power of middle-class Black Bay Area residents and to their attendant political identities as consumers. In a May 1972 letter to United president Edward Carlson, requesting "an internal investigation" of United's employment practices, Carter reminded Carlson that "black citizens are well represented among the airlines' consumers," noting in particular that the NAACP's Western Region had recently chartered a United Airlines 727 to fly members to the NAACP's annual conference in Detroit.[73] Given that air travel was a large revenue and employment generator in the Bay Area, the AMEA argued that July, "the entire Black community is faced with the responsibility of carefully examining its relationship" to it. The organization called on Black travelers to evaluate airlines' affirmative action programs before purchasing flight tickets. Ultimately, they requested "that the Black traveler, and the Black job seeker, and the Black worker presently employed in the Airlines industry, form a coalition, or partnership to help each other. . . . This must be a first—the first time that the total unity of the Black community defeats the 'benign neglect' of racism and provides for a Black future in the Air industry."[74] This at a moment when local Black employees of TWA and United were developing marketing programs geared toward Black travelers as a means of tapping into their spending power and improving their employers' corporate images.[75]

Yet consumer pressure ultimately did little either to heal growing political, social, and economic divisions in Bay Area Black communities, as imagined, or to get airlines to change their behaviors. After learning that the Justice Department was considering filing a discrimination suit against United Airlines, Carter encouraged the department to follow through with it and pledged his office's cooperation.[76] The complaint, filed in 1973, excoriated the airline for a wide range of institutionalized, discriminatory practices against Blacks and women during hiring, recruitment, and promotion and for not taking reasonable affirmative action to correct the problems of which they were aware. The lawsuit also named five unions with which United had collective bargaining agreements, focusing on how union preferences for promotion, demotion, transfer, and layoff based on job seniority amplified their prior or ongoing discriminatory practices against Blacks and women as well as those of the airline.[77]

As the lawsuit proceeded, United initiated a variety of supplements to its local and national affirmative action programs and publicly called attention to its successes in minority and women's employment numbers throughout the ranks.[78] Still, the plaintiffs persevered. In 1975, the EEOC, recently substituted as a plaintiff, took the case to trial. In 1976, it negotiated a consent decree with the airline and the unions, which included five- to six-year targets for female and minority employment across a range of job categories; specific hiring rates by which to meet those targets; and revamped hiring selection procedures, seniority rules, and guidelines for terminations, demotions, and suspensions. Although United reported successes in implementing the decree over the next several years, it was not until 1995 that the EEOC, the airline and unions, and the court agreed that the decree requirements had been met.[79]

Although airlines were the major employers at SFO, contracts for goods and services were another focus of Black struggle at SFO. Such efforts were at once the product of the financial aspirations of Black businesspeople and, in some cases, the result of their Black Power–era vision that group empowerment could be advanced by linking their interests with those of workers, given the unequal, often duplicitous resource distribution economy at the facility. Such efforts developed hand in hand with the desires of civic and corporate elites who, during the Black Power era, wanted to capitalize, financially and symbolically, on Black economic success.

In 1968, Goodlett and three partners successfully bid on a three-year contract to take over the operation of SFO's parking garage, which the city was expanding pursuant to Proposition A funding. Goodlett viewed this as a potentially pathbreaking endeavor that would lead "other racial minorities throughout the nation to aggressively seek such public service contracts." He and his partners also saw it as a jobs program that other municipalities could emulate. Under their management, minority representation on the garage workforce grew from one-tenth to two-thirds. The group took particular pride in its on-the-job training of unskilled workers and its efforts to hire women, including female heads of households. They spoke of "break[ing] the cycle of poverty" and getting people off public assistance. They also donated shares of their profits to job training programs elsewhere at SFO.[80] The group's work paralleled airlines' efforts to reach the "hard-core" unemployed but did so in a way that sought to avoid the tokenism of such outreach efforts and provide a more systematic affirmative action at the interface of government largesse and capital accumulation.

Almost from the beginning, however, airport officials criticized and surveilled the operation, charging it with poor management, dubious accounting practices, inadequate security leading to auto thefts and burglaries, traffic congestion, and other issues. Goodlett and his partners were also increasingly at odds with city officials and the local white press, which described deficiencies in garage operations and even suggested complicity with an auto theft ring targeting the facility. The garage operators worked to remedy the issues—firing a manager, for example, who, they conceded, was not up to the task of running the large operation—but they insisted that fault for some problems, such as traffic congestion at the garage entrances and exits, lay with SFO management. They characterized the *San Francisco Examiner*'s 1969 campaign against them and subsequent journalistic coverage as racist responses to their antiracist affirmative action venture.[81]

Amid a new wave of mutual accusations in the spring of 1971, the recently established San Francisco Airport Commission, which took over SFO operations from the SFPUC in 1970, made clear that it wanted a different operator when it solicited bids that summer for a new lease. The commission requested that each bidder provide a $100,000 deposit—the same amount the City was trying to retrieve from the operators via a lawsuit for what it claimed was its unpaid share of parking revenue. The operators argued that the deposit requirement was effectively discriminatory by discouraging bids from minority contractors, and they brought the matter, via the NAACP and California Black Leadership Conference, to the attention of the US Department of Labor. Still, the group lost the concession after reportedly submitting the second-lowest bid.[82]

The garage operators suggested that one factor in their failure to maintain the operation was the fragility of political relationships that made such entrepreneurial affirmative action possible. According to their analysis, liberal San Francisco mayor Joseph Alioto took a political hit for insisting that the City follow its own guidelines and award the parking garage concession to the lowest bidder, Goodlett and company, back in 1968. Yet by not following the NAACP's and others' requests to appoint a Black airport commissioner, the group claimed, Alioto missed an opportunity, if he ever desired it, to protect this arrangement from its critics, who wanted to put the concession back in white hands at the earliest stage possible.[83]

The SFHRC turned its attention to airport contractors and concessionaires in the early 1970s. They monitored them for compliance with the city's antidiscrimination statutes and began conversations about developing affirmative action programs for such entities. From the beginning, this was a fraught process. It took several years for the SFHRC to convince the city that the new ordinance (now Chapter 12B of the municipal code) covering nondiscrimination in city contracts applied to hiring in leased space at the airport. Moreover, as the response to Nixon's Philadelphia Plan made clear, construction industry affirmative action programs were controversial in general, often pitting minority and white workers against one another, and limited in scope and effectiveness given resistance from unions.[84]

Airport construction affirmative action programs presented a particular challenge, since significant portions of the relevant work were being done by trades with low levels of minority and female participation (e.g., operating engineers) and since the SFHRC lacked influence over contractors based in San Mateo County and elsewhere outside of San Francisco.[85] Yet the SFHRC was still compelled to act given the limits of the programs geared toward direct hiring by airlines and in the wake of sustained activism by Black contractors since the mid-1960s to open up opportunity in the construction trades across the Bay Area.[86] Ultimately, the SFHRC's delicate dance with union officials, contractors, airport officials, and others led to a compliance policy but one that developed slowly—so much so that in 1974 the FAA and the Office of Federal Contract Compliance pressured the City to include "specific goals or quotas" within it.[87]

Minority and female contractors and vendors might have had it worse at SFO if not for major airlines developing their own programs. United Airlines, for example, established a nationwide minority vendor purchasing program in January 1973 and a minority construction program the following year. These programs paid some dividends to local Black businesses and generated hope in some quarters that future opportunities would materialize.[88] Yet others expressed significant frustration with their limits, noting that vending and construction contracts at the airport remained largely a form of "white welfare." Such thinking animated the *Sun Reporter*'s opposition to San Francisco's November 1977 Bond Measure C, designed to fund yet another airport expansion; its criticisms of Mayor George Moscone for his failure to replace William Chester (the departing Black airport commissioner, finally appointed in 1974) with another Black person, or otherwise rectify inequities in airport contracting; and its attempts to push Mayor Dianne Feinstein, who succeeded Moscone after his assassination, to take direct action against institutional racism at SFO.[89]

Eventually, the mix of local activism, federal pressure, and municipal and corporate affirmative action across the 1960s and 1970s pushed the SFHRC and the Airport Commission to develop a more comprehensive "affirmative action program for all phases of the airport's operation."[90] This 1979 initiative followed the 1977 passage of Chapter 12C of the City Administrative Code, which made clearer that municipal nondiscrimination provisions applied to "all property contracts" "entered into by any agency of the City and County" and empowered the SFHRC director to address any breaches of those provisions.[91] Meanwhile, the SFHRC reorganized its operation so that most professional staff "were moved into some affirmative action monitoring function or involvement." This focus was all the more important at SFO as the number of leases and concessions, as well as design, engineering, and construction contracts, increased with a series of airport expansion projects.[92]

Shaping the SFHRC's "involvement" was the Supreme Court's 1978 decision in *Regents of the University of California v. Bakke,* which affirmed the constitutionality of race-based affirmative action programs, so long as race was not the sole factor determining their outcome, but called into question the legitimacy of some quotas and set-aside programs. Although the post-*Bakke* terrain required caution, the SFHRC's interpretation of that case and contemporaneous court decisions was that they ultimately were "most supportive of affirmative action efforts, such as the SFHRC's, that are not exclusionary in nature." A centralized affirmative action project for the airport, the commission argued, would help ensure that post-*Bakke* restrictions were not violated.[93]

At the beginning of the 1979–80 fiscal year, the Airport Commission began funding two SFHRC staffers and a clerical support person for this program and soon passed a series of resolutions emphasizing its commitment to affirmative action and equal opportunity in response to ongoing complaints from SFO workers and their allies.[94] There were good reasons why complaints continued. In April 1979, total minority employment among SFO lessees and tenants continued to fall short of goals based on Bay Area demographics, with numbers particularly low for "minority females." And that was among businesses willing to report their data. The only two minority-owned "tenant concessions" at the end of that year were "a Black-owned shoeshine stand and a Hispanic-owned barbershop."[95]

The SFHRC and the Airport Commission secured new affirmative action agreements with SFO tenants, including airlines, on behalf of minority businesses and workers. These led to improvements, but they were once again limited and complicatedly so. By the fall of 1984, minority employment at SFO had grown since the institutionalization of this latest affirmative action plan. It was up to 31.6 percent from the 28 percent reported in 1980. The percentage of minority women in the airport workforce had increased to 10.9 percent in 1984 from 7.5 percent in 1983, and the percentage of minorities in the laborer category had decreased from 61 percent to 46 percent as they made inroads in clerical and office work. Yet representation in the professional ranks remained woefully low at 2.6 percent, even below the 3 percent reported in 1980. The SFHRC could only conclude—when comparing the percentages of women and minority workers in different airport occupations to the percentage of available minority workers in those categories in San Francisco and the Bay Area as a whole—that significant work remained to be done.[96]

As to Black workers specifically, the history of activism, corporate reforms, and affirmative action had led to an improved yet ultimately precarious and patchy inclusion in airport employment. By 1985 the percentage of Black employees in SFO's permanent and temporary workforce had improved slightly from the 1980 figure of 8 percent to 10.4 percent. This number exceeded that of the Black population of San Mateo County (6.6 percent) and the Black population of the nine-county Bay Area (9.9 percent), but it remained below that of San Francisco (12.4 percent). Black workers remained underrepresented in the professional ranks, and Black women fared much worse than Black men, representing just 3.8 percent of the airport permanent workforce compared to 6.6 percent for Black men.[97] While 75 percent of Black male airport workers were employed by one of the airlines, with their generally better benefits and pay scales, only 56 percent of Black women had airline jobs, with 34 percent in generally lower-paid work at concessions.[98]

These statistics signal how extant airport affirmative programs had only gone so far in ameliorating the legacies of previous generations of discrimination and could provide only inadequate protection to Black, women, and other SFO workers in the wake of the Airline Deregulation Act, signed by President Jimmy Carter in 1978. This act prompted airlines to seek to reduce labor costs by implementing two-tier wage systems, with lower pay and benefits packages for recently hired employees, and by subcontracting with businesses to provide labor done by even lower-paid workers. Union bargaining power in the industry took a hit as well during this period, as symbolized by President Ronald Reagan breaking the air traffic controllers' union in 1981. Although workers across categories (even pilots) were affected by these changes, the impact was longer-lasting and more significant for lower-wage workers, who at SFO, as at many airports in the United States, were disproportionately women and people of color. It also limited opportunities for professional advancement, which tended to affect most significantly minorities, women, and others who had been hired into professional positions most recently.[99]

Then, of course, there were the lower-income and poor members of the Bay Area's Black community whose interests were simply not served at all by the coming together of various aspirations and networks in airport affirmative action programs. For them, SFO work was never a reasonable possibility given their child-rearing responsibilities, lack of access to transportation, entanglement in the carceral system, long-term mental health costs, insecure housing, and other factors that airport employment and contracting programs and struggles coinciding with them could not adequately address.

Black businesspeople faced their own challenges. Black-owned firms did have their moments, such as 1983, when Black-owned/controlled construction firms managed to secure a percentage of airport construction contracts (8.8 percent) more or less in line with their Bay Area population. Yet the mainstays of Black business at the airport on the concession side were the (now two) shoeshine stands.[100] The Black political and entrepreneurial class, relatively well connected politically and economically in comparison to other minority groups, had, after all, begun to lose some of its clout. Post-1965 demographic transformations began to decenter Black political agency and need in public discourse. Indeed, San Francisco's and San Mateo's Black populations began their precipitous decline in real numbers circa 1980 as a result of out-migration to farther-flung suburbs and other regions, gentrification and urban renewal, the rising cost of housing, the disappearance of jobs and public housing, mass incarceration, and other factors. And while the greater Bay Area's Black population remained steady between the 1980 and 2010 US Censuses, their percentage in this rapidly growing region declined significantly, in large part because of expanding populations of Latinxs and Asian/Pacific Islanders.[101] Meanwhile, white-controlled unions and contractors remained hostile to the interventions that threatened to disrupt their special hold on resources funneled through contracts for goods and services. As minority and female contractors (and those passing as them) lined up to get their "fair share" of available resources, claims of Black and female incompetence fomented a backlash against affirmative action and governmental largesse that was never adequate to begin with when it came to fundamental structural and institutional change.[102]

In other words, the exclusionary assemblage that was SFO had been remade through workers' and entrepreneurs' struggles against discrimination, transformations in civil rights and affirmative action law and policy at different levels of government, shifting corporate practices, and other factors. All of this led to very real progress in workplace mobility and professional advancement. Yet this was progress defined by its limits, as reflected by persistent raced and gendered imbalance in airport hiring, the overrepresentation of Black workers in lower-wage, nonprofessional positions at the facility, the only intermittent successes of the Black business elite through construction-, concession-, and vendor-oriented affirmative action programs, and the lack of access to airport employment at all for some lower-income people. Deregulation in the commercial aviation industry brought even more diminishing returns for many.

Two early 1980s complaints brought to the SFHRC made clear these impacts. In the summer of 1982, the BRAC filed a complaint with the

SFHRC on behalf of seventy-five Allied Maintenance Corporation sky-caps against their employer and fourteen airlines that still contracted skycap services from the company. At issue was a recently completed agreement between the Airport Commission and the airlines that fol-lowed the deregulation of the industry. The agreement increased the carriers' power over their contracted labor, effectively enabling them to nullify the 1963 collective bargaining agreement that spelled out provi-sions for wage standards, sick leave, paid vacations, and other benefits. In order to continue working for the airlines through Allied, skycaps would have to forgo many of these benefits, and their pretip base pay would be reduced to the minimum wage of $3.35 per hour.[103] In other words, the good job the Allied skycaps had fought for in 1970 was now not as good a job, as airlines, ancillary companies, and local authorities colluded to lower worker pay and benefits at a moment of trying finan-cial times for local and federal governments and the airline industry alike.[104]

The skycaps had unsuccessfully pursued an action with the National Labor Relations Board (NLRB), but they argued that the SFHRC should intervene because this agreement was in violation of a subsection of Chapter 12B of the San Francisco Administrative Code that required contractors and subcontractors working for the City to provide a pre-vailing wage. A key question was whether this regulation applied to arrangements that had been "negotiated through the collective bargain-ing process pursuant to the National Labor Relations Act."[105] In Janu-ary 1983 the SFHRC's director, on the advice of the City Attorney's Office, determined that other sections of the code suggested that the NRLB was the ultimate authority in this case. The skycaps used several strategies to appeal, but in February 1984 a special committee upheld the original decision.[106]

A more successful 1982 case involving the prevailing wage clause featured a multiracial group of eighty-five union aircraft and terminal cleaners who lost their jobs when American, Pacific Southwest, and Western Airlines terminated their custodial work agreements with Allied and contracted instead with Western Service Incorporated. This Texas-based company employed a crew of primarily Korean nationals who were housed in company dormitories, were paid "minimum and subminimum wage," and were forced to reimburse the company for room and board. These Allied workers' union, Service Employees Inter-national Union (SEIU) Local 77, filed a complaint with the SFHRC against Western Service and the three airlines.[107]

A city attorney opinion that hurt the skycaps' cause—that the SFHRC had authority to act under the city's prevailing wage provision only if the failure to pay such a wage was "itself a discriminatory employment practice or violate[d] an element of an affirmative action program"—provided a basis for finding in favor of the janitors. The SFHRC argued that the shift to a contractor employing lower-wage foreign nationals had a discriminatory effect on minority workers in the United States by obviating the airport's affirmative action goals. The SFHRC also seems to have taken to heart the wave of organized labor protests over prevailing wages and working conditions for subcontracted airport labor, including a March 1983 protest over the janitor and skycap cases, sponsored by the San Mateo County Labor Council and the San Francisco Airport Labor Coalition, that drew 250 picketers to the airport. Protesters linked these cases to "a systematic wave of union busting at the airport" and insisted that the city needed to do more to protect and enforce the prevailing wage provisions in its charter.[108]

Yet the limits of the janitors' victory were soon made clear. Western Airlines terminated its relationship with Western Service and hired back the union janitors through Allied, but only after renegotiating the contract with decreased wages. Pacific Southwest and American dragged their feet, ultimately refusing to sign an SFHRC-negotiated affirmative action plan, which would have allowed Western Service to remain their subcontractor for janitorial services on the condition that it try to increase its "non-Korean" workforce to 50 percent. Subsequently, Pan Am and other international carriers began their operations out of the revamped international terminal using Western's janitorial services. They got around the SFHRC's ruling by subcontracting to a Lockheed subsidiary that, in turn, subcontracted to Western Service. Infuriated by the City's apparent lack of response and efforts to "rehabilitate" Western Service, SEIU Local 77 filed a lawsuit, albeit one that was quickly dismissed, against the Airport Commission, its director, and the City and County of San Francisco, for failing to comply with the provisions of Chapter 12B of the Administrative Code.[109]

A brief hope arose that these cases would otherwise revamp municipal regulations pertaining to living wages for airport workers more generally. In 1984, following pressure from the San Mateo Central Labor Council and the Airport Labor Coalition, San Francisco amended its Administrative Code to require that airport workers be paid prevailing wages in the region for their respective categories of employment. But a group of twenty-one airlines quickly and successfully were able to get the ordinance, as it applied to them, struck down by a federal court on the grounds that it changed the terms of their recently signed leases. Beyond that, the ordinance was seldom enforced when it came to other airport leaseholders and concessionaires, and it was eventually dropped from the Code.[110]

Ultimately, the Allied skycaps were symbolically projected back in time to the 1950s, when union protections were fewer (or nonexistent) and they relied more on tips for their livelihood. But that was also a moment when more elite, less harried travel made their servility more valuable and remunerative. The janitors' case provided a ray of hope, as it gestured to the growing visibility and power of the SEIU as a representative of low-wage, service sector workers, many of them migrants, immigrants, and/or people of color. Yet their victory, such as it was, also marked the limits of what had been and could be achieved for low-wage workers, Black and non-Black, at this moment of deregulation, outsourcing, impermanence, and post-Fordist restructuring of the economy. The larger irony, of course, is that the airport work that people struggled for was at a facility that provided some of the infrastructural support for the acceleration of these changes into the future. Reminiscing decades later about the vibrancy of Black San Francisco in the late 1950s, before Black neighborhoods were decimated by urban renewal projects, gentrification, automation and deindustrialization, and insufficient funding for schools, parks, and social services, and more foundationally by the upward redistribution of wealth in the city, longtime *Sun Reporter* newspaper columnist Rochelle Metcalfe mentioned skycap jobs at SFO as one of the important ways that "the average working man, without a college degree," could make a "decent living."[111] The figure of the skycap thus remains a significant symbol of Black incorporation into the complex, colonial assemblage of Bay Area work and urban life that was from the outset destined to be defined by the limits of its rewards.

CHAPTER 5

The Politics of Jet Noise

As Black skycaps protested changes to their working conditions during the spring and summer of 1970, a different group of activists, largely white and operating primarily as homeowners rather than as workers, were engaged in their own SFO-focused struggle. The issue was jet noise, a long-standing nuisance that had become more unbearable as the airport grew and as environmentalists and government agencies deemed it a form of pollution that could have detrimental effects on human well-being. That November, after months of unsuccessfully lobbying airport and government officials for changes to SFO flight operations, thirty-two property owners from South San Francisco, a then largely white working- and middle-class suburb located northwest of the airport, filed claims with the San Francisco Airport Commission seeking compensation for the disruptions caused by jets taking off over their neighborhoods. The commission denied the claims, so the following February the South San Franciscans filed a $320,000 lawsuit ($10,000 per plaintiff) against the City and County of San Francisco on the grounds that jet noise had "diminished and damaged" the "reasonable use and quiet enjoyment of their property." Subsequently, ten individuals from the tonier suburbs of Woodside and Portola Valley, located southeast of the airport, filed their own lawsuit, requesting the same per-person damages caused by noise from aircraft on approach to SFO.[1]

These lawsuits, ultimately settled by the Airport Commission's promise to institute a $5 million noise mitigation program, were among the

many antinoise actions undertaken by outraged SFO neighbors following the introduction of jet aircraft to the facility in 1959. Their communities had grown in symbiotic relationship with SFO in ways physical, social, political, and economic. Jet sounds helped to compose their
soundscapes, or acoustic environments, offering their inhabitants referents through which they conceptualized and lived their urban experiences. The sounds oriented local residents toward the sky, providing a
generalized sense of being urban, while also defining their relationships
to SFO through the horizontal positioning of homes, workplaces, recreation sites, schools, and other places they inhabited in relation to
takeoff and landing vectors and the facility itself.[2]

How people experienced this relationship to place via jet sounds—
whether positive, negative, or ambivalent—was affected by people's
proximity to such sounds, the frequency and duration of them, their
relative audibility in relation to other components of the soundscape,
and the social and political meanings they were conditioned over time
to hear in them. When Bay Area residents heard jet sounds as "noise,"
it was often simply because they were loud and profoundly disruptive.
But at other moments jet noise was a more subjective, socially determined "unwanted sound." Such determination happened, in part, as
anthropologist Marina Peterson's work on LAX and its environs helps
us understand, because of what these insistent sounds had come to sym-
bolize as they catalyzed relationships among an expanding ensemble of
individuals and community groups; government officials, agencies, and
regulations; activists and their organizations; scientists and other
researchers; the airport and its operations; and a broad set of social,
political, and economic forces.[3]

Some local residents were willing to tolerate the noise. It was an
inconvenience to be put up with in exchange for the benefits of living,
working, or doing business near the airport. Noise itself, and the impu-
nity to make it, might have signified the financial and political interests
of airlines, airport officials, and other powerful interests, but these entities offered something (jobs, construction contracts, airport employee
spending, convenient travel, and so on) in return. For others, however,
this loud component of the soundscape signified differently on the pros
and cons of living near the airport as well as on the relationships in
which they were immersed. Jet noise, in other words, could be heard as
a manifestation of the forms of power that defined the regional colonial
present, and it raised the question of how local residents would live out
their attachments to them.

Anti–jet noise activism by individuals, homeowner associations, political figures, environmental groups, and others around SFO usually reflected their relative degrees of privilege and aspiration as mostly white beneficiaries of accumulated colonial power in the region. Yet their activism simultaneously articulated critiques, explicit and implicit, of the ways elements of the power—economic, legal, bureaucratic, and so on—that lay behind the noise had diminished human thriving in the region more generally. Airport and local government officials, labor unions, and others who opposed, deflected, or sought to incorporate strategically the goals of these activists also expressed or otherwise engaged multiple forms of social, economic, and bureaucratic power while seeking to advance or protect their own accumulated interests.

The activists had some successes. SFO and its surrounding communities eventually became less noisy because of changes in aircraft technology (especially engine technology) and also because the FAA, airport operators, civic leaders, and others eventually started to listen to antinoise activists and made significant efforts to mitigate jet noise. But jets continued to generate noise at and near SFO, and some people are still complaining about the problem today. Still, the history of antinoise activism around SFO—the version in this chapter runs from the late 1950s into the 1980s—is still worth exploring because it makes audible some of the complex ways that challenging and reproducing power in the mid- and late twentieth-century regional colonial present occurred through the synergies, conflicts, and missed opportunities for cooperation among largely white homeowner, environmentalist, and worker movements when they collided with SFO as manifestation of broader economic transformations and modes of governmental infrastructure development and resource stewardship.

. . .

Aircraft noise had been the subject of intermittent complaints in the Bay Area going back to the early days of aviation. Concern that loud airplanes might depress real estate prices was among the factors that led to the shuttering of San Francisco's early civilian airstrip in the Marina District.[4] Noise was initially not a problem around Mills Field. Aircraft of the 1920s and 1930s were not terribly loud, and there was little residential development nearby. That began to change after World War II as commercial air operations at what became SFO increased, aircraft grew in size and sound-generating capability, and residential neighborhoods encroached upon the airport. As was the case elsewhere in the

FIGURE 18. SFO and its environs in 1960. As surrounding communities encroached upon the airport and grew denser after World War II, some of their residents were put into closer proximity to the noisy aircraft operations. These operations had become significantly noisier with the advent of commercial jet service at SFO in 1959. Collection of SFO Museum.

United States, growing local concern about airport noise dovetailed with fears of aircraft crashing into homes or businesses below, as happened near the Newark and Idlewild airports in late 1951 and early 1952. Two pre–jet age incidents of aircraft developing engine trouble after taking off over South San Francisco increased the level of anxiety about that community's proximity to SFO in particular.[5]

Complaints, emanating primarily from five surrounding cities, grew exponentially with the arrival of jet aircraft in April 1959. Residents of San Bruno, Daly City, and, most vocally, South San Francisco were primarily affected by aircraft departing to the northwest from runway 28, oriented to allow aircraft to take off into the wind through the "gap" between San Bruno Mountain and the Santa Cruz Mountains. South San Franciscans formed neighborhood jet noise committees, but their complaints were often channeled through city councilman and later mayor Leo Ryan and City attorney John Noonan. The two officials began a dialogue with airport representatives, pilots, airlines, and federal officials about the coming jet noise problem in 1957, commissioned an engineer's report on the matter, and stepped up their efforts after the jets arrived.[6]

As complaints from South San Francisco increased, and as technological advancements permitted more takeoffs in crosswinds or slight tailwinds, flights were shifted to the intersecting, perpendicular runway 1 in an effort to redistribute aircraft noise. This made things more difficult for residents of Millbrae and northeastern Burlingame and especially for those living in Bayside Manor, a Millbrae neighborhood established in 1943, across the Bayshore Freeway from the end of the runway. Bayside Manor residents were primarily affected by the "jet blast" (i.e., noise, vibration, and fumes) from aircraft as they began their takeoffs just seven hundred feet away from the edge of the development. Residents organized primarily through the Bayside Manor Improvement Association, formed in 1948, which had for several years been fighting the placement of industrial facilities on undeveloped land near their subdivision.[7]

Local residents experienced a variety of dramatic and disruptive effects from jet engine-produced sound waves. According to a Millbrae woman, "We thought the old planes were bad enough. But jets are terrible. The house shakes, light bulbs burn out from the vibration, and we can't hear TV programs when the planes are taking off." People also complained about frightened and crying children, sleepless nights, distractions in schools, disrupted church and funeral services, interrupted in-person and telephone conversations, jumping phonograph needles, the inability to entertain outside, and actual physical damage to their property from sonic vibrations: cracked walls, stucco, chimneys, fireplaces, gas lines, and windows, as well as dishes breaking after falling from shelves. They worried about falling home values and about their physical and mental well-being. Some were exhausted. Others complained of headaches, earaches, temporary hearing loss, and other ailments. According to one petition, some South San Franciscans were "in a constant state of anxiety and have had to undergo medical treatment for nervous conditions said to have been induced by the noises created by the jet aircraft and the anxiety due to the passage of jet aircraft over their homes."[8]

The areas most affected by jet noise were relatively modest working- and middle- class neighborhoods. They were also, in 1960, affirmatively and restrictively white. Millbrae was 99.9 percent white, while South San Francisco was 98.3 percent white, albeit with 8.7 percent of the population listed in the census as white with a "Spanish surname."[9] Whether they consciously embraced the fact or not, residents of these communities had collectively benefited from generations of state-sanctioned white settler development in the area as well as more recent state investments in their whiteness. After World War II, whiteness was consolidated and maintained in San Mateo County—as elsewhere, as George Lipsitz makes clear—through supposedly race-neutral liberal state policies that allocated resources to largely white groups of citizen-consumers and protected their claims on them.[10] Subsidized whiteness went hand in hand with active discrimination on the ground, and their combined effects helped airport neighbors secure homes, maintain and increase the value of their real property investments, and obtain (at least the men among them) significant advantages at work.

South San Francisco, Millbrae, and nearby municipalities benefited from the federally funded rerouting and transformation of the Bayshore Highway (101) into the Bayshore Freeway, which facilitated suburban development by creating easier access to jobs in San Francisco and stimulating economic activity locally.[11] The San Mateo County workforce was largely segregated and otherwise exclusionary in 1960. Most airlines and air transport industry unions, as discussed earlier, still practiced systematic racial and gender discrimination, and airport work for people of color was, with some exceptions, largely restricted to low-paying (or, in the case of skycapping, high-paying) service work. Also largely off limits to nonwhites were lucrative airport vending and construction contracts.

Homeownership was a particularly important mechanism for white structural advantage. As Daniel Martinez HoSang argues, the very "social and political identity" of California "homeowner" going back to the late nineteenth century was generally assumed to be white (and heteronormative), and such identities were further consolidated by state and commercial practice. Home sales in the cities that encroached upon the airport, as elsewhere in San Mateo County, were largely limited to whites by racially restrictive covenants placed on deeds by individuals and homeowner associations. These were encouraged and sometimes required by insurers, realtors, and, for a time, the Federal Housing Authority (FHA). Ostensibly, FHA support for covenants ended after the 1948 *Shelley v. Kraemer* decision determined that they could not be enforced, but the FHA continued to back mortgages to buyers in racially segregated communities while redlining communities with larger populations of people of color. Intimidation from established residents was also a factor. In a nationally and internationally visible 1952 episode, for example, residents of South San Francisco's Southwood neighborhood successfully pressured Pan-Am mechanic Sing Sheng, his wife Grace, and their young son to cancel plans to move into the community after he had put a deposit down on a home. Shortly thereafter, white residents nearly succeeded in chasing a Black family from their new San Bruno home by means of threats and broken windows.[12]

Jet noise provided the occasion for local residents (especially homeowners) to consider what costs (economic, environmental, social, and so on) they were willing to live with in order to preserve their way of life with its attendant, albeit relative, economic and social privileges. Some airport neighbors heard jet noise favorably as a by-product of the urban economic and infrastructural development that defined these largely white suburban spaces and integrated them into a Bay Area metropolitan region whose growth was intimately tied to the expansion of US empire. Some realtors even used proximity to airport work and views of arriving and departing aircraft as selling points for homes in Millbrae and San Bruno, at least in neighborhoods that were not too adversely affected by jet noise.[13] Other neighbors heard jets as a component of the urbanized, suburban soundscape that they could live in so long as it was not too loud and so long as other benefits came with it. Such was the case with some of those who remained silent on the issue or who sided with local political representatives who explained that any large-scale noise abatement project would jeopardize the airport's function as an economic engine for the Peninsula as it potentially lost business to Oakland's facility when it began jet operations.[14]

Yet many airport neighbors never accepted jet noise, whether they stopped complaining about it or not. "Progress," as one local resident put it, "does not have to embody torture." Jet noise threatened their ability to enjoy the fruits of their racialized positions as blue- and white-collar workers, businesspeople, and home-owning consumers. Their social and political identities as such gave them the status and voice to try to do something about it. Airport neighbors' complaints and demands for changes to SFO operations reached a fever pitch in the fall of 1959 and early 1960, energized in part by a contemporaneous national outcry about jet noise. Residents hired consultants to document the noise in their communities and voiced their concerns in face-to-face interactions and correspondence with government and SFO officials; at public meetings held by SFO and municipal organizations; through letters to newspaper editors; at an April 1960 public hearing on jet noise held at the airport Hilton by a subcommittee of the House Committee on Interstate and Foreign Commerce; and that same month at a panel discussion recorded and later broadcast by local television station KPIX.[15] Residents also expressed their displeasure through calls to SFO's Sound Abatement Committee, launched in February 1960, the stated mission of which was to collect and map complaints about noise, assess their legitimacy and cause, and address them to the extent they were able.[16]

The Sound Abatement Committee notwithstanding, SFO acted slowly on the complaints. The 1946 US Supreme Court decision in *United States v. Causby* had determined that noisy aircraft rendering a property uninhabitable or unusable constituted a "taking" for which its owners were entitled to compensation. But that decision, pertaining to military aircraft that had literally frightened to death a North Carolina farmer's chickens, left unresolved the question of liability in cases involving civilian aircraft and airports operated by local governments. One problem was the number of entities that put humans in proximity to jet operations. Airport owners and operators determined the location of airports and the orientation of runways; municipalities and developers put homes in proximity to airports; the Civil Aeronautics Administration (CAA) (and subsequently the FAA) determined flight paths and set rules for flight operations; airlines scheduled flights; pilots made decisions about takeoff directions and angles of ascent and descent; and aircraft manufacturers and their subcontractors designed and built jet engines. At the dawn of the jet age these entities sought to shift liability and responsibility to one another and hoped the public would to some extent get used to the noise.[17]

SFO officials also tried to deflect complaints and proposals for mitigation via cost-benefit arguments. More radical suggestions, like moving the airport to the Central Valley, would be absurdly expensive and inconvenient. More practical measures, like eliminating nighttime flights, would diminish airport operations and therefore threaten the airport's role as employment generator. Officials described jet noise as a necessary by-product of a new technology that enabled people to travel to faraway places at greater speeds. And nighttime flights were a product of consumer demand and a necessity in cases of medical emergencies. Moreover, public safety trumped all other considerations, and some proposals, such as altering takeoff and landing speeds and climbing angles, might prove too dangerous to implement.[18]

Yet some San Mateo County residents continued to react negatively to the noise, hearing it as a manifestation of a different cost-benefit calculus. As local antinoise activist F. Thomas McDonnell argued decades later, the airport and its users (airlines, contractors, passengers, and workers) benefited from an "indirect, nonvoluntary" subsidy in the form of an array of costs, "external to the pricing systems of the air transport business," that were borne by surrounding communities. In the case of noise, costs came in the form of quantifiable "damages to property," primarily in the form of decreased home values, and less quantifiable "damages to people," in the form of classroom interruptions, middle-of-the-night awakenings, psychic distress, physical discomfort, and so on. Officials' opposition to or slow implementation of sound abatement measures perpetuated this subsidy. So did local and national legal and bureaucratic entanglements that made unclear the extent to which actors involved in making jet noise were legally responsible for reducing it or liable for its effects.[19]

Developers and local planning bureaucracies also helped shift costs onto local residents while exposing them to environmental hazards. Developers' search for profit coincided with a rapidly expanding Bay Area population as well as municipal and county planners' pursuit of metropolitan growth and lack of vision (and will) when it came to foreseeing that housing infill surrounding a major airport might be incompatible with its operations. Developers secured at relatively low costs open space and sites zoned for industrial use near SFO and built upon them often cheaply constructed homes with little or no insulation to protect residents from noise. Cities often approved such projects to increase tax revenues. As a result, homeowners-as-consumers saw their ability to reap the rewards of their investments diminished by the same forces that had helped make the realization of them possible in the first place.[20]

City attorney Noonan addressed displaced costs when he complained in the press that while SFO officials had, in the late 1950s, spoken about noise mitigation as a "price of progress" *the airport* would have to pay for doing business in San Mateo County, they now described jet noise as a cost *airport neighbors* would have to bear in exchange for the economic benefits of the facility.[21] Similar outrage was evident in a series of letters to the editor of a local newspaper after it reported that jets were being "accepted as part of the 1960's by the people who watch them and hear them, as by those who ride in them." As one respondent argued, any reduction in the number of complaints stemmed not from acceptance but from frustration and helplessness in the face of the airport's and air industry's intransigence. "People in this area are becoming nervous wrecks because of the campaign of noise making carried on as a consequence of 'progress' and disregard for the rights of other people."[22]

Eventually, pressure from the San Mateo County citizenry, their representatives, and the local press convinced SFO and San Francisco officials to look harder for solutions to the jet noise problem. There emerged a rough consensus in the summer of 1960 among local representatives, airport officials, and some residents that ameliorating jet noise without severely affecting airport operations could be accomplished in several steps. Extending the left-hand portion of runway 28 into the bay would allow flights to take off farther from neighborhoods to the northwest, thus enabling planes to achieve a higher elevation by the time they reached them, or to turn right over the water on their ascent and thus avoid them altogether. Building a baffled sound wall between the airport and Bayside Manor would ameliorate noise, vibrations, and fumes during departures from runway 1. And if the wall was effective, more takeoffs could be moved to that runway, further reducing noise northwest of SFO. Plans also included eliminating jet training flights from the airport and moving preflight testing of jet engines at night to remote parts of the airport.[23]

There was a brief period of optimism after these plans were publicized. Local congressional representative J. Arthur Younger secured full funding for the runway extension in late July 1960, and work began on the project soon thereafter. An announcement that training flights would soon end came early in August. Meanwhile, plans for the sound wall moved forward.[24] But complaints and frustration with SFO officials were on the rise again that fall. It became clear that the large infrastructural solutions would take time to realize, and the elimination of training flights did not help that much given that the overall number of jet flights was increasing.[25] Moreover, the sound wall protecting Bayside Manor did not materialize in the end. The City of San Francisco agreed to finance it in exchange for a commitment from Millbrae to block additional residential construction near the airport. But this agreement fell apart near the end of 1960 when San Francisco officials learned that Millbrae planners had given permission to a developer to build an apartment building that was even closer to runway 1 than areas with noise levels neighborhood activists had deemed "intolerable."[26]

Activism on jet noise around 1960 reproduced resident-consumers' individual investments in their homes and collective investments in their communities—with whiteness structuring both—while commenting on and illustrating, in the end, how these were investments with a low rate of return. Although their struggles do not fit neatly into the history of green-oriented Bay Area environmentalism, these anti–jet noise activists were concerned, ultimately, with the multifaceted ways that power was shaping their lived environment, the systems that defined it, and the health of their communities. Their activism illustrates, as urban geographer Richard Walker points out, that the Bay Area suburbs did not just produce the environmentalists who shaped the movement in the late 1960s and 1970s but also were the site of industry- and developer-wrought environmental transformations with which individual homeowner-consumers and their community associations were compelled to contend. This environmental activism would be foundational to the antinoise struggles that emerged later in these communities and elsewhere, for better and for worse, as neighborhood-focused concerns developed in synergistic ways with a reinvigorated environmental movement.[27]

The US Supreme Court's March 1962 *Griggs v. Allegheny County* decision finally made clear that civilian airport owners and operators bore some responsibility and liability for commercial jet noise because of their role in the design and situation of airports. Along with a series of decisions by state courts that ruled individuals could be entitled to compensation for damages from noise to their property that did not reach the threshold of a "taking" and that such damages could stem from proximity to aircraft operations rather than solely from direct overflights, it opened the door to airport noise litigation against local governments.[28] Within days, SFO officials admitted that a wave of property damage lawsuits was likely coming their way. In April, four Bayside Manor residents confirmed those fears by filing lawsuits, and close to sixty of their neighbors added their own in July.[29] Although these lawsuits were ultimately unsuccessful—a judge ruled in favor of the defendants in 1967, noting statute-of-limitations issues and rejecting the argument that the plaintiffs had "suffered a permanent, substantial or total deprivation of the free use of their properties"—the lawsuits marked San Mateo County communities' continuing concerns about jet noise and pointed to a mode of activism that would be used more effectively later.[30]

Indeed, complaints from the communities most directly affected by SFO jet noise were again on the rise in the late 1960s. Larger versions of popular DC-8 and Boeing 727 planes, introduced in the mid-1960s, made more noise as they strained to lift their heavier loads into the sky. Night operations continued and at times increased, as when the US

Armed Forces in 1966 expanded overnight airmail and military cargo flights to Southeast Asia to seven per day as they pursued the explicitly military side of empire.[31] Even without the sound wall, a higher percentage of flights had been shifted onto runway 1, making matters difficult for Millbrae residents. Meanwhile, more flights were leaving SFO in general, mitigating the relief that the runway 28 extension and the shifting of flights to the intersecting runways offered to people living northwest of the airport.[32]

The noise problem and activism around it were also expanding geographically. The planned community of Foster City, built, beginning in 1963, on the reclaimed salt marsh of Brewer's Island to the southeast of the airport, put thousands of people in proximity to the overwater approaches to runway 28 and inspired an emergent wave of antinoise activism by city residents and officials alike.[33] Inhabitants of the wealthy exurban communities of Portola Valley and Woodside southeast of the airport began to complain vociferously about airport noise in late 1969 after FAA-changed flight patterns brought jets heading to runway 28 over their communities more frequently and at lower altitudes than before.[34]

Local residents' dissatisfaction with jet noise at this moment was increasingly shaped by environmental thinking and activism, locally and nationally, in part because of growing public concern about noise pollution as disturbance and potential health hazard. A 1968 amendment (implemented in 1969) to the Federal Aviation Act of 1958 empowered the FAA to create noise control and abatement regulations. The 1970 amendments to the Clean Air Act drew additional attention to noise pollution, with more emphasis coming with the Noise Control Act of 1972 and the concomitant creation of the Environmental Protection Agency's Office of Noise Abatement and Control.[35] Closer to home, the California legislature, via a 1969 bill coauthored by now assemblyman Leo Ryan, commissioned CALTRANS' Division of Aeronautics to institute airport noise standards that went into effect in 1972, despite ongoing efforts by the airline industry group Air Transport Association to undermine them.[36]

Fears that Bay Area residents would have to contend with the Supersonic Transport (SST) aircraft then being developed were another factor in the growing outrage over jet noise. Environmentalist pressure led to the US Congress's decision to stop government funding for the SST and, shortly thereafter, to the California legislature passing a bill that would ban the aircraft from the state if it was found to create excessive noise from sonic booms at altitude or from takeoffs and landings. But concerns remained that the aircraft might still ply Bay Area airspace.[37] Sensitivity to jet noise was heightened by growing dissatisfaction with the aviation industry more generally as it fell upon difficult financial times at the end of the 1960s with concomitant bad publicity about poor service, safety breaches, air disasters, long waits at airports, hijackings, terrorist attacks, and traffic problems in surrounding communities.[38]

The late Vietnam War–era economic downturn was more generally a moment of rising frustration in suburban communities across California, as the privileges of living there were seemingly under threat from declining services, rising property taxes, roadway congestion, and other factors. Even members of upper-middle-class Bay Area enclaves, many of whom had participated in and benefited from the corporate management, research and development, and finance facets of the region's militarized economy, experienced a "frustrated advantage," as Clarence Lo puts it, when it came to their ability to leverage governmental action through regular channels on the issues that were impinging on their ability to enjoy the fruits of their privilege.[39] Suburban communities did, of course, have differing investments in the noise issue as defined by demographics and proximity. Still, as the population of educated, professional people across San Mateo County grew along with airport operations, more of them were living in relatively close proximity to SFO and its vectors of approach and departure. Even if they did not experience as much noise as those living closer to the airport, they often had less tolerance for it and more status and skills to try to do something about it.

The Woodside and Portola complaints brought a degree of class- and gender-based backlash, including from some long-suffering individuals living northwest of the airport. A December 1969 *San Mateo Times* piece disparaged a Portola Valley group presenting complaints to the airport's Sound Abatement Center as "housewives" while reporting on a San Bruno city councilman's dismissive response that the jet noise on approach they heard was inconsequential compared to the takeoff noise his constituents and residents of South San Francisco had to endure. A United Airlines mechanic from San Mateo repeatedly referred to the Portola Valley activists as "rich ladies" in his subsequent letter to the *Times* editor. He knew jet noise was a problem from his work on engines, but he emphasized that north county residents endured much worse noise than the well-heeled set to the south, who should understand that the minor sonic inconvenience they experienced was a small price to pay for their ability to take quick jaunts by jet to New York. Ultimately, "The work [jet engines] produce far outweighs the noise they make. . . .

If the ladies can come up with a quieter engine with the same efficiency, their suggestions would be more than welcome."[40] Yet activism from Portola Valley and Woodside inspired some north county residents and officials to rearticulate their own concerns, and the shared experience of noise in some cases brought people together across social distance and enabled them to present the problem as a metropolitan one.[41]

The individuals from these middle-income and wealthy communities who filed the February 1971 lawsuit mentioned at the beginning of this chapter were buoyed by a recent Los Angeles County Superior Court decision involving noise exposures near LAX. The judge ruled in *Aaron v. City of Los Angeles* that a compensable "property taking" was not restricted to physical damage or a decline in market value but could also stem from the "substantial interference with the use and enjoyment of [the] property."[42] In July 1971, the City and County of San Francisco, aware of its vulnerability in light of the legal precedent from Southern California and bad industry publicity, settled the case, not with individual payments to residents, but with a promise to institute a five-point program to reduce noise: lengthen the right-hand portion of runway 28; seek approval from the FAA for new takeoff patterns; redistribute more flights to runway 1; install noise and flight monitoring systems; and hold more substantive sound abatement meetings with community members. But it was a hollow victory for the plaintiffs in the end. Some of these improvements were already under way as part of the expansion funded by the 1967 bond initiative, with only some of the justification for noise reduction.[43] Others were either slow to develop or relatively ineffectual given the ever-expanding airport operations. Complaints about noise continued, now with reference to the limits of the lawsuit settlement and concern that things would get even worse.[44]

Subsequently, some airport neighbors joined forces with environmental organizations that were more generally concerned with urban growth and concomitant degradation in the region. This followed SFO's publicized updates on the expansion projects in December 1972 and its release of a state-mandated Environmental Impact Report (EIR) in January 1973. These documents made clear that the scope of the 1967 bond measure–funded work had increased, with costs escalating dramatically. Also worrisome were estimates that by 1985 the airport would be accommodating thirty-one million passengers per year, doubling the 1972 number. Activists raised concerns that the expansion project would lead to "unwanted" population growth and development on the Peninsula and in San Francisco; increased traffic requiring new freeway construction; exposure to noise pollution for those living near the airport and under flight paths; and other "nuisances."[45]

Opponents of expansion charged that such futures were not fully addressed in the inaccurate and misleading EIR. They had a point. The report, which blithely predicted minimal environmental impact, was authored anonymously by Bechtel Corporation, a paid consultant on the construction project that was no stranger to controversy.[46] The venerable and powerful San Francisco–based company had long been an object of critique for, among other things, its close ties to the CIA and government power brokers, its roles in building up the US nuclear arsenal and nuclear power industry, and its work advancing US imperial interests (as well as its own) through overseas engineering and construction services and strategic consultation.[47]

Activists raised their concerns at a series of March 1973 meetings in San Francisco and San Mateo County where the EIR and expansion plans were assessed. These meetings were both a reflection of and a further catalyst for a growing alliance among aggrieved airport neighbors and environmentalists. Longtime community activist Rose Urbach of San Bruno represented the airport neighbor perspective, as she spoke at the March 6 Airport Commission meeting about the "intolerable" noise levels in her community that would likely grow worse with expansion. Olive Mayer, a Sierra Club environmentalist and mechanical engineer, was from Redwood City and thus outside of the areas most affected by jet noise. At the March 6 meeting she emphasized a broader set of environmental concerns, speaking primarily about the EIR's failure to take into account the possibility of future fossil fuel shortages and the economic impact they would have on the air transport industry and, by extension, the taxpayers who underwrote the airport expansion. But at a March 28 San Mateo County Planning Commission meeting, she rearticulated concerns about noise as expressed by those living close to the airport. Others spoke consistently from their positions as environmentalists *and* as people living with aircraft noise. Sally Cooper of Woodside, an official with the Loma Prieta chapter of the Sierra Club, spoke about the inadequacies of the EIR as both cause and effect of broader patterns of unsustainable growth in the Bay Area, but she concluded by emphasizing the particular problem of noise. Sylvia Gregory of San Bruno, future chairwoman of that city's environmental committee, testified about the airport's impact on the soundscape and on available energy reserves.[48]

Despite the opposition, the Airport Commission, at its May 1, 1973 meeting, sided with expansion supporters—airport officials, airline and union representatives, local businesspeople, and others—and unanimously approved the EIR as well as a resolution to continue the construction. The commission then sent the matter on to the San Francisco Board of Supervisors for consideration, ushering in a two-year process of lawsuits, appeals, more contentious commentary at public meetings, and public relations campaigns by airport officials and environmentalists alike. A critical step in this process occurred on May 17, when the environmental organizations San Francisco Ecology Center (SFEC), Friends of the Earth, and San Francisco Tomorrow, as well as eight individuals, including Cooper and Gregory, filed a Superior Court lawsuit, *San Francisco Ecology Center et al. v. City and County of San Francisco,* seeking to block the project on the grounds that the airport was moving forward with an inadequate EIR.[49]

As the plaintiffs prepared their case and the San Francisco Board of Supervisors considered whether to green-light the expansion, the SFEC published a report, *The San Francisco Airport Expansion Plan: A Critical Study,* for the board's and the broader public's consideration. The report assembled correspondence and memoranda from most of the eleven organizations that signed off on it, as well as newspaper clippings and supporting documentation from consultants, city officials, and representatives of state agencies. Some of this commentary was critical of the airport expansion or the planning process for it, while other pieces evaluated the EIR itself. Aircraft noise was one of the primary concerns articulated throughout the report, as well as in a special section dedicated to the issue.[50]

There were strategic reasons for environmentalists to foreground the antinoise cause. Emphasizing such community concerns provided a rejoinder to charges by airport officials and others that environmentalists were elitist outsiders whose concerns did not jibe with those of local residents, many of whom supported expansion because of the new jobs that would come with it.[51] Bringing in the human element vis-à-vis commentary on noise also provided a mechanism for asserting citizens' interpretive authority in the face of scientific and bureaucratic planning discourse that minimized the noise problem, labeled it as difficult to measure, or suggested that any human environmental costs would be mitigated by social and economic benefits. Sally Cooper's "Statement of the Loma Prieta Chapter of the Sierra Club," for example, claimed that "no public agency" had systematically surveyed members of communities affected by jet noise. "Such information would have been immeasurably helpful in putting the human element into the planning process for future developments." "It is important to remember," the SFEC added, "that no matter how skillful science becomes in telling us what we are doing to ourselves, the perception of the human senses of the same information cannot be ignored. In no environmental subject is this more true than that of noise pollution."[52]

Beyond strategy, the report's analysis of the jet noise problem reflected complex understandings of the rippled effects of SFO expansion on the Bay Area as a network of economic, social, resource, and environmental relationships. After all, local residents had been engaging noise as an undifferentiated atmospheric force that audibly defined the region's sprawling urbanity through overflight noise and as an array of high-volume sonic vectors accompanying takeoffs and landing that hailed people in specific neighborhoods as disgruntled citizens and sometimes as activists.

A letter from the local environmental group Environmental Quality Control Committee (EQCC), signed by research scientists and prominent Peninsula environmentalist Claire Dedrick, and written as a follow-up to a public meeting the group held about the expansion, suggested that the project, even if it included plans for noise mitigation, would bring unanticipated consequences. Changes in runway preferences would likely just shift the noise problem from one community to another. Increasing traffic at other Bay Area airports might still create a problem for San Mateo County residents if aircraft using those airports flew over county airspace. Even the strengthening of antinoise laws as a means of mitigating the effects of expansion could result in noise levels adjacent to the airport remaining at the present intolerable levels if the number of flights increased as expected. In other words, the Bay Area was a complex urban system that could quickly begin to fail its inhabitants if environmental, economic, and social factors were not intelligently taken into consideration together.[53]

Other report contributors railed against corporate greed, the government's complicity with the aviation industry, and, again, the ways these entities were trying to externalize their costs onto the public. Noise was the price nearby residents had to bear because the air industry did not want to outlay the capital necessary to address the problem. Noise, and the possibility of more noise with the airport expansion, also signified the risk the public was taking in financing a project that was dependent on continued access to a resource (oil) whose future availability was in doubt. Air travel and related noise would increase if the resource held out, said local environmentalist and mechanical engineer Olive Mayer in testimony to the Airport Commission reproduced in the report, but the people of San Francisco might end up paying for a "white elephant" if oil supplies were compromised.[54]

The Ecology Center's Gil Bailie, noting that the health of the airline industry had been flagging over the past several years, suggested that SFO's expansion should also be seen less as a stimulus for the Bay Area economy than as a bailout of the airline industry. It was environmentalists' duty, then, as they did through their opposition to the SST, to save the industry and Bay Area governments from themselves. "Airport expansion is a gamble on the part of an industry that is rapidly running out of options. The industry is already heavily mortgaged to the massive capital investment of wide-bodied jets. The question is: Can a big airport do for the airlines what big airplanes failed to do?" The answer, of course, was no. If the bailout succeeded, "it will commit this region (and nation) to an extravagantly wasteful and environmentally disastrous mode of transportation." If not, then the results would be "free enterprise offered once again on the sacrificial altar of poor planning. Higher taxes."[55] Cooper addressed the job engine argument offered by the expansion projects supporters, suggesting that such justification was "not only unimaginative thinking, but extremely wasteful and destructive of both natural and human resources." This expansion was not in the interest of workers, she argued, but in that of "industry" and the "particular segment of society that can afford air travel on demand."[56]

Cooper, Mayer, and Bailie offered a critique of airport expansion rooted in an understanding of the urban environment as a potentially healthy ecology, composed of human and natural systems, that was under threat from the combined effects of state action and inaction and the interests of those with the strongest investments in capital accumulation. Jet noise, then, was both signifier of these forms of power and catalyst for trying to come to terms with the complexity of their interfaced operations. In addition to building upon the legacy of antinoise activism that had developed over the past fifteen years or so near SFO, these activists' attention to noise as pollution reflected the coming together of several additional trajectories of environmental thought and activism that Richard Walker and others have identified. One was a long-standing commitment to preserving nature within and adjacent to the cities that had "co-evolve[d]" with it. Such work in San Mateo County had, over the decades, often been the province of the white techno-scientific class developing around Stanford and Silicon Valley, but it was growing at this moment through northern San Mateo County movements to limit freeway construction and housing developments. There was also a concomitant critique of out-of-control urbanization, with roots in Bay Area urban and regional planning networks going back to the 1930s. Coalescing with these concerns were those regarding environmental pollution, which became a prominent struggle in the Bay Area in the wake of federal and state legislation around it in the late 1960s and early 1970s.[57]

As is evident in their public testimony and contributions to the Ecology Center report, women from the northern and southern San Mateo County cities played a more central role as leaders in antinoise activism in the early 1970s than they had a decade earlier, when their voices were often mobilized by men to testify about the disruption of domestic space by noise. Now, they were leading much of the organizing around such domestic concerns themselves. Their work was emblematic of how white women were playing particularly important roles, as leaders and as rank and file, in redefining environmentalism in the Bay Area away from the romantic conservation of individuals like David Brower or John Muir and in shifting more of its focus to local environments with constitutive elements like housing, jobs, and schools. The coalition of north and south county residents also reflected the increasingly broad base (in terms of class, if not yet in terms of race and ethnicity) of environmentalism developing in the Bay Area.[58]

It is important to keep in mind, however, that the resulting critique was, to some degree, rooted in the elitism of environmental and suburban politics circa 1973, with a certain amount of attention to the preciousness of domestic space and homeowning consumer satisfaction. It was, in other words, still foundationally predicated on an investment in suburban whiteness, in terms of who was speaking and for whom, that was shaped in part by the anxieties produced by its diminishing returns. This activism should also be understood as part of the history of the "fragmentation" of activism opposing the "destructive majoritarianism" of postwar urban growth in the Bay Area, as Alex Schafran discusses. One critical factor here was the inability of antigrowth environmentalists to find consistent common cause with advocates for racial justice and lower-income people more generally. One of the outcomes of this history has been that many communities across the Bay Area, including in San Mateo County, became greener and more sustainable while remaining racially and economically exclusionary, albeit in sometimes complicated ways.[59]

Still, these activists did offer an insightful analysis of air transportation as a system riven by inequality while using huge amounts of natural resources. The industry was more egalitarian in the 1970s than earlier in terms of ridership, but it still primarily served those who were well off. Although antidiscrimination activism and affirmative action programs had created more opportunities over the previous decades, white men were still by far the largest economic beneficiaries of commercial aviation—whether through direct employment at the airport or by airlines or via the businesses providing contracts for various goods, services, or construction at the airport. More broadly, jet noise, as a sonic force and as the object of these activists' critiques, made clear the costs of empire in a region that was asymmetrically benefiting from its development. The most tangible manifestation of the critique was the growing opposition to nighttime cargo flights, often on older, noisier planes, whose numbers were to rise steadily across the 1970s along with international trade. Some of these transpacific flights left in the middle of the night to avoid night flight curfews in Japan and Hong Kong. Of particular concern was a regularly scheduled Japan Airlines flight to Tokyo that typically left SFO around 3:00 a.m.[60]

In that sense, then, this early 1970s anti–jet noise and anti-SFO expansion commentary and activism, began to approach an environmental justice frame, even if not yet attuned to pertinent questions regarding race and class, and even though jet noise exposures around SFO were not in a systematic way determined by race and class exclusions. Moreover, this was the moment when some of the previously exclusionary white communities around SFO, especially South San Francisco, were becoming more racially and ethnically diverse. Significant factors here were changes to US immigration law via the 1965 Hart-Celler Act and the eventual affirmation of the civil rights activists–inspired California Fair Housing Act of 1963 (or Rumford Act)—following its quick overturning by state ballot initiative Proposition 14—by California and US Supreme Court decisions and the Congressional Fair Housing Act of 1968.[61] Antinoise activists' comments about asymmetrical benefits, even if not explicitly linked to contemporaneous racial justice struggles, anticipated the changing demographics of who was getting exposed to jet noise as a manifestation of multiple forms of power in these traditionally working-class and lower-middle-class neighborhoods.

Despite the growing public critique, planning commissions in both San Mateo and San Francisco Counties approved going forward with expansion in late 1973 on the logic that the social and economic benefits outweighed the local environmental and human costs.[62] As it became clear that the 1973 lawsuit would not halt the expansion—it eventually lost on appeal in May 1975—activists tried again via a federal lawsuit, *Friends of the Earth v. Coleman,* filed in US District Court on September 30, 1974. Friends of the Earth and the dozen San Mateo County residents who joined as plaintiffs, again including Cooper and Gregory, sought to halt construction on the basis that the FAA should have been required to submit a federal EIS given that it was providing $34 million in federal funds for the expansion project. The plaintiffs asked for an injunction against any further federal funding for the expansion until the EIS was prepared and approved.[63] This new lawsuit ultimately failed to achieve activists' goal of scaling back the expansion, but it blocked the release of federal funds for additional work until a new EIS was filed, and it halted the entire project for a few weeks in the spring of 1975 while the court worked out whether an EIS would be required for the non–federally funded expansion components to proceed.[64]

Although members of prominent environmental organizations such as Friends of the Earth and the Sierra Club would continue to fight for a quieter San Mateo individually and as members of other organizations, the lawsuit marked the apex of these environmental groups' visible leadership in antinoise struggles around SFO. More radical environmental critiques and analyses of jet noise as related to corporate and state power would also diminish somewhat in public debates about it. Yet a broadly conceived environmentalism would influence subsequent struggles against jet noise that were more focused on the annoyance it presented to suburban dwellers whose advantages were frustrated. Such a vision would also shape the perspectives, or at least the self-presentation, of those pushing back on these movements.

Some opponents, to be sure, continued to reject environmentalists' concerns out of hand and positioned them as antithetical to the needs of both business and labor. Responding at a March 31, 1975, press conference to the injunction temporarily halting the expansion, a San Mateo County Building Trades Council representative said, "I don't think Friends of the Earth are the Friends of Man," given that unemployment in building trades in the county was at about 50 percent.[65] But a significant mode of opposition to environmentalists' challenges moving forward involved a partial incorporation of their rhetoric and concerns, while pushing back on what some saw as their elitist and exclusionary dimensions. In response to the injunction halting expansion, a San Francisco Labor Council representative said at the March 1975 press conference that his group was proenvironment but that there "must be a balance" between protecting the environment and promoting job-creating development as the recession of 1974–75 continued to take a toll on local workers. A Peninsula-based, prodevelopment women's organization expressed such sentiment in their name, AWARE (Active Women Advancing a Responsible Environment).[66]

Airport and municipal officials also positioned themselves as responsible stewards of an urban environment that included human, financial, and cultural economies as well as the land, air, and water. Airport officials had been visibly doing this to some degree since the 1971 noise settlement, and they ramped up those efforts a few years later in response to the opposition to the expansion by emphasizing that certain elements of the project, including new industrial waste and water treatment plants, the noise-monitoring system, and the paving of the runway 28 extension, were motivated by environmental concerns.[67] In a 1974 "Fact Sheet," SFO officials claimed they had done the best they could over the preceding two decades to protect the environment. They were, after all, "interface[ing] with residents of neighboring communities and those who espouse the causes of conversation and ecology, attempting to satisfy conflicting expectations and demands of diverse and powerful systems while maintaining the viability of the airport."[68] A December 1975 report, authored by a public relations firm hired by San Francisco to shift the conversation about expansion in the airport's favor, argued that SFO would do more in the future do more to protect the Bay Area's urban environment. Although it was not "directly responsible" for the environmental issues of current concern, it was "involved" in them and therefore had a duty to "use its power and prestige to take a forefront position in the effort to find solutions. It should be a leading voice, not just an observer, in regional planning committees. It should bring greater pressure to bear on federal agencies and the airlines for compliance with noise standards." But it could only take this on if "allowed to update and improve itself."[69]

SFO's efforts to "update and improve itself" by being a good steward and responsible neighbor were, not unexpectedly, uneven. The noise-monitoring system agreed to in the 1971 settlement finally came on line early in 1975, but even that effort was mired in controversy. A 1975 UC Davis study, commissioned by the EPA, claimed that SFO officials had been trying to reduce aircraft noise but also had colluded with the state's Aeronautics Division to avoid complying with state noise regulations. Later that year the California attorney general launched an investigation into whether the division had improperly given SFO a "zero variance" rating, allowing it to exceed state noise limits without violating them.[70] A 1977 report issued by Hillsborough engineer Arthur Hollo-way further challenged the accuracy of the airport's noise-monitoring system. Also raising local concerns was renewed discussion about bring-ing the SST to SFO. The November 1977 San Francisco bond measure securing additional funds for the ongoing, and now more expensive, expansion project inspired even more opposition.[71]

In this context activists created new organizations that kept the issue of jet noise as nuisance in the local news and maintained pressure on SFO and San Francisco city officials to do more about it. Several plain-tiffs in the Friends of the Earth lawsuits were central players in the Airport Impact Reduction Force (A.I.R. Force). Started in early 1975, with Sylvia Gregory as its coordinator, this group, with members from San Francisco and San Mateo County, was also active in the public debates about expansion that year and efforts to bring construction to a halt. It subsequently brought attention to the noise problem and pres-sured elected officials, planning organizations, and state agencies to force the airport to comply with extant noise regulations and to engage in more rigorous assessments of its environmental impacts.[72] A more locally constituted group, San Mateo County Residents for a Less Noisy Airport, was founded in 1977, with Burlingame's Delores Huajardo and Linda Dyson as its most visible leaders. Both were part-time work-ers and "homemakers," and Huajardo had formerly worked as a flight attendant. Their group drew attention to the problem through partici-pation at public meetings, letters to newspaper editors, and an October 30, 1977, protest at SFO involving simultaneously a picket line and a "drive-in" that slowed airport automobile traffic during the afternoon rush hour, a few hours before Britain's Prince Charles was scheduled to depart the facility.[73] A 1977 call to action by A.I.R. Force's South San Francisco coordinator, Kathleen Van Velsor, published in the local Sierra Club chapter newsletter, illustrated how at least some members of both groups emphasized jet noise's threat to domestic space, family life, and the quality of the urban environment more generally. Van Velsor described her group's members as people "who are fed up, who are playing a high-stake game to protect our urban environmental [sic] from auditory, olfactory, and visual deterioration."[74]

Thanks in part to the work of these activists, airport noise dimin-ished somewhat in the coming years, though the modes of activism and opposition to it by labor groups at the end of the 1970s and into the 1980s still speak of missed opportunities when it came to developing a sustained critique and possible movement oriented to supporting human thriving in the Bay Area's colonial present across a diversity of communities. Fights over jet noise at this moment illustrate further how SFO's taking into account environmentalists' concerns and presenting itself as an environmentally conscientious steward were becoming even more central to its justifications of its operations in the face of a growing web of environmental regulation and in light of the continuing need to secure public expenditures to keep itself going.

As the San Mateo Board of Supervisors, with a proenvironment majority as of 1976, and the Regional Airport Planning Committee pressured San Francisco to expand its mitigation efforts, they encountered a new San Francisco mayor, George Moscone, and airport director, Richard Heath, who, despite some critiques to the contrary by upset SFO neighbors, were more sympathetic to their protests than their predecessors. And this at a moment that saw growing cooperation among San Francisco and San Mateo County officials regarding SFO matters more generally. One manifestation of the more cooperative atmosphere was the Joint Land Use Study, a large undertaking begun in 1976, via a newly created Joint Powers Board, designed to set the parameters for future land use within the airport boundaries and in its surrounding areas. SFO submitted a new noise mitigation plan to the Association of Bay Area Governments / Metropolitan Transportation Commission's Regional Airport Planning Committee in May 1978, and in 1979 the focus of the Joint Land Use Study was shifted to noise mitigation.[75]

"A Plan for Reducing Aircraft Noise" was one of three components of the Board's Joint Action Plan. Its dozens of recommendations informed SFO's Airport Noise Mitigation Action Plan, released in 1981. SFO proposed to expand its noise-monitoring system; establish the Airport/Community Roundtable, a voluntary committee made up of elected officials that addressed "community noise impacts"; and make a series of requests to airlines to comply with California airport noise standards by shifting flight patterns, using quieter aircraft at the facility, and restricting nighttime cargo flights, which had risen steadily across the 1970s along with international trade, between 2 a.m. and 5 a.m.[76]

As this plan unfolded, it did not sit well with airport labor groups. They saw noise not as an involuntary subsidy provided by neighbors but as a cost that all had to bear to maintain a healthy society where working people could thrive. The San Francisco Airport Labor Coalition, for example, was formed in the summer of 1979 under the auspices of San Mateo County's Central Labor Council. It included representatives from a host of airport worker unions (machinists, flight attendants, pilots, and others), Teamsters, and the Building Trades Council. It came into being after union officials learned, belatedly, of the Joint Land Use Study and the ways environmental and community groups were steering its focus to noise mitigation. Union officials were particularly concerned, in the words of acting secretary Peter Cervantes-Gautschi, that "proposals to control noise caused by aircraft landings and takeoffs," including the banning of nighttime flights, "could cause layoffs of thousands of workers." The group was also troubled by proposals, such as altered flight patterns involving steep banks, that were "potentially dangerous to our members living near the airport in that they could reduce safety margins."[77]

Airport labor groups recognized noise as a potential health issue both for airport workers exposed to jet engine noise on the job and for those who lived in the surrounding communities and had to deal with overflight and takeoff noise at home. But this was a moment when airline deregulation was putting a squeeze on airport workers, as airlines— under financial pressure from increased competition as well as from rising fuel costs, inflation, and other economic shocks earlier in the decade—were speeding up work by funneling more flights through hub cities like San Francisco while also laying off workers or reducing their hours, renegotiating union contracts, and replacing union workers with nonunion contract labor.

The Airport Labor Coalition was "most interested in some proposals which in varying degrees could lessen noise and improve the living environment of our members living adjacent to the airport while also providing additional jobs." Such attempt at balance was evident in the coalition's proposal to the Joint Powers Board that it consider the use of engine sound–dampening devices, or "hush boxes," on planes during engine run-ups before nighttime takeoffs, maintenance, and repairs. Given that these noisy run-ups of the engines were necessary to their safe operation, the coalition presented this proposal as one that could mitigate noise for neighbors and airport workers and ensure the safety of passengers and workers on the airplanes without eliminating airport jobs. And they found common cause for this proposal with airport officials, local politicians, and at least some environmentalists and community activists.[78]

Desperate to protect jobs, some union groups also supported the continued operation of noisy nighttime flights. Protecting these manifestations of the growing reach of global capital, ironically, became a means of countering some of the other manifestations of it that were brought to bear upon them as workers. Their support of continuing noisy operations was also wrapped up in an alternative ecological vision that sought to balance the need to protect the health and sensibilities of workers and residents with the need to protect continued access to good jobs. The goal according to United pilot and chairman of the Airlines Pilots Association Council 34 Walter Ramseur, in an address to a local labor group in 1980, should be to find the best balance for all involved. "We need a little education—that everyone depends on everyone else, and whether or not we like everything our neighbors do, we're going to have to be a little cooperative with each other."[79]

But cooperation was not the outcome when nighttime cargo flights continued after the Airport Noise Mitigation Action Plan's release. These flights were a major motivation for a spate of small claims lawsuits filed in September 1981 against the City and County of San Francisco by primarily middle- and upper-middle-class homeowners from eight surrounding communities. These were organized in large part by Burlingame residents Huajardo and Dyson, who were frustrated by the slow pace of change locally and emboldened by the California Supreme Court's recent ruling in *Westchester Homeowners Association v. City of Los Angeles*, a case originally filed in 1968 by neighbors of LAX, that affirmed residents' right to compensation for damage to persons from the "annoyance, inconvenience, discomfort, mental distress, and emotional distress" brought about by jet noise as well as from damages to their property. As the Westchester case also made clear, civil noise suits could be tremendously time consuming and involve substantial attorney fees. Upon the advice of a local attorney, and in consultation with Ralph Warner, the "do your own law" doyen and owner of Nolo Press in Berkeley, Huajardo, Dyson, and their neighbors filed 172 $750 claims against the City and County of San Francisco in San Mateo County Small Claims Court.[80]

The plaintiffs were initially successful. In January 1982, a judge awarded 116 of them damages of $750 apiece, for a total of $87,000. They subsequently filed three more waves of small claims cases based on the determination in *Westchester* that airport noise was a "continuing nuisance" that could be the object of serial litigation until the problem was rectified. San Francisco effectively appealed the first wave of lawsuits in superior court on the grounds that the airport had responded adequately to noise complaints by adhering to FAA regulations and that going beyond that would lead to job loss at the airport and in airport-related industries. The victory, however, was costly. San Francisco had at that point spent over $800,000 to defend and appeal the lawsuits. With the other three sets of lawsuits still in process—two on appeal, one yet to be tried—the airport and the neighbors engaged in settlement negotiations in the summer of 1983. In exchange for most of the neighbors dropping current and future claims, the airport agreed to improve its response to jet noise. The SST was officially banned from the airport. Moreover, more engine noise–dampening equipment was required on planes using the airport, night flight patterns were altered, and the airport banned some older, noisier jets that exceeded local noise limits.[81]

One notable step in this process occurred in August 1982 when California Assembly Speaker Willie Brown, under pressure from the airport and its supporters, succeeded in securing passage of an amendment (AB2909) instituting a two-year moratorium on small claims nuisance lawsuits by San Mateo residents for San Francisco Airport noise. Huajardo, Dyson, and others initially went to Sacramento to voice their opposition, but they ultimately decided to focus on their current claims rather than their right to file future ones.[82] One of the bill's supporters was the Airport Labor Coalition, which lobbied in Sacramento in support of it. As the bill awaited the governor's signature, the coalition explained its position to the public. Contrary to coverage in the press, the small claims lawsuits were not "another case of 'Big Business and Big Government' versus the people." This was about relatively powerful local residents, via "a well-organized **political** effort" (emphasis in the original), trying "to inflict sufficient financial hardship on the City and County of San Francisco to force it to shut the airport down at night." Although they acknowledged that a ban on nighttime flights would make things quieter, and affirmed the need for reasonable noise abatement measures, they again raised the specter of job loss and the need to maintain a perspective on the economic effects of any environmental action. "The San Francisco Airport is the sixth busiest airport in the world! It is the lifeline to many of the most important industries in the Bay Area and has a ripple effect that touches most of the others. A major international airport like this cannot be shut down at night without disastrous consequences for the entire Bay Area economy."[83]

For middle- and upper-middle-class airport neighbors, then, the struggle for a quieter urban environment was, again, launched from a position of their relative but frustrated advantage in the regional colonial present. It was directed against forms of power manifest in noise that was helping to reproduce their privilege as homeowners, consumers, and workers—at least for those who stayed employed and housed during a period of inflation and rapid increases in the price of housing—

but was making living this privilege less than desirable because of noise among other factors. Their struggle was now shaped by a decade of environmental activism that framed the discourse about noise pollution as a threat to human health and expanded their expectations and knowledge about how one might act upon such perceived injustice.

Their antinoise activism continued to be predicated on a suburban outlook that was framed racially at its inception in terms of whiteness and was carried forward as a specific set of quality-of-life and public health concerns distinct from those of greatest concern to lower-income neighborhoods and communities of color. Still, such investments were now being articulated by a more ethnically diverse (and wealthier) community surrounding the airport, even in tonier areas like the Burlingame Hills. For some well-off residents, exposure to jet noise was the price to pay for their incorporation into a spatial regime of whiteness. Back of this was the fact that higher costs were also being incurred by middle- and working-class people of color—Asian Pacific Islander and Latinx primarily—moving into even noisier areas of South San Francisco, San Bruno, Foster City, and Daly City. Their exposure to jet noise still reflected the spatial limits vis-à-vis class and race of their incorporation into this suburban social order, even if the modes of opposing this situation were not rooted in an environmental justice perspective.

The Airport Labor Coalition—representing unions that had long maintained the privileges of whiteness but had taken some steps toward integration over the previous decade and a half—was pushing back on what it perceived as the powers lined up against it: politically connected airport neighbors and the forces that were making their existence as workers (some more than others) more precarious. Although the coalition was aligned with the airlines and industry groups on this matter, invested as they were in local economic growth and the air industry's imperial reach, their attempts to limit community pressure on airport operations, and night flights in particular, were also responses to the postderegulatory, globalist pressures they were feeling. And they too were operating in a more environmentalist frame, even as they pushed back on a version of environmentalism that they did not think was adequately attuned to workers' concerns. By trying to preserve noisy nighttime cargo flights, they were trying to maintain their hold on resources at a moment when broader economic transformations were putting the squeeze on them.

SFO, for its part, by scaling back but not ultimately banning night-time cargo flights, was presenting itself as a steward of the environment up to a point, as it tried to manage the political and economic forces from which it drew its power but that also represented threats to its continued exercising of it. This challenge became clear in a series of conflicts with the FAA and cargo carriers beginning in 1985 after the airport finally instituted the policy preventing carriers from operating noisy Boeing 707s that had been modified to meet FAA standards but still exceeded SFO noise limits. The airport ultimately lost approximately $18 million in federal airport aid after defying the agency's demand that the ban be rescinded.[84]

Struggles over noise continue. Today, jets are less "noisy" on the whole through a combination of changes to aircraft technologies, noise abatement efforts instituted by SFO, including an extensive program for soundproofing people's homes, and the fact that rising ambient noise levels in some areas have made the jet sounds less disruptive.[85] But people still complain. One phenomenon is that shifts to departure and arrival flight paths—sometimes for noise abatement reasons, at other times to improve operational efficiency—bring jet sounds above neighborhoods where they were not heard so keenly before. Such was the case when the FAA in March 2015 began instituting NextGen, a massive transformation of air traffic management meant to improve air traffic efficiency. SFO's Noise Abatement office received the highest volume of complaints in its history during the six months following its rollout.[86] In other words, the terms of the struggles staked out during these earlier episodes have been differently reproduced in the decades that followed, as those living near SFO negotiated the costs and benefits of shifting regional colonial presents, the lived contradictions of which, manifest in airport operations, were sometimes catalyzed and made audible by jet noise.

CHAPTER 6

Differing Degrees of Welcome

Thousands of protesters converged on SFO's International Terminal on Saturday afternoon, January 28, 2017, after learning that US immigration officials were detaining travelers there following recently inaugurated president Donald Trump's "Muslim ban" issued the day before. Among other things, Executive Order 13769 blocked for ninety days the entry into the United States of foreign nationals from seven primarily Muslim countries, prohibited most refugees from entering the country for 120 days, and suspended indefinitely the entry of refugees from Syria. As with actions at other US airports, the SFO protesters that day and the following one included prominent local power brokers, including California's lieutenant governor (and former San Francisco mayor and future governor) Gavin Newsom and Google cofounder Sergey Brin. Also present were police in riot gear guarding the security checkpoints. So were thirty immigration attorneys who vowed to remain at the facility until all detainees were released. That finally happened Sunday afternoon following a federal judge's Saturday night injunction that the order could not be enforced on those with valid visas and the eventual determination, following two days of contradictory statements by federal officials, that the order did not apply to green card holders from the seven countries or to those holding dual citizenship from both banned and nonbanned countries.[1]

The protest provided the occasion for many Bay Area residents to voice their outrage over the ban and the new president's racism and

FIGURE 19. The January 2017 SFO protest against the Trump administration's "Muslim Ban," accompanied by the Brass Liberation Orchestra, continues into the early morning of its second day in the International Terminal. Police in riot gear guard the security gate while airport screeners labor on. Photo by Brooke Anderson.

xenophobia. Some did so by juxtaposing the region's values with those of the new administration, emphasizing San Francisco's current status as a sanctuary city or noting the Bay Area's previous welcomes to European Jewish, Iranian, and other refugees.[2] This invocation of the region's hospitality, however, glossed over the roles that the Bay Area's residents, government officials, institutions, and infrastructures (including its airports) had played in a longer history of exclusionary and punitive immigration practice. A 1948 deportation, for example, was the occasion for what was then California's worst aviation disaster, memorialized in Woody Guthrie's song "Plane Wreck at Los Gatos (Deportee)," when a plane full of expelled migrant Mexican farmworkers (some of them Bracero guest workers) broke apart in midair on the way from Oakland to El Centro, killing everyone on board.[3]

That some foreign nationals were still more welcome in the Bay Area than others was evident in local politicians' and business elites' concern that the Trump administration's policy would hurt the local economy, particularly its technology sector. Some pointed out that American hospitality had made possible the success of Apple cofounder Steve Jobs, the son of a Syrian refugee. Within a week, some of the Bay Area's most prominent corporate executives had become visible members of the resistance, signing onto a legal brief opposing the travel ban on the grounds that it was bad for businesses that had long depended on foreign-born engineers and executives and was thus un-American. Even coverage of an ACLU lawsuit on behalf of a Yemeni student at Stanford and an Iranian student at UC Berkeley emphasized their comments that the ban would prevent them from landing coveted Silicon Valley jobs.[4]

The 2017 event was not the first time SFO had been the location or the referent of protest addressing how members (or, at least, certain members) of different groups had been excluded from the nation or, as scholars such as Yên Lê Espiritu and Catherine Ramírez argue, "differentially included" in socially, economically, or politically subordinate or marginalized ways.[5] Across such protests, activists (whether travelers or their allies) voiced their criticisms and demands by, in a sense, acting like travelers: that is, by making themselves visible and insisting on their (or others') deservingness as temporary or permanent participants in a new place.

Indeed, travelers at international airports are surveilled and profiled with attention to racial, religious, ethnic, and gendered difference. Some are screened for their assumed, terroristic threat to the state and public safety. Others are sorted into processing categories—citizens, permanent residents, immigrants, work visa holders, tourists (visa-holding and not), refugees, political agitators, and so on—while their right to enter is determined. Such processes have been enhanced since September 11, but they have been developing at airports for as long as these have been ports of entry. The goal of such management of traveling bodies—often executed by government agents with a good deal of discretionary power to enforce immigration and transit rules as they see fit—is to cultivate certain national or regional futures and to prevent others from occurring. Travelers, in turn, perform their deservingness—and their own participation in such futures—by presenting documents, answering questions, permitting themselves and their belongings to be scanned and searched, and queueing up with only minimal complaint. Accepting the protocols of identification bound up in the intersecting systems of governance that come together at airports or having such protocols imposed on an individual or group has tended to reproduce the colonial present as designed. Refusing those protocols or insisting on their transformation has been where the politics of belonging intensify, where aspects of power and its exclusions have been made visible, challenged to various extents, but generally, in the end, reconstituted.[6]

Activists who engaged in SFO-focused protests around travel and immigration negotiated the particulars of SFO as a manifestation of layered, inconsistent, and often contradictory demands of the national security state with its shifting racial (and other) investments. And sometimes they contended simultaneously with the airport as a scene of racially and otherwise exclusionary labor practices.[7] As they did so, they often drew upon local and farther-reaching activist networks to counter the exclusionary power of the federal government. They simultaneously drew sustenance and rhetorical power from the idea that the Bay Area was more progressive and welcoming than the nation itself. They were, to some extent, successful. They helped ameliorate discriminatory and punitive federal immigration and immigrant labor policies and inspired local protections that otherwise countered the effects of those policies. They also helped to engender an expanding array of political identities.

Yet local actors' engagements with protocols of identification—whether in the street, at SFO, or in the halls of government—were still facilitated and constrained by shifting, region-defining assemblages of sociality, governance, and economic transformations that reproduced asymmetrical difference. They could not fully escape the logics of deservingness that had long shaped immigration policies in the United States. Whether intentional or not, demands for inclusion for some often enhanced the exclusion of others or consigned them to be differentially included as more subordinate or vulnerable members (or potential members) of Bay Area communities. Thus, SFO-focused activism around immigration and immigrant work was a direct affront to the nation's and the region's colonial and imperial legacies and a component of their future management.

. . .

Mexican dress designer Jaime Chavez arrived at SFO on a Mexicana Airlines flight on the Saturday night of December 29, 1979. He was on his way to deliver dresses to a client, Patricia Volti, and to stay with her and her husband for his yearly, two-week San Francisco vacation. He announced his brown queerness, as he traversed the airport, with what appeared to be makeup on his face and women's rings on his fingers. When he presented himself to US Immigration and Naturalization Service (INS) agents, they tagged him as a suspected "homosexual," who, given the current state of US immigration law, could be barred from entering the United States. The dresses the agents found in Chavez's luggage confirmed their assessment. The agents strip-searched Chavez, who spoke only Spanish, and convinced him to sign a statement in English admitting his homosexuality and to withdraw his application to enter the United States. During his detention, Chavez contacted Volti, who advised him to withdraw his confession. She then talked the INS into removing him from a deportation flight bound for Mexico City. Rather than releasing him, the INS instructed Mexicana to hire private security guards to hold Chavez in a room in the nearby Airport Hilton. Volti also reached out to Gay Rights Advocates (GRA), a law firm that had recently worked on similar immigration cases. Lawyers were finally able to secure Chavez's release on Sunday. He was paroled into the United States for the duration of his intended stay, albeit with the understanding that he could be deported at any time following a hearing with immigration officers later in the week. And his future entry would be jeopardized if his "homosexual" designation were confirmed.[8]

Chavez was deemed suspect because he, his Mexican body, and his queer accoutrements walked into a multifaceted, homophobic, and racially exclusionary immigration apparatus. It was, at that moment, a porous system for some LGBTQ travelers given the ambiguity of many signifiers of same-sex desire and queer gender identification as well as border agents' preoccupations with other putative threats to the nation. But the apparatus was at that moment under siege, and some of its agents, at the local and national levels, were desperately holding onto their assumed duty to exclude aliens that they identified as deviant.

The United States had a long history of barring entry to and deporting foreign nationals based on their sexualities, often as linked to race, as Siobhan Somerville, Eithne Luibhéid, and other scholars have made clear. The Bay Area figured into that story as well. The 1875 Page Act, precursor to the Chinese Exclusion Act, for example, forbade the recruitment of Asian laborers for "lewd and immoral purposes." The act targeted Chinese women arriving in the Bay Area, putatively destined for sex work, who were detained at Angel Island while awaiting word about whether they would be granted entry or deported. The policing of suspected queer immigrants and travelers was consolidated with the Immigration and Nationality Act of 1952 (also known as the McCarran-Walter Act). Passed at a moment when Cold War hysteria positioned homosexuality and communism as mutually constitutive threats to the nation, the act defined homosexuals as excludable from entry into the United States by virtue of their "psychopathic personalities." While doing away with explicitly racist proscriptions against the naturalization of Asians, McCarran-Walter also, as Somerville points out, maintained national origin quotas and carried with it a racial logic rooted in eugenicist discourse in its determination that homosexuals deemed psychopathically deviant (whatever their perceived race) were a threat to the body politic understood generally as heterosexual *and* white.[9]

Aliens suspected of homosexuality were to be examined by a psychiatrist upon arrival to assess whether or not they could enter the United States or remain there. But often matters at ports of entry did not get that far, as confrontations with INS agents caused some to turn themselves away. This exclusion was challenged in the courts during the 1960s, in part because of the vagaries of the psychopathological definition of homosexuality that was falling out of favor in the medical community. But the US Supreme Court's 1967 decision in *Boutilier v. Immigration and Naturalization Service* affirmed the intent of McCarran-Walter by remaking the medical definition of excludable homosexuality into more of a "legal-political identity category," even as psychiatrists continued to wield authority over one's capacity for entry.[10]

Legal-political status was, of course, what some people embraced as they continued to push back on immigration laws and the medicalized definitions of homosexuality that informed them. During the early 1970s, LGBTQ activists successfully lobbied the American Psychiatry Association (APA) to remove homosexuality from the *Diagnostic and Statistical Manual of Mental Disorders,* which it did in 1973. The following year, the head of the APA asked the INS to refrain from excluding gay and lesbian aliens from the United States, commencing several years of debate over the issue among the INS, a succession of surgeon generals, the American Civil Liberties Union, and the National Gay Task Force. In November 1977, the office of President Jimmy Carter's surgeon general, Julius Richmond, wrote to INS commissioner Leonel Castillo, informing him that the US Public Health Service (PHS) should no longer participate in the evaluation of suspected homosexual travelers given the APA's recent actions. The INS, in turn, insisted that the PHS did not have the authority to step away from its legislatively determined responsibility to exclude homosexuals and insisted on continuing its own practice of trying to identify them at the nation's borders.[11]

In June 1979, Carl Hill, a white British antique restorer and photographer for the *London Gay News,* arrived at SFO and walked into this impasse while wearing a Gay Pride button. He was traveling with his partner, Michael Mason, the *News*'s editor, to celebrate their anniversary and attend San Francisco's pride festivities. Mason, who was also white and wore no sign of his sexuality obvious to border control, was admitted to the United States with minimal hassle. But INS agents pulled Hill aside and asked him if he was homosexual. When he answered in the affirmative, they told him he could not freely enter the country. After being detained for several hours, during which time the INS considered putting him on a return flight to London, he was released on his own recognizance pending a hearing with the PHS on the question of whether his admitted homosexuality was evidence of a psychopathic personality.[12]

Local government officials expressed their outrage. This was a moment when many were trying to rebuild support in San Francisco's gay community in the wake of former police officer and supervisor Dan White getting off with a voluntary manslaughter conviction for the assassinations of Supervisor Harvey Milk and Mayor George Moscone. Hill received public support from the local political establishment, including California senator Alan Cranston, congressmen Phil and John Burton, assemblyman Art Agnos, and openly gay San Francisco supervisor Harry Britt. He also secured the services of GRA, which promptly sued Surgeon General Richmond to prevent the examination from going forward before Hill's and Mason's scheduled return home. With supporting affidavits by prominent psychiatrists decrying the politicization of medical science, the suit challenged the INS guidelines more generally. Hill delayed his departure so he could pursue his case and, among other things, march at the front of the city's Gay Freedom Day Parade. Predisposed to supporting his legal adversary, the surgeon general settled the case in late July, once again affirming the redesignation of homosexuality as an identity category rather than a disease. On August 2 he announced that the PHS would no longer assist the INS with its evaluation of suspected homosexual travelers.[13]

This respite for gay travelers did not last long. The following day, August 3, Arturo Javier Cruz Garcia and Eduardo Ramon Martinez were detained by the INS upon their arrival at SFO from Mexico. One wore an earring while the other carried what appeared to be a woman's purse, and both likely received additional scrutiny as Mexican nationals. Agents claimed to find cosmetics and an address book with an "excessive" number of men's names in their luggage. Their incommunicado detention inspired a small protest of sorts when friends and reporters gained entry to the room where they were being held. GRA secured their entry into the country, pending a formal deportation hearing. There was even more local political backlash against the INS—from congressional representatives, acting San Francisco mayor Dianne Feinstein, the San Francisco Board of Supervisors, and others, but the INS held firm for the time being, declaring it would be working "to find a way to enforce the law" with or without the PHS's help.[14]

Eventually, the political pushback helped. On August 14 the INS announced it would no longer detain suspected homosexuals trying to enter the country. The service would, instead, allow them to enter with evaluations of their right to be in the United States deferred until the legal issues could be resolved. But what remained clear over the ensuing weeks was that the INS was populated nationwide by individual officials and agents with widely differing ideas about the rights of LGBTQ people to enter the United States and whose judgments were also affected by different interpretations of the markers of travelers' race, nation, and sexuality. There were numerous incidents of INS officials interrogating suspected homosexuals at various ports of entry and barring some of them from entering the United States. And then on December 26, 1979, the Department of Justice weighed in with its opinion that the INS was still required to enforce the "exclusionary provisions" established by McCarran-Walter.[15]

This was the situation facing Chavez a few days later as he presented himself as Brown and queer at the SFO terminal. According to John C. Knutson of GRA, the Justice Department opinion was not binding. Rather, agents' harassment of Chavez was a product of their or their supervisors' homophobia—of which there was no short supply among Bay Area law enforcement in the wake of a growing, more militant gay rights movement and the polarizing effects of Dan White's lenient verdict and the subsequent White Night Riots, during which outraged gay protesters fought with the police—and a linked impetus to "settle a score" with gay travelers given the affronts to protocol and the embarrassing press occasioned by the detentions several months earlier.[16]

Although Chavez was not the typical Mexican object of the INS's scrutiny—that is, a migrant worker crossing the border by car or foot—his more cosmopolitan gay body still bore the weight of the vexed history of relationships between the United States and Mexico and their people.[17] This history was defined by, among other things, the US colonization of what was now its Southwest and its continuing imperialist economic ventures in what remained Mexico; shifting US immigration policies geared to the delicate dance of maintaining the United States as a white nation (and California as a white state) while retaining access to sufficient quantities of Mexican labor to keep aspects of its economy going, and contemporaneous anti-Mexican sentiment in California amid growing fears over "illegal" immigration. McCarran-Walter's lingering consolidation of foreign queerness as a threat to a white and heterosexual body politic was another factor. In other words, Chavez presented a twinned affront to INS agents, commissioned to protect the sanctity of a racial and straight state but to some extent left to their own devices as to how to do so given the ambiguity of the law.

The Chavez case also provoked an outcry among local activists and elected officials, although their critique was generally focused on Chavez's sexuality rather than his race or national origin. GRA quickly filed a lawsuit on his behalf for the harassment he had endured and prepared a class action suit against the INS and PHS in an attempt to end the exclusionary policy. Within days, the progressive Harvey Milk Gay Democratic Club announced it would hold a mass demonstration at the INS office in downtown San Francisco. The offices of Mayor Feinstein and California governor Brown issued statements condemning Chavez's detention, calling into question its constitutionality and marking it as a human rights violation. Supervisor Britt vowed to fight the practice from his local position as he demanded that President Jimmy Carter be held accountable.[18] By the time two hundred people, including Britt, attended the protest at the INS building two weeks later, others had jumped into the fray. Milton Marks, a state senator representing San Francisco who had a history of supporting gay rights, introduced legislation that would ask the president and the Congress to eliminate the homosexual exclusion from US immigration law. San Francisco's John Burton was among several members of California's congressional delegation who drafted or signed on to letters to the Carter administration protesting the policy and demanding its termination.[19]

The protests quickly went international. A self-proclaimed "Homosquad" donned borrowed police uniforms and demonstrated their contempt for the US policy by interrogating arriving American travelers about their sexualities after they cleared immigration at Amsterdam's Schiphol airport. In February the Dutch parliament wrote a letter to the US Congress to protest the policy, which it described as "incompatible with human rights." Dutch representatives to the UN Human Rights Commission complained about the policy at its meeting that month in Geneva. They and other European officials promised to revisit the issue at an upcoming meeting of the Council of Europe and reconvening of the nations that had signed the Helsinki Accords.[20]

An appeal to human rights also figured prominently in San Francisco assemblyman Art Agnos's own letter to Carter. Not only was the "violation of basic human rights" "grossly inconsistent with this nation's principles," Agnos argued, but it also ran contrary to the administration's professed "commitment to global human rights as a foundation of American foreign policy." Agnos pointed out in a newspaper editorial accompanying a published version of his letter that there was something fundamentally hypocritical in the actions of a nation that would exclude foreign nationals "whose only crime is loving the officially defined wrong gender" while offering "sanctuary and haven to criminals and murderers" such as deposed Nicaraguan dictator Anastasio Somoza and former South Vietnamese general Nguyen Ngoc Loan, who became infamous for summarily executing a Viet Cong prisoner on camera.[21]

Agnos's and other local politicians' support for Chavez's human rights defined the Bay Area as a region that was more welcoming of queer people and immigrants than the United States generally. Such perspectives, importantly, were being shaped increasingly by the demands of gay rights activists that built upon a longer history of local rights struggles emanating from antiracist, social justice, and political Left movements. Support for and identification with the gay traveler, whether Mexican or British, also drew upon and refreshed a regional cosmopolitanism—that is, the sense that the Bay Area could be a more welcoming and more enlightened home to a diverse population from across the globe than the nation itself—in increasingly queer-friendly ways.

While affirming, the policy effects of the outcry and political lobbying only went so far. Within weeks GRA was in Washington meeting with Justice Department officials, who indicated interest in a settlement (of both Chavez's and Hill's cases) that would include a scaling back of enforcement of the ban, if not change in the law itself. In September 1980, the INS declared that border guards could enforce the exclusion of homosexual aliens without a medical certificate but would no longer be permitted to ask those seeking admission to the United States whether they were homosexual, unless said applicants outed themselves or were outed by a third party. The issuance of this guideline occasioned another round of political and editorial debate, but the Justice Department stood firm in its conviction that it must to some extent uphold the intended exclusion of the 1952 law. Thus, while enforcement of the regulation abated somewhat over the course of the Reagan era, in part because of injunctions GRA secured in the Hill and Chavez cases, some gay and lesbian travelers continued to be excluded, and there was growing fear that the new conservative administration, in debt to the Religious Right for its support, might expand its efforts to exclude.[22]

The public identification with these relatively elite travelers, moreover, spoke to the limits of this queer-friendly cosmopolitanism as defined against the values of the nation and its immigration apparatus. Hill was an antique restorer and photographer, Chavez a dress designer, Cruz Garcia a bar owner, and Martinez a quality control inspector at a nuclear power plant. They had the ability to travel internationally and were rather seamlessly presented as welcome temporary visitors by virtue of professional standing and ability to contribute to the local culture and economy as tourists. At a moment of growing anti–Latinx immigrant backlash across the state of California, Mexican travelers and workers (whether queer or straight) crossing the border by car or on foot were unlikely to be the objects of a cause célèbre.

Moreover, the identification with these exceptional, traveling figures stood in contrast to and elided the marginalization and sometimes outright racism facing LGBTQ Latinx people at this moment in San Francisco's white dominant gay social and political scene, as documented by Horacio Roque Ramírez. The asymmetries were products of the longer history of Mexican subordination in the Bay Area noted earlier. They were also products of emergent conflicts between Latinx people and white lesbians and, especially, gay men in the late 1970s that accompanied the gentrification of San Francisco's Mission District and attendant struggles over political representation in the neighborhood and antigay hate crimes committed by Latinx youth.[23]

In other words, while the homophobic dimensions of the immigration apparatus were laid bare in the various political appeals to these travelers' human rights, some of its racial dimensions—as inflected by divergent sexualities, class, immigration status, and so on—were not. And, by extension, even as Bay Area political and civic culture was becoming more queer-friendly and multicultural at this moment, a great many people (LGBTQ and not) remained subordinate and only differentially included into this more expansive cosmopolitan scene. Such marginalization was a significant part of the motivation for the creation of queer of color activist and community organizations, like the Gay Latino Alliance, in the Bay Area during the 1970s.[24]

The homosexual exclusion would not be removed from US immigration policy until the Immigration Act of 1990, signed into law by President George H. W. Bush in November of that year. Although the move was welcomed by many LGBTQ activists in the Bay Area and elsewhere, its limits were already apparent after three years of controversy regarding, and increasingly militant action against, the exclusion from the United States of people who were HIV positive or who had developed acquired immunodeficiency syndrome (AIDS). Again, SFO, foreign travelers, and San Francisco activists and city officials figured prominently in this story that showed that entry exclusion often targeted some foreign nationals differently than others.

For several years, the politics of working in the air and traveling by air with HIV/AIDS had been complex and often tragic. US flight attendant ranks were hit hard by the AIDS epidemic in the early 1980s, given how significantly gay and male the profession was at that moment and as a result of the high rates of infection in some hub cities where flight crews were based. By 1983 airlines started grounding flight attendants who had contracted the disease given fears in-house, as well as among a larger public, that it could be spread through casual contact. Among them was Los Angeles–based Gär Traynor, who was put on permanent medical leave by United Airlines that May. Traynor fought the decision in arbitration and, while his case was under way, moved to San Francisco, where he secured the support of the local AIDS activist community. One group, People with AIDS–San Francisco, called for a national boycott of the airline. United, weighing concerns about potential bad publicity from having obviously ill flight attendants against concerns stemming from discriminating against people with a chronic illness, settled with Traynor in late 1984. The airline allowed him to return to work and gave him eighteen months of back pay. The agreement may well have represented the first time in US jurisprudence that a person with AIDS successfully fought to get their job back, and it set employment protection precedent for future court decisions and legislation, including provisions in the 1990 Americans with Disabilities Act.[25]

One factor in the airlines' development of increasingly gay-friendly policies toward workers was the need to make amends after a series of embarrassing episodes involving airline personnel engaging in AIDS-phobic behavior. SFO was a key scene of debates and protests over this issue as well. Most airlines did not have clear policies when it came to transporting people with AIDS. Generally speaking, they left it up to their personnel to determine whether a passenger should be barred from a flight because they were not well enough to travel or their illness posed a threat to other passengers.[26] In the summer of 1987, Northwest and United received unfavorable attention by refusing to transport a gravely ill US citizen with AIDS home from China on the grounds that he was too ill to travel. The man's family ended up paying $40,000 to have him transported home on an air force medevac plane before he died one week later. Subsequently, Northwest instituted a policy excluding people with AIDS from all of its flights, and it received further bad press when San Francisco activist Leonard Matlovich, accompanied by reporters, showed up at Northwest's SFO ticket counter wearing a T-shirt bearing the words "I'm a Human with AIDS" and tried to purchase a ticket. Just that day Northwest had revised its policy to allow passengers with AIDS to travel so long as they had a physician's certification of fitness. Matlovich did not have this and left the airport without a ticket. This incident helped to generate outcry locally and nationally over such restrictions, and in the coming months most (although not all) airlines began to lift them. Reportage of these less punitive corporate policies instituted at the end of the 1980s indicated that they were based in part on a growing awareness of some LGBTQ individuals' consumer spending power.[27] Still, residual and emergent homophobia and entrenched government policy helped to set the limits of such inclusiveness along national and racial lines.

On April 2, 1989, Dutch national and AIDS activist Hans Paul Verhoef was detained at the Minneapolis airport pursuant to a 1987 change to federal policy that barred people with AIDS from immigrating to the United States. In May of that year, the Reagan administration, via the PHS, issued a directive recommending mandatory HIV infection testing for all immigrants and added HIV infection to the list of "dangerous and contagious diseases" that could prevent one from entering the United States. Shortly thereafter, North Carolina senator Jesse Helms sponsored an amendment to a bill funding the HIV/AIDS treatment drug AZT that included the HIV immigration exclusion. Although congressional debate made clear that the law was intended to apply only to those seeking to immigrate to the United States, the INS chose to apply the exclusion to short-term visitors and tourists displaying signs of the illness as well, albeit inconsistently. In such cases, travelers could be detained and returned home or admitted to the United States through a waiver to policy. In Verhoef's case, US Customs agents found AZT, sex paraphernalia, and some of his writing about traveling with AIDS in his luggage. They turned him over to the INS, which held him for five days, first in the Scott County Jail and then in the Oak Park Heights state prison, pending a medical examination.[28]

Verhoef's detention in Minnesota sparked outrage among local activists and those elsewhere—including in San Francisco, where he was on his way for the Eleventh National Lesbian and Gay Health Conference, which began on April 5. The following day conference attendees protested Verhoef's detention outside of San Francisco's Federal Building. In an address to the conference (now) mayor Art Agnos declared April 6 "Hans Paul Verhoef Day" in the city and slammed the federal government for "put[ting] its resources to work stopping people with AIDS instead of stopping the epidemic of AIDS." He also used the occasion to announce that he would soon sign San Francisco's domestic partner benefits ordinance. The outcry eventually led the INS to grant Verhoef a waiver to enter the United States and continue on to San Francisco. Supporters met him at SFO with flowers, and Agnos's limousine took him into the city so he could attend the final hours of the conference. Verhoef announced after his arrival in San Francisco that he hoped to return to the city to attend the International AIDS Conference, scheduled to be held there in June 1990. But almost immediately his arrest prompted proposals to move the conference to a site outside of the United States because of its government's immigration policy, and there were otherwise fears that the conference might be jeopardized if foreign travelers with AIDS were prevented from attending.[29]

San Francisco conference organizers, city officials, activists, and others quickly began their own debates over whether the conference should go forward, as the issue of access for seropositive travelers exacerbated tensions already brewing among the "fragile coalition" that had been gathering at the yearly international meetings designed to further AIDS research. Members of the San Francisco Public Health Commission, for example, threatened to withdraw sponsorship of the conference if the US government did not amend its visa requirements regarding persons with AIDS or HIV infections. Some local activists promised mass protests to shut down the conference, which coincided with the city's Gay Freedom Day parade. On the other hand, Dr. John Ziegler of UCSF, conference cochair with his colleague Dr. Paul Volberding, while critical of the immigration policy, argued that the meeting must go forward. Ziegler cautioned that only the organizers had the right to cancel the conference and emphasized the annual event's importance to researchers' efforts to develop HIV/AIDS treatments. San Francisco's Convention and Tourist Bureau also expressed concerns about a possible conference cancellation given the potential revenue losses for local businesses.[30]

Meanwhile, politicians, scientists, and activists in the United States and elsewhere fought for an exception to the policy that would permit foreign nationals with AIDS to attend the conference. Representative Barney Frank's immigration reform bill, which passed committee in mid-April, sought to loosen restrictions on both travelers and immigrants with AIDS. In May 1989, with talk of a resolution at the upcoming Montreal AIDS conference to cancel future AIDS conferences in the United States, the Justice Department proposed a shift in policy that would allow foreigners with AIDS to enter the United States to attend conferences, engage in commerce, visit relatives, or seek medical care.[31]

There was, from the beginning, worry that this revised policy would be applied inconsistently across the nation's airports. The concern was realized when a British traveler on the way to San Francisco to receive experimental AIDS treatment was turned back in Minneapolis after refusing the six-week jail stay he was told he would have to endure while waiting for a waiver.[32] Moreover, as an editorial in the *Bay Area Reporter* pointed out, this policy still discriminated against those hoping to enter the United States for other important reasons—say, to visit a lover in the hospital or attend a funeral—and "perpetuates the xenophobic misconception of the United States as a pure nation that requires defending against infested, invading hordes. It overlooks the fact that HIV infection cannot be spread casually, and it denies the right of HIV-positives and people with AIDS to associate, congregate, converse, and, yes, have sex, with whomsoever they please."[33]

Much of this activism was not, however, coming to terms with how the exclusion often posed a more dire set of circumstances for those hoping to enter or remain in the United States permanently. The Justice Department's small concession was achieved, in part, by politicians and some activists making a distinction between the needs of travelers and immigrants. San Francisco's representative Nancy Pelosi, for example, did so early on while lobbying for Verhoef's release from detention. She emphasized that the restriction was intended only to prevent immigrants who were HIV positive or suffering from AIDS from entering the United States and was not supposed to apply to tourists.[34] Indeed, the political and social status of international travelers with AIDS led to their differential treatment from immigrants—despite those cases of very real humiliation and physical endangerment—and was a key factor in the international outcry over US immigration policy.[35]

But other Bay Area activists were at that moment insisting that the precarious status of lower-profile immigrants with AIDS or HIV infection be addressed. A June 1989 protest, for example, brought together members of Instituto Familiar de la Raza (a Latinx community health care organization) and its Latino AIDS Project, the Coalition for Immigration and Refugee Rights and Services, the AIDS Coalition to Unleash Power (ACT UP)/San Francisco, and other groups to protest the United

States' policies toward travelers and immigrants alike at the INS's San Francisco headquarters. This came at a moment when AIDS activists of color in San Francisco, many of whom had long-developed experiences working on queer, immigrant rights, labor, and community of color struggles, had been pushing for greater access to educational resources, social services, and medical care on behalf of their communities, broader public knowledge about the prevalence of the disease within them, and more attention from researchers so as to better address their needs. The protest also reflected the growing roles that immigrant activists, some of whom were members of multiple organizations, were playing within and in dialogue with ACT UP/San Francisco to push the group to devote more attention to the twinned vulnerabilities to the disease and social marginality facing immigrants of color. In addition to protesting governmental policy, for example, ACT UP would soon be offering legal assistance and counseling services to HIV-positive immigrants.[36]

At the protest, one ACT UP activist read a statement from Verhoef, decrying his treatment by the INS and suggesting that the new May guidelines for travelers with HIV/AIDS were still discriminatory toward them. But another member of the group, like other speakers, noted that the stakes were higher for immigrants. Those seeking citizenship, visas, or green cards—including undocumented immigrants hoping to secure permanent residence under the amnesty provision of the Immigration Reform and Control Act of 1986—could be disqualified because of their seropositive status. As was pointed out at the rally, some undocumented people went underground after receiving a diagnosis to prevent deportation, jeopardizing their access to treatment for the disease. The protest concluded with some street theater. Demonstrators played a game of "Red Rover," in which white, presumably heterosexual individuals were permitted to "come over" while people of color, those marked as HIV positive, and those who appeared to be queer were not. The final act was the destruction of a Jesse Helms piñata filled with condoms. When the Instituto's executive director Concha Saucedo affirmed the day's camaraderie, praised ACT UP's involvement in immigration issues, and hoped that more solidarity between white gays and people of color would be forthcoming, she implicitly critiqued what some saw as the racist practices of majority-white liberal and radical AIDS activist groups while simultaneously signaling growing commitments to antiracist work within them.[37]

By this time, there was a rough consensus among AIDS conference organizers and many local and international activists that the conference should go forward, with a tacit understanding that more people with HIV/AIDS, people of color, LGBTQ individuals, activist groups, and AIDS service providers should be involved in conference planning and that organizers would have to contend with the politics of US immigration policy before and during the conference. Still, much of the debate in late 1989 and early 1990 revolved around the extent to which a conference going forward would be boycotted, because of a policy that still allowed only select HIV-positive people into the country for a narrow set of purposes and via a process that potentially stigmatized them by marking their status on official documents.[38] Meanwhile, President George H. W. Bush ensured that the conference would move forward in an antagonistic relationship with the US federal government when his office announced in February that he had declined what organizers admitted was a lukewarm invitation to attend.[39]

On-the-ground organizers in San Francisco continued to protest the exclusionary border policy and its ameliorations, with some activists insisting that the conditions of immigrants and alien residents with HIV/AIDS be foregrounded even more. At a February 1990 action at San Francisco's INS offices, organized by ACT UP/San Francisco members Jorge Cortiñas and Kate Raphael, and coordinated with a protest in Washington, D.C., the group publicized the plight of people already living in the Bay Area who were facing deportation. Part of the motivation for this action at which seven people were arrested was the recent news that two people (one German, one Mexican) had had their applications for exceptions to the immigration policy excluding HIV-positive individuals denied. According to Cortiñas, himself a Mexican immigrant, people with HIV/AIDS, regardless of immigration and citizenship status, shared a kind of "second-class citizenship," but it was incumbent on activists to recognize and respond to the overlapping racist dimensions of US immigration policy with a long history back of it. Immigrants with HIV/AIDS were particularly vulnerable. "Nearly all immigrants who are HIV-positive contracted the virus in this country. They have already been denied access to health care and education, which might have prevented their becoming infected. Now they are being sent to die in countries where treatments are not available?"[40]

The waves of activism had an impact on federal policy but only on some of the goals established the previous year vis-à-vis conference attendees. The PHS announced in April 1990 that those entering the country for certain approved conferences could be granted a ten-day visa without being required to inform immigration officials about their HIV status. But some quickly pointed out that this policy did nothing to address the needs of other travelers while granting the government undue authority to determine whether a gathering was legitimate enough to generate a waiver to policy.[41] A *Bay Area Reporter* article suggested that the "real dirt" behind the recent decision was that "the administration really doesn't mind if a few scientists and community organizers from Europe with HIV visit the U.S. for a conference. But they don't want thousands of HIVers from Third World countries flocking across the borders because this is their only hope of treatment for HIV. And if any of the world's tired, homeless, etc. (but particularly sick) do happen to wander across the border, they want to have the right to ship them back pronto without any talk of their being 'entitled' to expensive treatment." At a moment when the administration was hesitant to pay for its own citizens' HIV treatment, "it goes without saying . . . that they don't want to pay for the care of a bunch of immigrants, particularly when these are mostly people of color."[42] But, again, as pointed out, among other places, at a May Day protest by Stop AIDS Now or Else (SANOE) at the San Francisco INS building—which involved the occupation of INS official David Ilchert's office and the arrest of two dozen demonstrators (and police-inflicted injuries to demonstrators and a member of the press)—the ten-day visa policy also left in the lurch the many long-term United States residents whose citizenship, green card, or, in the case of the undocumented, amnesty applications could be denied because of their HIV-positive status.[43]

Calls for a conference boycott continued in the run-up to it, especially among representatives of foreign governments and organizations. There were attendant fears that a diminished conference would be the site of mass protests and might even be shut down. A local group proposed civil disobedience actions at customs at JFK and SFO, and rumors circulated that some foreign activists would challenge the broader, Cold War–era homophobic immigration policy by announcing their homosexuality upon arriving at US ports of entry. New York-based ACT UP founder Larry Kramer's widely syndicated article "A Call to Riot" gained serious traction as the conference neared with its call to shut down the event itself.[44] Others insisted that they would attend but would put US immigration policy toward people with HIV/AIDS front and center at the conference—as did Bay Area Physicians for Human Rights, whose members promised to wear and distribute red arm bands supporting the boycotters and the various efforts to change policy.[45]

The conference, which coincided with the city's Gay Freedom Day Parade, was not, in the end, shut down, but it was not as international as it might have been. It was, however, something of a riot, albeit not quite in the way Kramer initially proposed. In fact, Kramer had embarrassed himself in the eyes of some commentators by walking back his call for a shutdown, accepting an invitation to speak at the conference after earlier excoriating organizers for not extending one, and then backing out at the last minute.[46] Organizers had ameliorated the situation to some degree by giving community and activist groups a voice in planning the conference and some prime speaking spots. A heavy police presence at some events delimited protest as well. But there was still significant disruption over the several days of the meeting. Over three hundred people were arrested, with a good deal of the civil disobedience focused on US immigration policy.[47]

On the eve of the conference, ACT UP/San Francisco led a march of an estimated one thousand demonstrators through downtown San Francisco to a protest at the INS office, coordinated with similar actions elsewhere in the United States and Europe, which resulted in a violent encounter with the police and several arrests. Although the protest and accompanying civil disobedience had been planned for weeks, they were animated in the moment by the recent news that the INS had rejected requests for waivers to policy excluding HIV-positive individuals from immigrating to the United States from thirty-three more HIV-positive, undocumented immigrants seeking amnesty under the 1986 Immigration Reform and Control Act. These decisions seemed particularly outrageous when news emerged of a recent decision by the US comptroller general that the 1987 Helms Amendment did not bar a secretary of health or president from removing HIV infection from the list of diseases that prevented one from gaining entry to the United States. The protest was accompanied by an "Open Letter to President Bush," signed on to by a range of AIDS, immigrant rights, Latinx community, and other groups, that demanded an end to exclusionary immigration policy, which was now known to be within the president's purview, and a reconsideration of the waiver applications.[48]

Outrage over US immigration policy continued at the opening conference session the following afternoon. Several speakers spoke out against it, thousands of attendees wore the red armbands that signified their concerns about it, and most audience members heeded ACT UP/New York's Peter Staley's call to rise from their seats in a statement of opposition to it.[49] The government's exclusion of HIV-infected people from entering the United States was among the targets of ACT UP's protest on the final day of the conference. Activists rushed the stage as

Secretary of Health and Human Services Louis Sullivan was being introduced and proceeded to disrupt his speech with chants, whistles, and
airhorns while they and other members of the audience stood with their
backs turned with them. Sullivan was an obvious target as the representative of the Bush administration. He not only had a say in the government's support for AIDS drug research but was statutorily positioned
to help enforce the immigration policy. Sullivan continued his speech
with the microphone turned up. While he decried the discriminatory
provisions of the proposed Chapman Amendment to the American with
Disabilities Act, which would have required businesses to remove workers with AIDS and other contagious diseases from food-handling jobs,
he made no mention of immigration policy.[50]

As the conference concluded, some hoped the protests would help
to shift federal policy. The following week the House considered an
amendment to the major immigration bill currently making its way
through Congress that would allow Sullivan to revise the list of contagious diseases that would bar those infected with them from entering
the United States without restriction. It was expected that he would act
quickly to remove HIV/AIDS from the list.[51] As passed and then signed
into law by President Bush in November, the Immigration Act of 1990,
among other things, eliminated the exclusion of "suspected homosexuals" based on the psychopathic personality definition and theoretically
gave government health officials the power to determine the list of infec-
tious diseases that could bar one entrance to the United States. At the
beginning of January 1991, Sullivan's office announced he would indeed
strike HIV/AIDS from the list.[52]

But social conservatives and other federal officials had different ideas.
Within weeks of Sullivan's announcement, conservative groups and
religious fundamentalists began pressuring Bush to block Sullivan's recommendation. Particularly effective in this regard was notoriously
homophobic Orange County representative William Dannemeyer, who
organized a postcard-writing campaign by people on the right. Shortly
before the immigration law went into effect on June 1, 1991, the Bush
administration reversed course and decided to maintain the ban, following additional pressure from a Justice Department that confirmed its
critics' analyses by justifying its position with the argument that the lifting of the ban would lead to a sharp rise in government spending on
medical treatments for foreign nationals with HIV/AIDS.[53]

The question of how to move forward to protect the rights of immigrants with HIV/AIDS would be a difficult one in Bay Area activist

FIGURE 20. English-language poster for ACT UP/San Francisco protest against the travel and immigration restrictions on people with AIDS and HIV, with Senator Jesse Helms as the stars and barbed wire as the stripes of the US flag. The protest took place on the eve of the 1990 International AIDS Conference in San Francisco, reflecting both a legacy of grassroots activism on behalf of seropositive immigrants and travelers and the prominence of this issue at the conference. From the Jorge Cortiñas Papers, Collection #98-42, courtesy of Gay, Lesbian, Bisexual, Transgender Historical Society, San Francisco. (See figure 21 for Spanish version.)

communities, particularly for ACT UP/San Francisco. At an event in the days before the 1990 conference, ACT UP/San Francisco organizers stated that the organization now "consider[ed exclusionary borders to be a primary obstacle to ending the AIDS pandemic. We oppose restrictive immigration laws, particularly those that exclude HIV positive individuals, and all the borders established by those in power."[54] But this

FIGURE 21. Spanish-language poster for ACT UP/San Francisco protest against the travel and immigration restrictions on people with AIDS and HIV. From the Jorge Cortiñas Papers, Collection #98-42, courtesy of Gay, Lesbian, Bisexual, Transgender Historical Society, San Francisco. (See figure 20 for English version.)

would not be a consensus position. In the months after the conference, there were growing conflicts in the organization over whether to refocus on AIDS treatment and research, as progress on drug treatment research slowed and the death toll from the disease mounted, or to maintain focus on structural issues like racism and sexism, both inside the organization and as social phenomena that shaped access to treatment and the impact of the disease more generally. Given these and other disagreements, and with the group's membership growing rapidly in the wake of the conference, the more treatment-focused ACT UP/Golden Gate split off from the organization in September 1990.[55]

Despite the disappointment and acrimony surrounding the split, some members of the two groups found common cause fighting for the rights of immigrants with HIV/AIDS. Members of both groups devoted significant time during the spring of 1991, operating at times through the two chapters' Immigration Working Group(s), to get the Bush administration to keep its promise to remove HIV/AIDS from the list of "dangerous and contagious diseases."[56] Once the promise was broken, they organized, along with members of other groups, a series of protests and other actions to get the administration to reverse course. That June, for example, on the occasion of the 1991 International AIDS Conference in Florence, and in coordination with protesters across the globe, members of ACT UP/San Francisco, ACT UP/Golden Gate, and Queer Nation engaged in yet another protest at and occupation of the San Francisco INS office. A second INS protest nine days later brought together the SF AIDS Foundation, Project Inform, and Instituto Familiar de la Raza in an expression of widespread opposition to the policy among public health and immigrant and refugee rights groups.[57]

Then, as it became clear that the administration would not reverse course, Bay Area activists, now at times operating through a joint Immigration Working Group of the two ACT UP chapters, played key roles in building support in local, national, and international political, scientific, and activist circles for the idea that future International AIDS Conferences should not be held in the United States until the travel ban was lifted. An important first step in what would become a long-term absence from US soil was Harvard University's August announcement that it would not host the 1992 conference as planned.[58]

The situation facing immigrants and travelers with HIV/AIDS would not get better for some time. There was briefly hope that the newly elected president Bill Clinton would remove the HIV restriction in US immigration policy, but he also retreated in the face of conservative pressure. The ban was reaffirmed by a 1993 supplement to the 1990 Immigration Act, and it would remain in place until that provision was repealed in 2010.[59] The situation became worse for particular groups. Perhaps most notable was the situation facing refugees from Haiti in the aftermath of the coup and canceled election that unseated President Jean-Bertrand Aristide. Haitian immigrants, along with Africans, had briefly in 1990 been discouraged from donating blood in the United States, though the Haitian incidence of HIV infections was not higher than that of neighboring countries whose citizens were not subject to ban or that of certain areas in the United States. Based on misinformation and stereotypes about Black promiscuity and unnatural exchanges of blood, the short-lived ban enhanced scrutiny of this potential immigrant population and led to discrimination against those already in the United States. Beginning in November 1991, the INS, which took over the processing of Haitians seeking political asylum in the United States in the wake of the coup, started detaining those infected with HIV in what eventually became an unsanitary, overcrowded facility at Guantanamo Bay.[60]

Spanish national, US permanent resident, and activist Tómas Fábregas addressed the dire situation facing Haitians in compelling terms in an August 1992 commentary in the *Bay Area Reporter*. Fábregas was a key figure in ACT UP's Immigrant Working Group and a member of ACT UP/Golden Gate and the San Francisco AIDS Foundation. In the summer and fall of 1991 he helped consolidate support locally and nationally for the cancellation of the Harvard conference, and he had, over the past months, along with Jorge Cortiñas and other local activists, brought attention to the plight of HIV-positive Haitian immigrants and lobbied for their better treatment.[61] In his commentary, Fábregas linked the outrage of Haitian detention and, in some cases, repatriation to a country with inadequate HIV treatment options to the situation facing immigrants in the Bay Area. The INS policy, he argued, drove people without secure immigration status underground, distancing them from AIDS education and prevention services and medical treatment. It also potentially positioned them as objects of more discrimination and violence given the increased xenophobia occasioned by being deemed possible sources of infection. The INS policy was thus itself a public health hazard that needed to be opposed.[62]

The occasion of Fábregas's piece was his return from the recent International AIDS Conference in Amsterdam, the replacement site for the meeting originally planned for Boston. Fábregas had attended the conference as a representative of ACT UP's Immigration Working Group, and he had moderated the panel "National Policies on International Mobility." He announced at a press conference in the Netherlands that, as someone who had been diagnosed with AIDS in 1989, he would be returning to San Francisco in violation of US immigration law, and he dared President Bush to keep him from doing so.[63] Rather than being kept out, he was welcomed at SFO by his partner, other supporters, the media, and even the INS, which opened up "a special immigration desk" to "expedite" his return. Echoing the welcome given to Hans Paul Verhoef three years earlier, San Francisco mayor Frank Jordan proclaimed the day of Fábregas's return (July 25) as Tomás Fábregas Day in the city. The event received national and international press coverage.[64]

Fabregas concluded his piece by documenting the extraordinary amount of work done by collaborations among queer and immigrant rights activists (and those, like himself, who were both) in the Bay Area over the past few years. This struggle had not been easy, as the ACT UP/San Francisco split, among other things, made clear. Still, often working across ideological and racial lines, activists showed that the immigration ban, which had been brought to prominence in public discourse because of the experiences of elite travelers, had more serious ramifications for those already living in the Bay Area with a precarious citizenship status or more generally at its margins.[65]

By making such issues visible, while attending to the specific needs of diverse members of their own communities, these groups joined others working on a range of issues to shape a regional culture in the 1990s that was decidedly more queer-friendly, including for queer people of color, than many places in the country or the state of California—and more immigrant-friendly, and more queer immigrant–friendly as well.[66] But inclusion always had its limits, even when its temporarily preferred subject spoke forcefully and eloquently against them. As an HIV-positive person, Fábregas faced a real chance that he would have been prevented from entering the United States upon his arrival at SFO. But as he realized himself, his status as a relatively elite and visible person of European background and as a legal permanent resident created an avenue of welcome, by the INS and others, that would not be possible for differently situated travelers and immigrants. His experience thus exemplified how ideas about deservingness, based simultaneously on race, national origin, sexuality, class, and other factors still factored in when it came to who would be accepted on an exceptional basis.[67]

Speaking of such contingencies, immigrant airport workers rather than travelers were at the center of coordinated noontime protests at San Francisco, Oakland, and San Jose airports on February 19, 2002. Organized by local unions, civil rights groups, and immigrant rights activists under the theme "Justice for Airport Workers, Safety for Passengers," the protests were a response to the US citizenship requirement for airport security workers that had been written into the Aviation Transportation and Security Act (ATSA), signed into law the previous November in the wake of the September 11 terrorist attacks. Held on the day the federal government officially took over airport security across the United States, it drew hundreds of protesters. Most were

Filipinx, as were most of the security workers at Bay Area airports likely to lose their jobs. Local Filipina activist Rhonda Ramiro suggested that the "legislation would result in the racial and ethnic cleansing of Filipinos at these airports" and wondered, rhetorically, about the reason for its passage: a belief that "Filipinos are not smart enough to do federal screening? Or are the Filipinos simply not trusted?"[68]

The ATSA had put into place a variety of security measures for aviation and other forms of transportation. These included the establishment of the Transportation Security Administration, which was designated to take over security screening at commercial airports in the United States, with a workforce of US citizens, by November 19, 2002. Up to this point airport security was generally overseen by the FAA but carried out by private security firms hired by airlines operating out of the departure terminals where they were based. The ATSA's citizenship requirement was motivated in part by assumptions that US citizens (especially white ones) would be less likely to have allegiance with terrorists and would have backgrounds more easily investigated, but the restriction clearly had a performative dimension as well. At a moment of heightened xenophobia and general nervousness about flying, many congressional representatives, especially but not exclusively Republicans, were invested in demonstrating their nationalist bona fides while providing a sense of security to airline passengers who might be more comfortable flying with less foreign-appearing people working the gates.[69]

Noncitizens made up around 25 percent of the airport screeners nationwide in 2001, but at SFO that number was approximately 80 percent. Most of them were Filipinx, who constituted the largest ethnic group of low-wage workers at the airport. There were reasons for this. One was a long history of Filipinx immigration to the Bay Area that followed the shifting dynamics of US colonialism and militarism in the Philippines going back to the beginning of the twentieth century. Another was the availability of less-than-desirable airport screener jobs. Airport security was one of the fixed costs of airport operations for which airlines were responsible. Given the financial pressures and attacks on unions that followed the deregulation of the industry in 1978, airlines cut costs by outsourcing and depressing in-house worker wages. They did so in the realm of security by contracting those operations to private companies, which reduced their own costs through low pay, minimal benefits, and, therefore, a heavy reliance on immigrants and US-born people of color. Argenbright Security, an Atlanta-based company that was a major contractor at SFO and other US airports pre-9/11, recruited workers directly from the Philippines. Long hours, difficult interactions with hostile travelers, and modest compensation led to high turnover in the occupation. Over the previous few decades, Filipinx immigrants, who had few other options, even though some of them had relatively high levels of education, had been drawn to these often-available jobs. Some had settled in Daly City, South San Francisco, and San Bruno—cities near the airport notable for their relatively large Filipinx populations.[70]

The high number of *noncitizen* Filipinx workers was, in part, a product of the lengthy process for securing citizenship, which included long waits for processing as well as a five-year residency requirement. On top of this was the somewhat anomalous situation facing those wanting to bring family members to the United States. Circa 2000, Filipinxs were the only group of foreign nationals for whom the queue for a family-based immigrant visa was significantly shorter for green card holders than for citizens. Many opted to remain legal permanent residents until family members could join them rather than applying immediately for citizenship.[71]

Airport security work at SFO had become somewhat better recently following union organizing of screeners (among other low-wage workers) and in the wake of another and more successful series of living wage campaigns and municipal mandates in and around San Francisco. Most relevant of the latter was the Quality Standards Program, approved by the Airport Commission in January 2000 and implemented in April of that year. This program sought to improve airport security by establishing minimum compensation levels for all SFO employees working in safety and security-related positions and by improving standards for hiring, training, and oversight. By January 2001, security screeners had seen their average pay rise from $13,400 a year with no benefits to $20,800 plus full benefits, an increase of 55 percent in wages and 75 percent in total compensation. The job turnover rate dropped 80 percent, and the security process was reported to have improved in the process.[72]

In the wake of the passage of the ATSA, Bay Area and Southern California union officials, politicians, and activists sought in various ways to protect noncitizen security screeners' now-better jobs. They were part of a nationwide campaign to pressure Congress to amend the law. Within weeks Senator Diane Feinstein and Representative Mike Honda of San Jose sponsored companion bills that would allow noncitizen screeners to keep their jobs while expediting their applications for naturalization. Closer to home, union and immigrant rights activists convinced the San Francisco Board of Supervisors to pass a resolution in December 2001 opposing the citizenship requirement. In January, the ACLU of Southern California, the Service Employees International Union (SEIU), and the National Asian Pacific American Legal Consortium filed a federal lawsuit based on the citizenship requirement being unconstitutional and discriminatory. In protests in San Francisco, Oakland, and elsewhere at the end of 2001 and early 2002, screeners and other Filipinx activists, alone and in coalition with broader Asian American constituencies, Muslims, and others, linked the plight of airport screeners to widespread surveillance, detention, and deportation of immigrants as well as to ascendant US militarism that followed the September 11 terrorist attacks.[73]

When Filipinx security screeners promoted their own cause, they were often critical of these xenophobic dimensions of the current political climate and recent government regulation that threatened their livelihoods. At other moments, however, they relied upon and helped reproduce this web of social differentiation and exclusion in which they were themselves enmeshed. Sometimes their strategy was to prove their loyalty to the nation and their embrace of its ideals by emphasizing the deficiencies of other constituencies in that regard. One Oakland International Airport screener and supervisor deployed the trope of the hardworking immigrant to push back on the citizenship exclusion by casting aspersions at, presumably, other people of color working these low-wage jobs. "I see that some of my co-workers who are citizens are not performing their jobs as well as some of the immigrants. Many immigrants are hardworking people."[74] Moreover, some activists struggling for racial justice on behalf of Filipinx screeners reported that they were compelled to push back on screeners' assumptions about Muslims' predilection for terrorism and their willingness to racially profile Muslim travelers.[75]

Over the spring and summer of 2002, it seemed unlikely that the citizenship requirement would be lifted. In March, as part of its nationwide Operation Tarmac, the INS arrested and, in some cases, deported undocumented San Francisco and San Jose airport workers as well as noncitizen workers with felony convictions who had access to secured areas of the airport.[76] SFO screeners and their allies rallied at the airport in June after screeners and union activists Erlinda Valencia and Aurora Rallonza were threatened with termination by one of the three security contractors operating at SFO after speaking to the media about their situation.[77]

In this climate, activist screeners and their allies began focusing on helping *noncitizen* screeners naturalize in the hopes of getting Transportation Security Administration (TSA) jobs while helping *citizen* screeners

negotiate a complicated, time-consuming, and what they saw as culturally biased application process for those jobs by, for example, working
with them to meet the English proficiency requirement. Dozens of screeners and their supporters, some of whom were members of the Bay Area
Organizing Committee, showed up to a May 7 Airport Commission
meeting and presented a five-point proposal for maintaining current
workers' jobs. The proposal included a request to the INS to expedite the
naturalization process for noncitizen screeners and to hire them provi-
sionally until the process was complete.[78] Meanwhile, San Francisco
mayor Willie Brown struck a deal with Secretary of Transportation Nor-
man Mineta, of San Jose, to secure SFO's participation, along with that
of four other airports, in a pilot program, via an "opt-out" clause in the
ATSA, that allowed private contractors to maintain airport security
operations under the supervision of the TSA. When approved in June,
this Screening Partnership Program effectively gave some SFO screeners
a reprieve. They had until November to secure citizenship or otherwise
prepare to get rehired (e.g., through language study) into their current
positions.[79]

The Oakland and San Jose airports were not included in the Screening
Partnership Program. When the TSA took over at those locations at the
beginning of October 2002 to a renewed round of airport protests, many
of the Filipinx workers, citizens and noncitizens alike, lost their jobs to a
much whiter cadre of replacements.[80] There was brief hope for a reprieve
for SFO's noncitizen screeners in the days leading up to the November
deadline. US District Judge Robert Takasugi issued a preliminary injunction in the lawsuit filed in January prohibiting their firing until the constitutionality of the citizenship requirement could be litigated, but it
quickly became clear that the scope of the injunction applied only to the
named plaintiffs rather than the entire class of noncitizen screeners. An
eleventh-hour amendment sponsored by Diane Feinstein that would
have given employment eligibility to noncitizen screeners passed the US
Senate but died in the House of Representatives. With options having
run out, five hundred noncitizen workers lost their jobs at SFO.[81]

Screeners and their allies continued to deploy tropes of patriotism
and security as they sought to soften the blows of the new regulations.
Noncitizens could not keep their jobs, but the People's Association
for Workers and Immigrants (PAWIS), one of the coalitions that had
emerged from the screeners struggles, secured "Patriot Bonuses" of
$500 to $700 for noncitizen workers who stayed on the job until their
date of termination.[82] The use of "Patriot" here is instructive, demon-

strating again how, in various registers, Filipinx screeners and those supporting them continued to mobilize the idea that those deemed a threat to the nation were in fact loyal to it and, by extension, had the skills and commitment to keep it safe. The ATSA opt-out clause provided a mechanism by which the airport and the City of San Francisco could affirm and extend the Quality Standards Program. It was justified by a framing of it as exemplary in its twinned commitments to low-wage airport workers' rights and to making the air industry more secure.[83]

Others, however, explicitly called into question the work that loyalty did in the post-9/11 world. Some screeners and their allies linked their own marginalization by the state as racial outsiders, undeserving of TSA employment, to the fortunes of those that they were asked to profile. The airport screener struggle was one catalyst for coalitional antiwar mobilizations among Filipinx people in the Bay Area during the run-up to the Iraq War. Filipinos for Global Justice Not War, for example, tried to highlight the threat to members of this diasporic community through the targeting of airport screeners in the United States and through a resurgent US militarization in the Philippines in the form of military aid to support the nation's fight against Abu Sayyaf, a militant Islamist organization, and the use of military bases to launch US operations directed elsewhere. At times such activism involved solidarity work with Arab and Muslim groups opposing a twenty-first-century expansion of US imperialism.[84]

Yet these solidarities were difficult to sustain given the different analyses and needs of movement participants, and, as ethnic studies scholar Nadine Naber points out, the political projects they advanced tended to get lost in the liberal multiculturalist rhetoric that defined media coverage of the Bay Area antiwar movement.[85] And even some of the minor successes of the airport screeners' struggles were scaled back with the further development of the security state and its local inflections. Ten days after former Filipinx security screeners were a visible presence at huge antiwar march in San Francisco on February 16, 2003, PAWIS held a protest at the city's Federal Building, demanding that the Patriot Bonuses promised to those terminated noncitizen workers who had stuck with their jobs actually be paid. They also insisted that those citizen workers who had lost the jobs for which they were previously qualified—because of supposed deficiencies in verbal English skills, deference to authority, or other relatively subjective criteria—be reinstated. Although some got their jobs back after reapplying or received their bonuses (especially at the San Jose airport, where a high percentage of laid-off screeners were PAWIS members), many did not.[86]

Ultimately, the screeners who kept their jobs continued to reap the benefits, such as they were, that the union and the Airport Commission had put into place through the Quality Standards Program and the Screening Partnership Program. The SEIU continued to represent security workers in the face of layoffs, a site-specific right-to-work movement, and other subsequent efforts to scale back wage and benefit protections established by the collective bargaining process and the municipal program.[87] Workers benefiting from such support were standing behind the police in riot gear who guarded the security gates during the 2017 anti-Trump protests. They were better paid because they, the city, and the union remained vigilant about their wages and benefits, and because they had made themselves visible and been made visible as a group of people who were making the nation safer on the terms that some in the region could embrace as marking its distinctiveness.

Those workers were multiracial and not "all-white" and "all-male," as some activists had feared a TSA-controlled security apparatus would be, but they were all citizens with fewer Filipinxs within their ranks. In other words, the entry and exit points of SFO's security area in 2017 constituted a zone where the war on terror had been brought to bear on noncitizens with differing degrees of welcome to a region that distinguished itself against its colonial and imperial past while, once again, cultivating its present and future through its asymmetrical and sometimes punitive incorporation of difference. That certain green card workers were eventually told they could pass through customs but other green card workers were no longer screening their carry-on luggage the next time they left town was just one more example of how this complex politics of welcoming has quite often played out at SFO and in the Bay Area more generally.

CHAPTER 7

Sanctuary's Gateway

The International Terminal where travelers, screeners, immigration agents, lawyers, protesters, and others encountered one another in January 2017 had opened in December 2000. SFO had marked that occasion, one week before the facility officially starting serving passengers, with a black-tie gala at which one thousand VIPs gathered in the terminal's expansive, luminous glass and steel departure hall. The $1.25 billion centerpiece of a new, roughly $2.5 billion international complex—which would eventually include a long-awaited connection to the BART system—had been in the works for over a decade, with ground broken in 1995. Its architecture spoke to its intended function. With its double-arcing roof and daylight-filled interior space, the departure hall was described as the "the West's winged gateway to the Pacific" and as akin to the "great halls of European train stations." SFO officials and supporters claimed that better serving international business travelers and tourists would be good for the local economy. The new terminal would provide good jobs for Bay Area residents, they said, and, after the massive capital investment was recouped, it would improve SFO's own financial fortunes through revenues from concessions, of which foreign travelers contributed a growing share through purchases at restaurants, duty-free shops, rental car counters, and other airport businesses.[1]

Coverage of the terminal opening, like much of the reportage as it neared completion, paid close attention to the new facility's artworks and cultural displays. One reporter marveled at James Carpenter's *Four*

FIGURE 22. Su-Chen Hung, *Welcome,* International Terminal, SFO. The piece consists of twenty-two glass panels mounted on eleven rectangular columns with the word *welcome* displayed in different combinations of languages on the panels. The piece was inspired by the artist's experience of encountering a welcome banner at SFO upon immigrating to the United States with her mother in August 1976. Collection of the City & County of San Francisco. Photograph by Su-Chen Hung. Courtesy SF Arts Commission and Su-Chen Hung.

Sculptural Light Reflectors (see figure 3), an installation commissioned for the new building. Composed of sheets of silicon-coated fiberglass stretched over elongated, bowed metal frames, these large pieces, suspended below the skylights of the main hall, were meant to recall the construction of the Wright brothers' first flying machine. Four SFO Museum "mini-exhibitions"—of wooden ancestor figures from New Guinea, California Indian basketry, European mechanical dolls, and Japanese parasols—expressed the cultural breadth that had long defined that institution's temporary exhibits dispersed across the airport's

FIGURE 23. Su-Chen Hung, *Welcome*, International Terminal, SFO. Collection of the City & County of San Francisco. Photograph by Su-Chen Hung. Courtesy SF Arts Commission and Su-Chen Hung.

terminals. At one end of the International Terminal sat the museum's new offices, research facility, and exhibition space, the latter replicating the 1937 terminal's two-story passenger lounge. And this represented only what could be seen in the departure hall. The display of art and artifacts proliferated across concourses, gates, the customs area, and elsewhere in the terminal.[2]

The art pieces and temporary exhibitions represented the latest chapter of a then two-decades-old, twinned program of permanent and temporary art and material cultural installations at the airport, carried out by SFO and the San Francisco Arts Commission.[3] The International Terminal display may well have reflected what some described as the current desire of "selling the city" to a growing population of well-heeled, high-spending international travelers "by showcasing the art," but it was also part of a longer process by which Arts Commission members, airport curators, artists, and others had used the opportunity provided by SFO patronage to support local artists (and the art scene more generally), envision the Bay Area as an exceptionally diverse cultural and political space, and put SFO at the cutting edge of airport curatorial practice. As these programs developed over the 1980s and 1990s, they portrayed the Bay Area's past, present, and future, while increasingly emphasizing SFO's role, like that of the new terminal itself, as "an international gateway and point of exchange for world cultures."[4]

Among the pieces commissioned for the new International Terminal were two by local artists that emphasized the Bay Area as a space of welcome and sanctuary, albeit with explicit and implicit commentary about the limits of the region's hospitality. Su-Chen Hung's *Welcome* consists of eleven thirty- by sixty-inch rectangular columns, with cast green glass panels (one smooth, one serrated) mounted on each side. Behind the serrated sides are acrylic panels with the word *welcome* displayed in several languages commonly spoken in the Bay Area or among travelers passing through SFO. Twenty-two languages in all are represented on the panels. Inspired by her own experience of encountering a welcome banner at SFO upon immigrating to the United States with her mother in August 1976, the piece extends that welcome to "all the people who arrive in San Francisco." Passengers encounter these panels while approaching customs and immigration, with the words of welcome on the serrated side disappearing, because of an optical illusion, as the passenger walks by.[5]

Juana Alicia and Emmanuel C. Montoya's mural *Santuario/Sanctuary,* situated at one of the concourse gates, uses *fresco buono* (pigment mixed into wet plaster) and sculpture to portray SFO as "the setting for some of the most dramatic moments and milestones in our lives" and the Bay Area as a place of sanctuary for diverse peoples. Such sentiments are expressed through an ethnically diverse, multigenerational cast of roughly twenty individuals, most of whom appear to be greeting or separating from one another. Among them is a representation of Montoya, lifting his and Alicia's daughter off of the ground. As they radiate out from a young girl throwing a paper airplane at the center of the mural, its subjects are, in one respect, situated in the interior space of a version of SFO as defined by a background wall with art deco-ish design elements and windows looking out onto San Bruno Mountain and San Francisco Bay. But the presence of bas-relief, basswood pelicans, gulls, cormorants, avocets, and other species of native and non-native shorebirds at the edges of the mural and the multicolored floor suggestive of water and earth simultaneously places the human subjects

FIGURE 24. Juana Alicia and Emmanuel Montoya's *Santuario/Sanctuary*. Consisting of a *fresco buono* mural and basswood bas-relief sculpture, this piece sits at one of SFO's International Terminal gates. It celebrates the airport as a site of "greetings and leave-takings" and the Bay Area as a place of sanctuary for humans and nonhumans. Collection of the City & County of San Francisco, photo provided by the artists. Courtesy SF Arts Commission, Juana Alicia Araiza, and Emmanuel Montoya.

outdoors, participating in the migratory processes of the natural world. As Alicia put it, the piece "celebrate[s] issues of permanence and impermanence, of migration and indigenousness, of the peoples of the Bay Area who have come and gone, who have sought sanctuary here in a political sense, of the natural sanctuary that this place is for animal forms and natural forms aside from the human ones, and the sacred bienvenidas y despedidas that go on between peoples . . . the greetings and leave-takings that go on between peoples in public spaces."[6]

Yet *Welcome* and *Santuario/Sanctuary* offer their messages of inclusiveness in a facility that, as the previous chapters have shown, has welcomed people to or sustained them in the Bay Area unevenly (or has not welcomed or sustained them at all). SFO's new International Terminal, designed as it was to facilitate the Bay Area's ever-growing integration into the neoliberal global economy and bring capital investment to the region, is an architectural manifestation of the ever-growing inequality and displacement in the Bay Area that the airport as infrastructure, and the economic, political, and economic, and social relationships that interface there, have helped to reproduce.

These and other terminal artworks signal the ways that Bay Area artists have pushed back on the exclusionary and exploitative dimensions of political-economic transformation in the region. But, as situated in the airport, they also call attention to how powerful state and corporate actors have put a benign face on and extended such trends, some of which have taken a toll on artists whose work is displayed in the facility, through the cultivation of multicultural public art. Indeed, as anthropologist Arlene Davila argues, evaluation of public art in the neoliberal moment, when culture more generally is "asked to do" so much, must be attuned to the entangled injustices (racial and other) inherent in the selections of artworks for public exhibition; in the transformation of the meanings of such works once they are displayed; in the local political and economic priorities shaping the operations of and sometimes the very existence of the infrastructures and institutions where such works are placed; and in the shifting statuses and mobilities of those individuals who commission, create, consume, and labor to maintain access to such cultural works. This is always a complicated story, Davila insists, whether we are looking at shopping malls, museums, corporate office towers, or, in this case, an airport.[7]

The very funding mechanisms that facilitated the emergence and thriving of SFO's public art and museum program were manifestations of unequal patterns of public arts patronage developing in the Bay Area that were, in turn, products of asymmetrical political-economic restructuring in the region and beyond. One significant component of California's neoliberal retreat from the public funding of human thriving and various individuals' acquiescence to this project, for example, was Proposition 13 and the concomitant "taxpayers' revolt" by homeowners and commercial property owners. This movement responded to the very real issue of unaffordable property tax bills for those with modest incomes while also reflecting the greed of large, corporate property holders and a rising tide of white grievance about government subsidies being more fairly distributed among an increasingly, racially diverse population. In the wake of Proposition 13's passage and the state and municipal budget cuts that followed, many publicly funded arts programs in San Francisco and other communities—especially though not exclusively those serving lower-income communities and communities of color—suffered tremendously.

Because San Francisco continued to find the funds to build and expand municipal infrastructures like SFO that were deemed good for the region's economic development, and because the city's code dictated that public art be budgeted into construction costs for new civic buildings, SFO's arts programs thrived even as programs elsewhere were being cut. Later, venture capitalists and other private investors would help to revamp the local established art scene by contributing huge sums of money for the construction of a new San Francisco Museum of Modern Art (SFMOMA) in the mid-1990s and a new DeYoung Museum in the mid-2000s. These projects, along with SFO International Terminal completed in between them, spoke loudly of the ways that the burgeoning wealth in the region—enabled by both state intervention in some sectors and its neoliberal retreat from others—in the 1990s and later supported the growth of arts institutions as well as the marginalization of some of the artists and patrons they purported to serve.

Whereas the 1954 Flight Festival, with its militaristic and floral splendor, showcased the airport's function as assemblage that was part and parcel of the region's growing economic and imperial expansion at a moment when its white supremacist elements were only beginning to be troubled, the 2000 International Terminal gala spoke to a Bay Area whose imperialistic reach and settlement were cast in more benign frames of multicultural exchange and understanding. The politics of that display and the funding behind it had their own racial logics that reflected and facilitated both emergent and residual exclusions and displacements.

. . .

The San Francisco Arts Commission (then known as the *Art* Commission) began installing public art at SFO in the late 1970s. The program developed under the auspices of San Francisco's Arts Enrichment Ordinance—first passed in 1965 and put into practice during the 1966–67 fiscal year—which designated that up to 2 percent of construction costs of public buildings be dedicated to art, with selection and installation of works falling under the jurisdiction of the commission. By 1969, the commission claimed that the funds generated by the ordinance, on top of its regular operating budget, had led the City of San Francisco to become "the largest patron of the arts in the Bay Area."[8] That there would be significant resources devoted to an arts program often described as "humanizing" the airport made sense at the end of the 1970s. Not only did massive expenditures for SFO's recent expansion discussed in chapter 5 provide an avenue for earmarking funds for public art; the decade had also seen a rapid growth of "anti-airport sentiment," in the words of critic Alastair Gordon, with airports often "seen as an allegory for all that was dehumanizing in modern life."[9]

In 1977, the Art Commission selected ten Bay Area painters for purchase awards at the commission-sponsored San Francisco Arts Festival, paying them $5,000 apiece for artworks to be installed in the under-construction North Terminal Complex (now Terminal 3).[10] The program ramped up the following year when a joint Airport/Art Commission Committee expanded the North Terminal art program to forty-four works, at a total cost of $1.7 million by the time all of its spaces had opened in 1981. As it quickly grew in these early years through purchases and commissions (most notably, large sculptures by Bruce Beasley and Freda Koblick), the collection continued to emphasize Bay Area artists across a range of realist, abstract, and mythic approaches. SFO also made efforts to broaden the scope of its holdings by purchasing *Figure,* a significant piece by the Japanese American sculptor Isamu Noguchi, works by several Southern California artists, and a handful of pieces by international figures, including Canadian textile artist Micheline Beauchemin. The artists represented in SFO's early collection trended white and male, as was then common curatorial practice in the art world, but this first wave of airport acquisition, as indicated by the aforementioned artists, was praised for its relatively "diverse ethnic and gender representation." As a later assessment pointed out, however, this commitment to diversity was not carried out in a systematic way, with consistent attention to quality in terms of the artists' reputations or the integrity of the collection as a whole.[11]

This early wave of SFO art procurement was not without controversy in the moment, with some of that stemming from the question of how best to balance a commitment to supporting Bay Area artists with one to broaden the "international" aspects of the collection. In the spring of 1979, members of the Art Commission and the Airport Commission on the Joint Committee found themselves at odds over the question. Members of the Art Commission were generally more committed to Bay Area artists, while the Airport Commission desired to bring in more major international figures. Complicating such disagreements over vision was the fact that the Airport Commission provided the finances for the project and wanted significant input, while the Art Commission, per the city charter, maintained its authority to "supervise and control" the procurement and installation of artworks in public buildings. Its position was that the Joint Committee was only advisory. Things came to a head when the Art Commission approved cost increases and design changes for the Beasley and Koblick pieces without full consultation with SFO-affiliated committee members. In the wake of the controversy, the Joint Committee was reconfigured with new membership and more authority, and Mayor Diane Feinstein was empowered to arbitrate disputes.[12]

Feinstein created a new controversy the following spring. She threatened to stop new art commissions at the airport because of the municipal budget cuts that followed Proposition 13. By doing so, she helped to illuminate the funding climate in which SFO's early arts and cultural programs must be understood. According to local art critic Alan Temko, Feinstein's move was primarily a public relations stunt designed to sell a MUNI fare increase to voters who might be put off by the knowledge that the city was spending large sums of money on "adornments" in public facilities. Temko claimed that Feinstein admitted later that any monies saved from the airport's public art program could not be repurposed for other civic needs. Funding for airport art (like the North Terminal construction costs more generally) came from the sales of revenue bonds that were repaid by airport leases and fees.[13]

Indeed, the airport art program was prospering, by virtue of being the beneficiary of fees generated from publicly supported infrastructural and, by extension, corporate growth, at precisely the moment when other city art programs were being scaled back in the wake of post–Proposition 13 municipal budget cuts. Among other things, funding for the city's nationally acclaimed Neighborhood Arts Project, with cultural centers and other programming designed in part to meet the needs of lower-income communities, with particular attention to communities of color, was dramatically decreased, free public music concerts were cut, and the city began to ask artists to pay to participate in the Arts Festival.[14]

Post–Proposition 13 belt tightening also provided some of the impetus for what eventually morphed into SFO Museum. Established by the Airport Commission, this program began operations in 1980 in the North Terminal as the Bureau of Temporary Exhibition and Cultural Programs. The initiative was designed to "humanize the Airport and to create an atmosphere which reflects the sophistication and cultural diversity of the City of San Francisco and the entire Bay Area." Its first director, Elsa Cameron, and two staff members were transferred from Fine Arts to the airport, bringing with them curatorial expertise in popular, "ethnic," and folk art, after it became clear that their current project of taking art out of the more established museums into exhibition spaces downtown was likely be defunded amid ongoing budget cuts. Small exhibits at SFO in 1980 included a collection of historical photographs of San Francisco borrowed from the De Young Museum and paintings by schoolchildren from San Mateo County.[15] SFO's "breakthrough" exhibit in terms of publicity and critical acclaim was "New Glass," a spring 1981 display that had originated at the Corning Museum and had recently been at the Metropolitan Museum in New York. SFO's nascent exhibition program, with its bond measure funds in hand, landed the traveling show after San Francisco's Palace of the Legion of Honor determined that it could not afford to host it given recent Proposition 13 budget cuts.[16]

As the exhibition program ramped up to museum status by practice and nomenclature and moved into the other terminals, it filled a niche in Bay Area curatorial practice given the region's lack of a museum dedicated to craft and design. Its locally based, temporary exhibits promoted the work of other museums, as well as that of nonprofit institutions, like the San Francisco Opera and San Francisco Zoo, while compensating them with SFO funds for the use of their materials and their conservation and installation services. Its third exhibit, for example, coinciding with Day of the Dead 1981, featured works from San Francisco's Mexican Museum and provided publicity for the sometimes-troubled institution as it prepared to move into a more spacious new home at Fort Mason.[17]

Over the next two decades cultural programming at SFO grew dramatically. By the time the new International Terminal opened in 2000, what was now known as SFO Museum had presented around 375 locally and externally focused exhibitions on crafts, folk art, pop culture, photography, local and aviation history, social movement ephemera, natural history, and much more—everything from carousel animals from Golden Gate Park to Navajo weavings to African barbershop signs to vintage ukuleles to airport architecture. SFO Museum now had an annual operating budget of $2.3 million, a staff of twenty-nine, and the capacity to curate forty exhibitions a year. It also had a tremendous influence on other airports, inspiring them to start their own museums or exhibition programs. In 1999 it became the first airport museum to be accredited by the American Alliance of Museums.[18]

SFO's public art program had experienced similar, though uneven, growth across the terminals. While various pieces and the collection as a whole won a good deal of praise over the years, there were also criticisms of the shortcomings of the collection, the poor placement of individual pieces, and the airport's inability to keep artworks clean and free from damage. A January 1995 Arts Commission–sponsored report by local arts professionals Karen Tsujimoto and Katherine Holland offered a mostly positive assessment of SFO's collection of works by Bay Area artists, noting particularly strong holdings in realist and abstract painting. Although their report generally praised SFO's commitment to ethnic and gender diversity, it argued for more careful collecting practices in this area while marking some weaker pieces and others seen to have anachronistic racial representations for deaccessioning. Subsequently, Lenore Chinn's *Los Indios de Mexico*, an original North Terminal acquisition and the object of complaints from the local Latinx community, and Edith Hamlin's *Map for the Pacific and Orient Steamship Lines* were removed from display. The report acknowledged important works by Southern California, national, and international artists but again noted weaknesses with individual pieces and with the scope of these collections more generally.[19]

Ultimately, Tsujimoto and Holland's recommended path forward for SFO was to develop a finer-tuned set of collecting philosophies that would bring more consistent quality and coherence, with a simultaneous eye toward procuring pieces that worked within the physical space of the airport and that could withstand its well-traveled environment. Regarding the collection of work by the Bay Area artists, the ideal way forward would be to continue to acquire work in this area "with an emphasis on large scale works that give context to those already in the collection." Judiciously expanding the Southern California collection seemed prudent given the vibrancy of the region's art scene, and the report also recommended growing the international collection with a handful of "very strong" works that would help to "emphasiz[e] the fact that the airport is the gateway to the Pacific Rim." Interpretive materials, artwork installation and storage, and coordination between curatorial personnel and airport management should also be improved.[20] Tsujimoto and Holland made these recommendations with an eye toward the upcoming airport expansion, with the new International Terminal at its center, which would provide new procurement funds through the Art Enrichment Ordinance.[21]

By the time the report was issued, the Airport Art Steering Committee, an updated collaboration between the Airport Commission and the Arts Commission, had already selected several artists for commissions in the terminal and had been working with them to develop mutually agreeable pieces for installation. One was Su-Chen Hung, an immigrant from Taiwan, living in San Francisco after receiving a BFA and an MFA from the San Francisco Art Institute. Her work appealed to committee members because it could showcase "the affectionate link between East and West," a theme for airport art procurement that had been emphasized for over a decade.[22] Travel themes in Hung's work were also likely of interest. Hung's 1994 video installation *On the Way Home* was part of the exhibition *Asia/America: Identities in Contemporary Asian American Art* at San Francisco's Yerba Buena Center for the Arts. The piece, consisting of six video monitors, with images reflected in a tank of water, shows scenes from a moving train, with time lag across monitors, which further reproduces for the viewer the experience of looking out from a railroad car.[23]

Yet there was also a critical edge to some of Hung's engagements with intercultural exchanges and the ways they shaped individuals. Her 1984/87 video work *East/West*, based on her US citizenship interview, uses a split screen to portray her mouth with one side speaking Mandarin and the other English. Although her lips occasionally move in unison, for the most part they do not, illustrating the challenges that often arise when trying to negotiate multiple cultural backgrounds and attachments. As Hung put it, "The lips never perfectly overlap because of the fundamental differences between my native and my adoptive country. Although I've been living in the US for many years now, it took me some time to feel more comfortable with my double identity. It's like walking on the top of a roof and trying to keep myself balanced."[24]

Hung and the committee came to an agreement for *Welcome* to speak to a vision of the airport as a node of global transit and the Bay Area as a home of a diverse immigrant population. Among the changes the Steering Committee recommended to Hung's original design welcoming international visitors to SFO, in order to strike the right balance of representing Bay Area diversity and appealing to travelers: adding Celtic, seldom spoken in the Bay Area, but theoretically representative of the region's large Irish American population; scaling back the plan to use locally dominant English, Spanish, and Chinese on every panel, displaying these on two-thirds of the panels instead so more languages could be presented; and increasing iterations of Japanese and French welcomes to appeal to large numbers of tourists from those countries.[25]

Alicia and Montoya's *Santuario/Sanctuary* was one of the pieces subsequently selected by the Steering Committee for the International Terminal after the release of the Tsujimoto/Holland report. The two consultants were part of an Airport Art Steering Committee selection panel that also included local artists Armando Rascon and Raymond Saunders as well as airport commissioner William Coblentz.[26] As Alicia and Montoya developed their proposal, the Steering Committee, after hearing concerns from airline liaisons, required them to make several changes to the designs as sketched to avoid emotionally difficult concourse experiences. The representation of Montoya, back to the viewer, with the couple's daughter flying from his arms was changed so that, now in profile, he was lifting her up while still holding her, thus avoiding any misconception that the child was dangerously slipping from the grasp of the adult or perhaps was even a detached, recently departed spirt on her way to the afterlife. The foregrounded figures of an African man and an African American woman embracing and a Cambodian mother and child clasping one another's hands were to be rendered with facial expressions clearly expressing joy rather than with those that might signify a sad goodbye. And an image of an airplane flying over hills had to be removed given the restrictions on images of aircraft in the gate rooms to prevent nervous flyers from thinking too much about what they were about to do with its implied risk of disaster. Alicia was, however, able to bring a version of the image back into the work in the form of the paper airplane being released by the young girl at the center of the mural.[27]

Alicia said after the fact that the insisted-upon changes, communicated to her and Montoya in what she considered a "sort of brutal" fashion, were difficult to countenance during the development of the piece, raising as they did the specter of "compromise." But in the end, she contended, the piece "actually improved overall after their attempts at censorship. . . . I don't feel like we sold out or that we lost too much of what we wanted to do. In fact, I don't think we lost anything." Another challenge to her vision inspired by her long-standing "dream" of having an artwork at SFO that would welcome people seeking refuge in the Bay Area: passengers disembarking from international flights do not actually get to view the piece. Rather, they are, after deplaning, directed into a "sterile corridor" that circumvents the boarding area and takes them directly to customs and by Hung's and other artworks instead. Still, Alicia took solace in the fact that some passengers might see the work as their jet pulls to the gate and they wait to unload. Others might get a kind of deferred welcome upon their return home from that SFO gate.[28]

Sanctuary/Santuario, with its goal of "trying to set a humane and sanctified environment for people who ordinarily don't see their images in those environments," builds upon Alicia's work over the previous decades. Born in Newark and raised in Detroit, Alicia moved to California's central coast in the early 1970s at the invitation of United Farm Workers leader Cesar Chávez, whom she met at a rally in Detroit. She worked on the UFW newspaper *El Malcriado,* picked berries and lettuce in Salinas, taught in Salinas and Watsonville, and pursued a BA and a graduate degree in education at UC Santa Cruz. Landing in San Francisco in the early 1980s, Alicia established herself as a major figure in the Mission District mural scene, with her work addressing local and transnational social movements, anti-imperial critique, coalitional feminisms, antiracist politics, spirituality, and other issues. *Las Lechugueras* (1983), for example, originally painted on the wall of a Mission District meat market, portrayed six women engaged in different tasks associated with harvesting lettuce. Among the issues invoked in the mural are the toxic exposures that women farmworkers, including those who were pregnant, endured in the fields—something Alicia had experienced herself while expecting her first child. Another prominent piece, *Te Oímos Guatemala* (1985), representing a Guatemalan woman weeping over the body of her deceased husband, was one of thirty-six murals painted in the Mission's Balmy Alley by artists organized under the name PLACA in a gesture of critique of contemporaneous US military and political interventions in Central America and solidarity with its people.[29]

Like others in the Mission District mural movement, Alicia was committed to producing a kind of "academy of the street for everybody": creating art that would be accountable to communities where murals were situated by allowing community members to see themselves represented at some level, to help to reclaim public space for them, to be attentive to their social and political needs, and perhaps to inspire them to action as well. Her work, like that of other Mission District muralists, had developed in tune with—and sometimes in productive critique of—local Chicanx and Latinx social movements, women of color coalitional feminisms, Central American solidarity work, and grassroots, community-based efforts to fight displacement and gentrification that went back to the late 1960s and early 1970s.[30]

Alicia also had long experience improvising productive compromises given the challenges presented by the various systems of patronage that she, like others, had to negotiate. She had encountered challenges with Arts Commission sponsorship before. She received funding for *Las Lechugueras,* but only after a supportive commission member intervened on her behalf in the face of hostile comments from another member. Such experiences were, on the one hand, simply part of the challenge of "mak[ing] a living in the context of a capitalist society, while at the same time creating alternatives to that paradigm."[31]

Yet Alicia eventually faced the specific challenge of the rapidly increasing cost of living in what was already one of the more expensive cities and regions in the United States in which to live. After being evicted from their Mission District apartment circa 1986, she and Montoya moved to San Francisco's Lower Haight neighborhood. They were subsequently priced out in 1995 and moved to Berkeley in the East Bay.[32] It is no small irony that Alicia and Montoya left the city shortly before being selected to create a kind of welcome message for SFO's tony new terminal and that one of the first large pieces Alicia completed in San Francisco after moving to the East Bay was *Cross-Pollinate,* a mural for a new Whole Foods at California and Franklin featuring a multiracial cast of people growing food and feeding one another.

Alicia was well aware of how locally produced Latinx cultural expression had been exploited for financial gain by various entities and incorporated into branding and development projects that helped produce the Mission as a multiculturally friendly yet racially and economically divided space in the late twentieth and early twenty-first centuries. As American studies scholar Cary Cordova notes, an elite embrace of the "Mission School" of art in the early twenty-first century came roughly a decade into "a dot-com gold rush" that brought to the Mission and other neighborhoods new start-ups, live-work lofts, fancy shops and eateries, and well-off, young, and predominantly white (although increasingly East and South Asian American and international) workers (permanent and temporary) who would pay ever-increasing housing costs. The result, not surprisingly, was a rapid acceleration of income inequality in the neighborhood, as elsewhere across San Francisco, a wave of evictions and rent hikes, and the displacement of low-income and middle-class residents, which by definition included many people of color.[33]

The highly visible and much commented upon tech-boom gentrification in San Francisco, however, was only one component of the changing demographic mosaic that geographer Alex Schafran describes as the result of the "resegregation" of the Bay Area over the past several decades. Layered over earlier forms of segregation stemming from mid-twentieth-century government subsidies of white communities, successive regimes of housing and job discrimination, and disinvestment in communities of color, these newer forms of spatial division (which are, ironically, constituted in part by the proliferation of extraordinarily integrated communities in the region) were products of many intersecting factors. These included deindustrialization, demilitarization, globalization, and asymmetrical wage growth in the finance, service, and technology sectors; a lack of political will (or funds) post–Proposition 13 for municipalities to address the concomitant social problems and inequalities that emerged in their wake; lenders' and bond holders' insistence that cities invest in more market-friendly infrastructure rather than on municipal projects (schools, social services, and so on) geared toward people of color, immigrants, and other residents with lower status and fewer resources; and antigrowth politics in core Bay Area cities and prohousing and pro–commercial development policies in those farther afield that pushed much of the newer housing stock and many jobs to its periphery. All the while a multihued cast of immigrants and migrants came to the region in search of opportunity, while whites (and others) continued to work hard to protect what they viewed as their professional, private property, and social resources from encroachment by these newcomers.[34]

The multicultural Bay Area, then, is what Schafran calls a "complex, hyperdiverse archipelago." It includes, among other places, a gentrifying but still significantly Latinx Mission District; a gentrifying and no longer very Black Fillmore District; longtime Black neighborhoods like San Francisco's Bayview–Hunters Point, West Oakland, and Richmond's Iron Triangle that have suffered immensely from job loss and divestment, toxic exposures, crime, punitive policing and prosecutions, piecemeal redevelopment and gentrification, and a concomitant displacement of many residents; well-to-do and formerly very white suburbs in Santa Clara, Alameda, and San Mateo Counties that have become significantly more diverse, in some cases majority East and South Asian American; old white bastions in these same counties and, especially, Marin County that remain so; multiracial, majority-minority working- and middle-class Contra Costa County suburbs like Antioch and Pittsburg, which have offered opportunities for Blacks, Latinxs, Filipinxs, Southeast Asians, and others seeking refuge from high housing costs and deteriorating social conditions in the core Bay Area but which also suffered tremendously during the 2008 foreclosure crisis; and rapidly growing white flight destinations even farther afield, like Brentwood and Oakley, that have been populated in part by those fleeing the multiracial suburbs.[35]

The complex face of Bay Area multiculturalism on any given day is also defined by job sprawl in the region and the long commutes people do. San Francisco, for example, may be home to a wealthier, whiter, more East and South Asian, and international population, but more of its residents are now doing the reverse commute to sites of recent capital investment in Silicon Valley and Alameda and San Mateo Counties. These workers are temporarily replaced in the city, over the course of day, evening, and night shifts, by lower-wage Black and Brown workers, many of whom now live in the farther-flung cities of the East and North Bay.[36]

Building on a history of Bay Area arts activism, Alicia and Montoya's *Santuario/Sanctuary* and Su-Chen Hung's *Welcome* counter the regional colonial present's contemporary logics of displacement and exclusion. They are, after all, situated in a port of entry for many of the immigrants that have made the region more diverse. SFO is also a key assemblage that connects Bay Area residents from across the hyperdiverse archipelago. These works critique the Bay Area's ongoing project of producing a multicultural array of subjects and incorporating them into and across the metropole unequally and in exclusionary ways. At a moment when many elite Bay Area residents are more likely to connect professionally and personally—via SFO and virtually—with those living in other global centers of finance and technology than to connect to the working-class members of the region living in the periphery or working for low wages in the core, these artworks insist instead on a continuing, central, and thriving presence of those populations (as well as those who might someday join them) in the face of some of the intersecting economic, political, and social forces that make them necessary to the region's operations but socially and symbolically marginal within it.

Yet much as radical Mission District art makes a gentrified city aesthetically pleasing and helps to brand it, even *Santuario/Sanctuary* is incorporated rather seamlessly—despite some contemporaneous criticism for what one writer called "excessive political correctness"—into a space in which a vision of economic progress, unfettered mobility, cosmopolitanism, and sophisticated consumerism dominates.[37] The success of such aesthetic integration was likely facilitated by the Steering Committee's insistence that the piece's potentially, emotionally disruptive elements be toned down. And this attempt by the committee to soften the piece's radical edges, even if not fully successful, gestures more broadly to the ways that multicultural celebration has at times been the terrain upon which unequal material distribution and outright displacement have been smoothed over and enacted in the Bay Area and elsewhere during the 1980s, 1990s, and beyond. Such pluralistic visions may well be generative of collective sustenance for those on the margins and of important progressive, even radical, critique, but, as Lisa Lowe, Marina Peterson, and other scholars have argued, their display in depoliticized, consumer-friendly spaces can elide the material and historical conditions that produced cultural difference as represented while softening the political demands that stem from them through visual, textual, or sonic grammars of inclusion.[38]

A reading of *Santuario/Sanctuary,* like that of many other artworks at the airport, must also contend with the fact that it is one of the pieces of public art and cultural exhibitions that sit behind the security gates, thus largely limiting access since 9/11 to ticket-holding passengers and certain airport workers, whose attention (except in cases of excessive travel delays for the former) is likely directed elsewhere.[39] Moreover, international travelers typically get to view *Santuario/Sanctuary* only when waiting to leave the Bay Area; upon arrival, they bypass the gate area as they depart their aircraft and move toward Customs and Immigration. Along the way some may well find encouragement or solace in Hung's *Welcome* panels, and this may be sustained through the process of entering or reentering the United States. But, as has been discussed, that process (reflective as it is of the needs of the state and capital) will be exclusionary and traumatic for others.

Ironies have proliferated as the airport public art and museum exhibition programs have grown and broadened, along with the airport, in the years since the International Terminal's opening. The reopening of Terminal 2 (the old Central Terminal built in 1954) in 2011, after extensive renovation, provided the occasion for five newly commissioned works and the reinstallation of twenty pieces from the permanent collection. New works included the nature-oriented, interactive pieces *San Francisco Bay Area Bird Encounters* and *Butterfly Wall,* created respectively by Walter Kitundu and Charles Sowers, whose day jobs were at San Francisco's educational tourist destination, the Exploratorium.[40] The completion of an update to Terminal 3 in 2014 provided another occasion for reinstallation and the commissioning of new works, including Janet Echelman's *Every Beating Second,* a fiber art piece evoking local natural landscapes and cultural histories.[41]

The renovation and reopening in 2019 of Terminal 1 as the Harvey Milk Terminal, paying homage as it did to the slain civic leader and gay rights icon, provided a similar expansion of the collection. In the words of airport director Ivar Satero, the "museum exhibits and public artwork together tell a story about what makes San Francisco great, and how people like Harvey Milk continue to serve as an inspiration for our region." In addition to hosting subject position– and perspective-challenging pieces by Hank Willis Thomas (*They Are Us, Us Is Them*) and Tammy Rae Carland (*Untitled (On Becoming: Billy + Katie 1964 #1–8)*), Terminal 1 featured a temporary SFO Museum exhibit, *Harvey*

Milk: Messenger of Hope, put together from materials located in local archives and submitted in response to the museum's public call for materials. Launched in conjunction with the terminal's reopening in 2019, portions of the exhibit remain on long-term display in other terminal locations.[42]

Although limited in terms of access by its location at the airport, some of the Milk exhibit can be viewed outside the security area. But it is still part of an exhibition space (SFO) that, while exposing artworks to a broader, less traditional museum-going public, lies within a built infrastructural space that, through various modes of mobility, consumption, and employment, continues to reproduce colonialism's and empire's tentacular networks and afterlives. Moreover, the socially differentiating practices of local museum patronage (despite and as a function of the radical appeal of artworks under scrutiny) have been brought into a space that reproduces many of those same differentiations through other means—such as access to lounges, seat assignments, queuing practice, the purchases of expensive food, drinks, and gifts, and the occupations held by different classes of airport workers. Such practices of differential incorporation at the cultural level were established at SFO, one must remember, because of the earlier limits that reconfigurations of capital accumulation placed on public arts institutions. As funding for some of the tonier cultural institutions in the region—the new SFMOMA and DeYoung Museum, for example—was ramped up through large-scale private investments, the differentiating project of SFO's cultural displays and those elsewhere could work more synergistically with them.

The agreement between SFO and SFMOMA for the latter to open a museum store in the presecurity area of the International Terminal is a useful case in point. Designed in part to further SFO's "goal of making the new International Terminal reflect the sophistication of the Bay Area," in the words of then airport director John Martin, it was also, according to SFMOMA director David Ross, a chance to expose more international travelers both to "extraordinary works of art and design" and to the operations of local art institutions.[43] In other words, it was a chance to expand the reach and to draw upon other mechanisms of support for a local art world by linking it to the experience of a differently configured consuming public and by tapping into capital generated by public investment in the air travel industry. Political or aesthetically radical artworks within the airport space remind at least some airport patrons of such contradictions—as they sometimes did me while waiting to board flights, albeit in an analytically abbreviated sense given I did not yet have some of the background laid out here—while simultaneously assimilating them, differentially, as travelers and consumers, into the habitus of the regional colonial present.

Writers, filmmakers, and even philosophers have examined the possibility of living in airports, airplanes, and their connected infrastructures as a window into conditions of late twentieth-century or early twenty-first-century life.[44] In 2017, one local journalist ran with this practice to comment on the high cost of living in the Bay Area. The catalyst was the opening in the International Terminal of Freshen Up, a business providing nap and shower rooms, computer access, and amenities to travelers with lengthy layovers. At $140 per eight-hour shift, the journalist surmised, a month living at the airport with a private room would cost one $4,200. But that was not so bad given that, according to one rental website, the average cost for a one-bedroom apartment in the Mission District at the time was $3,981 (not counting utilities). While airport food was a bit on the expensive side, the Wi-Fi was free, as were the public art and museum exhibitions. In other words, "Living at the airport—and having a really cool address—would only cost you $22 a month more than in town. . . . And you'd never be late for a flight." To make the point further, the article offered a map of various high-end airport amenities, including the SFMOMA store, the SFO Museum, and some of the locally relevant public artworks.[45]

Tongue-in-cheek as it might have been, the article spoke to the staggering costs of living (even for more well-to-do residents) in San Francisco and the Bay Area more generally. It also called attention to a decades-old shift of some of the city's cultural resources to SFO intended to serve the linked projects of branding and economic development. These projects served the needs of local and transnational capital while providing an asymmetrical system of rewards for local workers and residents. This during a period when the airport and privately funded, revamped major facilities were thriving but when other public arts programming locations in the city were still poorly maintained and faced other problems that stemmed at least in part from intermittent budget cuts.[46] Some of the facility's artworks and exhibits asserted the presence and rights of people—including artists and art world workers—who benefited less from the Bay Area's assembled relations, exposing as they did their limits and contradictions, but they simultaneously contributed to a multicultural political culture that made those relations more livable outside and within a more "humanized" SFO.

Yet livability must be maintained for any survivable future for the objects and subjects of the regional colonial present. This message is clear in Alicia and Montoya's *Santuario/Sanctuary,* and it extends to nonhuman lives as well—namely, the shorebirds threatened by the airport's "incursion into that estuary." Alicia surmised that the symbolism of their bas relief birds may have been one element that the Airport Commission missed when scrutinizing the mural for potentially controversial images.[47] But perhaps not, given that at this moment SFO was updating its self-representation as a paragon of environmental stewardship, joining other airports in developing sustainability programs, and actually engaging in efforts to protect shorebirds and other nonhuman species living near the facility.

CHAPTER 8

Shoreline Futures

Bayfront Park, located along Millbrae's shoreline, on land owned by the airport and leased back to the city at a nominal price, is a good vantage point for observing SFO. Largely built on landfill, the small park is defined by a breakwater, walking paths, benches, planted beds, grassy areas, trees, and a small marsh off its northern end. It offers a view of jets approaching runway 28 across the water to the southeast. With its northern end only about one thousand feet from the beginning of runway 1, the park also positions one well to see and, more dramatically, to hear aircraft throttle up their engines and begin their takeoffs to the northeast.

Bayfront Park is also a fine place to birdwatch. During a brief visit on a sunny March afternoon, I observed what seemed to my nonexpert eye to be an extraordinary number and range of native and migrating shorebirds, congregating primarily in the marsh or adjacent waters. I recognized on the fly or later, after reviewing my mobile phone–generated photos with a guidebook in hand, Canada geese, California gulls, Western gulls, Western sandpipers, American avocets, snowy egrets, American coots, snowy plovers, long-billed curlews, American wigeons, and canvasbacks. And I likely would have identified at least several additional species if I were an actual birder with a pair of binoculars and a better camera.[1]

In other words, despite the threat to wildlife from what Juana Alicia described as SFO's incursion into the estuary—brought home to me that brisk afternoon by the intermittent blasts of takeoff noise and the

FIGURE 25. SFO as seen from Bayfront Park in Millbrae, a good place to watch both planes and, surprisingly, birds. Canada geese figure prominently in this image, but a number of other shorebirds are evident behind them on the water and in the marsh. Photo by the author.

persistent smell of jet fuel—and despite the trash in the water and marsh grass and who-knows-what in the runoff draining into the bay from the adjacent Millbrae Canal, the birds in the immediate vicinity seemed generally to be thriving. Moreover, the avian presence at Bayfront Park has likely been enhanced over the past few decades by SFO actions. Not only has the airport helped to keep the space open by leasing it back to Millbrae at virtually no cost; it also committed funds for the expansion of the park as part of a program to preserve, restore, and create 558 acres of tidal marshes and wetlands on its own property and elsewhere around the bay as mitigation for the 32-acre encroachment into the bay by its 1992 Master Plan expansion that, among other things, included the new International Terminal.[2]

Such mitigation efforts have been part of an array of sustainability projects that SFO has undertaken in recent decades, both by choice and by necessity, in the wake of new government regulations, scientific studies, lawsuits, and protests. The specter of human-created climate change has loomed large across these efforts, in no small part because of SFO's role—directly and as a nodal point in the global commercial aviation industry—in the release of greenhouse gases into the atmosphere and because of the threats rising sea levels pose to its own operations. Like other entities engaged in "market-oriented sustainabilities," SFO has tried to walk a fine line between being environmentally responsible and maintaining operations as usual. All the while it has sought to distinguish itself from similar facilities through its "green" commitments that reflect some hard work on environmental issues while simultaneously serving as public relations cover for the destructive impacts to the planet that it, as an airport, has by definition been making.

SFO's self-representation through its sustainability programs calls attention to its continuing function as an assemblage in analytically useful ways. It makes visible the array of environmental regulations at the federal, state, and municipal levels that have shaped airport operations in the late twentieth and early twenty-first centuries while signaling the ways the natural environment has been part of the contingently obligatory relationships that have defined the facility and been shaped by it. Attending to such matters in this concluding chapter brings this book full circle, after beginning with the story of how the land (and water) upon which the airport was built were radically transformed by successive waves of colonial encounter.

The effects and repercussions of climate change in the present are simultaneously manifestations of the deep time of geological process and products of the sum total of human history. Such human-wrought changes to the earth have, more specifically, been one of racial capitalism's most profound legacies. Many observers have argued that Indigenous dispossession, extractive colonialism, chattel slavery, global trade, and attendant environmental transformations ushered in the new geological epoch of the Anthropocene—or Capitalocene, as some prefer—beginning more or less in the early seventeenth century.[3] That SFO is now under threat from rising sea levels speaks to this longer history of planetary warming that, ironically, has put in harm's way many of the oceanfront imperial and colonial metropolises that facilitated the fossil fuel consumption, deforestation, and other processes behind it.[4] As with other phenomena discussed in this book, the accumulated relationships contributing to planetary warming have benefited the already powerful (and those becoming powerful) while posing some of the most dire climate-related threats to those already living on the margins because of other effects of those same relationships (lack of access to safe land or safe housing, for example).[5]

Waterfront airports have played particular roles in their own potential demises by facilitating commercial aviation's relatively small but still significant (and growing) contributions to fossil fuel consumption across the twentieth and into the twenty-first century. The fact that the effects of sea-level rise promise to be even more pronounced at SFO because it is sinking—as the fill upon which it was built compresses from the weight of its largely concrete and steel infrastructure—speaks to the legacies of the specific set of relationships that transformed the site over regional colonial presents.

Climate change has been a story shaped most profoundly and for longer periods by wealthy nations and empires, their corporations, certain oil companies, and the hubris, greed, complacency, and denial of social elites of various stripes. But SFO's growth as a global hub is also representative of how decolonization, modernization, and growing levels of energy consumption in India, China, and other more recently industrialized countries have contributed to the acceleration of the climate crisis over the last several decades.[6] Closer to home, SFO's growth has been facilitated by the partial democratization of air travel since the mid-twentieth century and the concomitant relevance of the infrastructure as a site of consumption and labor for a growing number of Bay Area residents. In other words, commercial aviation, like other contributions to the growing climate crisis, is the outgrowth of a long history of dispossession, exploitation, and profound and irrevocable changes to the earth as well as of concomitant, collective efforts by a wider range of people to live life conveniently and comfortably.

SFO sustainability programs generally, and the airport's efforts to address climate change in particular make clear some of the planetary costs accrued as people and things have been swept into the assemblages that have defined the region. With a foundational commitment to remain economically viable and operational, but influenced by environmentalist thinking and, more recently, questions of social justice, these efforts demonstrate the ways progressive politics has shaped the operations and rhetoric of local government and industry over the past half century or so. But what SFO claims is an attempt to develop a more equitable ecology of humans and things in and around the airport speaks just as loudly of the limitations of its sustainability programs and, as discussed in previous chapters, of the shortcomings of previous modes of social inclusion and environmental stewardship at and near the airport. Thinking into the future envisioned by such sustainability efforts compels us to confront the likely persistence of exclusion, inequality, and environmental degradation in the region in times ahead that may well witness the reclamation of the former salt marsh, mud flats, and open water by a larger San Francisco Bay.

. . .

The comprehensive sustainability plan that SFO began to promote in the mid-2000s had its roots in a series of policies and programs it put in place during the 1990s and early 2000s in response to a mix of government mandates and incentives. The airport's ongoing solid waste recycling program, for example, pursued goals established by the State of California's 1989 Integrated Waste Management Act (Assembly Bill 939) and San Francisco's subsequent Resource Conservation Ordinance directing municipal departments to reduce landfill waste and to purchase recycled products to the extent possible. An upgrade to the facility's wastewater treatment plant was the latest effort to remain in compliance with the 1972 Clean Water Act and amendments. And, to provide one more example while not exhausting the list, a 2000 program piloting the use of low-emission vehicles at the airport was funded by a $2 million FAA grant.[7]

Other programs responded to, and were designed in part to defuse, environmentalists' critiques about the ecologically destructive aspects of airport operations. In 1998 SFO and San Francisco officials began pushing a massive runway expansion plan that would have involved filling between six hundred and nine hundred square acres of the bay. As part of the public relations efforts designed to build support for the controversial project, SFO offered to contribute up to $200 million for additional wetlands restoration around the bay (i.e., beyond that related to the 1992 Master Plan) as mitigation for the project. Although the runway plan was ultimately delayed in the wake of the post-9/11 downturn in air commerce and then at least temporarily abandoned in the face of public opposition, the city did take steps, with federal and state support in some cases, to secure privately held wetlands for restoration.[8] SFO's award-winning efforts to maintain habitat for and restore populations of the endangered San Francisco garter snake and, by association, the threatened California red-legged frog on the 180-acre parcel of airport property sandwiched between US 101 and the cities of South San Francisco, San Bruno, and Millbrae was put into place in 2008. But SFO developed its earlier efforts to protect the species, which involved a switch from heavy machinery to a herd of goats to clear vegetation at the site, in response to concerns raised by individual scientists and, ultimately, the US Fish and Wildlife Service that these species, per the Endangered Species Act, needed protection.[9]

Eventually, SFO incorporated these and other programs and initiatives into the multifaceted sustainability program that has recently informed the airport's operations and public relations. SFO's efforts on this front followed state and municipal mandates for more climate-friendly policies at public agencies and institutions. The *Climate Action Plan for San Francisco*, issued in 2004, put into practice a 2002 San Francisco Board of Supervisors' resolution calling upon city departments to reduce greenhouse gas emissions 20 percent from 1990 levels by 2012. The resolution also offered recommendations for solid waste management, renewable energy use, and other sustainability actions. California governor Arnold Schwarzenegger's 2005 Executive Order S-3-05 established statewide greenhouse gas reduction targets that would result in a return to the 1990 level by 2020 and an 80 percent drop from 1990 levels by 2050. Such goals were affirmed by the California Global Warming Solutions Act of 2006 (AB 32). Subsequently, San Francisco, with its Climate Change Goals and Action Plan (Ordinance No. 81-08), revised its goals to reach a 40 percent drop in 1990 greenhouse gas levels by 2025 and an 80 percent drop by 2050.[10]

SFO was also tapping into broader trends of government and corporate green branding, including those specific to aviation. Studies investigating aviation's impact on climate change go back to the late 1960s and early 1970s, but the early and mid-1990s saw invigorated investigation of such connections with attendant public attention. The promotion of sustainable aviation, holding that industry growth and environmental protection were not mutually exclusive, was increasingly deployed by airport operators, governments, airlines, and others across the globe, often in locally inflected ways, to justify the continuation and indeed expansion of airport operations in the face of withering critiques from environmentalists and other concerned citizens. Pro-aviation entities proposed, with varying levels of success when it came to convincing a skeptical public, that the industry could be committed to environmental stewardship while playing an important, indeed necessary, role in local economic development.[11] In other words, arguments similar to those mobilized in earlier years to deflect criticisms of local traffic and noise nuisance, environmental pollution, taxpayer burdens, and the like were now rearticulated to address the global climate crisis and air industry's role in it.

In its 2007 *Sustainability Report* SFO defines its efforts in this area as a project encompassing commitments to "reducing its contribution to global warming, to improving air and water quality, to reducing noise impacts, and to preserving natural resources." These commitments, it argues, are an "integral part" of its mission "to provide a safe, secure, customer-friendly, and economically-sound facility."[12] The report foregrounds SFO's recent efforts to meet the municipal and state mandates to reduce greenhouse gas emissions through conservation, the use of renewable energy sources, the procurement of materials with smaller carbon footprints, and so on, while emphasizing San Francisco's status as the first city to register its greenhouse emissions with the California Climate Action Registry.[13] Not only is the report's description of the airport's efforts to reduce jet noise in surrounding neighborhoods by monitoring noise levels, altering aircraft operations, installing insulation in homes, and other measures an updated attempt to frame its efforts to placate angry neighbors as an expression of its environmental stewardship; it also symbolizes how SFO's articulated vision for sustainability, like San Francisco's and that of other local governments, has emphasized human thriving in the economic, cultural, and social spheres along with care for the environment.[14]

SFO foregrounded social responsibility as a constituent part of its public-facing sustainability program even more over the following decade, as the airport adhered to local mandates and to visions developed in collaboration with other airport operators who were seeking to deflect criticism by presenting themselves as stewards of their regions' natural and human ecologies. SFO's 2014 *Sustainability Report* describes a program now defined by the four "EONS" guidelines— economic viability, operational efficiency, natural resource conservation, and social responsibility—recently proposed by the airport operator trade organization, Airports Council International–North America. "Natural resource conservation" is no doubt important, but the sequential logic of the EONS acronym prioritizes the "significant economic benefits for the entire Bay Area, through direct employment, induced employment, and business revenues," as well as via benefits to local companies through its facilitation of business travel.[15]

As to social sustainability, not only does the facility adhere to state and local laws and regulations pertaining to nondiscrimination and equal opportunity in employment and contracting, the report argues, but SFO distinguishes itself through its generous employee benefits, cooperation with unions, health and wellness programs, progressive approaches to discipline, job training, and willingness to incorporate workers into its strategic planning activities. Airport neighbors, meanwhile, benefit from the noise reduction program as well as from partnerships with schools and local hiring incentives. Passengers' needs are met through a variety of on-site amenities, including, of course, the SFO Museum and public art program.[16]

SFO extended its self-presentation in this direction a few years later with the release of its 2018–19 *Sustainability and Social Equity Plan.* This revised accounting of the facility's sustainability's efforts, which was linked to the airport's 2016 Strategic Plan for future growth and operations, framed the moment of crisis defined by climate change, the looming end of peak oil, and growing social inequalities as one of opportunity as well. Up to that point, 2015 through 2017 were the warmest years recorded on earth, and global awareness and outrage about climate change had been catalyzed in 2015 by, among other pronouncements, the Paris Climate Agreement and *Laudato Si'*, Pope Francis's encyclical letter on climate change. What SFO now described as its "holistic sustainability" was built upon the EONS framework as well as environmental protection standards established by the UN's International Civil Aviation Organization (ICAO) and its wider set of Sustainable Development Goals (SDGs). It would further be defined by SFO's future carbon neutrality and its "unparalleled economic and social benefits to the San Francisco Bay Area and beyond." Such efforts could be achieved by "deepening the airport's engagement with stakeholders and building relationships based on transparency, trust and credibility."[17]

More so than in articulations of its sustainability visions from several years earlier, SFO presents itself in the *Sustainability and Equity Plan* as an agent of reform. It references its Quality Standards Program living-wage standards and promises to make additional efforts to improve worker safety and satisfaction in the future and draw upon workers' insights when further developing its visions for growth. Increased economic mobility for diverse members of local communities, the report argues, will develop hand in hand with the airport's long-term financial viability.[18]

The plan's description of SFO's social equity planning reads like an updated summary of the affirmative action and nondiscrimination programs (e.g., outreach efforts, antibias trainings, apprenticeships, and so on) developed in the wake of Black (and other minority) airport activism going back to the 1960s. The fact that such programs were still a yet-to-be-realized component of SFO's holistic sustainability vision speaks simultaneously of the limits of previous efforts to promote social equity in the arenas of airport and airline employment and contracting; to the persistence and reconfigurations of racial, gender, and other modes of discrimination in these areas; to the ongoing commitments of workers, activists, and some SFO and city officials to make things better; and to the branding power of the incorporation of such goals into the airport's self-presentation in the late 2010s.

Airport catering workers and their allies made clear the limits of such branding at a pre-Thanksgiving 2019 sit-in for better wages and health benefits at SFO's Terminal 2 organized by Unite Here Local 2. Focusing on two catering companies and American Airlines, the protest led to the arrests of close to fifty workers and three San Francisco supervisors.[19] The fact that the plan rewrote SFO's own recent history in a more socially inclusive *and* environmentally responsible manner must also be read as an attempt to incorporate, at least at the rhetorical level, the concerns of environmental justice activists into its branding in order to advance some measure of equity within its operations while deflecting their more radical critique.

Such moves make sense given that the plan was generated at a moment of growing demands by environmental justice activists that governmental and corporate sustainability projects, including those intended to address climate change, be more attentive to the needs and aspirations of low-income people and communities of color who stood to lose the most both from ongoing environmental degradations and from the exclusions that were often produced in efforts to mitigate their effects. Such concerns were quite visible at the California Global Climate Action Summit held in San Francisco in September 2018. This conference was hosted by Governor Jerry Brown as a follow-up to the 2015 Paris Climate Summit, in which he participated, out of which came the aforementioned Paris Agreement setting forth a path for mitigating global warming. Given President's Trump's announcement in 2017 that the United States would leave the agreement, the summit positioned California as a model for responsible state action on climate change in the absence of such responsibility at the federal level.

Yet, in many people's eyes, questions of climate justice did not get nearly the attention they deserved at the celebrity- and corporate-friendly 2018 California meeting. In anticipation of such shortcomings, thousands of protesters gathered a few days before the summit for the Rise for Climate, Jobs and Justice March in San Francisco, coordinated with similar actions across the globe. Many in attendance, as well as those engaged in critical dialogue about the summit, decried Brown's sanguine acceptance of society's carbon dependence and his attempts to strike a balance between commitments to environmental protections and those protecting the interests of oil companies and other large carbon emitters. Although he had signed Senate Bill 350, requiring the state to increase its energy efficiency and use of electricity generated from noncarbon sources, some criticized him for striking a provision in the 2015 legislation to expedite its passage that would have required a 50 percent reduction in the state's oil consumption. Others decried his support for cap-and-trade policies or emphasized that government climate policies and programs, while necessary, were inadequate to the extent that they did not address in intentional and specific ways the environmental inequities brought to bear on Black, Indigenous, POC, and low-income communities. This perspective was brought home to conference-goers by Kanyon Sayers-Roods, a member of the Indian Canyon Mutsun Band of Costanoan Ohlone, who welcomed them with a song at the opening plenary session but also criticized cap-and-trade programs that allowed some industrial sites to remain dirty with often-grave implications for people living near them.[20]

Speaking of the limits of governmental and corporate sustainability projects, the 2018–19 *Sustainability and Social Equity Plan* only touched briefly on the program that was, ultimately, at the core of the airport's recent turn toward sustainability: efforts to lower greenhouse gas emissions. SFO's success in this regard was impressive, at least by the measures emphasized in the report. The airport's array of carbon-reducing activities implemented since the development of its 2008 Climate Action Plan included conserving energy in airport buildings, increasing the percentage of electricity generated by renewable sources, encouraging carpooling among airport employees, recycling solid waste, partially funding the BART extension to the airport, and planting trees across the airport facility. By fiscal year 2018–19, the airport could boast that it was on track to achieve a 50 percent reduction in 1990 level greenhouse gas emissions by 2021. This would be a significantly greater decrease than the City of San Francisco's goal of a 40 percent reduction by 2025, which, with the help of some small purchases of carbon offsets, would make the facility, in its own estimation, carbon neutral.[21]

But there was a significant catch. The carbon reduction measurements applied only to what are known as Scope 1 and Scope 2 greenhouse gas emissions, as established by the Kyoto Protocol and further defined by the World Resources Institute and World Business Council for Sustainable Development. Scope 1 emissions were those produced directly by the airport, such as those emanating from the natural gas burned to heat airport buildings. Scope 2 referred to "indirect emissions" generated off-site to produce energy used at the airport, though SFO had not been responsible for any of these since 2012, when it stopped using fossil fuel–generated electricity. Scope 3 emissions, which did not factor into SFO's carbon reduction accounting, were produced by activities that were not controlled by the airport but that occurred at or above it up to an altitude of three thousand feet. Also included in the category were some off-site activities undertaken by airport personnel and passengers. Scope 3 emissions thus included, among other things, those produced by aircraft takeoffs and landings over the airport property, powered-up aircraft parked at gates, vehicular traffic on airport roadways, airport tenants' use of natural gas, construction operations by private contractors, employee and passenger commutes to and from the airport, and employee business travel.[22]

Scope 3 emissions in fiscal year 2018 were about 1.7 million metric tonnes, with roughly 70 percent of that amount stemming from aircraft operations and most of the rest coming from passenger and employee travel to and from the airport. Scope 1 emissions amounted to only about 18,000 metric tonnes. In other words, Scope 3 emissions that year were about 95 times more than Scope 1 activities. Moreover, Scope 3 emissions were increasing along with the number of flights operating in and out of the facility, as had been the case for decades, even as jet engines and automobiles had become significantly more efficient. And those aircraft emissions produced between the gates and the ends of the runways, of course, represented only a small percentage of the total produced in flight.[23]

SFO was compelled, per its participation in the Airport Council International (ACI)'s Airport Carbon Accreditation program, to monitor Scope 3 emissions and work toward mitigating them in collaboration with other stakeholders, but this was a heavy lift. SFO had, for example, encouraged airport and airline employees to purchase electric vehicles, carpool, and use mass transit as a way of reducing their collective footprint; incentivized rental car agencies and transportation network companies like Uber and Lyft to use more electric vehicles, and urged airlines to spend more time at the gate plugged into the airport's electrical power system rather than generating power from their running engines. But all such measures presented challenges. For instance, the costs of vehicular upgrades, the wide dispersion of SFO employee residences across the Bay Area, and the limits of Bay Area mass transit made dramatic changes to commuting behaviors difficult to enact.[24]

Moreover, any piecemeal carbon savings that might come from altering employee, tenant, and passenger behaviors would still be dwarfed by the carbon expenditures produced by aircraft operations at and beyond the airport. SFO officials, along with representatives of airlines, oil companies, aircraft manufacturers, government agencies, and others, had been looking at the problem, focusing primarily on how to make the use of sustainable aviation fuels safe, technologically viable, and cost effective. Added incentive for moving in this direction, of course, had been the projected moment of peak oil and subsequent decline in production and rise in fossil fuel costs. SFO began convening meetings among these stakeholders in 2017, secured some incentives for a biofuels program from the California Air Resources Board, and sponsored test flights using such fuels beginning in 2018. Although results were promising, progress has remained slow given production, supply chain, and cost challenges. But even if the rather rosy prediction presented in SFO's 2018 *Climate Action Plan* were to materialize, with 50 percent of California's total aircraft fuel consumption in 2050 coming from sustainable fuels, the total use of fossil fuels by aircraft would decline only minimally given the likely growth in airport operations. Furthermore, today's sustainable jet fuels reduce carbon emissions by only 30 to 50 percent of those produced from conventional fuel.[25]

It is no surprise, then, that the inevitability of the effects of human-produced climate change would also creep into the 2018–19 *Sustainability and Social Equity Plan*. Buried toward the middle, in a section on current and future partnerships among SFO departments and regional agencies, is a brief mention of current efforts to "create a plan for sea level rise and resilience and integrate it into the airport's development plan, guidelines for planning, design and construction, and its master plans."[26] For SFO, like other airports situated along or near oceans, seas, and estuaries across the globe, is under direct threat from future sea-level rise stemming from racial capitalism's long development as it has interfaced with atmospheric and geological processes. The question is not whether the airport will be significantly affected by sea-level rise in the future but rather when and by how much.

Knowledge of this threat is nothing new. The sea level has been rising in the Bay Area—about eight inches over the past one hundred years—and common sense has long told observers that runways situated just several feet above bodies of water would be flooded, at least intermittently, if sea levels were to rise significantly. The 1980s witnessed a flurry of government and academic studies prognosticating the effects of sea-level rise on San Francisco Bay and its surrounding communities and infrastructures (including SFO).[27] During this decade SFO took some preliminary steps to address the problem by updating and adding earthen berms and seawalls around the facility's perimeter. In 2015, the Airport Commission secured approval from the San Francisco Board of Supervisors for a $58 million Shoreline Protection Program to improve about one-half of the facility's existing bay-facing seawall system. Designed to protect the airport against eleven inches of sea-level rise, the plan was based on some of the rosier estimates from recent studies detailing the potential impacts of rising bay waters on the region by 2050.[28]

Yet the State of California's 2017 report, *Rising Seas in California,* and a 2018 follow-up report, *Sea Level Rise Guidance,* compelled SFO officials to take into account researchers' more dismal sea-level rise predictions while also addressing the possibility of additional flooding from one-hundred-year storm surges. According to some of the recent research, including that addressing melting ice sheets, the effects would likely be minimal before 2050 but would increase rapidly after that. Therefore, sea-rise planning should look at 2100 estimates of sea-level rise as well as 2050 estimates. Although one study projected that sea levels could rise about ten feet above 2000 levels by 2100, the report recommended planning based on the more likely scenario that they would increase between 2.4 and 3.4 feet by that date.[29]

The release of *Sea Level Rise Guidance* coincided with publication of a study indicating that various parts of the Bay Area, including SFO, were at even great risk from sea-level rise given that they were sinking by as much as ten millimeters a year as a result of the compaction of the landfill and underlying mud deposits upon which they were built. If these predictions were accurate, its authors argued, over half of the airport's runway and taxiway area might well be underwater by 2100.[30] This and other studies published at the end of the 2010s projected that SFO was on its way to becoming part of a mosaic of inundation across the Bay Area that could include Oakland International Airport and the Moffett Airfield, shoreline freeways and other major roadways, parts of San Francisco's financial district, South Bay technology corporation campuses, tony bayside residential enclaves in Marin County, generally more middle-class communities like Alameda and Foster City, and already-vulnerable low-income, primarily Black and Brown neighborhoods in East Oakland, East Palo Alto, and Marin City.[31]

SFO's updated Shoreline Protection Plan is best understood within this broader and worsening context of vulnerability. The current plan, as of this writing, is to build steel and concrete walls rising in some areas fifteen to twenty feet above sea level along the eight miles of the airport's shoreline; add concrete walls to the airport sides of the San Bruno and Millbrae Canals, at the northern and southern ends of the airport respectively; and create an as-yet-to-be-determined barrier to protect the airport from water spilling over from what could be flooded land to the west. SFO pitched the plan to the San Francisco Board of Supervisors by emphasizing the tremendous economic benefit the facility was providing to the city and the Bay Area more generally in the form of jobs, fees, tax revenues, contracts, purchases, and so on that stemmed directly and indirectly from airport operations. All told, "SFO's total economic footprint within the Bay Area," SFO claimed, amounted "to approximately $62.5 billion in business sales, including $20.9 billion in total payroll, and more than 300,000 jobs in the region." The supervisors approved the $590 million project (with an ultimate cost after interest of as much as $1.7 billion) in September 2019. It was to be paid for with airport revenue bonds that would, in turn, be reimbursed with funds generated by airport leases and concession revenues. Pending environmental review and permitting, the project is scheduled to begin in 2025.[32]

Other local entities have been moving forward with their own plans for protecting themselves against sea-level rise. The Port of Oakland has embarked on a $46 million project to raise the dike protecting Oakland Airport's runways and terminals by two feet, although this project would address only estimated sea-level rise through 2050.[33] In November 2018, San Francisco voters approved a $425 million project to rebuild the seawall running along the city's Embarcadero.[34] San Mateo County cities along the bay near the airport have been developing their own plans for building or strengthening seawalls.[35] In ongoing attempts to raise capital to pay for such mitigation, Oakland, San Francisco, San Mateo County, and Marin County were among the municipal, county, and state governments across the United States that in 2017 filed lawsuits against oil, natural gas, and coal companies that sought, unsuccessfully so far, to hold them liable for costs associated with sea-level rise.[36]

There have been efforts to coordinate Bay Area sea-level rise mitigation plans so that there is some measure of fairness and equity in this process when it comes to vulnerable populations and municipalities and so that an unsystematic approach to building them does not make sea-level rise worse in some places by diverting water in their direction. The *San Francisco Bay Shoreline Adaptation Atlas* (2019), for example, encouraged planners to think beyond infrastructural and municipal boundaries and collaborate with others when addressing sea-level rise given that the bay is an "interconnected physical system" that does not adhere to such boundaries. It suggested that Bay Area planners think instead about how their communities (or parts of them) were components of one or more of the thirty "operational landscape units" (OLUs) surrounding the bay that were defined by common physical attributes. The report encouraged local entities to work with other constituencies that shared their OLUs and, when possible, "to identify where nature-based approaches, such as beaches, marshes, and subtidal reefs, can help create a resilient shoreline with multiple benefits."[37]

By the time SFO submitted its Shoreline Protection Plan proposal to the San Francisco Board of Supervisors for approval, it had been exploring the possibility of coordinating its efforts not only with those of San Mateo County and the California Department of Transportation but also with the surrounding communities of South San Francisco, San Bruno, Millbrae, and Burlingame. This made sense given that SFO and the four cities were all part of the same OLU as identified by the *Atlas*. But SFO pointed out that these other entities were only just beginning to identify their vulnerabilities and that it was very unlikely that they would have their protection systems in place within the next ten years.[38] The uncertain plans for a seawall on the western side of the airport, then, reflected the contingency that SFO might have to go it alone to protect its own interests, leaving its neighbors to fend for themselves, should collaborative projects not be feasible.

The Shoreline Protection Plan was in these ways another articulation of the bottom-line sensibility governing SFO's vision of "holistic sustainability." It represented the facility as both site and facilitator of overlapping webs of social, economic, governmental, and environmental relationships that defined the region and enabled it to survive. Climate change represented an existential threat to the facility through sea-level rise, but it also offered a possibility for reimagining airport operations and their role in activating the relationships that sustained the Bay Area. In SFO's and its supporters' publicly expressed views, these relationships would ideally be fair and equitable and encourage thriving for the human and nonhuman entities dependent on or protected by a still-functioning airport but only so far as the airport's own operational survival could be preserved.

It is in part on these terms that SFO moves into the future as an infrastructural manifestation of a succession of regional colonial presents, layered on top of sinking concrete, steel, and landfill upon mud. The airport continues to draw Bay Area inhabitants, human and nonhuman, into contingent, exclusionary, and incorporative relationships, some of which are becoming more visibly bound up in the survival of the planet itself. As before, the reproduction of power through these relationships stems from the operations of the things themselves in complex, multidirectional ways as well as through attempts to mitigate them. So, what might that look like, as SFO, like other airports, tries to sustain itself—and, by extension, as multiple constituents try to sustain themselves—into an uncertain future? And how will such work help to define the Bay Area's future regional colonial presents?

Whatever happens will remain part of a global story of how, in Julie Sze's words, "capitalism and carbon live out and through systematic dispossession, production, extraction, and disposability—in short, death and violence."[39] The neocolonial- and neoliberal-wrought environmental devastation and the killing fields in the Niger Delta and the Amazon headwaters are among the latest manifestations of this history, and over one billion people possibly displaced across the globe by various effects of climate change (water shortages, extreme heat, stronger storms, wildfires, armed conflicts, and, of course, rising seas) by 2050 represents its short-term future.[40] But a significant part of this global story of the exercise of asymmetrical power will be the efforts to mitigate and repair the damage wrought by this devastating history linked to the pursuit of wealth and convenience.

The recent past, globally, has been defined not only by new forms of political and economic sovereignty across the globe (albeit often limited and contradictory) but also by the ability of growing numbers of humans to consume more fossil fuels after having that expression of modernity "suppressed" by Western powers.[41] Yet the economic growth of developing countries—much deserved, by a certain calculation, after being stymied by European and US interests—and the attendant rise of their carbon emissions have helped bring home the fact that a just distribution of resources and consumption of them rooted in our fossil fuel–based economy is an unfolding disaster that may culminate in the end of humans on earth.[42]

SFO, as international hub for passengers and cargo, has helped to facilitate this dynamic at a global as well as a local scale. On the one hand, international airports reproduce unequal economic relationships that go hand in hand with continued asymmetries in carbon emission levels. One recent study shows that 1 percent of flyers account for 50 percent of all aircraft emissions, while only 11 percent of the world's population fly at all in the given year.[43] Scaling that up, we know that global megacities, enriched by technology and finance, are leaving cities

in "flyover country" behind.[44] And we cannot forget that the proliferation of global systems of finance and goods, facilitated by air travel and
commerce, is also the path to short-term immiseration for those still left
out of this redistribution of resources. Consider what global capital
accumulation has done for female Bangladeshi garment factory workers; young men mining coltan for mobile phones in the Democratic
Republic of Congo; migrants of all ages and genders risking being
caged, being raped, or dying in the desert along the United States' southern border; the unhoused living in tents, collecting cans, and trading
bicycle parts in an increasingly unaffordable Bay Area (and where I live
in Santa Cruz), and . . . that list goes on.

Yet airborne commerce simultaneously represents the possible amelio-
ration of some exclusions and inequalities. Industry champions often
point out that such commerce fuels economic growth in countries with
developing economies such as China, India, and Kenya, enriching the
elite, of course, but also sustaining electronics manufacturing, agriculture,
and other industries that are lifting at least some workers and their families out of poverty.[45] Ditto for the rapidly growing travel and tourism
sector—approximately 10 percent of the global economy before the
Covid-19 pandemic—which, while leading to profoundly uneven economic development in tourist areas and a decline of status for farmers,
factory workers, and others engaged in longer-standing means of supporting themselves, also leads to significant social advancement for others.[46]

Some have argued that the relatively limited current impact of aviation on global warming for the time being (perhaps 3.5 percent now)
relative to its economic benefits suggests that air travel for business and
leisure and cargo operations should be encouraged while the world
focuses on reducing the greater threat of emissions from burning coal.
Yet such a strategy, which could see aviation's share of global emissions
rise to 15–20 percent, might at best only keep the world on the perilous
path being defined by current levels of emissions given how entangled
air travel and cargo are with other economic sectors (manufacturing,
ground transportation, agriculture) that otherwise rely on fossil fuel
use.[47] Consider, for example, SFO's claims about its indirect impact on
the Bay Area economy. And, of course, if the world becomes more economically just, as the wages of workers across the world increase, even
if minimally, in a global economy stimulated by air commerce, those
workers will use more fossil fuel directly to heat their homes, cook their
food, and get to work, and, indirectly, to grow their food and manufac-
ture the material goods they purchase.[48]

Wealthier nations and urban areas across the global North will generally be in a better position to mitigate the effects of climate change than
their poorer counterparts in the South, but there will be differential
responses among rich and poor constituents in both North and South.[49]
There will no doubt be some measure of displacement from sea-level rise
around the Bay Area, perhaps by 2050, certainly by 2100, and everyone
will feel some effects. Most likely, poor and working-class people, especially those who are Black, indigenous, and people of color, will be
affected more dramatically by sea-level rise in the region. There is, after
all, greater probability that wealthier low-lying neighborhoods or what
are deemed essential or commercial or transportation infrastructures will
be better protected by government-funded mitigation projects than will
lower-income flatland neighborhoods.[50] If communities are intermittently
or permanently inundated, wealthier individuals and small businesses in
those areas, generally speaking, as was evident in Houston, New Orleans,
and elsewhere in recent decades, will be better equipped, given their
social and financial capital, to address their circumstances by rebuilding,
relocating, negotiating legal and federal aid systems, and so on.

Yet a future of neoliberal depredation and asymmetrical social power
may be complicated by the contingently obligatory relations of people,
power, and things defining the region. There may be differential outcomes for lower- or middle-income people in low-lying areas, depending on the extent to which their neighborhoods, by virtue of proximity,
fall within the areas covered by projects geared toward protecting
wealthier neighborhoods or critical infrastructures. Residents living in
modest neighborhoods near US 101 in Marin or San Mateo Counties or
Interstate 880 in East Oakland could be protected by projects designed
to keep open these major transportation corridors. A multiracial coalition of community activists, environmentalists, and municipal officials
in East Palo Alto are already engaged in an impressive array of efforts
to make their community more climate resistant, but they could addi-
tionally benefit if plans for collaborative shoreline protection ventures
with wealthier, neighboring communities and regional planning agencies materialize.[51]

Also potentially playing a role moving forward is gentrification. Formerly a majority-African American city, now majority-Latinx, East Palo
Alto is again undergoing transformation as wealthier, young technology
sector workers are moving in. As of this writing, the median home price
was just under $1 million. Although it is unclear what this and similar
communities will look like decades from now, growing populations of

wealthier residents may be able to leverage more clout, tax base, and networks to mitigate the effects of rising bay waters, thus increasing the likelihood that lower-income residents will be protected too—at least those who are not displaced by rising housing costs.

SFO, as assemblage, will continue to play its own role in the local human drama of sea-level rise, displacement, and mitigation. The relatively modest—albeit with extraordinarily high home prices—neighborhoods of Bayside Manor in Millbrae and Lomita Park in San Bruno might benefit from a successful collaboration between SFO and its neighbors. But if SFO ends up acting on its own to build a seawall on the landward side of its perimeter before those cities complete projects of their own, their low-lying neighborhoods may experience even greater flooding. And even a successful collaboration between SFO and its immediate neighbors may well increase flooding in areas elsewhere near the bay that remain unprotected.[52]

Meanwhile, sustained employment at SFO may indeed enable some residents of these and other low- and middle-income neighborhoods to better endure the effects of climate change. As discussed earlier, airport work for Black and Filipinx workers has been a site of advancement but also of marginality, as it has been for others. SFO is a site where racial and gendered asymmetries emanating from long histories of colonial encounter and labor exploitation continue to play out. Even with newfound commitments to "social equity," hierarchies of status, pay, and relative permanence are likely to be exacerbated by job cuts and reductions of hours stemming from climate-related rising operational costs and disruptions. Yet for some, SFO will remain a source of steady work, enabling them and their families to maintain some measure of stability amid challenging circumstances.

But workers in a future "carbon-neutral" airport that facilities the release of huge amounts of Scope 3 emissions will, of course, be implicated in further climate change. Not as much as the oil companies who made great profits and exacted exorbitant human and environmental costs extracting fossil fuels over the years and then did what they could since the 1960s, and especially since the late 1970s, to diminish public knowledge of the long-term climatic impacts of the burning of these fuels and to stymie government regulation of that burning.[53] And not as much as the local governments now suing the oil economies that have up until very recently promoted carbon-centered development. And not as much as the airlines, and not as much as frequent-flying cosmopolitan business and leisure travelers. But to the extent that airport workers sustain the operation, commute to and from work, and use their wages to travel by air, they will, collectively, like other less wealthy people across the globe, play a growing role in the deterioration of the planet as populations grow and individuals use more carbon resources.

SFO as heavy infrastructure on sinking Ramaytush Ohlone land, dumping carbon into the atmosphere even as the facility becomes greener, will in these and other ways reproduce the Bay Area's multiple colonial pasts and presents, articulated or disarticulated as they will be, to and from the colonial pasts and presents of other places. SFO's "sustainability," then, is ultimately a descriptor of a current set of environmentally and socially focused policies and of present and future manifestations of a history of reproducing power in the Bay Area. SFO does not represent the whole story of our networked, regional colonial present and its possible futures, yet as a uniquely visible, spectacular and mundane, deeply symbolic assemblage, it offers insights about the social, political, cultural, and economic dynamics that have shaped the layers of colonial encounter that have defined the region over the past century and will do so into as much as we have of a future.

How humans will ultimately respond to the climate crisis remains an open question. Despite the recent and more obvious local signs of the crisis—fires and smoke, drought and excessive heat, floods and mudslides when rainstorms do actually happen—there are signs all around the region that the forces of business as usual hold firm, that many people are too entrenched in their routines and their investments in comfort, convenience, God, or ideology to move beyond denial. Some, well aware of what's coming, are moving forward with a cynical understanding, shared by elites and members of the middle classes across the globe, that poor people, Indigenous people, and people of color—by virtue of previous acts of marginalization and dispossession that put them in harm's way in urban heat islands, low-lying areas, and marginal reservation lands with limited resources to take action on their own behalf—will just have to bear the brunt of the effects of global warming.[54] Such awareness is often paired with the belief that new security measures will be necessary to keep their responses to those effects (both political and migratory) in check.[55] Some are paralyzed by the unfathomableness of it all, while governments are paralyzed by partisan, bureaucratic, or budgetary dysfunction. Some are putting their faith in technological or market-based fixes. Some of the most marginalized and aggrieved are simply trying to survive other crises.

But California and the Bay Area in particular remain key nodes of activism around climate change, and many of their residents, individually and collectively, are working toward a reparative future by engaging in important small acts in the arenas of environmental justice, ecological restoration, scientific and social research, education, urban gardening and food redistribution, and old-fashioned protest.[56] Local Indigenous peoples have been important leaders in such efforts. Members of the Association of Ramaytush Ohlone, for example, have been working with state agencies and conservation groups on ecological restoration projects on the Peninsula that "seek to show how Indigenous practices of land management are critical in addressing climate collapse." These include the restoration of trout and salmon habitats in San Mateo County creeks.[57] The Indigenous women-led Sogorea Te' Land Trust in the East Bay has dedicated itself "to heal and transform the legacies of colonization, genocide, and patriarchy and to do the work our ancestors and future generations are calling us to do." At the time of this writing they were in the process of establishing a series of Himmetkas, or "culturally based emergency response hub[s]," designed to ameliorate the effects of the Covid-19 pandemic, climate change, and other crises through the creation of ceremonial space, food and medicine gardens, stores of medicine and clean water, and other community resources.[58]

Such work is necessary: small acts, as they are, they stem from broader projects of sovereignty and cultural revitalization that remain, as they always have been, the most foundationally important responses to the networked colonialisms and imperialisms set in motion in the region by Spanish soldiers and missionaries, Californio ranchers, and Anglo financiers, and lived by most of the rest of us through a multiplicity of historically unfolding assemblages. These decolonial responses point to a possible future, very different from the one most of us who live in and around the Bay Area have the capacity to pursue. Perhaps there is hope for a successful movement—and real reform, with land repatriation and wealth redistribution accompanying environmental repair—to follow this lead despite the proliferation of signs that the enormity of the problems generated by climate change and the sum total of human refusals to deal with it will just be too extensive to overcome, by anyone. Some of that struggle may well manifest itself at and around SFO as long as it remains open, and SFO, in turn, may well continue to be a touchstone for analyzing the relationships that have defined the region—at least as long as people still have the luxury of analyzing things.

It is fitting that San Francisco Bay will be a primary agent in what comes next. After long being filled, silted, polluted, littered, sonically assaulted, and warmed over, the bay (and whatever living things are left in it), with its expanding waters most recently the product of the longer durée of racial capitalism, will continue its epochal processes of rising and falling, moved by the earth's and moon's gravitational pulls and changing winds. As it transforms the contours of surrounding tidelands and makes new tidelands, it will approach, surround, and perhaps even move within the airport. The bay will thus, by extension, help redefine the colonial presents of the future, with its intrusive, brackish water demanding of those people who inhabit it a more holistic, planetary perspective than many of us hold today when it comes to understanding connections among humans, other forms of life, and their built and nature-made surroundings.[59]

Whatever the case may be, the shorebirds will continue to bear witness to all of this, although their shore may end up being quite some distance away.

Acknowledgments

I have been thinking about doing a book on the metropolitan Bay Area for quite a long time. A version of it crept into my graduate school applications, and I mentioned it as the semifictional "next book" in cover letters and interviews for assistant professor positions. It took a few decades for the project to actually materialize, albeit in a very different form than originally imagined, but it was always there in the background. I am grateful, then, to all the friends, mentors, and colleagues who have kept me going over the years with their brilliance, support, and kindness.

This project began to come together in earnest about a decade ago, as Lewis Watts and I were completing a book on New Orleans. Thinking with Lewis about urban relationships in post-Katrina NOLA provided important inspiration for a study about a place closer to home. I also benefited during the early stages of conceptualizing this work from being in dialogue with Miriam Greenberg and other members of the Urban Studies Research Cluster and Critical Sustainabilities projects at UC Santa Cruz. Reading with these colleagues and hearing presentations of their work, some of it focused on the Bay Area, similarly inspired me to rekindle the long-dormant project. This was around the time that my original home department at UC Santa Cruz, American studies, imploded and I began working in the Departments of History, History of Consciousness, and Critical Race and Ethnic Studies. I value the intellectual camaraderie and support I've received from folks in all three units while working on this book.

A year off from teaching provided by a University of California Presidential Faculty Research Fellowship in the Humanities was instrumental in helping me get this project off the ground (pun intended). I am grateful to the selection committee as well as to Nathaniel Deutsch and Irena Polic of the Humanities Institute at UC Santa Cruz for helping me with my application for this award and more generally supporting the work. Also helpful along the way were several small Faculty Research Grants awarded by the Committee on Research at UC Santa Cruz. As I worked to finish this up during the difficult days of the pandemic, I was sustained by Friday afternoon hikes in DeLaveaga park with Chris Bratt and Stephen Snyder.

History of Consciousness graduate students Adrian Drummond-Cole, Stephen Engel, and Patrick King provided excellent research assistance and helpful feedback on the work. Julie Takata of SFO Museum, Catherine Powell of San Francisco State University's Labor Archives and Research Center, and Isaac Fellman of the GLBT Historical Society in San Francisco offered invaluable assistance with navigating their collections and securing images for the project. I am also grateful for the research assistance and image procurement provided by staff at the Bancroft Library at UC Berkeley, the California State Library's California History Room, the California Historical Society in San Francisco, the Golden Gate National Recreation Area Park Archives and Record Center, the Moorland-Springarn Research Center at Howard University, San Francisco Public Library's San Francisco History Center, the San Mateo County Historical Association Archives in Redwood City, UC Santa Cruz's McHenry Library, and the US Library of Congress. I am especially grateful to Su-Chen Hung, Juana Alicia Araiza, and Emmanuel Montoya for allowing me to reproduce images of their art in the book and to Susan Pontious and Tara Peterson of the San Francisco Arts Commission for helping to make that happen.

Far too many people to name (and remember adequately) provided useful information about sources, events, and airport-related phenomena over the years, but conversations with the following individuals come to mind now as helping me better conceptualize and move this project forward at key moments: Lindsey Dillon, Daniel Fischlin, Debbie Gould, Herman Gray, Christine Hong, and Gabriel Mindel. Chapter 5 benefited from comments and questions by audience members at talks at UC Santa Cruz and UC Berkeley, and chapter 4 was improved by feedback from *California History* editor Mary Ann Irwin and two anonymous readers for the journal. It goes without saying, of course, that any errors of fact or analysis and all other missteps in these and other chapters are entirely my own doing.

I am grateful to Niels Hooper, my editor at UC Press, for his interest in this project and for his encouragement and support as I completed it. Along the way, I benefited from the generative feedback offered by an anonymous reader, George Lipsitz, and Danny Widener on a proposal and sample chapters and then on the full manuscript. Danny provided particularly useful guidance and support in a follow-up conversation at a moment of some uncertainty on my part. Naja Pulliam Collins of UC Press did an excellent job keeping me on track (and on schedule) as the book went into production, at which point I also benefited from the keen eye of copyeditor Elisabeth Magnus. Recent experience has also given me a sense of how many UC Press workers are involved with getting these books out there in the world, and I thank all of them for their labors.

My parents, Scipio and Barbara, and my brother, Scott, in many different ways have inspired the intellectual work that I do. I remain, as always, grateful for that. My father died during the writing of this book, as did his sisters (and my aunts), Mary and Arlene. The three of them composed an entire generation of our branch of the Porter family. I also lost my uncle John on my mother's side. The passing of these elders over just a few short years was a profound loss with which we continue to try to come to terms. I wish they could have seen this book materialize, and I dedicate it to their memory.

I am enriched by the love, support, and luminescence of Catherine Ramírez, and I am grateful that we chose each other as partners in life. More prosaically, I appreciate the time she has spent over the past decade listening to half-baked theories about airports and reading chapter drafts. Finally, I treasure the inspiration and distraction of our children, Carmen and Omar, who grew up over the years I spent writing this book.

Notes

INTRODUCTION

1. Bhimull, *Empire in the Air;* Van Vleck, *Empire of the Air.*
2. Flynn, *Men, Money and Mud,* 54–56.
3. The nine estuary-bordering counties generally understood as constituting the Bay Area are Alameda, Contra Costa, Marin, Napa, San Francisco, San Mateo, Santa Clara, Solano, and Sonoma. What we generally think of as San Francisco Bay also includes its extensions, San Pablo Bay and Suisun Bay.
4. This follows Derek Gregory's use of "the colonial present" to analyze the early twenty-first-century "war on terror." Gregory uses *colonial* instead of *imperial* "to retain the active sense of the verb 'to colonize.'" *Colonial Present,* xv.
5. Brechin, *Imperial San Francisco.*
6. In Mark Salter's words, "Airports represent an assemblage of multiple actors operating according to different and often conflicting logics that lacks a single root-branch architecture, but nevertheless expand across the urban and global landscape." Salter, "Global Airport," 9. As Fuller and Harley describe it, "The networked and dispersed city of the air . . . turns mobility and connection into a productive force that produces value and in the process reshapes a city and its infrastructure." *Aviopolis,* 140. Such conceptualizations follow the lead of Gilles Deleuze and Félix Guattari's theorizations of assemblages in *A Thousand Plateaus* and elsewhere.
7. See Gordon, *Naked Airport,* Schaberg, *End of Airports,* and Schaberg, "Mini Object Lesson," for accounts of contradictory meanings and feelings around airports.
8. I join scholars who have analyzed the role of airports in the development of specific metropolitan regions. See, e.g., Bloom, *Metropolitan Airport,* and Kim, "Airport Modern." I also build on work attending to how colonial, racial, and other forms of power have structured the development of transportation

infrastructures and vice versa—e.g., Avila, *Folklore of the Freeway*, and Karuka, *Empire's Tracks*.

9. Robinson argues that "the social, psychological, and cultural origins of racism and nationalism both anticipated capitalism in time and formed a piece with those events which contributed directly to its organization of production and exchange." *Black Marxism*, 9. For an excellent, brief synopsis of Robinson's concept, see Kelley, "What Did Cedric Robinson Mean." For recent elaborations of Robinson's work, see, for example, Lowe, *Intimacies of Four Continents*; Jenkins and Leroy, *Histories of Racial Capitalism*; and Byrd et al., "Economics of Dispossession." As these studies (and many others) show, racial capitalism fundamentally shaped the world through colonial settlement, occupation, and the dispossession and removal of Indigenous peoples; the concomitant rise of plantation economies and the chattel enslavement of (primarily) African people; subsequent colonial and imperial enterprises arising from European, Asian, and American metropoles; and associated state-building projects and movements of people (forced and otherwise) as slaves, indentured servants, migrants, immigrants, and refugees.

10. See Patel and Moore, *History of the World*, for a survey of racial capitalism's transformation of the natural world.

11. My account of how geopolitical and social formations, ideas, rules, identities, and relations of production transposed from the past (and sometimes from other places) combine with emergent phenomena that are specific to given times and places is influenced by S. Hall, "Race, Articulation," and Saldaña-Portillo, *Indian Given*.

12. Assemblage theorist Manuel DeLanda thinking about "contingently obligatory" relationships is useful here. See his *New Philosophy of Society*. Also shaping my analysis throughout this project are thinkers who fuse assemblage thinking with critical race and gender and decolonial perspectives. See, e.g., Escobar, *Territories of Difference*, Puar, *Terrorist Assemblages*, and Weheliye, *Habeas Viscus*.

13. I am inspired by Christina Sharpe's elegant formulation, crafted with specific attention to slave ships, afterlives of slavery, and anti-Blackness: "Racism, the engine that drives the ship of state's national and imperial projects . . . cuts through all of our lives and deaths inside and outside the nation, in the wake of its purposeful flow." Sharpe, *In the Wake*, 3.

14. Augé, *Non-places*. To be fair to Augé, given how arguments about the local specificity of airports often use him as a foil, he makes clear in the introduction to the second edition of this volume that nonplaces for some can be places of locally relevant social bonding or collective history for others (viii).

15. "concourse, n." OED Online, June 2021, www-oed-com.oca.ucsc.edu /view/Entry/38377?redirectedFrom=concourse&.

16. See Mimi Sheller's discussion of "differential mobilities" in "Air Mobilities."

17. Fuller and Harley, *Aviopolis*; Adey, *Aerial Life*; Salter, "Global Airport"; Schaberg, *End of Airports*.

CHAPTER 1. OUT OF THE MUD

1. Flynn, *Men, Money and Mud*, 5.
2. J. Hill, *SFO*, 13, 95.
3. Booker, *Down by the Bay*, 16–17; Scott, *San Francisco Bay Area*, 1.
4. My references to the original inhabitants of the Peninsula follow the lead of the Association of Ramaytush Ohlone, on that association's website; see "Terminology: On the Terms Costanoan, Ohlone, Ramaytush, and Yelamu," accessed March 25, 2022, www.ramaytush.org/terminology.html.
5. Cronon, *Nature's Metropolis*, 149–50; Booker, *Down by the Bay*, 18–21; M. Anderson, *Tending the Wild*, 57.
6. Milliken, Shoup, and Ortiz, *Ohlone/Costanoan Indians*, 3, 291–92; Stanger, "California Rancho," 245; John Dury and Laird Townsend, "Shellmound at San Bruno Mountain," *Found SF*, accessed March 25, 2022, www.foundsf .org/index.php?title=Shellmound_at_San_Bruno_Mountain.
7. Milliken, Shoup, and Ortiz, *Ohlone/Costanoan Indians*, 87, 96–100, 291–92; Booker, *Down by the Bay*, 23.
8. Milliken, Shoup, and Ortiz, *Ohlone/Costanoan Indians*, 295–98; Lightfoot, *Indians, Missionaries, and Merchants*, 66–68.
9. Haas, *Conquest and Historical Identities*, 29–33; Hynding, *From Frontier to Suburb*, 25–26; Skowronek, "Sifting the Evidence," 683–90; Lightfoot, *Indians, Missionaries, and Merchants*, 68–70, 188–89, 199–202.
10. M. Anderson, *Tending the Wild*, 5–6.
11. Stanger, *South from San Francisco*, 18–21; Stanger, "California Rancho," 245–46; Hynding, *From Frontier to Suburb*, 20–23.
12. Stanger, "Californio Rancho," 246–49; Stanger, *South from San Francisco*, 24–26.
13. Booker, *Down by the Bay*, 24–26, 116; M. Anderson, *Tending the Wild*, 76–77.
14. Milliken, Shoup, and Ortiz, *Ohlone/Costanoan Indians*, 153–57; Haas, *Conquest and Historical Identities*, 32–37; Pitti, *Devil in Silicon Valley*, 21–23.
15. Stanger, "California Rancho," 249–52; Kinnaird, *History*, 1:205–6, 262–63.
16. Stanger, "California Rancho," 252; Scott, *San Francisco Bay Area*, 18.
17. Milliken, Shoup, and Ortiz, *Ohlone/Costanoan Indians*, 168, 171–74, 184–87.
18. Stanger, *South from San Francisco*, 39; Haas, *Conquest and Historical Identities*, 37; S. Smith, *Freedom's Frontier*, 19–22.
19. Sanchez will, translation by Frank Stanger, p. 3, documents folder 179, San Mateo County Historical Association Archives (hereafter cited as SMCHAA).
20. Milliken, Shoup, and Ortiz, *Ohlone/Costanoan Indians*, 187.
21. Milliken, Shoup, and Ortiz, *Ohlone/Costanoan Indians*, 179–81, 187; Booker, *Down by the Bay*, 26.
22. Pitt, *Decline of the Californios*, 84–103.
23. Stanger, "California Rancho," 253–57.
24. Stanger, *South from San Francisco*, 53–73.

25. Milliken, Shoup, and Ortiz, *Ohlone/Costanoan Indians*. 179–80, 184–85, 187–88.

26. Du Bois, *Black Reconstruction in America*, 700.

27. Milliken, Shoup, and Ortiz, *Ohlone/Costanoan Indians*, 299–304; Almaguer, *Racial Fault Lines*, 26–41; S. Smith, *Freedom's Frontier*.

28. Milliken, Shoup, and Ortiz, *Ohlone/Costanoan Indians*, 179, 187–95.

29. Hubert Howe Bancroft, "Biography of Darius Ogden Mills," undated manuscript, Bancroft Library, University of California, Berkeley, 2–4; Cross, *Financing an Empire*, 1:78, 81; Mills, Mills, and Miller copartnership agreement, February 18, 1856, box 369, National Bank of D. O. Mills and Company Collection, 1847–1927, California State Library, California History Section (hereafter cited as D. O. Mills Collection); stock certificates: Bear River and Auburn Water & Mining Company, Bradley-Berdan & Co., Eureka Canal Company of El Dorado, and Last Chance Copper, Gold and Silver Mining Company, box 374, D. O. Mills Collection.

30. Stanger, "California Rancho," 254–55; 1868 map of San Mateo County, A. S. Easton, County Surveyor, S.M.C., SMCHAA; trust agreement, D. O. Mills, A. I. Easton, and Henry Miller, October 9, 1867, box 368, D. O. Mills Collection.

31. Dow, "Bay Fill in San Francisco," 7–9, 14–19; Dillon, "Civilizing Swamps in California," 264–65.

32. 1909 map of San Mateo County, J. V. Neuman, county surveyor, SMCHAA.

33. Joan Levy, "What Happened to the Rancho?," *Daily Journal*, January 22, 2007, 3; Stanger, *South from San Francisco*, 107; Igler, *Industrial Cowboys*, 47–49.

34. San Bruno Turnpike Road Company stock certificates, Box 371, D. O. Mills Collection; Hynding, *From Frontier to Suburb*, 119.

35. Stanger, *South from San Francisco*, 93–95; 1868 map of San Mateo County, A. S. Easton, County Surveyor, S.M.C., SMCHAA; San Francisco and San Jose Rail Road Company certificates, Box 375, D. O. Mills Collection.

36. Kinnaird, *History*, 2:36–37; Walker, *Country in the City*, 39–41; agreement between D. O. Mills and A. F. Green, January 1, 1865, Box 368, D. O. Mills Collection.

37. Brechin, *Imperial San Francisco*, 41; Wurm and Demoro, *Silver Short Line*, 28–41; "Bank Crowd," in *Online Nevada Encyclopedia*, accessed November 19, 2020, www.onlinenevada.org/articles/bank-crowd; articles of agreement between D. O. Mills and William Sharon, Carson and Colorado Railroad, Box 375, D. O. Mills Collection.

38. Central Pacific Railroad Company mortgages, January 1, 1867, and October 1, 1870, Box 375, D. O. Mills Collection; Hunter, *Partners in Progress*, 34.

39. Karuka's concept of "railroad colonialism" is useful here. He defines it as "territorial expansion through financial logics and corporate organization, using unfree imported laborers, blending the economic and military functions of the state, materializing in construction projects across the colonized world." *Empire's Tracks*, xiv.

40. Karuka, *Empire's Tracks*, 85–86.

41. Beebe and Clegg, *Steamcars to the Comstock*, 11.

42. "Regents of the University of California," University of California History Digital Archives, accessed July 19, 2021, www.lib.berkeley.edu/uchistory/general_history/overview/regents/index.html; Brechin, *Imperial San Francisco*, 282.

43. Hunter, *Partners in Progress*, 27–28, 43; Wilson, *400 California Street*, 22, 33–37; Brechin, *Imperial San Francisco*, 67, 218–21, 334; Igler, *Industrial Cowboys*, 7, 44; "Life of Mr. Mills," *New York Tribune*, January 5, 1910; "Fix Mills Estate Total $36, 227, 391," *New York Times*, April 18, 1914; representative documents from the D.O. Mills Collection: Bank of California circular, box 368; agreement with Oriental Bank Co., January 1, 1866, box 368; deed (January 3, 1877) and livestock sales record (July 28, 1885) with Leonidas B. Benchley, box 368; list of shareholders, n.d., Hayward Petroleum Company, box 369; receipt for shares, San Francisco Pacific Sugar Co., September 1865, box 371; promissory note, Father DeSmet Consolidated Gold Mining, July 6, 1880, box 374; purchase agreements, Quicksilver Mining Company, February 10, 1870, and June 20, 1872, box 374; assessment, White Pine Water Co., 1869, box 374; trust deed, Southern Pacific Railroad, November 1, 1870, box 375; trust mortgage, Southern Pacific Railroad, April 1, 1875, box 375.

44. Brechin, *Imperial San Francisco*, 218–21.

45. Brechin, *Imperial San Francisco*, 41–43.

46. Deverell, *Railroad Crossing*, 35–39.

47. George, *Our Land*, 53, 55, 75.

48. George, *Our Land*, 69–93.

49. Henry George, "The Chinese in California," *New York Tribune*, May 1, 1869.

50. George, "Chinese in California," *New York Tribune*; Chang, "Chinese Railroad Workers," 33.

51. Regnery, "Oldest Railroad Station," 5, 9; Hynding, *From Frontier to Suburb*, 166; Kinnaird, *History*, 2:39–40. Mills contributed his part by serving as Southern Pacific's treasurer for a time.

52. Day, *Alien Capital*, 42.

53. Issel and Cherney, *San Francisco*, 125–30; Saxton, *Indispensable Enemy*, 113–37.

54. Gyory, *Closing the Gate*, 103; "Local Miscellany," *New York Tribune*, December 18, 1877.

55. Stanger, *South from San Francisco*, 107–8; Hynding, *From Frontier to Suburb*, 121, 166; Michael Svanevik, "A Glimpse into D.O. Mills' Life," *San Mateo Times*, February 21, 1986; "Bay Shore," 8.

56. See Chan, *This Bittersweet Soil*, 160–85, for an account of Chinese workers on Delta and Central Valley reclamation projects. Mills may also have been familiar with marsh and tideland reclamation projects in San Francisco, significantly carried out by Irish laborers during the 1850s. See Dillon, "Civilizing Swamps in California," 259, 267–69.

57. "Life of Mr. Mills," *New York Tribune*, January 5, 1910.

58. Brechin, *Imperial San Francisco*, 77–80; Hynding, *From Frontier to Suburb*, 74–77; Svanevik and Burgett, *San Mateo County Chronicles*, 18.

59. Brechin, *Imperial San Francisco*, 84–90; Cross, *Financing an Empire*, 1:401–7; receipt, United States Trust Co. of New York, box 371, D.O. Mills Collection.

60. Brechin, *Imperial San Francisco*, 98–99; Stanger, *South from San Francisco*, 145–51; 1877 map of San Mateo County, J. Cloud, county surveyor, SMCHAA; 1909 map of San Mateo County, J. V. Neuman, county surveyor, SMCHAA, 1927 map of San Mateo County, George Kneese, county surveyor, SMCHAA; "History," City of San Bruno website, accessed March 25, 2022, https://sanbruno.ca.gov/264/History.

61. Mitchell Postell, "The Legacy of a Lost Resource: The History of the Fishing Industry off the San Mateo County Line," unpublished paper, October 1985, 2–9, manuscript file 88-169, SMCHAA; Booker, *Down by the Bay*, 112–16, 119–20, 126, 135–36.

62. Brechin, *Imperial San Francisco*, 33–38, 48–49, 60–61; Booker, *Down by the Bay*, 120–22.

63. Postel, "Legacy," 5–7, 10–16; Booker, *Down by the Bay*, 136–39; "Bay Shore," 4.

64. Postel, "Legacy," 38–41; Booker, *Down by the Bay*, 139–45.

65. Postel, "Legacy," 16–21; Hynding, *From Frontier to Suburb*, 84–85; Chris Carlsson, "Chinese Shrimping Village," *FoundSF*, accessed June 15, 2021, www.foundsf.org/index.php?title=Chinese_shrimping_village.

66. Postel, "Legacy," 21–37; Carlsson, "Chinese Shrimping Village."

67. Postel, "Legacy," 37; Carlsson, "Chinese Shrimping Village."

68. "Mills Divides His Estate among Children," *San Francisco Chronicle*, January 18, 1910; "Millbrae Estate to Be Subdivided," *San Francisco Chronicle*, February 10, 1912; "J. Ogden Mills, Philanthropist, Dead," *San Mateo County Times*, January 29, 1929.

69. Booker, *Down by the Bay*, 145; "Land Deeded to Mills Field," *San Mateo County Times*, December 18, 1935.

70. "The Columbus Group," *Sacramento Daily Union*, December 24, 1883.

CHAPTER 2. MAKING SAN FRANCISCO AIRPORT

1. Arthur L. Price, "Deadly Bomb Drops from Biplane," *San Francisco Call*, January 16, 1911; Flynn, *Men, Money and Mud*, 8–10.

2. Lotchin, *Fortress California*; Lotchin, "City and the Sword"; Lotchin, "Darwinian City"; Lotchin, "Political Culture."

3. Bednarek, *America's Airports*, 14–15, 18–27, 31–32; Edward A. Keogh, "A Brief History of the Air Mail Service of the U.S. Post Office Department (May 15, 1918–August 31, 1927)," Air Mail Pioneers, 1927, www.airmailpioneers.org /content/Sagahistory.htm; H.I. Brock, "Transport by Air Enters a New Stage," *New York Times*, August 29, 1926.

4. "Round-the-Rim Plane Lands at Presidio Field," *San Francisco Chronicle*, October 11, 1919.

5. "Air Gymnastics above City to Be under Ban," *San Francisco Chronicle*, January 30, 1920; "Air Mail Service," *San Francisco Examiner*, February 9, 1925; Paul Freeman, "Montgomery Field / Marina Airfield, San Francisco,

CA," in his "Abandoned and Little-Known Airfields: California: San Francisco Area," accessed April 15, 2021, www.airfields-freeman.com/CA/Airfields_CA_SanFran.htm#marina; Flynn, *Men, Money and Mud,* 11; San Francisco Board of Supervisors, *San Francisco Airport,* 23.

6. Bednarek, *America's Airports,* 44–48; San Francisco Board of Supervisors, *San Francisco Airport,* 9, 23–24; J. Hill, *SFO,* 16.

7. San Francisco Board of Supervisors, *San Francisco Airport,* 9, 11; Gordon, *Naked Airport,* 48–54.

8. Bednarek, *America's Airports,* 62.

9. Brechin, *Imperial San Francisco,* 132–57.

10. Bhimull, *Empire in the Air,* 33–39, 45–64.

11. Van Vleck, *Empire of the Air,* 31–40.

12. Flynn, *Men, Money and Mud,* 13; San Francisco Board of Supervisors, *San Francisco Airport,* 9–12.

13. Scott, *San Francisco Bay Area,* 133–34, 141–47, 188–96; Brechin, *Imperial San Francisco,* 269–70.

14. San Francisco Board of Supervisors, *San Francisco Airport,* 12–13, 16–17; Scott, *San Francisco Bay Area,* 145–46.

15. Scott, *San Francisco Bay Area,* 183; Hynding, *From Frontier to Suburb,* 197–99.

16. San Francisco Board of Supervisors, *San Francisco Airport,* 11–12, 19–21.

17. J. Hill, *SFO,* 17; San Francisco Board of Supervisors, *San Francisco Airport,* 17–21; Bednarek, *America's Airports,* 51–52.

18. Flynn, *Men, Money and Mud,* 15–16; J. Hill, *SFO,* 17–18; San Francisco Board of Supervisors, *San Francisco Airport,* 17–19; "Mills Field at Bay Dedicated," *Los Angeles Times,* May 8, 1927.

19. "Coolidge Lauds Air Trade," *Los Angeles Times,* May 5, 1927.

20. Van Vleck, *Empire of the Air,* 44–47; Bhimull, *Empire in the Air,* 88–95; Bay, *Traveling Black,* 194–95.

21. "Bay City Opens Airport Today," *Los Angeles Times,* August 1, 1927; Hawkins, "James D. Dole," 153–56.

22. Van Vleck, *Empire of the Air,* 53–72; Bhimull, *Empire in the Air,* 110–16; Sampson, *Empires of the Sky,* 44–46; George Wheeler Hinman Jr., "President Coolidge Will Sound Keynote for U.S.," *San Francisco Examiner,* January 15, 1928.

23. J. Hill, *SFO,* 18, 31–32; San Francisco Board of Supervisors, *San Francisco Airport,* 24–28; "Air Mail Row Hits Bay City," *Los Angeles Times,* December 12, 1927.

24. J. Hill, *SFO,* 18–19; Bednarek, *America's Airports,* 67–92.

25. San Francisco Board of Supervisors, *San Francisco Airport,* 31–35, 39, 57–61, 66–70.

26. Mills Field flyer, 1930, "San Francisco Municipal Airport, Mills Field" folder, ephemera files, California Historical Society.

27. San Francisco Board of Supervisors, *San Francisco Airport,* 39–50.

28. San Francisco Board of Supervisors, *San Francisco Airport,* 39–42, 45, 49–50; Kinnaird, *History,* 2:445–46.

29. Flynn, *Men, Money and Mud,* 19–20; San Francisco Board of Supervisors, *San Francisco Airport,* 50–51; Baldwin, *Urgent Importance,* 4, 22–27.

30. Flynn, *Men, Money and Mud,* 20–26; V. Northrop and Doolin, *Preliminary Study,* n.p.

31. Armstrong, *History of Public Works,* 193–94.

32. US Federal Works Agency, *Final Report,* 1–10, 51; Armstrong, *History of Public Works,* 193–194; Bednarek, *America's Airports,* 101–4; Mooser, *Report on Progress,* unpaginated introduction.

33. Armstrong, *History of Public Works,* 193–94; Leighninger, *Long-Term Public Investment,* 36–39, 62–63; Public Works Administration, *First 3 Years,* 2, 17, 33.

34. "New Runway Open at Mills," *San Mateo County Times,* July 24, 1936; "San Francisco Municipal Airport," in V. Northrop and Doolin, *Preliminary Study,* n.p.; L. T. McAfee to A. G. Lang, August 12, 1933, folder B, SFPUC Airport Contract No. 31, SFO Museum; E. G. Cahill to Crocker Estate Company, August 21, 1934, folder B, SFPUC Airport Contract No. 31, SFO Museum; SFPUC, *San Francisco Airport 1937,* 8–10, 13–15, 25–27; J. Hill, *SFO,* 43; Bednarek, *America's Airports,* 98.

35. Unpaginated documents in V. Northrop and Doolin, *Preliminary Study:* "State Aeronautical Program for California, Statistical Summary"; B. M. Doolin to Federal Aviation Commission, November 7, 1934; Vernon D. Northrop to Harry L. Hopkins, FERA, October 31, 1934; Seth E. Howard to Harry L. Hopkins, FERA, November 2, 1934; "San Francisco Municipal Airport."

36. Bednarek, *America's Airports,* 102; J. Smith, *Building New Deal Liberalism,* 114; Drew Pearson and Robert S. Allen, "Washington Merry Go Round," *San Mateo County Times,* September 8, 1936.

37. SFPUC, *San Francisco International Airport 1937,* 25.

38. Lotchin, "Darwinian City"; Lotchin, *Fortress California,* 10–21; Shanken, "How to Celebrate," 49–50.

39. SFPUC, *San Francisco International Airport 1937,* 22–30; Flynn, *Men, Money and Mud,* 29–31; J. Hill, *SFO,* 44–46; "San Mateo to Be Made Terminus for World's Premier Ocean Air Line," *San Mateo County Times,* December 5, 1935.

40. Flynn, *Men, Money and Mud,* 29; SFPUC, *San Francisco International Airport 1937,* 25; Healy, *San Francisco Improved,* 22; Mooser, *Report on Progress,* chart between pp. 158 and 159; "Equipment for Mills Fld. Work," *San Mateo County Times,* December 9, 1935; "Land Deeded to Mills Field," *San Mateo County Times,* December 18, 1935.

41. Gordon, *Naked Airport,* 101–2.

42. Kinnaird, *History,* 2:254–85.

43. McWilliams, Meier, and García, *North from Mexico,* 15–25.

44. Kropp, *California Vieja,* 8. Kropp applies this interpretation to Southern California, but it works well for the North.

45. Singh, *Black Is a Country,* 60–64, 86–88.

46. SFPUC, *San Francisco International Airport 1937,* 7.

47. Van Vleck, *Empire of the Air,* 72–82, 92–97.

48. "San Mateo to Be Made Terminus for World's Premier Ocean Air Line," *San Mateo County Times,* December 5, 1935; "S.F. Selected as Permanent Clipper Base," *San Francisco Examiner,* December 5, 1935.

49. Flynn, *Men, Money and Mud,* 29; SFPUC, *San Francisco International Airport 1937,* 11–13, 21–24.

50. Issel, "New Deal," 69–75; "Traffic Police Quell Mills Field WPA Riot over Delay in Pay," *San Mateo County Times,* March 7, 1936; "Man Shortage Confronts S.M.," *San Mateo County Times,* June 5, 1936.

51. J. Smith, *Building New Deal Liberalism,* 15.

52. A.D. Wilder to E.G. Cahill, December 18, 1933, folder F, Airport Contract No. 31, SFO Museum; Airport Contract No. 31 (July 1934), p. 32, folder B, SFO Museum.

53. Broussard, *Black San Francisco,* 48–49, 113–30; "Dozen Injured in Series of Accidents on Highway," *San Bernardino Sun,* December 1, 1936; Kruman, "Quotas for Blacks," 40–44; Leighninger, *Long-Range Public Investments,* 39; Airport Contract No. 31 (July 1934), p. 31, folder B, SFO Museum; Airport Contract No. 38 (April 1936), pp. x, 27, folder B, SFO Museum; G.H. Reed to SFPUC, June 5, 1936, folder A, Airport Contract No. 38, SFO Museum.

54. Baldwin, *Urgent Importance,* 7, 27–29, 58–61; Shanken, "How to Celebrate," 52–55.

55. Shanken, "How to Celebrate," 55–59, 65–66; Shanken, *Into the Void Pacific,* 26–28, 32–34; Rubens, *1939 San Francisco World's Fair,* 15–20.

56. Shanken, "How to Celebrate," 57, 60–65; Rubens, "1939 San Francisco World's Fair," 18–23; Reinhardt, *Treasure Island,* 36–37; Lawson, *Achievements,* 94; Healy, *San Francisco Improved,* 16, 52–53; "Shoals Get PWA Airport Fund," *San Mateo County Times,* September 30, 1935.

57. "County Move Under Way to Acquire Port," *San Mateo County Times,* August 2, 1935; "San Mateo to Be Made Terminus for World's Premier Ocean Air Line," *San Mateo County Times,* December 5, 1935.

58. SFPUC, *San Francisco International Airport 1937,* 9–10; J. Hill, *SFO,* 57; Armstrong, *History of Public Works,* 194.

59. SFPUC, *Report,* fiscal year 1939–40, 189.

60. American Municipal Association, *Airports,* 1–2; Armstrong, *History of Public Works,* 195; Bednarek, *America's Airports,* 118–20.

61. Armstrong, *History of Public Works,* 190, 193–96; Bednarek, *America's Airports,* 120–21; Public Works Administration, *America Builds,* 191–92.

62. "Spend Bill Gives S.M. 6 Million," *San Mateo County Times,* June 22, 1938; Flynn, *Men, Money and Mud,* 30–32; Hill, *SFO,* 46.

63. SFPUC, *Report,* fiscal year 1939–40, 5; Flynn, *Men, Money and Mud,* 32–34.

64. Lawson, *Achievements,* 94.

65. Rubens, "1939 San Francisco World's Fair," 91–95, 107–9, 112–20; J. Hill, *SFO,* 56.

66. Rubens, "1939 San Francisco World's Fair," 48–90; Shanken, *Into the Void Pacific,* 10–25, 94–107, 148–77; Schrenk, "Visions of Progress," 78. The Rivera mural, better known as *Pan American Unity,* resides at City College of

San Francisco. "*Pan American Unity*," CCSF Diego Rivera website, accessed April 1, 2018, www.ccsf.edu/en/about-city-college/diego-rivera-mural.html.

67. J. Hill, *SFO,* 56; Reinhardt, *Treasure Island,* 133, 140–41; Rubens, "1939 San Francisco World's Fair," 86–87.

68. SFPUC, Report, fiscal year 1939–40, 189–90.

69. J. Smith, *Building New Deal Liberalism,* 201–10; Bednarek, *America's Airports,* 153–63; US Federal Works Agency, *Final Report,* 51.

70. Van Vleck, *Empire of the Air,* 106–118.

71. SFPUC, *Report,* fiscal year 1939–40, 120, and *Report,* fiscal year 1940–41, 5–6, 121, 209; "History: Treasure Island Naval Base." Former Bases, website, accessed April 11, 2018, www.formerbases.com/cal_no_treasureisland_history.htm.

72. SFPUC, *Report,* fiscal year 1941–42, 124–25; "Treasure Island Accord," *San Francisco News,* March 19, 1942, www.sfmuseum.net/hist9/tilease.html; "Treasure Isle Goes to Navy," *San Francisco News,* April 17, 1942, www.sfmuseum.net/hist9/tiseizure.html; Lotchin, *Fortress California,* 139–40.

73. SFPUC, *Report,* fiscal year 1942–43, 199, 202, and *Report,* fiscal year 1943–44, 107, 189, 193–95; J. Hill, *SFO,* 61; Flynn, *Men, Money and Mud,* 36–37; Lotchin, *Fortress California,* 139–40; Kinnard, *History,* 2:400–403.

74. SFPUC, *Report,* fiscal year 1943–44, 193–95; Flynn, *Men, Money and Mud,* 37.

75. SFPUC, *Report,* fiscal year 1944–45, 216–20, *Report,* fiscal year 1942–43, 202, and *Report,* fiscal year 1943–44, 195.

76. J. Hill, *SFO,* 52, 62; SFPUC, *Report,* fiscal year 1941–42, 206, *Report,* fiscal year 1942–43, 4, and *Report,* fiscal year 1944–45, 188, 190.

77. SFPUC, *Report,* fiscal year 1941–42, 206, 210–11, 217, *Report,* fiscal year 1943–44, 198–201, and *Report,* fiscal year 1944–45, 191–92; Flynn, *Men, Money and Mud,* 36–38.

78. SFPUC, *Report,* fiscal year 1944–45, 183–88; SFPUC, *Proposed Expansion Program*; SFPUC, *Factual Data.* Plans for moving the Bayshore had been under way for some time. See "$2,000,000 for Airport Sought," *San Mateo County Times,* June 4, 1942; "New Bayshore Route Favored," *San Mateo County Times,* August 19, 1943.

79. SFPUC, *Report,* fiscal year 1944–45, 183–85; SFPUC, *Proposed Expansion Program,* 1.

80. Flynn, *Men, Money and Mud,* 40–43; Lotchin, *Fortress California,* 163–64; Issel, "New Deal," 75–85.

CHAPTER 3. OF FIGHTING PLANES AND FLOWERS

1. "9000 Employed at Airport," *San Mateo Times,* August 25, 1954; SFPUC, *Report,* fiscal year 1953–54, 44–45.

2. Gordon, *Naked Airport,* 141–214; Bloom, *Metropolitan Airport,* 63–96.

3. SFPUC, *Report,* fiscal year 1954–55, 9.

4. Scott, *San Francisco Bay Area,* 271–309.

5. "So That Those Who Have Built It May Enjoy It . . . " (advertisement), *San Mateo Times,* August 25, 1954; "San Francisco International Airport Terminal Dedication and Flight Festival Program," *San Mateo Times,* August 25, 1954; "'See the World' at Flight Festival Friday," *San Mateo Times,* August 25, 1954; Stan Wiseman, "338,000 Counted at Air Fete Closing," *San Mateo Times,* August 30, 1954.

6. "Gov. Knight to Dedicate New Air Terminal," *San Mateo Times,* August 25, 1954; "San Francisco International Airport Terminal Dedication and Flight Festival Program," *San Mateo Times,* August 25, 1954; photo, "San Francisco International Airport (SFO), Terminal Building Dedication, United Air Lines," 1954, SFO Museum Aviation Collection, www.sfomuseum.org/aviation-museum-library/collection/14850.

7. Bay Area Census, "San Francisco Bay Area, Decennial Census Data, 1950–1960," www.bayareacensus.ca.gov/bayarea50.htm. The exact figure per the census was 91.6 percent white (80.7 percent "native" and 10.9 percent foreign-born). This total did include 5 percent of the population described using the contemporary census category of "white persons with a Spanish surname."

8. See, for example, two photos, both titled "San Francisco International Airport (SFO), Terminal Building Dedication, United Air Lines," 1954, SFO Museum Aviation Collection, www.sfomuseum.org/aviation-museum-library/collection/14862, and www.sfomuseum.org/aviation-museum-library/collection/14873.

9. Record, *Minority Groups,* 10.

10. Jenkins, *Bonds of Inequality.*

11. J. Hill, *SFO,* 80–81.

12. "8 Queens Set for Fete Friday," *San Mateo Times,* August 25, 1954.

13. Barry, *Femininity in Flight,* 114–15.

14. "San Francisco International Airport Terminal Dedication and Flight Festival Program," *San Mateo Times,* August 25, 1954.

15. US Coast Guard, "Coast Guard Air Station San Francisco," accessed January 18, 2021, www.pacificarea.uscg.mil/Our-Organization/District-11/District-Units/Air-Station-San-Francisco/.

16. SFPUC, *Report,* fiscal year 1949–50, 29, *Report,* fiscal year 1950–51, 25, and *Report,* fiscal year 1951–52, 25.

17. Van Vleck, *Empire of the Air,* 179.

18. Gordon, *Naked Airport,* 142; Van Vleck, *Empire of the Air,* 202.

19. "San Francisco International Airport Terminal Dedication and Flight Festival Program," *San Mateo Times,* August 25, 1954.

20. Gordon, *Naked Airport,* 142; Van Vleck, *Empire of the Air,* 201–02; Bednarek, *America's Airports,* 166–70.

21. SFPUC, *Report,* fiscal year 1945–46, 199, *Report,* fiscal year 1947–48, 123, *Report,* fiscal year 1948–49, 128, 130, and *Report,* fiscal year 1949–50, 29; "World War II Boosted S.F. Airport into 'Major League' Status," *San Francisco News,* August 25, 1954; Flynn, *Men, Money and Mud,* 46–48.

22. SFPUC, *Report,* fiscal year 1949–50, 37; 1949 Air Fair brochure, SF International Airport, Fairs and Exhibitions ephemera file, San Francisco History Room.

23. 1949 Air Fair brochure.

24. Armstrong, *History of Public Works*, 196–97; Bednarek, *America's Airports*, 170–77.

25. SFPUC, *Report*, fiscal year 1954–55, 11.

26. Van Vleck, *Empire of the Air*, 167–98.

27. SFPUC, *Factual Data*, 6; SFPUC, *Proposed Expansion Program*, 5; SFPUC, *Report*, fiscal year 1949–50, 30; Lotchin, *Fortress California*, 252.

28. Scott, *San Francisco Bay Area*, 258–63; Lotchin, *Fortress California*, 155–56, 166–68.

29. Bay Area Airport Planning Group, *Airport Plan*, i–xi, 9, 18.

30. SFPUC, *Report*, fiscal year 1949–50, 35, and *Report*, fiscal year 1950–51, 30.

31. Lotchin, *Fortress California*, 252–53; SFPUC, *Report*, fiscal year 1948–49, 130, 133; Flynn, *Men, Money and Mud*, 49–50.

32. "Congratulations City and County of San Francisco" (advertisement), *San Mateo Times*, August 25, 1954.

33. "An Invitation to the Residents of San Mateo County from the City and County of San Francisco" (advertisement), *San Mateo Times*, August 25, 1954.

34. "S.F. Airport Festival," *San Francisco Examiner*, July 19, 1954; "S. Mateo AFL'ers Are Named to S.F. Airport Dedication," *San Mateo County Union Gazette*, August 13, 1954; "S.M. Labor Chiefs Aid Airport Fete," *San Mateo Times*, August 25, 1954.

35. "Gateway to Millions," *San Mateo Times*, August 26, 1954.

36. "San Francisco International Airport Terminal Dedication and Flight Festival Program," *San Mateo Times*, August 25, 1954; "Plan S.M. Floral Greetings," *San Mateo Times*, August 25, 1954; "Gateway to Millions," *San Mateo Times*, August 26, 1954; "338,000 Counted at Air Fete Closing," *San Mateo Times*, August 30, 1954; Will Stevens, "338,000 Turn Out for Last Airport Show," *San Francisco Examiner*, August 30, 1954.

37. "200,000 Free Flowers for Visitors," *San Francisco Examiner*, August 27, 1954.

38. "Airborne Freight First in Flower Flight Move," *San Mateo Times*, August 25, 1954; Bloom, *Metropolitan Airport*, 48–49; "S.F., L.A. Fight for Continental Airport Traffic," *San Mateo Times*, August 25, 1954; Snow, *Air Freight Forwarding*, 487; Flynn, *Men, Money and Mud*, 59–60; Airborne Flower and Freight, Inc. advertisement, *San Mateo Times*, August 25, 1954.

39. Van Vleck, *Empire of the Air*, 215–17, 248–52, 259–60; Gordon, *Naked Airport*, 155–62 "PAA Credit Plan Spreads Sept. 15," *San Mateo Times*, August 25, 1954; "'See the World' at Flight Festival Friday," *San Mateo Times*, August 25, 1954.

40. "9000 Employed at Airport," *San Mateo Times*, August 25, 1954.

41. "United Airlines Story of Flight Progress in U.S.," *San Mateo Times*, August 25, 1954.

42. Chinn, Lai, and Choy, *History of the Chinese*, 60–61; Hynding, *From Frontier to Suburb*, 191.

43. "Gateway to Millions," *San Mateo Times,* August 26, 1954; SFPUC, *San Francisco International Airport* (pamphlet), "San Francisco International Airport" ephemera file, California Historical Society.

44. "Pan-Am Moving into Air Terminal," *San Mateo Times,* August 25, 1954.

45. "Airport Story Told in Book Form at Fete," *San Mateo Times,* August 25, 1954; Flynn, *Men, Money and Mud,* 54–56.

46. "Floor-by-Floor Tour of Terminal," *San Mateo Times,* August 25, 1954; SFPUC, *Report,* fiscal year 1949–50, 35, and *Report,* fiscal year 1953–54, 38–39; SFPUC, February 23, 1950, meeting minutes, PUC 2/1950 to 7/1950 folder, WP Day Collection, California Historical Society.

47. Flynn, *Men, Money and Mud,* 38; SFPUC, *Report,* fiscal year 1947–48, 75; Scott, *San Francisco Bay Area,* 281–83.

48. "Standard Supplies Airport Gasoline," *San Mateo Times,* August 25, 1954; SFPUC, *Report,* fiscal year 1953–54, 39–40, 43.

49. SFPUC, *Report,* fiscal year 1952–53, 31; Scott, *San Francisco Bay Area,* 278–80; Kinnaird, *History,* 2:509–12.

50. SFPUC, *Report,* fiscal year 1948–49, 135, 139.

51. SFPUC, February 23, 1950, meeting minutes, PUC 2/1950 to 7/1950 folder, WP Day Collection, California Historical Society.

52. Flynn, *Men, Money and Mud,* 46; Simard, "Portion of Bayshore Freeway," 12.

53. "338,000 Counted at Air Fete Closing," *San Mateo Times,* August 30, 1954.

54. Bloom, *Metropolitan Airport,* 106–9; Gordon, *Naked Airport,* 189.

55. Will Stevens, "30,000 See Great Airport Dedicated," *San Francisco Examiner,* August 28, 1954.

56. SFPUC, *Report,* fiscal year 1951–52, 26; President's Airport Commission, *Airport and Its Neighbors,* iii–vii, 45–47, 101–9; Bednarek, *Airports, Cities,* 155–56.

57. Van Vleck, *Empire of the Air,* 206–8; Lotchin, *Fortress California,* 245–46.

58. Boeing, "B-47 Stratojet," accessed September 3, 2021, www.boeing.com/history/products/b-47-stratojet.page; Mike Lombardi, "Why 7's Been a Lucky Number," *Frontiers Online* 2, no. 10 (March 2004), www.boeing.com/news/frontiers/archive/2004/february/i_history.html.

59. J. Hill, *SFO,* 73.

CHAPTER 4. A BLACK FUTURE IN THE AIR INDUSTRY?

1. Birney Jarvis, "Skycaps Arrest United Executive," *San Francisco Chronicle,* July 11, 1970; "Judge Continues Air Arrest Case," *San Francisco Chronicle,* July 14, 1970; "Unfriendly Skies Fall over United," *Sun Reporter,* July 18, 1970. The idea for the citizen's arrest was suggested by the skycaps' attorney, Aubrey Grossman, a well-known and outspoken Bay Area civil rights and labor lawyer.

2. "Court Throws Out Skycap Case," *San Francisco Examiner,* July 17, 1970.

3. H. Northrup, Thieblot, and Chernish, *Negro,* 58–59.

4. Kelley, *Race Rebels,* 55–75; Bay, *Traveling Black;* Ortlepp, *Jim Crow Terminals.*

5. Gilroy, *Darker than Blue,* 4–54.

6. Influencing the analysis in this regard are studies that look at the interfaces of civil rights and Black Power struggles with municipal policy making, labor organizing, entrepreneurial endeavors, community development projects, and affirmative action programs. See, for example, Self, *American Babylon;* L. Hill and Rabig, *Business of Black Power;* Goldberg and Griffey, *Black Power at Work;* Weems, *Desegregating the Dollar.*

7. Dellums, *International President,* 97–99; Broussard, *Black San Francisco,* 133–65.

8. H. Northrup, Thieblot, and Chernish, *Negro,* 13–14, 17–27, 50, 61–64; Bay, *Traveling Black,* 196–206.

9. Broussard, *Black San Francisco,* 204–10; Murch, *Living for the City,* 37–40; Crowe, *Prophets of Rage,* 24–27, 39–40, 53–57; Miller, *Postwar Struggle,* 2–3; Self, *American Babylon,* 82–87; Record, *Minority Group,* 15–18; Lang, *Grassroots at the Gateway,* 132.

10. H. Northrup, Thieblot, and Chernish, *Negro,* 62–63; Bay, *Traveling Black,* 205–9; Babow and Howden, *Civil Rights Inventory,* 26–28, 101–2, 117–24, 146–47; Schafran, *Road to Resegregation,* 138.

11. "First with Airlines," *Jet,* May 1956, 6; "Discrimination by Major Airlines in Flight Capacity Employment," *NAIRO Reporter,* February 1956, 3; "US Airlines and Racial Discrimination," *NAIRO Reporter,* October 1957, 3; "Employment: Fair Employment Laws—New York," *Race Relations Law Reporter,* June 1958, 502–3; "Mich. Negro Pilot Accuses Airline of Bias," *Jet,* May 22, 1958, 29; H. Northrup, Thieblot, and Chernish, *Negro,* 30–31, 34–35; Broussard, *Black San Francisco,* 212; Crowe, *Prophets of Rage,* 103–105; Miller, *Postwar Struggle,* 22, 30; Babow and Howden, *Civil Rights Inventory,* 303–5; Schiller, *Forging Rivals,* 82–83, 111–12.

12. Babow and Howden, *Civil Rights Inventory,* 276.

13. Untitled photo, July 1958, *The Shield,* 17; Gene Robertson, "On the Beam," *Wing Tips,* July 1959, 12; "TWA Hires Negro in Personnel Spot," *Amsterdam News,* August 31, 1957; "Plinton Serves as Professional Liaison," *Negro History Bulletin,* February 1958, 118; "People Make the Difference," *The Shield,* October–November 1957, n.p.

14. Ortlepp, *Jim Crow Terminals,* 36–60; Bay, *Traveling Black,* 268–305.

15. Self, *American Babylon,* 180–82.

16. Joseph L. Howerton, "Statement before the Finance Committee," May 26, 1967, container 23, folder 38, National Association for the Advancement of Colored People, Region I, Records, BANC MSS 78/180 c, Bancroft Library, University of California, Berkeley (hereafter cited as NAACP Region I Records).

17. "Public Leaseholders vs. Fair Employment," *Sun Reporter,* July 30, 1960; Thomas C. Fleming, "Weekly Report," *Sun Reporter,* December 9, 1961.

18. Mary Ellen Rose, "UC Students Picket Employment Offices," *Sun Reporter,* May 4–11, 1961. Blake later coauthored Huey P. Newton's autobiog-

raphy, *Revolutionary Suicide,* and was founding provost of Oakes College at UC Santa Cruz. For more on his activism at UC Berkeley, see Murch, *Living for the City,* 76, 83.

19. Bill Sherman, "NALC Charges Discrimination by United Airlines," *Sun Reporter,* September 28, 1963.

20. John F. Kennedy, Executive Order 10925—Establishing the President's Committee on Equal Employment Opportunity, March 6, 1961, American Presidency Project, www.presidency.ucsb.edu/documents/executive-order-10925-establishing-the-presidents-committee-equal-employment-opportunity.

21. H. Northrup, Thieblot, and Chernish, *Negro,* 37–38; Bay, *Traveling Black,* 282–83; Orenic, *On the Ground,* 166.

22. "Plans for Progress Plan Announced," *The Shield,* December 1964, 4–6.

23. H. Northrup, Thieblot, and Chernish, *Negro,* 38–41, 47–48, 53–59.

24. Barry, *Femininity in Flight,* 115–116; "New Yorker to Testify at Airline Bias Probe," *Jet,* June 1957, 10; "TWA Hires First Negro Flight Hostess," *New York State Commission against Discrimination Newsletter,* June 1958, 1, 3; "Employment: Airlines—New York," *Race Relations Law Reporter,* Spring 1960, 263–80; "Hire Negro Flight Personnel, Capital Lines Ordered," *Jet,* March 24, 1960, 4.

25. H. Northrup, Thieblot, and Chernish, *Negro,* 50; Murch, *Living for the City,* 37.

26. Barry, *Femininity in Flight,* 117; H. Northrup, Thieblot, and Chernish, *Negro,* 51; George Dacres to Leonard H. Carter, October 18, 1963, plus attachment, container 104, folder 29, NAACP Region I Records.

27. Classified advertisements, *Sun Reporter,* January 11, May 2, May 9, and May 23, 1964.

28. "UAL Seeks Stewardesses," *Sun Reporter,* February 20, 1965; advertisement, *Sun Reporter,* April 24, 1965.

29. Leonard H. Carter to Samuel Jackson, April 1, 1966, Carter to Edward Howden, April 1, 1966, and George Holland to Carter, April 19, 1966, all in container 104, folder 36, NAACP Region I Records.

30. H.K. Schlinker to NAACP Regional Office, San Francisco, April 27, 1966, container 104, folder 29, NAACP Region I Records.

31. H. Northrup, Thieblot, and Chernish, *Negro,* 105–6; Ortlepp, *Jim Crow Terminals,* 6–7; Weems, *Desegregating the Dollar,* 70–79.

32. L. Hill and Rabig, *Business of Black Power,* 3.

33. "Negro Named Director of Special TWA Markets," *Jet,* July 30, 1964, 48; "Profiles in Print," *The Shield,* April 1965, n.p.; front cover, *The Shield,* June 1967; "Her Dream Came True," *The Shield,* March 1968, 4–5; "Annual Meeting of Stockholders," *The Shield,* May 1968, 8–9.

34. Barry, *Femininity in Flight,* 117–18.

35. Van Vleck, *Empire of the Air,* 259–61.

36. "City's Minority Coalition Makes Recommendation," *Sun Reporter,* February 29, 1964; Thomas Fleming, "Mayor to Ask Supervisors for Human Rights Commission," *Sun Reporter,* March 7, 1964; "An Auspicious Beginning," *Sun Reporter,* March 28, 1964; "Supervisors to Vote on Human Rights

Commission," *Sun Reporter,* May 30, 1964; San Francisco Human Rights Commission (hereafter SFHRC), *Annual Report,* no. 1, September 1965, 1–11; Schiller, *Forging Rivals,* 161–63.

37. Advertisements, *Sun Reporter,* October 29, 1966; Jenkins, *Bonds of Inequality,* 135–38.

38. "Statement before the Finance Committee of the Board of Supervisors of the City and County of Francisco, Joseph L. Howerton, Field Director, West Coast Region, NAACP," May 26, 1967, NAACP Region I Records, container 23, folder 38.

39. For a discussion of the uprising, see Dunn-Salahuddin, "Forgotten Community."

40. SFHRC, *Annual Report,* no. 2, September 2, 1965, to September 2, 1966, 8–12; Schiller, *Forging Rivals,* 163–88.

41. "Negroes in Public Utilities," *Sun Reporter,* June 10, 1967.

42. "Negroes in Public Utilities," *Sun Reporter;* "NAACP's Doubts on Airport Bonds," *San Francisco Chronicle,* July 4, 1967; George Rhodes, "City PUC to Establish an Equal Hiring Officer," *San Francisco Examiner,* July 19, 1967; "NAACP Council Presents PUC with 12 Conditions on Airport Bond Issue," *Sun Reporter,* July 29, 1967; "It's Still No! on Airport Bonds," *Sun Reporter,* August 26, 1967; SFHRC, *Annual Report,* no. 3, September 1966 to September 1967, 6–7; advertisement, *Sun Reporter,* October 21, 1967.

43. "Carlton Goodlett, Negro Leader, Announces Opposition to Bond Measure," *San Francisco Chronicle,* September 16, 1967; "Vote No! on A" and advertisement, *Sun Reporter,* November 4, 1967; Schiller, *Forging Rivals,* 182–85; Guthrie, "Examining Political Narratives," 286–372.

44. SFHRC, *Annual Report,* no. 3, September 1966 to September 1967, 6; SFHRC, *Meeting Minutes,* May 9, 1968, 2–3; SFHRC, *Annual Report,* no. 4, January 1968 to January 1969, 7–9; Schiller, *Forging Rivals,* 163–88; "Annual Meeting of Stockholders," *The Shield,* May 1968, 8–9; Robert L. Fienberg, "New Lifeline for the Disadvantaged," *The Shield,* June 1968, 3–4; Robert L. Fienberg, "Building a Bridge of Understanding," *The Shield,* August 1968, 12–13.

45. Leonard Carter to John Soltys, May 2, 1968, container 105, box 47, NAACP Region I Records; G.B. Koch to Carter (plus attachment) May 22, 1968, container 105, box 47, NAACP Region I Records; Leonard Carter to D.N. Waite (plus attachment), May 25, 1968, container 27, box 15, NAACP Region I Records; SFHRC, *Annual Report,* no. 4, January 1968 to January 1969, 7–9, and *Annual Report,* no. 5, January 1969 to January 1970, 4–5; "Airlines Hiring More Minorities," *Sun Reporter,* July 5, 1969.

46. SFHRC, *Annual Report,* no. 5, January 1969 to January 1970, 5, *Annual Report,* no. 6, January 1970 to January 1971, 13, and *Annual Report,* no. 7, January 1971 to January 1972, 10; H. Northrup, Thieblot, and Chernish, *Negro,* 69–106.

47. SFHRC, *Annual Report,* no. 4, January 1968 to January 1969, 8–9, and *Annual Report,* no. 6, January 1970 to January 1971, 13.

48. SFHRC, *Meeting Minutes,* June 10, 1982, 7; Scipio Porter, interview by Eric Porter, May 13, 2012; "Fleet Service Layoff at United," *Sun Reporter,* April 4, 1970; "I Heard That," *Sun Reporter,* September 29, 1977.

49. "Your Visit," *The Shield,* October and November 1967, 20; "Your Visit," *The Shield,* June 1969, 20–21; "Goals for 1970 Set," *The Shield,* February 1970, 3–5; "A $3.8 Million Problem, Pt. 2," *The Shield,* April 1970, 3–4; "1970: Year of the Red Ink," *The Shield,* November–December 1970, 3–5; Ken Bracken, "'People Power' in Action," *The Shield,* November–December 1970, 6; "United to Consider Layoffs," *Sun Reporter,* April 11, 1970; Ronald Stevens and Bettina Aptheker, "The Unfriendly Skies of United," *People's World,* September 5, 1970.

50. Almena Lomax, "Save Skycaps, Airlines Asked," *San Francisco Examiner,* April 2, 1970; Gary Dungan, "Friendly Skies of United May Fall," *Sun Reporter,* May 23, 1970.

51. "Fleet Service Layoff," *Sun Reporter;* George Rhodes, "City PUC to Establish an Equal Hiring Officer," *San Francisco Examiner,* July 19, 1967; "Skycap Shift Irks Blacks," *San Francisco Examiner,* April 10, 1970.

52. "Skycaps Fights: United Firm on Layoffs," *Sun Reporter,* April 18, 1970.

53. "$2.5 Million Skycaps' Suit," *San Francisco Examiner,* June 5, 1970; "United to Consider Layoffs," *Sun Reporter;* "Skycaps Fights," *Sun Reporter;* Dungan, "Friendly Skies," *Sun Reporter;* Jarvis, "Skycaps Arrest United Executive," *Sun Reporter.*

54. United Airlines SFO Employment Chart, July 1972, NAACP Region I Records, container 15, folder 33.

55. "Black Airline Employee Group for Personal, Community Gains," *California Voice,* June 8, 1972.

56. Schiller, *Forging Rivals,* 193–219.

57. United Airlines Black Caucus, "What the UABC Stands For," *Black Caucus Speaks* 1, no. 2 (February 1973); United Airlines Black Caucus, "BCS Probes Racism at SFOMB," *Black Caucus Speaks* 1, no. 3 (March–April 1973).

58. Black Caucus of TWA Employees, Bylaws, "Caucus Minutes, By-Laws, etc." folder, Materials relating to the TWA Black Caucus, [ca. 1960–ca. 1980], BANC MSS 85/138 c, Bancroft Library, University of California, Berkeley (cited hereafter as Black Caucus of TWA Papers).

59. "A Report to Management: Grievances of the Black Caucus of T.W.A. Employees," November 1968, container 27, folder 15, NAACP Region I Records.

60. R. V. Raine to Don Roberson, January 27, 1970, plus attachment, "TWA (Genl.)" folder, Black Caucus of TWA Papers; TWA Black Caucus to R. V. Raine, June 16, 1970, "TWA Minutes" folder, Black Caucus of TWA Papers; TWA meeting minutes, August 3, 1970, and October 1, 1970, "TWA Minutes" folder, Black Caucus of TWA Papers; R. D. Richmond, "Black Caucus 'Rap Session,'" March 1, 1971, "TWA Minutes" folder, Black Caucus of TWA Papers; Gary Duncan, "Racism at TWA," *Sun Reporter,* February 21, 1970.

61. EEOC, San Francisco, "Regional Director's Findings of Fact," November 30, 1970, "Caucus vs. TWA (Suit)" folder, Black Caucus of TWA Papers.

62. William Bennett Turner to Charles Stephen Ralston, February 9, 1971, box 125, folder 8, Herbert Hill Papers, Library of Congress (hereafter cited as Herbert Hill Papers); "Black Employees Sue TWA—'Discrimination,'" *San Francisco Chronicle,* March 9, 1971; "TWA Sued by Black Employees," *Sun*

Reporter, March 13, 1971; complaint, *Black Caucus of TWA Employees et al. v. Trans World Airlines, Inc.,* box 125, folder 8, Herbert Hill Papers.

63. NAACP Legal Defense and Educational Fund, San Francisco, press release, March 8, 1971, box 125, folder 8, Herbert Hill Papers.

64. Sources in the Herbert Hill Papers, box 125, folder 8: William Bennett Turner to William L. Robinson and Prof. Albert J. Rosenthal, May 18, 1971; Turner to Jack Greenberg et al., May 19, 1971; Turner to Robinson, September 15, 1971; Turner to Robinson, February 16, 1972. Sources in the "Caucus Minutes, By-Laws, etc." folder, Black Caucus of TWA Papers: Jack Carmichael to R. V. Raine, March 23, 1971; Raine to Carmichael, April 1, 1971; Black Caucus meeting minutes for November 16, 1970, August 17, 1972, August 23, 1972, December 21, 1972, and January 4, 1973.

65. Docket sheet, C 71 437 AJZ, *Black Caucus of TWA Employees et al. v. Trans World Airlines,* in author's possession; draft consent decree, *Black Caucus of TWA Employees et al. v. Trans World Airlines,* "Caucus vs. TWA (Suit)" folder, Black Caucus of TWA Papers; Donald D. Connors to R. R. Fletcher, March 2, 1972, "Caucus Material from In-House" folder, Black Caucus of TWA Papers; Dennis M. Sullivan to D. J. Crombie, March 28, 1972, and Sullivan to B. M. Fox, July 18, 1972, "TWA Confidential" folder, Black Caucus of TWA Papers.

66. T. Anderson, *Pursuit of Fairness,* 124–129; Weiss, *"We Want Jobs,"* 144–149; Schiller, *Forging Rivals,* 236.

67. Dennis M. Sullivan to B. M. Fox, November 9, 1972, "Caucus Material from In-House" folder, Black Caucus of TWA Papers.

68. "Interview," *The Shield,* March 1971, 8–10; documents from container 15, folder 33, NAACP Region I Records: EEO Bulletin from UAL Maintenance Operations Division; "1972 Affirmative Action Plan for San Francisco"; "1972 Affirmative Action Plan for San Francisco Maintenance Base Complex."

69. Correspondence from container 15, folder 33, NAACP Region I Records: Leonard Carter to Edward E. Carlson, May 12, 1972; Carlson to Carter, May 30, 1972; Guy London to Carter, June 1, 1972; Guy London to Carter, June 8, 1972; Al Cross to Carter, June 13, 1972; Carter to London, June 30, 1972; Carter to Cross, June 30, 1972; London to Carter, July 14, 1972; Carter to William H. Hastie Jr., August 21, 1972, with attached memorandum (Delores A. Isaac, "United Airlines Affirmative Action Plan"); Hastie to Carter, March 12, 1973.

70. "An Open Letter to United Airlines' Black Employees," *Sun Reporter,* October 28, 1972.

71. William H. Hastie Jr., "Memorandum Re: Possible Affirmative Action," container 15, folder 33, NAACP Region I Records.

72. Airlines' Minority Employees' Association statement (1972), "Black Caucus Corresp." folder, Black Caucus of TWA Papers. The politics around such tokenism were taken up in Sam Greenlee's 1969 novel about a black CIA agent-turned-revolutionary, *The Spook Who Sat by the Door,* which was made into a film in 1973.

73. Leonard Carter to Edward E. Carlson, May 12, 1972 and Carlson to Carter, May 30, 1972, container 15, folder 33, NAACP Region I Records.

74. "Travel Industry Blacks: Fight Airline Ripoff," *Sun Reporter,* July 15, 1972.

75. John Dorsey to Carl Hughes (plus attachment), March 22, 1972, "Jim" folder, Black Caucus of TWA Papers; "United Air Has: Something Special," *Sun Reporter,* July 1, 1972; United Airlines to Leonard Carter, undated, container 15, folder 33, NAACP Region I Records.

76. Leonard Carter to David Rose, December 8, 1972, Rose to Carter, April 26, 1973, and Carter to Rose, May 7, 1973, all in container 15, folder 33, NAACP Region I Records; "Major Airlines Named in Discrimination Suit," *Sun Reporter,* May 5, 1973.

77. Complaint, *United States of America v. United Air Lines et al.,* container 15, folder 33, NAACP Region I Records; Hansen and Oster, *Taking Flight,* 117; "Major Airlines Named in Discrimination Suit," *Sun Reporter.*

78. "Operation Bootstrap Seeks to Improve Communication," *Friendly Times,* December 1973, 3; "Affirmative Action Scorecard," *The Shield,* December 1973, 5–7; "United Pushes 1974 Affirmative Action Program," *The Shield,* June 1974, n.p.

79. Hansen and Oster, *Taking Flight,* 117–18; "Here's a Summary of Provisions in United/EEOC Court Decree," *Friendly Times,* June 1976, 8–9; "Affirmative Action Results Are Good," *Friendly Times,* April 4, 1979, 3.

80. Marian Fay, "S.F. Airport Garage—Racial Minorities Get Foothold in Big Business," *Sun Reporter,* December 6, 1969; Frank K. Laurent to Robert L. Goldman, November 11, 1971, Carlton B. Goodlett Papers, Manuscript Division, Moorland-Springarn Research Center, Howard University (hereafter cited as Goodlett Papers).

81. "The Examiner's Crusade against Airport Parking," *Sun Reporter,* October 11, 1969; correspondence from Goodlett Papers: Paul E. Boas to Frank K. Laurent, December 26, 1968; George F. Hansen to Laurent, June 10, 1969; Hansen to Laurent, July 2, 1969; Hansen to Laurent, August 19, 1969; Laurent to Hansen, August 26, 1969; Paul E. Boas to Laurent, September 5, 1969; Hansen to Laurent, September 30, 1969; Carlton B. Goodlett to Hansen, October 6, 1969; Hansen to Collins, Goodlett, Laurent, and Luster, October 28, 1969; Goodlett to Hansen (three letters), October 30, 1969; Hiram L. Pittman to Goodlett, Luster, Laurent, and Collins, December 3, 1969; Charles Boyd to Hansen, April 17, 1970.

82. "Race or Reason," *Sun Reporter,* February 6, 1971; "Airports Unit Backs Flights to China," *San Francisco Chronicle,* May 5, 1971; "S.F. Airport Parking," *Sun Reporter,* August 21, 1971; "The *Chronicle* Pushes the Big Lie," *Sun Reporter,* August 28, 1971; "Nailing Down a $100,000 Lie," *Sun Reporter,* September 4, 1971; Thomas C. Fleming, "City Files Suit against Parking Operators," *Sun Reporter,* September 4, 1971; "Goodlett & Co. Loses Airport Parking Bid," *Sun Reporter,* September 18, 1971; "The Grand Jury Farce," *Sun Reporter,* January 15, 1972; correspondence from Goodlett Papers: James K. Carr to Goodlett, Luster, Laurent, and Collins, February 18, 1971; Frank K. Laurent to Carr, February 26, 1971, March 4, 1971, March 15, 1971, March 18, 1971, March 24, 1971; George F. Hansen to Laurent, March 26, 1971; Laurent to Roy Samuels, April 7, 1971; Carlton B. Goodlett to William E.

Dacus, July 23, 1971; A. Cecil Williams to Dacus, August 29, 1971; Mildred Goodman to Carr, October 20, 1971.

83. "S.F. Airport Parking," *Sun Reporter*; "Race or Reason," *Sun Reporter*; "Alioto's Black Leadership," *Sun Reporter*, November 6, 1971; "Grand Jury Farce," *Sun Reporter*; "Alioto's Troubles at Home," *Sun Reporter*, July 24, 1972; Carlton B. Goodlett to James K. Carr, August 9, 1971, Goodlett Papers.

84. SFHRC, *Annual Report*, no. 6, January 1970 to January 1971, 1–5, 15; SFHRC, *Meeting Minutes*, October 4, 1973, 2–3; Schiller, *Forging Rivals*, esp. 251–55.

85. SFHRC, *Meeting Minutes*, November 9, 1972, 2–3, and *Meeting Minutes*, June 26, 1975, 3–4.

86. Rosen, "Work for Me," 68–89; SFHRC, *Annual Report*, no. 6, January 1970 to January 1971, 15.

87. SFHRC, *Meeting Minutes*, December 12, 1974, 7–8.

88. "Minority Vendor Plan Exceeds $500,000 Goal," *Friendly Times*, November 22, 1974; "UAL Buys Black Products," *Sun Reporter*, November 30, 1974; "Historical Understanding," *Sun Reporter*, June 5, 1976; "Minority Purchases by United Airlines Tops 5 Million in 1976," *Skanner*, March 24, 1977; "Minority Vendor Program Leaps and Bounds," *Friendly Times*, March 1977, 1, 14; "United Airlines Boasts Large Minority Contract, Purchasing Quotas," *Sun Reporter*, April 21, 1977.

89. Emory Curtis, "The Political Game," *Sun Reporter*, August 12, 1972; "Stop the Airport Bonds: Vote NO on C," *Sun Reporter*, October 13, 1977; Charles Belle, "Business in the Black: Vote No on Racist Issues: Bond Issues Bad for Blacks," *Sun Reporter*, November 3, 1977; *Sun Reporter*, "Moscone's Choice for Sheriff," February 16, 1978; "United We Stand," *Sun Reporter*, October 26, 1978; "Mayor Feinstein: 'Midstream Politics' Not Enough," *Sun Reporter*, December 7, 1978.

90. SFHRC, *Annual Report*, 1980–1981 (September 1981), 41; SFHRC, *Meeting Minutes*, February 8, 1979, 2.

91. SFHRC, *Annual Report*, 1984–1985 (December 1985), 3.

92. SFHRC, *Annual Report*, no. 14, January 1979 to January 1980, 6.

93. SFHRC, *Meeting Minutes*, October 26, 1978, 3; SFHRC, *Annual Report*, no. 14, January 1979 to January 1980, 5, 27.

94. SFHRC, *Annual Report*, 1980–1981 (September 1981), 41–43.

95. SFHRC, *Annual Report*, no. 14, January 1979 to January 1980, 6, 28–29.

96. SFHRC, *Annual Report*, 1980–1981 (September 1981), 42, 68–69, and *Annual Report*, July 1981–June 1982 (September 1982), 3–4, 54; Clemente Newball-Obregon, "Memorandum: Annual Airport Employment Profile," April 21, 1985, pp. 1–4, in SFHRC, *Annual Airport Employment Profile*, 1984 and 1985; SFHRC, *Meeting Minutes*, April 9, 1981, 6, and *Meeting Minutes*, May 27, 1982, 6–8.

97. SFHRC, *Annual Report*, July 1981–June 1982 (September 1982), 54; Newball-Obregon, "Memorandum," April 21, 1985, 3; Bay Area Census, "Population by Race/Ethnicity and County, 1980–2010," www.bayareacensus.ca.gov/historical/corace.htm.

98. Newball-Obregon, "Memorandum," April 21, 1985.

99. Orenic, *On the Ground*, 219–21; Reich, Hall, and Jacobs, *Living Wages*, 22–30; Hall, Jacobs, and Reich, "Liftoff," 72–75.

100. SFHRC, *Meeting Minutes*, April 24, 1980, 3; SFHRC, *Annual Report*, July 1981–June 1982 (September 1982), 53, and *Annual Report*, July 1982–June 1983 (May 1983), 46–48; SFHRC, *Meeting Minutes*, June 23, 1983, 9.

101. See Bay Area Census, "Population by Race/Ethnicity and County, 1980–2010," www.bayareacensus.ca.gov/historical/corace.htm.

102. SFHRC, *Annual Report*, July 1981–June 1982 (September 1982), 3, 56, 71; SFHRC, *Meeting Minutes*, April 24, 1980, 2, *Meeting Minutes*, September 25, 1980, 2, *Meeting Minutes*, February 26, 1981, 1, 3–5, and *Meeting Minutes*, April 29, 1982, 7. For a brief discussion of some of the complex elements of the backlash against Black people and others at this moment, see Porter, "Affirming and Disaffirming Actions."

103. SFHRC, *Meeting Minutes*, June 10, 1982, 7, *Meeting Minutes*, August 12, 1982, 2, and *Meeting Minutes*, February 24, 1983, 2; "Airport Coalition Opens Fight for Prevailing Wages," *San Mateo County Labor*, n.d., Box 5, 1982–84, *San Mateo County Labor*, San Francisco State University Labor Archives and Research Center.

104. The Allied skycaps' complaint followed several well-publicized protests across the nation by skycaps during the late 1970s and 1980s because of wage and benefit cuts as well as changes to the terms of their employment. "1,500 Black Skycaps Fight for Equality at Nation's Airports," *Tri-State Defender*, July 2, 1977; "Skycap!," *Black Enterprise*, January 1981, 15.

105. SFHRC, *Meeting Minutes*, June 10, 1982, 7, *Meeting Minutes*, August 12, 1982, 2, and *Meeting Minutes*, January 27, 1983, 1–2.

106. SFHRC, *Meeting Minutes*, February 24, 1983, 2, *Meeting Minutes*, March 10, 1983, 2–3, *Meeting Minutes*, May 26, 1983, 1, *Meeting Minutes*, July 7, 1983, 2–3, *Meeting Minutes*, August 24, 1983, 2, *Meeting Minutes*, November 10, 1983, 1–2, and *Meeting Minutes*, February 23, 1984, 1.

107. SFHRC, *Meeting Minutes*, January 13, 1983, 3, and *Meeting Minutes*, February 24, 1983, 2; "Airport Coalition Opens Fight for Prevailing Wages," *San Mateo County Labor*; "Local 77 Scores Big Airport Victory," *San Mateo County Labor*, May 1, 1983.

108. SFHRC, *Meeting Minutes*, March 10, 1983, 2–3, *Meeting Minutes*, April 14, 1983, 2–3, and *Meeting Minutes*, April 28, 1983, 2; Clemente Newball-Obregon, "Memorandum: Annual Airport Employment Profile," February 22, 1984, 2; "SEIU 77 Fights Airport Use of Alien Scabs," *San Mateo County Labor*, January 1, 1983; "Airport Workers Step Up Fight to Save Jobs, Wages," *San Mateo County Labor*, February 1, 1983; "Vigil Makes Powerful Statement," *San Mateo County Labor*, April 1, 1983; "Local 77 Scores Big Airport Victory," *San Mateo County Labor*, May 1, 1983.

109. Newball-Obregon, "Memorandum," February 22, 1984, 2; "SEIU 77 Fights Airport Use of Alien Scabs," *San Mateo County Labor*; "Local 77 Scores Big Airport Victory," *San Mateo County Labor*; "Chamber, Airlines Seek to Defeat Prevailing Wages," *San Mateo County Labor*, July 1, 1983; "Multimillion Lawsuit against City," *San Mateo County Labor*, August 1, 1983; SFHRC, *Meeting Minutes*, August 24, 1983, 3.

110. "Airport Pay Bill Moves to Board," *San Mateo County Labor,* April 1, 1984; "Airport Wage Bill on the Books," *San Mateo County Labor,* May 1, 1984; "CLC Moving Fast to Save Airport Pay Law," *San Mateo County Labor,* May 1, 1985; "SF Council, SEIU Locals Join Airport Pay Case," *San Mateo County Labor,* July 1, 1985; "CLC Acts to Bury Airlines' Claims," *San Mateo County Labor,* November 1, 1985; "Nos. 86-2520, 86-2530, 865 F.2d 1112 (9th Cir. 1989)," Justia US Law, accessed January 27, 2017, http://law.justia.com/cases /federal/appellate-courts/F2/865/1112/102317/; "Air Cal, Inc. v. City and County of San Francisco," Casetext, accessed January 27, 2017, https://casetext.com /case/air-cal-inc-v-city-cty-of-sf; Reich, Hall, and Jacobs, *Living Wages,* 27.

111. Rochelle Metcalfe, "I Heard That," *Sun Reporter,* May 10, 2007.

CHAPTER 5. THE POLITICS OF JET NOISE

1. "Residents Lose Bid for Damages," *San Mateo County Times,* December 16, 1970; "Airport Sued over Noise," *San Francisco Chronicle,* February 18, 1971; "Suit Filed on Jet Noise," *San Mateo County Times,* February 18, 1971; "Airport Noise Suit Settled; S.F. to Spend $5.2 Million," *San Mateo County Times,* July 21, 1971; Jerry Burns, "'Landmark' End to Airport Noise Suit," *San Francisco Chronicle,* July 21, 1971.

2. Influential here are Peterson, "Atmospheric Sensibilities," 69–70, and Feld, "Rainforest Acoustemology," 226.

3. Peterson, *Atmospheric Noise.*

4. San Francisco Board of Supervisors, *San Francisco Airport,* 23.

5. Moretti, "Communication and Problem-Solving Study," 8, 22; McDonnell, "San Francisco International Airport," 5–9; Bednarek, *Airports, Cities,* 154–55.

6. Moretti, "Communication and Problem-Solving Study," 11–13, 20; US House, *Aircraft Noise Problems,* 140–44, 148–51, 157–60; "Unit Acts for Lessening of Airport Noise," *San Mateo County Times,* February 26, 1958; "South City Jet Protests Termed Futile," *San Mateo County Times,* July 7, 1959; "Aroused South City Residents Demand Action on Jet Planes," *San Mateo County Times,* September 9, 1959. Ryan continued to work on jet noise, generally and on behalf of north county residents, after being elected to the California State Assembly in 1962 and then the US Congress in 1972. That work was cut short by his assassination on a Guyana airstrip while he was investigating the People's Temple in 1978, an event that was the catalyst for the Jonestown massacre.

7. Garbell, "Aircraft Noise Abatement," 4–6; Moretti, "Communication and Problem-Solving Study," 11; US House, *Aircraft Noise Problems,* 133–40, 161–62; "Bayside Manor Organizes Club," *San Mateo County Times,* May 12, 1948; "Millbrae to Fight Factories," *San Mateo County Times,* March 9, 1949.

8. "Younger Ask [*sic*] U.S. Funds for Jet Noise Relief to Millbrae," *San Mateo County Times,* March 24, 1960; US House, *Aircraft Noise Problems,* 133–48, 157–62; Moretti, "Communication and Problem-Solving Study," 22.

9. Census data from Bay Area Census: "City of Millbrae, Decennial Census Data, 1950–1960," www.bayareacensus.ca.gov/cities/Millbrae50.htm; "City of South San Francisco, Decennial Census Data, 1950–1960," www.bayareacensus .ca.gov/cities/SouthSanFrancisco50.htm.

10. Lipsitz, *Possessive Investment in Whiteness.*

11. McDonnell, "San Francisco International Airport," 5–6; Hynding, *From Frontier to Suburb,* 273–79.

12. HoSang, *Racial Propositions,* 54–58; Julia Scott, "Homeowners Guild Removes Racially Restrictive Language," *East Bay Times,* August 18, 2007; Cheng, "Out of Chinatown," 1082–88; Hynding, *From Frontier to Suburb,* 279–80.

13. Boubet, "Study of the Impact," 1.

14. Moretti, "Communication and Problem-Solving Study," 25, 117.

15. US House, *Aircraft Noise Problems,* 139; "U.S. Silencer Sought against Airport Noise," *San Mateo County Times,* August 28, 1959; "Aroused South City Residents," *San Mateo County Times;* "Noise Causes 'Emotional Disturbances,'" *San Mateo County Times,* March 23, 1960; "Aid Pledged in Jet Campaign," *San Mateo County Times,* April 21, 1960; "Jet Smoke at KPIX," *San Mateo County Times,* April 28, 1960, 13; Moretti, "Communication and Problem Solving Study," 20–21, 23.

16. Moretti, "Communication and Problem-Solving Study," 9–10; US House, *Aircraft Noise Problems,* 174–80.

17. Bednarek, *Airports, Cities,* 152–54, 158–65; US Federal Aviation Agency, *Sounds.*

18. Moretti, "Communication and Problem-Solving Study," 30–31, 53–55, 88–89.

19. McDonnell, "San Francisco International Airport," 39–43, 47–51.

20. McDonnell, "San Francisco International Airport," 5–8; Lo, *Small Property,* 36–37.

21. "Jet Noise Explanation Offered," *San Mateo County Times,* October 7, 1960.

22. Moretti, "Communication and Problem-Solving Study," 26–27.

23. Moretti, "Communication and Problem-Solving Study," 68–82, 124–26; "Sound Booklet Available at Airport," *San Mateo County Times,* July 4, 1960.

24. "Two Cities Spur Action to Abate Jet Noises," *San Mateo County Times,* August 2, 1960; "Airport Loses Jet Training," *San Mateo County Times,* August 4, 1960.

25. "Jet Noise Explanation Offered," *San Mateo County Times.*

26. "Millbrae Frowns on Apartment," *San Mateo County Times,* November 16, 1960; "Peaceful Solution to Jet Problem Disclosed," *San Mateo County Times,* March 2, 1961; "Noise Group Meeting 'Cool,'" *San Mateo County Times,* March 4, 1961; "PUC Halts Work on Jet Wall," *San Mateo County Times,* June 14, 1961; Moretti, "Communication and Problem Solving Study," 58–59.

27. Walker, *Country in the City,* 82–104. When discussing such activism in the Bay Area, including San Mateo County, Walker draws from Rome, *Bulldozer in the Countryside.*

28. Bednarek, *Airports, Cities,* 165–66.

29. "S.F. Airport Faces Wave of Lawsuits," *San Francisco Chronicle,* March 10, 1962; "Airport Suit Asks $200,000," *San Mateo County Times,* April 21, 1962; "File More Jet Damage Suits," *San Mateo County Times,* July 4, 1962.

30. "Landmark Jet Noise Ruling," *San Mateo County Times,* September 20, 1967.

31. Bloom, *Metropolitan Airport,* 135; "New Airlift to S.E. Asia," *San Mateo County Times,* November 11, 1966.

32. McDonnell, "San Francisco International Airport," 80–85; "Ryan Suggests New Jet Noise Approach," *San Mateo County Times,* October 15, 1968.

33. George Golding, "Radar Problems over Foster City Reported," *San Mateo County Times,* February 10, 1967; "Foster City Noise Protest," *San Mateo County Times,* September 15, 1967.

34. "Jets Fly in New Pattern," *San Mateo County Times,* October 4, 1969; "Rustic Quiet Upset by New Jet Pattern," *San Mateo County Times,* November 8, 1969; "[sic] Seek to Block P.V. Jet Noises," *San Mateo County Times,* November 14, 1969.

35. Peterson, *Atmospheric Noise,* 77–103; Bednarek, *Airports, Cities,* 168–70.

36. Bednarek, *Airports, Cities,* 196; "Ryan Joins Protest on Jet Noise," *San Mateo County Times,* November 25, 1969; "Airline Group to Fight Noise Law," *San Mateo County Times,* July 10, 1971; "Aircraft Noise Control Law Takes Effect Friday," *San Mateo County Times,* November 28, 1972; "Airlines Sue over State Noise Law," *San Mateo County Times,* November 30, 1972.

37. George Golding, "Showdown Vote in Senate over SST Construction," *San Mateo County Times,* December 1, 1970; Theodore H. Long, letter to the editor, *San Mateo County Times,* December 16, 1970; "Jet Noise Bill Advances," *San Mateo County Times,* June 24, 1971.

38. Gordon, *Naked Airport,* 228–34.

39. Lo, *Small Property,* 41–42.

40. "Jet Roar Protested by 538," *San Mateo County Times,* December 6, 1969; Duncan R. McLean, letter to the editor, *San Mateo County Times,* December 13, 1969.

41. "Ryan Joins Protest," *San Mateo County Times*; Bob Peterson, "Jet Noise Meet [sic] Disappointment," *San Mateo County Times,* January 20, 1970.

42. "Charging for Noise," *San Mateo County Times,* February 14, 1970; McDonnell, "San Francisco International Airport," 50.

43. "Airport Noise Suit Settled," *San Mateo County Times*; Burns, "'Landmark' End," *San Francisco Chronicle*; "Carlos Firm Gets Airport Contract," *San Mateo County Times,* August 2, 1967; "Offer on Runway by Ecologists," *San Mateo County Times,* August 1, 1973.

44. "S.S.F. and San Bruno Hear Jet Complaints," *San Mateo County Times,* September 19, 1972; John M. Regan, letter to the editor, *San Mateo County Times,* January 6, 1973.

45. "Expansion Plan Details Revealed," *San Francisco Chronicle,* March 3, 1973; "S.F. Airport Details Expansion Program," *San Mateo County Times,* March 3, 1973; Alessandro Baccari and Associates, "San Francisco International Airport," 40–41.

46. Kevin Leary, "Airport Expansion to Resume," *San Francisco Chronicle,* May 2, 1973; Bolt, Beranek, and Newman, "Aviation Noise Evaluations," II-1, II-2; McDonnell, "San Francisco International Airport," 88–90.

47. Chris Carlsson, "Bechtel Corporation," FoundSF, accessed November 12, 2021, www.foundsf.org/index.php?title=Bechtel_Corporation.

48. Jerry Burns, "Expansion of S.F. Airport Fought," *San Francisco Chronicle*, March 7, 1973; George Golding, "Conservation Groups Attack Airport Plans," *San Mateo County Times*, March 7, 1973; "Millbrae Council Critical of Report," *San Mateo County Times*, March 10, 1973; "Airport Plan Gets Qualified Approval," *San Mateo County Times*, March 29, 1973; San Francisco International Airport Commission, *Environmental Impact Report*, 1-4 to 1-5, 1-10 to 1-12, 3–4.

49. Leary, "Airport Expansion to Resume," *San Francisco Chronicle*; "Airport Expansion OKd Despite Pleas," *San Mateo County Times*, May 2, 1973; "Airport Expansion Suit," *San Francisco Chronicle*, May 18, 1973; "Local Residents Sue S.F. Airport," *San Mateo County Times*, May 18, 1973.

50. SFEC, *San Francisco Airport Expansion Plan*, 42–47. This report is not paginated; my pagination begins on the page following the title page. Sponsoring organizations were San Francisco Ecology Center, San Francisco Tomorrow, Friends of the Earth, Peninsula Conservation Center, Save San Francisco Bay Association, Sierra Club-Loma Prieta Chapter, Sierra Club-Bay Chapter Conservation Committee, Environmental Quality Coordinating Council, San Mateo County Medical Society, Keep Pacifica Scenic, and San Francisco Loyal Opposition.

51. Golding, "Conservation Groups," *San Mateo County Times*; "The Hot Debate over Expansion," *San Francisco Chronicle*, May 27, 1973.

52. SFEC, *San Francisco Airport Expansion Plan*, 11, 29. Cooper originally presented her statement to the San Mateo County Planning Commission at its March 28 meeting

53. SFEC, *San Francisco Airport Expansion Plan*, 4–7; "S.C. Meeting on Airport," *San Mateo County Times*, March 14, 1973.

54. SFEC, *San Francisco Airport Expansion Plan*, 52–54.

55. SFEC, *San Francisco Airport Expansion Plan*, 58–59.

56. SFEC, *San Francisco Airport Expansion Plan*, 9–10, 12.

57. Walker, *Country in the City*, 5, 98–99, 106–8, 132–34, 206–7.

58. Walker, *Country in the City*, 8–13, 104–9, 240–41.

59. Schafran, *Road to Resegregation*, 18, 219, 243–44.

60. Boubet, "Study of the Impact," 48–49; "[sic] Seek to Reduce Night Noise at SF Airport," *San Mateo County Times*, August 4, 1973; George Golding, "Airport Noise Problems Continue," *San Mateo County Times*, September 15, 1977.

61. Bay Area Census, "City of South San Francisco, Decennial Census Data, 1970–1990," www.bayareacensus.ca.gov/cities/SouthSanFrancisco70.htm: In 1970 South San Francisco was 93.5 percent white, 1.3 percent Negro, 3.9 percent Asian (broken into different groups), and 0.5 percent Indian, with 15.4 percent of "Spanish origin." In 1980 it was 74.3 percent white, 3.8 percent Black, 14.5 percent Asian, and 0.4 percent American Indian, with 22.2 percent of "Spanish origin." See HoSang, *Racial Propositions*, 53–90, for more on the saga of the California Fair Housing Act.

62. SFEC advertisement, *San Mateo Times,* September 17, 1973; "Airports Unit Oks Planned Expansion," *San Francisco Chronicle,* November 8, 1973; Jerry Burns, "Lively Debate on S.F. Airport Expansion," *San Francisco Chronicle,* November 13, 1973; "New Suit to Halt Airport Expansion," *San Francisco Chronicle,* January 26, 1974.

63. "Lawsuit Filed on SF Airport Plan," *San Mateo County Times,* October 1, 1974; "Suit Seeks to Halt Airport Growth," *San Francisco Chronicle,* October 1, 1974.

64. "Judge Orders Airport EIR," *San Mateo County Times,* November 16, 1974; "Appeal on Airport," *San Mateo County Times,* November 23, 1974; "Airport Building Halted," *San Mateo County Times,* March 19, 1975; Kevin Leary, "Airport Expansion Halted," *San Francisco Chronicle,* March 20, 1975; "Court Oks Airport Construction," *San Francisco Chronicle,* April 11, 1975; Justia summary of *Friends of the Earth v. Coleman* (9th Cir. 1975), accessed February 19, 2017, http://law.justia.com/cases/federal/appellate-courts/F2/518/323/282024/.

65. "Environmentalist Foes to Fight for Bigger Airport," *San Francisco Chronicle,* April 1, 1975.

66. "Environmentalist Foes," *San Francisco Chronicle.*

67. George Golding, "Airport Noise," *San Mateo County Times,* April 25, 1972; "Airport Expansion Okd," *San Mateo County Times*; "Airport Suit Could Mar Noise Fight," *San Mateo County Times,* June 2, 1973.

68. San Francisco Airport Commission, "Facts, Questions and Answers about San Francisco International Airport," 1974, San Mateo County Historical Association Archives, folder 77-36.

69. "Airports Board Hires PR Firm," *San Francisco Chronicle,* April 2, 1975; Alessandro Baccari and Associates, *San Francisco International Airport,* 57.

70. George Golding, "Airport Avoided Noise Laws," *San Mateo County Times,* July 11, 1975; "Did State Err on Airport Noise Rule," *San Mateo County Times,* September 16, 1975.

71. "Expansion, Remodeling of S.F. Airport under Attack," *Los Angeles Times,* May 19, 1977; "Ryan to Call Concorde Hearing," *San Mateo County Times,* October 18, 1977; "Airport Sound Data Questioned," *San Mateo County Times,* November 1, 1977.

72. McDonnell, "San Francisco International Airport," 101–2; "Bruno Council Wants to Review Airport EIR," *San Mateo County Times,* April 15, 1975; Golding, "'Airport Avoided Noise Laws,'" *San Mateo County Times*; "State Noise Laws Debated," *San Mateo County Times,* October 16, 1976; "Airport Noise before Congress," *San Mateo County Times,* April 8, 1977; Sylvia Gregory, "Airport" (letter to the editor), *San Mateo County Times,* May 3, 1977.

73. McDonnell, "San Francisco International Airport," 102–3; Freeman and Farris, "Grassroots Impact Litigation," 262–63; Delores M. Huajardo, "Noise" (letter to the editor), *San Mateo County Times,* September 16, 1977; "Airport Had a Big Day," October 31, 1977; "Restricting Noisy Aircraft Just First Step at Airport," *San Mateo County Times,* November 30, 1977; Linda Dyson, "Noise" (letter to the editor), *San Mateo County Times,* December 2, 1977.

74. "AIR Force to the Rescue," *Loma Prietan* 8, no. 4 (May 1977), B.

75. Walker, *Country in the City*, 107; "Ward Hails Accord on Airport Board," *San Mateo County Times*, February 3, 1977; McDonnell, "San Francisco International Airport," 93–99, 106–9.

76. McDonnell, "San Francisco International Airport," 111–18. The Roundtable is still in operation as of this writing (http://sforoundtable.org, accessed April 7, 2017).

77. "Labor Council Initiates Airport Labor Coalition," *San Mateo County Labor*, August 1, 1979.

78. "Labor Council Initiates," *San Mateo County Labor*; "Airport Coalition Wins on Safety," *San Mateo County Labor*, March 1, 1980.

79. "Veteran Pilot Has His Own Ideas about Noise," *San Mateo County Labor*, May 1, 1980.

80. Freeman and Farris, "Grassroots Impact Litigation," 261–65; Eugene Robinson, "Top Court Widens Use of Airport Suits," *San Francisco Chronicle*, December 15, 1979.

81. Freeman and Farris, "Grassroots Impact Litigation," 265–70.

82. Freeman and Farris, "Grassroots Impact Litigation," 267. The legislature tried later to institute statewide prohibition along these lines, but their bill was vetoed by then governor Deukmejian. See "Noise Foes Hail Veto of Claims Bill," *Los Angeles Times*, September 18, 1983.

83. "The Ban on Airport Suits, Another View," *San Mateo County Labor*, October 1, 1982.

84. "S.F. Airport May Pay for Banning Noisy Jets," *San Francisco Chronicle*, December 7, 1985; "FAA Impounds $8.1 Million Grant to S.F. Airport," *San Francisco Chronicle*, August 6, 1986; "Big Defeat for SFO on 'Noisy' Jet Ban," *San Francisco Chronicle*, August 10, 1988.

85. For details on SFO's recent noise mitigation programs, see SFO, "Welcome to SFO's Aircraft Noise Office," accessed September 22, 2021, www.flysfo.com/noise.

86. Ana Santos, "New SFO Flight Paths Causing Record Airplane Noise Complaints," *Peninsula Press*, November 23, 2015, http://peninsulapress.com/2015/11/23/sfo-airplane-noise-complaints/.

CHAPTER 6. DIFFERING DEGREES OF WELCOME

1. Vivian Ho and Jenna Lyons, "Thousands at SFO Demand Detainees' Release," *San Francisco Chronicle*, January 29, 2017; Evan Sernoffsky, Joaquin Palomino, and Kurtis Alexander, "Main News," *San Francisco Chronicle*, January 30, 2017.

2. Ho and Lyons, "Thousands at SFO," *San Francisco Chronicle*.

3. For an account of the incident, see T. Hernandez, *All They Will Call You*.

4. Marissa Lang, "Edict Deeply Personal for Tech Workers," *San Francisco Chronicle*, January 30, 2017; Steve Rubenstein, "Metro," *San Francisco Chronicle*, February 4, 2017; Dominic Fracassa and Wendy Lee, "Tech Leaders Battling Trump," *San Francisco Chronicle*, February 7, 2017.

5. I draw primarily here from C. Ramírez, *Assimilation*.

6. Fuller and Harley, *Aviopolis*, 41–44; Adey, *Aerial Life*, 93–94; R. Hall, *Transparent Traveler*, 1–23; Browne, *Dark Matters*, 131–59.

7. Vernon, "Heathrow," addresses how racialized labor practices and immigration and security systems coincide at a different airport.

8. H. G. Reza, "Suspected Gay Detained at Airport," *San Francisco Chronicle*, December 31, 1979; Ronald D. Moskowitz, "Suspected Gay Allowed into S.F.," *San Francisco Chronicle*, January 1, 1980; Paul Lorch, "Lawsuits Filed on Behalf of Mexican Tourist," *Bay Area Reporter*, January 3, 1980; Wayne King, "Suit to Contest U.S. on Homosexual Ban," *New York Times*, January 3, 1980.

9. Luibhéid, *Entry Denied*, 5–7, 21; Somerville, "Sexual Aliens," 76–85; Bush, "Borderline Homophobia," 8–9.

10. Bush, "Borderline Homophobia," 8–9; Canaday, *Straight State*, 214–21, 241–48.

11. Bush, "Borderline Homophobia," 9; Canaday, *Straight State*, 248–50.

12. Ronald D. Moskowitz, "Gay Is Detained at S.F. Airport," *San Francisco Chronicle*, June 15, 1979; "Feds Flag Gays," *Bay Area Reporter*, June 21, 1979.

13. Ronald D. Moskowitz, "Gay Visitor Wins Mental Test Delay," *San Francisco Chronicle*, June 27, 1979; "British Tourist to Stay and Fight," *Bay Area Reporter*, July 5, 1979; "Gay Tourist Victory," *Bay Area Reporter*, August 16, 1979; "Statement of Donald C. Knutson," in US House, *Hearing before the Subcommittee*, 183–85; Bush, "Borderline Homophobia," 9–10; Canaday, *Straight State*, 250.

14. Bush, "Borderline Homophobia," 10; Ray P. Comeau, "The Mexican Tourists Caper," *Bay Area Reporter*, August 5, 1979; Ronald D. Moskowitz, "Immigration vs. Gays—The Latest Round," *San Francisco Chronicle*, August 7, 1979; Joseph B. Treaster, "Homosexuals Still Fight U.S. Immigration Limits," *New York Times*, August 12, 1979.

15. "U.S. Drops Rule Barring Suspected Homosexuals," *New York Times*, August 15, 1979; Carrie Dearborn, "Court Won't Dismiss Suit by Mexican against INS," *Gay Community News*, April 18, 1981, 1; Canaday, *Straight State*, 250–51; Bush, "Borderline Homophobia," 10–11.

16. Lorch, "Lawsuits Filed," *Bay Area Reporter*; Bobby Lester, "INS—Local Brass Should Go" (letter to the editor), *Bay Area Reporter*, January 31, 1980; Sides, *Erotic City*, 164–65.

17. Kelly Lytle Hernandez uses the term *Mexican Brown* to signify the "complexion-inflected class specificity" of such scrutiny when it came to US Border Patrol practices. See *Migra!*

18. Lorch, "Lawsuits Filed," *Bay Area Reporter*; "INS Protests," *Bay Area Reporter*, January 3, 1980; "Public Officials Protest INS Tactics," *Bay Area Reporter*, January 3, 1980.

19. "Immigration Office Picketed," *Bay Area Reporter*, January 17, 1980; "Officials Join I.N.S. Protest," *Bay Area Reporter*, January 17, 1980; "I.N.S. Policies Blasted by Congress," *Bay Area Reporter*, January 17, 1980.

20. "Dutch Gays Quiz U.S. Tourists," *Bay Area Reporter*, January 17, 1980; Bush, "Borderline Homophobia," 11.

21. "Agnos Responds on I.N.S. Flub," *Bay Area Reporter*, January 17, 1980; "Officials Join I.N.S. Protest," *Bay Area Reporter*.

22. "Gay Rights Advocates to Go to Washington, D.C.," *Bay Area Reporter*, January 17, 1980; Dearborn, "Court Won't Dismiss Suit," *Gay Community News*; "Statement of Donald C. Knutson," in US House, *Hearing before the Subcommittee*, 185–86; Konstantin Berlandt, "Another Gay Tourist Returned by INS," *Bay Area Reporter*, May 21, 1981; Konstantin Berlandt, "INS Can't Bar Gays," *Bay Area Reporter*, April 29, 1982; Canaday, *Straight State*, 251–53.

23. Roque Ramírez, "'That's *My* Place,'" 244–46; Roque Ramírez, "Communities of Desire," 172–74, 199–200, 225–36; Sides, *Erotic City*, 153–66. Most infamous among the hate crimes was the murder of Robert Hillsborough on a Mission District Street in June 1977.

24. I am influenced here by Jasbir Puar's analysis of how the recognition and incorporation of some "homosexual, gay, and queer bodies" vis-à-vis "liberal discourses of multicultural tolerance and diversity" can develop hand in hand with the marking of other people as a threat or as disposable. See Puar, *Terrorist Assemblages*, xii.

25. Tiemeyer, *Plane Queer*, 138, 142–43, 149–65.

26. Tiemeyer, *Plane Queer*, 180.

27. Tiemeyer, *Plane Queer*, 180–81; Allyn Stone and Jeff Pelline, "Airlines' Confusing Policy for AIDS Passengers," *San Francisco Chronicle*, August 15, 1987; Allen White, "Airline to Demand Medical Statement from Passengers," *Bay Area Reporter*, August 20, 1987; Fran Golden, "AIDS Victims Grapple with Travel Curbs," *Travel Weekly*, September 24, 1987, 1, 81.

28. Fairchild and Tynan, "Policies of Containment," 2016; Wachter, *Fragile Coalition*, 28–32; Ray O'Loughlin, "U.S. Officials Throw PWA In Jail," *Bay Area Reporter*, April 6, 1989.

29. Lori Olszewski, "S.F. Protest Planned over INS' Detaining of Dutch Man with AIDS," *San Francisco Chronicle*, April 6, 1989; Jay Newquist, "Dutch PWA Released from Prison Attends Final Hours of Health Conf.," *Bay Area Reporter*, April 13, 1989; Jay Newquist, "Agnos Honors Jailed AIDS Educator," *Bay Area Reporter*, April 13, 1989; Allen White, "1990 Conf. Endangered by U.S. Border Policy," *Bay Area Reporter*, April 13, 1989; Wachter, *Fragile Coalition*, 32–34.

30. Wachter, *Fragile Coalition*, 16–27; White, "1990 Conf. Endangered," *Bay Area Reporter*; Allen White, "City Prepares to Withdraw Sponsorship of '90 Conference," *Bay Area Reporter*, April 27, 1989; Randy Shilts, "Will AIDS Conference Be Canceled?" *San Francisco Chronicle*, May 8, 1989.

31. "Give Me Your Tired, Your Poor (Straight) Masses," *Bay Area Reporter*, April 13, 1989; Lori Olszewski, "New Immigration Plan to Let Some with AIDS In," *San Francisco Chronicle*, May 19, 1989.

32. Allen White, "Possibility of HIV Border Incidents Threatens Meeting," *Bay Area Reporter*, May 25, 1989; Rex Wockner, "Two More PWAs Nabbed at U.S. Border," *Bay Area Reporter*, June 15, 1989.

33. "Foul Play with Immigration Policy," *Bay Area Reporter*, June 1, 1989.

34. O'Loughlin, "U.S. Officials," *Bay Area Reporter*.

35. Fairchild and Tynan, "Policies of Containment," 2016.

36. Sides, *Erotic City*, 199–201; Roque Ramírez, "Communities of Desire," 352–57; flyers, "HIV, Rights and the INS" and "Inmigrante: ¡Conoce sus

derechos!," box 1, folder 2, Jorge Cortiñas Papers, GLBT Historical Society, San Francisco (hereafter cited as Cortiñas Papers).

37. Dennis McMillan, "ACT UP Demonstrates at INS against Deportation Threats," *Bay Area Reporter,* June 29, 1989; Gould, "ACT UP, Racism." Gould contends with the simultaneous existence of racist and antiracist practices in ACT UP, although her focus is not specifically on the Bay Area.

38. "Sixth Conference on AIDS Seeks Community Input," *Bay Area Reporter,* October 19, 1989; Rex Wockner, "Boycott of SF AIDS Conference Spreading," *Bay Area Reporter,* December 14, 1989; Elaine Herscher, "Shanti Project Protests AIDS Travel Policy," *San Francisco Chronicle,* January 25, 1990; Allen White, "HIV Policy Threatening SF's AIDS Conference," *Bay Area Reporter,* February 1, 1990; Wachter, *Fragile Coalition,* 34–38, 113–49.

39. "Bush Decides Not to Address AIDS Meeting," *San Francisco Chronicle,* February 2, 1990; Wachter, *Fragile Coalition,* 104–12. Bush was reinvited during the machinations over the ten-day visas a few months later but declined then as well. *Fragile Coalition,* 150–65.

40. Allen White, "ACT UP, CDC Target INS Policy," *Bay Area Reporter,* March 1, 1990; Michele DeRanleau, "Opposition to INS Policy Mounts," *San Francisco Sentinel,* March 1, 1990; Jorge Cortiñas, handwritten remarks, box 1, folder 12, Cortiñas Papers; ACT UP, press release, February 23, 1990, box 1, folder 12, Cortiñas Papers; Breu, "No Time," 31–35.

41. David Tuller, "HIV Travel Rules Eased," *San Francisco Chronicle,* April 14, 1990; Wachter, *Fragile Coalition,* 150–65.

42. Michael C. Botkin, "Immigration and HIV," *Bay Area Reporter,* April 12, 1990.

43. Peter Altman, "INS Office Occupied," *Bay Area Reporter,* May 3, 1990; Breu, "No Time," 35–36; Jennie McNight, "U.S. Unveils Insulting Visa Policy," *Gay Community News,* April 22–28, 1990.

44. Allen White, "Conference + Parade: Volatile Mix," *Bay Area Reporter,* April 26, 1990; David Perlman, "Conference on AIDS Picks 2,400 Reports," *San Francisco Chronicle,* April 26, 1990; Allen White, "Conference Boycott Widens," *Bay Area Reporter,* May 10, 1990; Allen White, "INS Ruling Stands," *Bay Area Reporter,* May 17, 1990; Lonn Johnston, "Bay Area Gays Upset over INS Decision," *San Francisco Chronicle,* June 4, 1990.

45. Richard L. Andrews, MD, "BAPHR Protest" (letter to the editor), *Bay Area Reporter,* June 7, 1990.

46. Michael C. Botkin, "When Latex Isn't Enough," *Bay Area Reporter,* June 14, 1990; Wachter, *Fragile Coalition,* 190.

47. Michael C. Botkin, "Conference Quieter than Expected," *Bay Area Reporter,* June 28, 1990; Dennis Conkin, "Reporter's Conference Notebook," *Bay Area Reporter,* June 28, 1990.

48. ACT UP/San Francisco to Friends, May 7, 1990, box 1, folder 16, Cortiñas Papers; Kate Raphael, "INS Denies Amnesty for HIV+ Immigrants," *San Francisco Sentinel,* June 14, 1990; David Tuller, "Uproar over INS Denial of Amnesty to 35 Aliens," *San Francisco Chronicle,* June 15, 1990; ACT UP/San Francisco, press release, June 18, 1990, box 1, folder 15, Cortiñas Papers; David Tuller and Dawn Garcia, "ACT UP Protesters Sit In at S.F.'s Marriott Hotel," *San Francisco*

Chronicle, June 20, 1990; Allen White, "Convicted ACT UP Protesters Tell of Police Brutality," *Bay Area Reporter,* December 6, 1990; "An Open Letter to President Bush," June 18, 1990, box 1, folder 15, Cortiñas Papers.

49. David Perlman and Lori Olszewski, "AIDS Conference Opens," *San Francisco Chronicle,* June 21, 1990; Charles Petit, "AIDS Delegates Join in Immigration Protest," *San Francisco Chronicle,* June 21, 1990; Allen White, "ACT UP/New York's Staley Fires Up Conference Opener," *Bay Area Reporter,* June 28, 1990.

50. Elaine Herscher and Lori Olszewski, "ACT UP Drowns Out Louis Sullivan's Speech," *San Francisco Chronicle,* June 25, 1990; Dennis Conkin, "AIDS Conference Culminates in Angry Demonstration," *Bay Area Reporter,* June 28, 1990; Michael C. Botkin, "Did Someone Say Something?," *Bay Area Reporter,* June 28, 1990; Wachter, *Fragile Coalition,* 227–30.

51. David Tuller, "The Future of Immigration Law Restricting People with AIDS," *San Francisco Chronicle,* June 27, 1990.

52. Dawn Garcia and David Tuller, "New Immigration Law Hailed," *San Francisco Chronicle,* December 1, 1990; Philip J. Hilts, "AIDS Taken Off List of Diseases Barring Foreigners," *San Francisco Chronicle,* January 4, 1991.

53. Dave Gilden, "HIV Reversal Threatens AIDS Meeting," *Bay Area Reporter,* May 30, 1991; ACT UP media advisory, June 19, 1991, box 1, folder 24, Cortiñas Papers.

54. Program, Speaking across Borders event, June 17, 1990, box 1, folder 14, Cortiñas Papers.

55. Tim Kingston, "Acting Up Is Hard to Do," *San Francisco Bay Times,* October 1990; Michelle DeRanleau, "ACT UP Blows Up," *SF Weekly,* September 19, 1990.

56. ACT UP/Golden Gate Immigration Working Group handout, May 1991, box 1, folder 18, Cortiñas Papers; Jorge Cortiñas to Friends, May 24, 1991, box 1, folder 19, Cortiñas Papers; press release, multiple organizations, May 30, 1991, box 1, folder 20, Cortiñas Papers.

57. ACT UP, press release, June 17, 1991, box 1, folder 22, Cortiñas Papers; Immigration Working Groups of ACT UP San Francisco and ACT UP/Golden Gate to Friends, June 14, 1991; ACT UP/Golden Gate press advisory, n.d., box 1, folder 23, Cortiñas Papers; "16 Activists Arrested at INS Offices," *Bay Area Reporter,* June 20, 1991.

58. Memorandum, Tomás Fábregas to ACT UP/Golden Gate, August 6, 1991, box 2, folder 8, Cortiñas Papers; "U.S. Immigration Policy Restrictions and the Eighth International Conference on AIDS," August 13, 1991, box 2, folder 8, Cortiñas Papers; Sabin Russell, "'92 AIDS Conference to Shun U.S.," *San Francisco Chronicle,* August 17, 1991.

59. Breu, "No Time," 22.

60. Fairchild and Tynan, "Policies of Containment," 2013–15.

61. Tomás Fábregas to Board of Directors, San Francisco AIDS Foundation, June 7, 1991, box 1, folder 9, Tomás Fábregas Papers, GLBT Historical Society, San Francisco (hereafter cited as Fábregas Papers); "Statement of Pat Christen, San Francisco AIDS Foundation, June 18, 1991, box 1, folder 9, Fábregas Papers; ACT UP/San Francisco "FYI," March 23, 1992, box 1, folder 1, Fábregas

Papers; flyer, ACT UP/Immigration Working group, n.d. (likely June 1992), box 1, folder 3, Fábregas Papers; ACT UP to Magic Johnson, February 27, 1992, box 1, folder 2, Fábregas Papers; Breu, "No Time," 36–39.

62. Tomás Fábregas, "Travel and Immigration Restrictions Foster Spread of HIV in US.," *Bay Area Reporter,* August 6, 1992.

63. Tomás Fábregas to panelists, June 23, 1992, box 1, folder 5, Fábregas Papers; media advisory, July 23, 1992, box 1, folder 11, Fábregas Papers.

64. Yasmin Anwar, "AIDS Activist Reenters U.S., Challenges Ban," *Oakland Tribune,* July 26, 1992; Marilyn Chase, "Spanish Man Who Has AIDS Defies U.S. Ban," *Wall Street Journal,* July 27, 1992; Alfonso Armada, "El gran día de Tomás Fábregas," *El Pais,* July 27, 1992; Breu, "No Time," 40–42.

65. Breu, "No Time," 42–43.

66. For more on this, see Roque Ramírez, "Communities of Desire," and Juana Rodríguez, *Queer Latinidad,* 37–83.

67. Roque Ramírez, "Communities of Desire," 409, 444–58; Susan Stern, "Battling AIDS' Borders," *Oakland Tribune,* July 25, 1992.

68. Ethen Lieser and Amita Teotia, "Filipino Americans Protest New Law at Three Bay Area Airports," *Asianweek,* February 27, 2002.

69. R. Rodriguez and Balce, "American Insecurity," 131–32; Joyce Nishioka, "Security Law to Axe Noncitizen Baggage Screeners, Many Filipino," *Asianweek,* December 20, 2001.

70. Reich, Hall, and Jacobs, *Living Wages,* 23–26, 32, 79; Steven Greenhouse, "Groups Seek to Lift Ban on Foreign Screeners," *New York Times,* December 12, 2001; Annie Nakao, "Airport Job Insecurity," *San Francisco Chronicle,* March 18, 2002; Acena, "Invisible Minority No More," 7, 19.

71. Ethen Lieser, "Policy on Airport Screeners Challenged," *Asianweek,* February 6, 2002; Bernice Yeung, "The Price of Citizenship," *S.F. Weekly,* February 13, 2002.

72. Reich, Hall, and Jacobs, *Living Wages,* 9–10, 13–18; Jacobs and Reich, "When Do Mandates Work?"; P. Hall, Jacobs, and Reich, "Liftoff."

73. Greenhouse, "Groups Seek," *New York Times;* Nishioka, "Security Law," *Asianweek;* Ethen Lieser, "Migrant Solidarity Fights Backlash," *Asianweek,* January 2, 2002; Lieser, "Policy on Airport Screeners," *Asianweek;* Nakao, "Airport Job Insecurity," *San Francisco Chronicle;* Naber, "So Our History," 228.

74. Greenhouse, "Groups Seek," *New York Times.*

75. Naber, "So Our History," 229.

76. Ethen Lieser, "Immigrant Activists Call for an End to INS Raids at Airports," *Asianweek,* May 1, 2002; INS, press release, March 26, 2002, www.oig .dot.gov/sites/default/files/pr20020326.pdf.

77. "Brown Bag," *Filipinas,* July 10, 2002.

78. R. Rodriguez and Balce, "American Insecurity," 133; Jim Doyle, "Feds Invite Applicants for SFO Security Jobs," *San Francisco Chronicle,* May 6, 2002; Ethen Lieser, "Screeners Speak Out at Airport Commission Meeting," *Asianweek,* May 22, 2002; SFO Commission, *Minutes,* May 7, 2002, www .flysfo.com/sites/default/files/default/download/about/commission/agenda/pdf /minutes/M050702.pdf.

79. "Federal Screener Deployment Runs behind Schedule," *Airport Security Report* (August 14, 2002), 1.

80. Steve Rubenstein, "New Airport Screeners Take Over at San Jose," *San Francisco Chronicle*, October 2, 2002; Alan Gathright and Henry K. Lee, "Screeners Call Off Planned Walkout," *San Francisco Chronicle*, October 5, 2002.

81. Bob Egelko and Alan Gathright, "Scope of Ruling on Screeners Limited," *San Francisco Chronicle*, November 21, 2002.

82. May Chow, "Demanding Patriot Bonus, Filipino Screeners Continue to Ask for Justice," *Asianweek*, March 12, 2003.

83. Reich, Hall, and Jacobs, *Living Wages,* 12.

84. Naber, "So Our History," 228; R. Rodriguez and Balce, "American Insecurity," 136–39; Joe Garofoli, "Bay Area Anti-war Coalition Building the Beginnings of a Rainbow," *San Francisco Chronicle*, February 17, 2003.

85. Naber, "So Our History," 230–31.

86. R. Rodriguez and Balce, "American Insecurity," 138; Chow, "Demanding Patriot Bonus," *Asianweek*.

87. May Chow, "Travel Woes Prompts Screener Layoffs," *Asianweek*, May 21, 2003; George Zornick, "It's Time to Give TSA Screeners Full Union Rights," *The Nation*, January 25, 2019; "Statement of John L. Martin, Airport Director, San Francisco International Airport" and "Statement of Valarie Long, Executive Vice President, Service Employees International Union (SEIU)," July 29, 2014, in US House, *Examining TSA's Management,* 62–67.

CHAPTER 7. SANCTUARY'S GATEWAY

1. David Littlejohn, "San Francisco Airport's High-Flying Art," *Wall Street Journal*, January 26, 2001; Zahid Sardar, "Flight Patterns," *San Francisco Chronicle*, September 3, 2000; J. Hill, *SFO,* 94–95.

2. Littlejohn, "San Francisco Airport's High-Flying Art," *Wall Street Journal*.

3. Information on the SFO Museum may be found on its website at www.sfomuseum.org. Descriptions of public artworks installed there may be found on the museum's "Public Art" pages at www.sfomuseum.org/public-art.

4. David Armstrong, "Making Impressions," *San Francisco Examiner,* August 8, 1999.

5. Email from Su-Chen Hung, September 12, 2021; "*Welcome* 2000," SFO Museum, "Public Art," accessed March 11, 2022, www.sfomuseum.org/public-art/public-collection/welcome.

6. Juana Alicia, "Santuario," *Blog*, accessed March 11, 2022, https://juanaalicia.com/content/santuario/; "*Santuario*/Sanctuary 2000," SFO Museum, "Public Art," accessed March 11, 2022, www.sfomuseum.org/public-art/public-collection/sanctuarysanctuario; Armstrong, "Making Impressions," *San Francisco Examiner*; Alicia, "Oral History Interview," session 1, tape 2, side A. At the time of this writing, Alicia goes by "Alicia Araiza," but I will use "Alicia" because the relevant artworks and other sources discussed here were created using or with reference to that name.

7. Davila, *Culture Works,* 1–20.

8. SFO Museum, "Public Art," www.sfomuseum.org/public-art; Snipper, "Art Commission," 366; San Francisco Art Commission, *Annual Report*, October 4, 1967, 4, and *Annual Report*, September 30, 1969, 4.

9. Gordon, *Naked Airport*, 228–31.

10. "Ten Paintings Win Purchase Awards," *San Francisco Chronicle*, September 23, 1977; Katherine Holland and Karen Tsujimoto, "The Art Collection of the City and County of San Francisco at the San Francisco International Airport: Assessment and Recommendations," prepared for the San Francisco Arts Commission, 1995, unpublished document in the author's possession.

11. Holland and Tsujimoto, "Art Collection," 2–3; San Francisco Art Commission, *Annual Report*, 1980–81, 6–7.

12. "Hullabaloo over Art for New Airport Terminal," *San Francisco Chronicle*, May 4, 1979; Eugene Robinson, "Art Commission Is Holding Firm," *San Francisco Chronicle*, May 8, 1979; "Airport Board OKs Solution in Art Feud," *San Francisco Chronicle*, June 6, 1979; San Francisco Art Commission, *Minutes*, May 7, 1979, 2.

13. Allan Temko, "Questions about Public Art Program," *San Francisco Chronicle*, April 1, 1980.

14. San Francisco Art Commission, *Annual Report*, 1978–79, 1–5, and *Annual Report*, 1980–81, 8–9.

15. "Collection Management Policy for SFO Museum, San Francisco International Airport," 5, last updated October 20, 2020, accessed October 18, 2021, www.sfomuseum.org/sites/default/files/inline-files/CMP_201020.pdf; Mark Gladstone, "Stumbling across the Old City," *San Francisco Examiner*, November 25, 1980; Allan Temko, "The Airport's Latest Flights of Fancy," *San Francisco Chronicle*, August 5, 1982; Blake Green, "The Biggest Museum without Walls," *San Francisco Chronicle*, May 1, 1984; Sam Whiting, "SFO Art— Culture to Go," *San Francisco Chronicle*, December 18, 1992.

16. San Francisco Art Commission, Joint Art Enrichment Committee, *Minutes*, October 9, 1980, 3; Allan Temko, "Glass Artistry in a Jet-Age Showcase," *San Francisco Chronicle*, March 29, 1981.

17. "SFO Museum Exhibitions," document generated by SFO Museum for author, April 2020; "Airport Commission Resolutions for SFO Museum," document generated by SFO Museum for author, April 2020; Georgia I. Hesse, "Passage to India," *San Francisco Chronicle*, February 2, 1986; Lloyd Watson, "SFO Sets the Pace in Airport Art Exhibits," *San Francisco Chronicle*, February 22, 1988; Allan Temko, "Mexican Art Show Takes Off Beautifully," *San Francisco Chronicle*, October 29, 1981.

18. "SFO Museum Exhibitions," document generated by SFO Museum for author; Peter Stack, "Airport Shoes," *San Francisco Chronicle*, December 2, 1987; Sam Whiting, "The Art of Flying," *San Francisco Chronicle*, November 12, 1999; Littlejohn, "San Francisco Airport's High-Flying Art," *Wall Street Journal*.

19. Holland and Tsujimoto, "Art Collection," 4–14; San Francisco Arts Commission, Airport Art Steering Committee, *Minutes*, November 30, 1995, 1–2, and *Minutes*, February 8, 1996, 1.

20. Holland and Tsujimoto, "Art Collection," 13–15.

21. Email from Susan Pontious, July 14, 2020.

22. San Francisco Arts Commission, Airport Art Steering Committee, *Minutes*, September 8, 1994, 1–6; San Francisco Arts Commission, Joint Art Enrichment Committee, *Minutes*, September 2, 1983, 3.

23. Kenneth Baker, "Asian Immigrant Arts Revealed," *San Francisco Chronicle,* October 12, 1995; *On the Way Home, video installation,* 1994, accessed June 30, 2021, https://vimeo.com/22055847.

24. Su-Chen Chung, *East/West,* video, 1984/1987, accessed October 18, 2021, www.suchenhung.com/gallery/video/eastwest/index.html (accessed October 18, 2021); Gabaldi, "Conversation with Su-Chen Hung."

25. San Francisco Arts Commission, Joint Art Enrichment Committee, *Minutes*, April 6, 1995, 1–2, and *Minutes*, June 12, 1997, 2–3.

26. Email from Susan Pontious, July 14, 2020; San Francisco Arts Commission, Joint Art Enrichment Committee, *Minutes*, May 23, 1996, 1–2.

27. San Francisco Arts Commission, Joint Art Enrichment Committee, *Minutes*, November 7, 1996, 1; Alicia, "Oral History Interview," session 1, tape 2, side A.

28. Alicia, "Oral History Interview," session 1, tape 2, side A.

29. Alicia, "Oral History Interview," session 1, tape 1, side A, and session 1, tape 2, side A; M. Ramírez, "Visual Solidarity," 115–20, 126; Mazurana, "Juana Alicia's *Las Lechugueras,*" 62–63, 74–78; Alicia's website at https://juanaalicia.com.

30. M. Ramírez, "Visual Solidarity," 126; Díaz-Sanchez, "'Yemaya,'" 173–76; Alicia, "Oral History Interview," session 1, tape 1, side B; Cordova, *Heart of the Mission,* 126–51.

31. Mazurana, "Juana Alicia's *Las Lechugueras,*" 63; M. Ramírez, "Visual Solidarity," 127.

32. M. Ramírez, "Visual Solidarity," 121.

33. M. Ramírez, "Visual Solidarity," 120; Cordova, *Heart of the Mission,* 1–2, 5.

34. Schafran, *Road to Resegregation.* See Jenkins, *Bonds of Inequality,* 219–22, for a relevant discussion of bond issues.

35. Schafran, *Road to Resegregation.*

36. Schafran, *Road to Resegregation.*

37. David Bonetti, "Art That Soars," *San Francisco Examiner,* October 8, 2000.

38. Lowe, *Immigrant Acts,* 85–86; Peterson, *Sound, Space,* 9–10. See also my "Jazz and Revival."

39. As of this writing, interested parties can arrange to view the artwork behind the security gates by prior arrangement during regular business hours with at least one week's notice.

40. Chloe Veltman, "Airport Art Is Not an Oxymoron," *New York Times,* April 1, 2011; "The Art of Terminal 2," *San Francisco Chronicle,* April 3, 2011; Sam Whiting, "Taking Wing at SFO's T2," *San Francisco Chronicle,* April 16, 2011.

41. SFO Museum, "Public Art," accessed August 20, 2020, www.sfomuseum.org/public-art; "*Every Beating Second* 2011," SFO Museum, "Public Art,"

accessed August 20, 2020, www.sfomuseum.org/public-art/public-collection
/every-beating-second.

42. San Francisco Arts Commission, "San Francisco's Public Art Program
Turns 50 and Debuts Five New Artworks at SFO," press release, May 31, 2019,
www.sfartscommission.org/our-role-impact/press-room/press-release/san-francis-
cos-public-art-program-turns-50-and-debuts-five; www.sfomuseum.org/public-
art/public-collection/they-are-us-us-them-and-impossibly; "*Untitled (Becoming:
Billy + Katie 1964 #1–8)*," SFO Museum, "Public Art," accessed August 17, 2020,
www.sfomuseum.org/public-art/public-collection/untitled-becoming-billy-
katie-1964-1-8; "*Harvey Milk: Messenger of Hope*," SFO Museum, "Exhibitions," accessed August 17, 2020, www.sfomuseum.org/exhibitions/harvey-milk-
messenger-hope; email from Kai Caemmerer, June 8, 2022.

43. "San Francisco Museum of Modern Art Store Lands at Airport," *Business Wire*, March 16, 1999.

44. See Alain de Botton's *A Week at the Airport*, Walter Kirn's novel *Up in
the Air* (2001) and its 2009 film adaptation, and Steven Spielberg's 2004 film
The Terminal, based loosely on the story of a stateless Iranian refugee living at
Charles De Gaulle Airport for eighteen years.

45. Spud Hilton, "Living at SFO?," *San Francisco Chronicle*, August 20,
2017.

46. Andy Wright and Reyhan Harmanci, "City's Art Is a Victim of Neglect,
Damage and Loss," *New York Times*, April 17, 2011.

47. Alicia, "Oral History Interview," session 1, tape 2, side A.

CHAPTER 8. SHORELINE FUTURES

1. For information on birds seen at Bayfront Park, see the continually
updated records at eBird's hotspot site for Bayfront Park-Millbrae, https://ebird
.org/hotspot/L1026132.

2. SFO Commission, *San Francisco International Airport 2007 Sustainability Report*, 12, 52.

3. See, e.g., Davis and Todd, "On the Importance"; Moore, "Rise of Cheap
Nature"; Ghosh, *Great Derangement*. These authors and others differ on the
question of whether capitalism and colonialism/imperialism should be seen as
part of the same complex of human actions or disentangled to some degree.

4. Ghosh, *Great Derangement*, 35–37, 54–55.

5. Somini Sengupta, "A Crisis Right Now," *New York Times*, February 13,
2020.

6. "The lurch into the Anthropocene," as Dipesh Chakrabarty notes, "has
also been globally the story of some long anticipated social justice, at least in the
sphere of consumption." "Climate and Capital," 15.

7. SFO Commission, *San Francisco International Airport 2007 Sustainability Report*, 25, 45–47, 55.

8. Save the Bay, "Impact: Prevented Bay Fill," accessed March 29, 2021,
https://savesfbay.org/impact/prevented-bay-fill; Marshall Wilson, "SFO Officials Dump 1 of the 4 Runway-Project Plans," *San Francisco Chronicle*, August
8, 2001; Phillip Matier and Andrew Ross, "O'Donoghue's Latest Tiff," *San

Francisco Chronicle, June 2, 2002; San Francisco Board of Supervisors, "Section 6," accessed March 29, 2021, https://sfbos.org/section-6-0.

9. SFO Commission, *San Francisco International Airport 2007 Sustainability Report*, 51–53; SFO, "Biodiversity," accessed March 29, 2021, www.flysfo.com/environment/biodiversity; DUDEK, "San Francisco Garter Snake," 2–3.

10. SFO Commission, *San Francisco International Airport 2007 Sustainability Report*, 17–18; San Francisco Ordinance 81-08 (as amended), accessed March 31, 2021, www.sfbos.org/ftp/uploadedfiles/bdsupvrs/ordinanceso8/00081-08.pdf.

11. Griggs and Howarth, *Politics of Airport Expansion*, 102, 129–30, 155.

12. SFO Commission, *San Francisco International Airport 2007 Sustainability Report*, 3. The report broke down the sustainability program into nine components: climate change/global warming; energy conversation / renewable energy; air quality enhancement; noise abatement; water conservation / water quality enhancement; natural resources management and remediation; solid waste reduction and recycling; hazardous material and waste management; and green buildings and facilities (5).

13. SFO Commission, *San Francisco International Airport 2007 Sustainability Report*, 17–21.

14. SFO Commission, *San Francisco International Airport 2007 Sustainability Report*, n.p., 39–43.

15. SFO Commission, *San Francisco International Airport 2014 Sustainability Report*, n.p.

16. SFO Commission, *San Francisco International Airport 2014 Sustainability Report*, 31–51.

17. SFO Commission, *San Francisco International Airport Sustainability and Social Equity Plan*, 5–8, 12.

18. SFO Commission, *San Francisco International Airport Sustainability and Social Equity Plan*, 12, 25, 58–60.

19. Mallory Moench, "Food Workers Arrested at SFO Pay Protest," *San Francisco Chronicle*, November 27, 2019.

20. Mark Hertsgaard, "Jerry Brown vs. the Climate Wreckers," *The Nation*, September 24/October 1, 2018, 10–13; Justine Calma, "Summit Protesters Want to Save the World without Screwing Over People," *Grist*, September 13, 2018, https://grist.org/article/climate-summit-protesters-want-to-save-the-world-without-screwing-over-people/; Melanie Curry, "The Point of California's Global Climate Action Summit," *Streetsblog CAL*, September 17, 2018, https://cal.streetsblog.org/2018/09/17/the-point-of-californias-global-climate-action-summit/.

21. SFO Commission, *San Francisco International Airport Sustainability and Social Equity Plan*, 7, 9; SFO Commission, *SFO Climate Action Plan*, fiscal years 2011–20. SFO pulled back somewhat from such estimates the following year in light of the expansion of the facility with the opening of the Harvey Milk Terminal and the Grand Hyatt at SFO as well as uncertainties about how the scaling up of operations after the Covid pandemic would affect energy consumption.

22. SFO Commission, *SFO Climate Action Plan*, fiscal year 2018, 6, 31–32.

23. SFO Commission, *SFO Climate Action Plan*, fiscal year 2018, 6, 13, 24–25.

24. SFO Commission, *SFO Climate Action Plan*, fiscal year 2018, 24–27.

25. SFO Commission, *SFO Climate Action Plan*, fiscal year 2018, 20, 25–26; SFO, "Sustainable Aviation Fuel," accessed April 1, 2021, www.flysfo.com/environment/sustainable-aviation-fuel; Niraj Chokshi and Clifford Krauss, "A Big Climate Problem with Few Easy Solutions: Planes," *New York Times,* June 2, 2021.

26. SFO Commission, *San Francisco International Airport Sustainability and Social Equity Plan,* 36.

27. Gleick and Maurer, "Assessing the Costs," 21–22.

28. SFO Commission, *Airport Shoreline Protection Project*, 2–3; San Francisco Bay Conservation and Development Commission, *Living with a Rising Bay*; San Francisco Board of Supervisors, Resolution No. 517-15, accessed April 2, 2020, https://sfbos.org/ftp/uploadedfiles/bdsupvrs/resolutions15/r0517-15.pdf.

29. SFO Commission, *Airport Shoreline Protection Project*, 3; California Ocean Protection Council and California Ocean Science Trust, *Rising Seas in California*, 3–4, 7, 26, 38–39; California Natural Resources Agency and California Ocean Protection Council, *Sea Level Rise Guidance,* 3–4, 12–13, 18.

30. Shirzaei and Bürgmann, "Global Climate Change"; Troy Griggs, "More of the Bay Area Could Be Underwater in 2100 than Previously Expected," *New York Times,* March 7, 2018.

31. Taylor Kate Brown, "What Readers Are Asking about Bay Area Impacts," *San Francisco Chronicle*, September 15, 2019; Lise Alves, "San Francisco Bay Area's Multifront Plans to Fight Sea Level Rise," *Miami Beach Times,* September 20, 2019.

32. SFO, "Shoreline Protection Program," accessed April 5, 2021, www.flysfo.com/about-sfo/environmental-affairs/shoreline-protection-program; SFO Commission, *Airport Shoreline Protection Project,* 9; Paul Rogers, "SFO to Build Sea Wall around Airport," *East Bay Times,* October 10, 2019.

33. Alex Davies, "How Airports Are Protecting Themselves against Rising Seas," *Wired Magazine,* December 2, 2019.

34. Lise Alves, "California May Need to Spend $12 Billion to Defend against Sea Level Rise by 2100," *Miami Beach Times,* April 6, 2019.

35. John Horgan, "Sea Level Rise," *San Jose Mercury News,* October 2, 2019.

36. Chris Mooney and Brady Dennis, "This Could Be the Next Big Strategy for Suing over Climate Change," *Washington Post,* July 20, 2017; Denis Cuff, "Oakland and S.F. Take Big Oil to Task over Climate Change," *East Bay Times,* September 21, 2017; Nicholas Iovino, "No Rehearing in Appeal over Big Oil's Liability for Climate Change," Courthouse News Service, August 4, 2020, www.courthousenews.com/no-rehearing-in-appeal-over-big-oils-liability-for-climate-change/.

37. Paul Rogers, "New Plan to Combat Sea Level Rise in the Bay," *East Bay Times,* May 2, 2019; SFEI and SPUR, *San Francisco Bay Shoreline Adaptation Atlas,* 4.

38. SFEI and SPUR, *San Francisco Bay Shoreline Adaptation Atlas,* 170–71; SFO Commission, *Airport Shoreline Protection Project,* 4.

39. Sze, *Environmental Justice*, 81.

40. Institute for Economics and Peace, *Ecological Threat Register 2020*, 4.

41. Ghosh, *Great Derangement*, 107–10; Mitchell, *Carbon Democracy*.

42. As Amitav Ghosh argues, "Inasmuch as the fruits of the carbon economy constitute wealth, and inasmuch as the poor of the global south have historically been deprived of this wealth, it is certainly true, by every available canon of distributive justice, that they are entitled to a greater share of the rewards of that economy. But even to enter into that argument is to recognize how deeply we are mired in the Great Derangement: our lives and our choices are enframed in a pattern of history that seems to leave us nowhere to turn but toward our self-annihilation." *Great Derangement*, 110–11.

43. "One Percent of the World's Population Accounts for More Than Half of Flying Emissions," Lund University, News, November 19, 2020, www.lunduniversity.lu.se/article/one-percent-worlds-population-accounts-more-half-flying-emissions.

44. Emily Badger, "The Megacity, Untethered," *New York Times*, December 24, 2017.

45. Kasarda and Lindsay, *Aerotropolis*, 337–38.

46. For an account of the contradictory effects of tourism on a region (specifically, Mexico's Yúcatan Peninsula), see Córdoba Azcárate, *Stuck with Tourism*.

47. Kasarda and Lindsay, *Aerotropolis*, 335–44; Griggs and Howarth, *Politics of Airport Expansion*, 67, 308–9; Ritchie, "Climate Change and Flying."

48. Chakrabarty, "Climate and Capital," 11.

49. Sengupta, "Crisis Right Now," *New York Times*.

50. Lise Alves, "San Francisco Bay Area's Multifront Plans," *Miami Beach Times*.

51. Kevin Stark and Ezra David Romero, "What Can the Bay Area Do about Rising Seas? East Palo Alto Has a Few Great Answers," KQED, April 22, 2021, www.kqed.org/science/1973805/climate-solutions-in-east-palo-alto; Gennady Sheyner, "With Baylands under Flood Threat, Palo Alto Explores Projects to Address Sea Level Rise," Palo Alto Online, September 8, 2020, www.paloaltoonline.com/news/2020/09/07/with-baylands-under-flood-threat-palo-alto-explores-projects-to-address-sea-level-rise.

52. The potential of local sea-rise mitigation projects to increase flooding elsewhere in the Bay Area is discussed in Hummel et al., "Economic Evaluation."

53. Rich, *Losing Earth*.

54. Brad Plumer and Nadja Popovich, "How Decades of Racist Housing Policy Left Neighborhoods Sweltering," *New York Times*, August 24, 2020; Christopher Flavelle and Kalen Goodluck, "Dispossessed, Again," *New York Times*, October 28, 2021.

55. Ghosh, *Great Derangement*, 143–49.

56. For a survey of such activity across California, see Merenlender and Buhler, *Climate Stewardship*.

57. Association of Ramaytush Ohlone, "Purpose Statement," accessed June 24, 2021, www.ramaytush.org/about.html.

58. Sogorea Te' Land Trust, "Our Vision," accessed July 20, 2021, https://sogoreate-landtrust.org.

59. Chakrabarty, "Climate and Capital," 23. As Chakrabarty puts it, "The realization that humans—all humans, rich or poor—come late in the planet's life and dwell more in the position of passing guests than possessive hosts has to be an integral part of the perspective from which we pursue our all-too-human but legitimate quest for justice on issues to do with the iniquitous impact of anthropogenic climate change."

Bibliography

ARCHIVES

Bancroft Library, University of California, Berkeley
California Historical Society, San Francisco
California State Library, California History Room, Sacramento
GLBT Historical Society, San Francisco
Moorland-Springarn Research Center, Howard University, Washington, DC
San Francisco History Center, San Francisco Public Library
San Francisco Public Library, Government Information Center
San Francisco State University Labor Archives and Research Center
San Mateo County Historical Association Archives, Redwood City
SFO Museum
University of California History Digital Archives
US Library of Congress, Washington, DC

MAGAZINES AND NEWSPAPERS

Airport Security Report
Amsterdam News
Asianweek
Bay Area Reporter
BBC News
Black Caucus Speaks
Black Enterprise
Business Wire
California Voice
Colorlines
Commonweal

Daily Journal
East Bay Times
Ebony
El Andar
Filipinas
Friendly Times
Gay Community News
Globe Mail
Inquiry
International Examiner
Jet
Keeping Posted
Loma Prietan
Los Angeles Times
Miami Beach Times
NAIRO Reporter
The Nation
Negro History Bulletin
New York State Commission against Discrimination Newsletter
New York Times
New York Tribune
Race Relations Law Reporter
Sacramento Daily Union
San Francisco Bay Times
San Francisco Call
San Francisco Chronicle
San Francisco Examiner
San Francisco News
San Jose Mercury News
San Mateo County Labor
San Mateo County Times
San Mateo County Union Gazette
S.F. Weekly
Shield
Skanner
Sun Reporter
Travel Weekly
Tri-State Defender
Washington Post
Wing Tips
Wired Magazine

OTHER SOURCES

Acena, Albert A. "Invisible Minority No More: Filipino Americans in San Mateo County." *La Peninsula* 37, no. 1 (Summer 2008): 3–41.

Adey, Peter. *Aerial Life: Spaces, Mobilities, Affects.* Malden, MA: Wiley-Blackwell, 2010.

Akins, Damon B., and William J. Bauer Jr. *We Are the Land: A History of Native California.* Oakland: University of California Press, 2021.

Alessandro Baccari and Associates. *San Francisco International Airport: A Socioeconomic View.* San Francisco: Alessandro Baccari and Associates, 1975.

Alicia, Juana. "Oral History Interview with Juana Alicia." Interview by Paul Karlstrom, Smithsonian Archives of American Art, May 8, 2000, and July 17, 2000.

Almaguer, Tomás. *Racial Fault Lines: The Historical Origins of White Supremacy in California.* Berkeley: University of California Press, 1994.

American Municipal Association. *Airports: A Brief Outline of the Municipal, State, and Federal Problems Arising from Air Traffic.* Chicago, 1936.

Anderson, M. Kat. *Tending the Wild: Native American Knowledge and the Management of California's Natural Resources.* Berkeley: University of California Press, 2005.

Anderson, Terry H. *The Pursuit of Fairness: A History of Affirmative Action.* New York: Oxford University Press, 2004.

Armstrong, Ellis L., ed., and Michael C. Robinson and Suellen M. Hoy, assoc. eds. *History of Public Works in the United States, 1776–1976.* Chicago: American Public Works Association, 1976.

Augé, Marc. *Non-places: Introduction to an Anthropology of Supermodernity.* Translated by John Howe. London: Verso, 1995.

Avila, Eric. *The Folklore of the Freeway: Race and Revolt in the Modernist City.* Minneapolis: University of Minnesota Press, 2014.

Babow, Irving, and Edward Howden. *A Civil Rights Inventory of San Francisco: Part I, Employment.* San Francisco: Council for Civic Unity, 1958.

Baldwin, Charles Hobart. *The Urgent Importance of Taking Immediate Steps to Provide Airports to San Francisco.* C.H. Baldwin: San Francisco, 1932.

Barry, Kathleen. *Femininity in Flight: A History of Flight Attendants.* Durham, NC: Duke University Press, 2007.

Bay, Mia. *Traveling Black: A Story of Race and Resistance.* Cambridge, MA: Harvard University Press, 2021.

Bay Area Airport Planning Group. *Airport Plan for the San Francisco Bay Area.* San Francisco: Bay Area Airport Planning Group, 1949.

"The Bay Shore: Otter, Oysters, Camps, Salt, and Land." *La Peninsula* 14, no. 5 (October 1968): 3–11.

Bednarek, Janet R. *Airports, Cities, and the Jet Age: US Airports since 1945.* New York: Palgrave Macmillan, 2016.

———. *America's Airports. Airfield Development, 1918–47.* College Station: Texas A&M Press, 2001.

Beebe, Lucius, and Charles Clegg. *Steamcars to the Comstock.* Berkeley, CA: Howell-North, 1957.

Bhimull, Chandra D. *Empire in the Air: Airline Travel and the African Diaspora.* New York: New York University Press, 2017.

Bloom, Nicholas Dagen. *The Metropolitan Airport: JFK International and Modern New York*. Philadelphia: University of Pennsylvania Press, 2015.

Bolt, Beranek, and Newman, Inc. *Aviation Noise Evaluations and Projections, San Francisco Bay Region*. Canoga Park, CA: Association of Bay Area Governments, 1971.

Booker, Matthew Morse. *Down by the Bay: San Francisco's History between the Tides*. Berkeley: University of California Press, 2013.

Boubet, Francois. "Study of the Impact of the Noise Originating from the San Francisco International Airport." MS thesis, San Francisco State University, 1981.

Brechin, Gray. *Imperial San Francisco: Urban Power, Earthly Ruin*. Berkeley: University of California Press, 1999.

Breu, Kevin-Niklas. "'No Time for National Solutions': ACT UP/San Francisco and the Politics of Border-Crossing." *Global Histories* 4, no. 1 (May 2018): 20–45.

Broussard, Albert S. *Black San Francisco: The Struggle for Racial Equality in the West, 1900–1954*. Lawrence: University of Kansas Press, 1993.

Browne, Simone. *Dark Matters: On the Surveillance of Blackness*. Durham, NC: Duke University Press, 2015.

Bush, Larry. "Borderline Homophobia." *Inquiry*, June 9, 1980, 8–11.

Byrd, Jodi, Alyosha Goldstein, Jodi Melamed, and Chandan Reddy, eds. "Economics of Dispossession: Indigeneity, Race, and Capitalism." Special issue, *Social Text*, no. 135 (2018).

California Natural Resources Agency and California Ocean Protection Council. *State of California, Sea Level Rise Guidance, 2018 Update*. 2018. https://opc.ca.gov/webmaster/ftp/pdf/agenda_items/20180314/Item3_Exhibit-A_OPC_SLR_Guidance-rd3.pdf.

California Ocean Protection Council and California Ocean Science Trust. *Rising Seas in California: An Update on Sea-Level Rise Science*. Sacramento: California Ocean Protection Council, 2017.

Canaday, Margot. *The Straight State: Sexuality and Citizenship in Twentieth-Century America*. Princeton, NJ: Princeton University Press, 2009.

Chakrabarty, Dipesh. "Climate and Capital: On Conjoined Histories." *Critical Inquiry* 41 (Autumn 2014): 1–23.

Chan, Sucheng. *This Bittersweet Soil: The Chinese in California Agriculture, 1860–1910*. Berkeley: University of California Press, 1986.

Chang, Gordon H. "Chinese Railroad Workers and the US Transcontinental Railroad in Global Perspective." In *The Chinese and the Iron Road: Building the Transcontinental Railroad*, edited by Gordon H. Chang and Shelley Fisher Fishkin, 27–41. Stanford, CA: Stanford University Press, 2019.

Cheng, Cindy I-Fen. "Out of Chinatown and into the Suburbs: Chinese Americans and the Politics of Cultural Citizenship in Early Cold War America." *American Quarterly* 58, no. 4 (December 2006): 1067–90.

Chinn, Thomas W., H. Mark Lai, and Philip P. Choy. *A History of the Chinese in California: A Syllabus*. San Francisco: Chinese Historical Society of California, 1969.

Córdoba Azcárate, Matilde. *Stuck with Tourism: Space, Power, and Labor in Contemporary Yucatán.* Oakland: University of California Press, 2020.

Cordova, Cary. *Heart of the Mission: Latino Art and Politics in San Francisco.* Philadelphia: University of Pennsylvania Press, 2017.

Cronon, William. *Nature's Metropolis: Chicago and the Great West.* New York: W.W. Norton, 1991.

Cross, Ira B. *Financing an Empire: History of Banking in California.* 4 vols. Chicago: S.J. Clarke, 1927.

Crowe, Daniel E. *Prophets of Rage: The Black Freedom Struggle in San Francisco, 1945–1969.* New York: Garland, 2000.

Davila, Arlene. *Culture Works: Space, Value, and Mobility across the Neoliberal Americas.* New York: New York University Press, 2012.

Davis, Heather, and Zoe Todd. "On the Importance of a Date, or Decolonizing the Anthropocene." *ACME: An International Journal for Critical Geographies* 16, no. 4 (2017): 761–80.

Day, Iyko. *Alien Capital: Asian Racialization and the Logic of Settler Colonial Capitalism.* Durham, NC: Duke University Press, 2016.

DeLanda, Manuel. *A New Philosophy of Society: Assemblage Theory and Social Complexity.* London: Continuum, 2006.

Dellums, C.L. *International President of the Brotherhood of Sleeping Car Porters and Civil Rights Leader: Oral History Transcript and Related Material.* Berkeley: Regents of the University of California, 1973. Online Archives of California, https://oac.cdlib.org/view?docId=hb938nb6fv&brand=oac4&doc.view=entire_text.

Deverell, William. *Railroad Crossing: Californians and the Railroad, 1850–1910.* Berkeley: University of California Press, 1994.

Díaz-Sanchez, Micaela. "'Yemaya Blew That Wire Fence Down': Invoking African Spiritualities in Gloria Anzaldúa's *Borderlands/La Frontera: The New Mestiza* and the Mural Art of Juana Alicia." In *Yemoja: Gender, Sexuality, and Creativity in the Latina/o and Afro-Atlantic Diasporas,* edited by Solimar Otero and Toyin Falola, 153–86. Albany: State University of New York Press, 2013.

Dillon, Lindsey. "Civilizing Swamps in California: Formations of Race, Nature, and Property in the Nineteenth Century U.S. West." *EPD: Society and Space* 40, no. 2 (2022): 258–75.

Dow, Gerald Robert. "Bay Fill in San Francisco: A History of Change." MA thesis, San Francisco State University, 1973.

Du Bois, W.E.B. *Black Reconstruction in America, 1860 to 1880.* New York: Free Press, 1998.

DUDEK. "San Francisco Garter Snake Recovery Action Plan 2019–2029, West-Of-Bayshore Property, San Francisco International Airport, San Mateo County, California." Oakland, CA: DUDEK, July 2019. https://www.flysfo.com/sites/default/files/media/sfo/community-environment/SFO_RAP_2019-2029.pdf.

Dunn-Salahuddin, Aliyah. "A Forgotten Community, a Forgotten History: San Francisco's 1966 Uprising." In *The Strange Careers of the Jim Crow North:*

Segregation and Struggle Outside of the South, edited by Brian Purnell and Jeanne Theoharis, 211–33. New York: New York University Press, 2018.

Escobar, Arturo. *Territories of Difference: Place, Movements, Life, Redes.* Durham, NC: Duke University Press, 2008.

Fairchild, Amy L., and Eileen A. Tynan. "Policies of Containment: Immigration in the Era of AIDS." *American Journal of Public Health* 84, no. 12 (1994): 2011–22.

Feld, Steven. "A Rainforest Acoustemology." In *The Auditory Culture Reader,* edited by Michael Bull and Les Back, 223–39. Oxford: Berg, 2003.

Field, Les W., and Alan Levanthal. "'What Must It Have Been Like!' Critical Considerations of Precontact Ohlone Cosmology as Interpreted through Central California Ethnohistory." *Wicazo Sa Review* 18, no. 2 (Autumn 2003): 95–126.

Flynn, William. *Men, Money and Mud: The Story of San Francisco Airport.* San Francisco: William Flynn Publications, 1954.

Freeman, Andrew D., and Juli E. Farris. "Grassroots Impact Litigation: Mass Filing of Small Claims." *University of San Francisco Law Review* 26 (Winter 1992): 261–81.

Fuller, Gillian, and Ross Harley. *Aviopolis: A Book about Airports.* London: Black Dog, 2004.

Gabaldi, Diana. "A Conversation with Su-Chen Hung: Resonances from the Past and a Look into Her Future Projects." *Droste Effect,* January 20, 2014. www.drosteeffectmag.com/conversation-san-francisco-based-artist-su-chen-hung-resonances-past-look-upcoming-projects/.

Garbell, Maurice A. *Aircraft Noise Abatement at the San Francisco International Airport.* San Francisco: Maurice A. Garbell Inc., 1971.

George, Henry. *Our Land and Land Policy: Speeches, Lectures, and Miscellaneous Writings.* Edited by Kenneth C. Wenzer. East Lansing: Michigan State University Press, 1999.

Gleick, Peter H., and Edwin P. Maurer. *Assessing the Costs of Adapting to Sea-Level Rise: A Case Study of San Francisco Bay.* Berkeley: Pacific Institute for Studies in Development, Environment, and Security, 1990.

Ghosh, Amitav. *The Great Derangement: Climate Change and the Unthinkable.* Chicago: University of Chicago Press, 2016.

Gilroy, Paul. *Darker than Blue: On the Moral Economies of Black Atlantic Culture.* Cambridge, MA: Belknap Press of Harvard University Press, 2010.

Goldberg, David, and Trevor Griffey, eds. *Black Power at Work: Community Control, Affirmative Action, and the Construction Industry.* Ithaca, NY: Cornell University Press, 2010.

Gordon, Alastair. *Naked Airport: A Cultural History of the World's Most Revolutionary Structure.* Chicago: University of Chicago Press, 2004.

Gould, Deborah B. "ACT UP, Racism, and the Question of How to Use History." *Quarterly Journal of Speech* 98, no. 1 (February 2012): 54–62.

Gregory, Derek. *The Colonial Present: Afghanistan, Palestine, Iraq.* Malden, MA: Blackwell, 2004.

Griggs, Steven, and David Howarth. *The Politics of Airport Expansion in the United Kingdom: Hegemony, Policy, and the Rhetoric of "Sustainable Aviation."* Manchester, UK: Manchester University Press, 2013.

Guthrie, Ricardo Antonio. "Examining Political Narratives of the Black Press in the West: Dr. Carlton B. Goodlett and the San Francisco *Sun-Reporter* (1950s–60s)." PhD diss., University of California San Diego, 2006.

Gyory, Andrew. *Closing the Gate: Race, Politics, and the Chinese Exclusion Act.* Chapel Hill: University of North Carolina Press, 1998.

Haas, Lisbeth. *Conquests and Historical Identities in California, 1769–1936.* Berkeley: University of California Press, 1995.

Hall, Peter V., Ken Jacobs, and Michael Reich. "Lift Off: Raising Wages at San Francisco Airport." In *When Mandates Work: Raising Labor Standards at the Local Level,* edited by Michael Reich, Ken Jacobs, and Miranda Dietz, 70–96. Berkeley: University of California Press, 2014.

Hall, Rachel. *The Transparent Traveler: The Performance and Culture of Airport Security.* Durham, NC: Duke University Press, 2015.

Hall, Stuart. "Race, Articulation, and Societies Structured in Dominance." In *Stuart Hall: Essential Essays,* vol. 1, edited by David Morley, 172–221. Durham, NC: Duke University Press, 2019.

Hansen, Janet S., and Clinton V. Oster Jr. *Taking Flight: Education and Training for Aviation Careers.* Washington, DC: National Academy Press, 1997.

Hawkins, Richard A. "James D. Dole and the 1932 Failure of the Hawaiian Pineapple Company." *Hawaiian Journal of History* 41 (2007): 149–70.

Healy, Clyde E. *San Francisco Improved.* San Francisco: City of San Francisco, 1939.

Hernandez, Kelly Lytle. *Migra! A History of the U.S. Border Patrol.* Berkeley: University of California Press, 2010.

Hernandez, Tim Z. *All They Will Call You.* Tucson: University of Arizona Press, 2018.

Hill, John H. *SFO: A Pictorial History of the Airport.* San Francisco: San Francisco Airport Commission, 2000.

Hill, Laura Warren, and Julia Rabig. *The Business of Black Power: Community Development, Capitalism, and Corporate Responsibility in Postwar America.* Rochester, NY: University of Rochester Press, 2012.

Horiuchi, Lynn, and Tanu Sankalia, *Urban Reinventions: San Francisco's Treasure Island.* Honolulu: University of Hawaii Press, 2017.

HoSang, Daniel Martinez. *Racial Propositions: Ballot Initiatives and the Making of Postwar California.* Oakland: University of California Press, 2010.

Hummel, Michelle A., Robert Griffin, Katie Arkema, and Anne D. Guerry. "Economic Evaluation of Sea-Level Rise Adaptation Strongly Influenced by Hydrodynamic Feedbacks." *Proceedings of the National Academy of Sciences* 118, no. 29 (July 2021). https://doi.org/10.1073/pnas.2025961118.

Hunter, James Joseph. *Partners in Progress, 1864–1950: A Brief History of the Bank of California, N.A., and of the Region It Has Served for 85 Years.* New York: Newcomen Society in North America, 1950.

Hynding, Alan. *From Frontier to Suburb: The Story of the San Mateo Peninsula*. Belmont, CA: Star, 1982.

Igler, David. *Industrial Cowboys: Miller & Lux and the Transformation of the Far West, 1850–1920*. Berkeley: University of California Press, 2005.

Institute for Economics and Peace. *Ecological Threat Register 2020: Understanding Ecological Threats, Resilience and Peace*. Sydney, Australia: IEP, September 2020. Available from: www.visionofhumanity.org/ wp-content /uploads/2020/10/ETR_2020_web-1.pdf.

Isenberg, Alison. *Designing San Francisco: Art, Land, and Urban Renewal in the City by the Bay*. Princeton, NJ: Princeton University Press, 2017.

Issel, William. "New Deal and Wartime Origins of San Francisco's Postwar Political Culture: The Case of Growth Politics and Policy." In *The Way We Really Were: The Golden State in the Second Great War*, edited by Roger Lotchin, 68–92. Urbana: University of Illinois Press, 2000.

Issel, William, and Robert W. Cherny. *San Francisco, 1865–1932: Politics, Power, and Urban Development*. Berkeley: University of California Press, 1986.

Jacobs, Ken, and Michael Reich. "When Do Mandates Work?" In *When Mandates Work: Raising Labor Standards at the Local Level*, edited by Michael Reich, Ken Jacobs, and Miranda Dietz, 1–43. Berkeley: University of California Press, 2014.

Jenkins, Destin. *The Bonds of Inequality: Debt and the Making of the American City*. Chicago: University of Chicago Press, 2021.

Jenkins, Destin, and Justin Leroy. *Histories of Racial Capitalism*. New York: Columbia University Press, 2021.

Karuka, Manu. *Empire's Tracks: Indigenous Nations, Chinese Workers, and the Transcontinental Railroad*. Oakland: University of California Press, 2019.

Kasarda, John D., and Greg Lindsey. *Aerotropolis: The Way We'll Live Next*. New York: Farrar, Straus, and Giroux, 2011.

Kelley, Robin D.G. *Race Rebels: Culture, Politics, and the Black Working Class*. New York: Free Press, 1994.

———. "What Did Cedric Robinson Mean by Racial Capitalism?" *Boston Review*, January 12, 2017. https://bostonreview.net/race/robin-d-g-kelley-what-did-cedric-robinson-mean-racial-capitalism.

Kim, Alice S. "Airport Modern: The Space between International Departures and Arrivals in Modern Korean National Imaginings." PhD diss., University of California Berkeley, 2013.

Kinnaird, Lawrence. *History of the Greater San Francisco Bay Region*. 3 vols. New York: Lewis Historical Publishing, 1966.

Kropp, Phoebe S. *California Vieja: Culture and Memory in a Modern American Place*. Berkeley: University of California Press, 2006.

Kruman, Marc W. "Quotas for Blacks: The Public Works Administration and the Black Construction Worker." *Labor History* 16, no. 1 (1975): 37–51.

Lang, Clarence. *Grassroots at the Gateway: Class Politics and Black Freedom Struggle in St. Louis, 1936–75*. Ann Arbor: University of Michigan Press, 2009.

Lawson, William R. *Achievements, Federal Works Agency, Work Projects Administration, Northern California: Jobs, 1935–1939.* San Francisco: Works Progress Administration, Northern California, 1939.

Leighninger, Robert D., Jr. *Long-Term Public Investment: The Forgotten Legacy of the New Deal.* Columbia: University of South Carolina Press, 2007.

Lightfoot, Kent G. *Indians, Missionaries, and Merchants: The Legacy of Colonial Encounters on the California Frontiers.* Berkeley: University of California Press, 2004.

Lipsitz, George. *The Possessive Investment in Whiteness: How White People Profit from Identity Politics.* Philadelphia: Temple University Press, 1998.

Lo, Clarence. *Small Property versus Big Government: Social Origins of the Property Tax Revolt.* Berkeley: University of California Press, 1990.

Lotchin, Roger W. "The City and the Sword: San Francisco and the Rise of the Metropolitan-Military Complex, 1919–1941." *Journal of American History* 65, no. 4 (March 1979): 996–1020.

——— "The Darwinian City: The Politics of Urbanization in San Francisco between the World Wars." *Pacific Historical Review* 48, no. 3 (August 1979): 357–81.

———. *Fortress California, 1910–1961: From Warfare to Welfare.* New York: Oxford University Press, 1992.

———. "The Political Culture of the Metropolitan-Military Complex." *Social Science History* 16, no. 2 (Summer 1992): 275–99.

Lowe, Lisa. *Immigrant Acts: On Asian American Cultural Politics.* Durham, NC: Duke University Press, 1996.

———. *The Intimacies of Four Continents.* Durham, NC. Duke University Press, 2015.

Luibhéid, Eithne. *Entry Denied: Controlling Sexuality at the Border.* Minneapolis: University of Minnesota Press, 2002.

Madley, Benjamin. *An American Genocide: The United States and the California Indian Catastrophe, 1846–1873.* New Haven, CT: Yale University Press, 2016.

Mazurana, Diane. "Juana Alicia's *Las Lechugueras* / The Women Lettuce Workers." *Meridians* 3, no. 1 (2002): 54–81.

McDonnell, F. Thomas. "The San Francisco International Airport Noise Problem." MA thesis, San Francisco State University, 1982.

McWilliams, Carey, Matt S. Meier, and Alma M. García. *North from Mexico: The Spanish-Speaking People of the United States.* 3rd ed. Santa Barbara, CA: Praeger, 2016.

Merenlender, Adina. *Climate Stewardship: Taking Collective Action to Protect California.* With Brendan Buhler. Oakland: University of California Press, 2021.

Miller, Paul T. *The Postwar Struggle for Civil Rights: African Americans in San Francisco, 1945–1975.* New York: Routledge, 2011.

Milliken, Randall, Laurence H. Shoup, and Beverly R. Ortiz. *Ohlone/Costanoan Indians of the San Francisco Peninsula and Their Neighbors, Yesterday and Today.* Oakland, CA: Archaeological and Historical Consultants, 2009.

Mitchell, Timothy. *Carbon Democracy: Political Power in the Age of Oil*. London: Verso, 2013.

Moore, Jason. "The Rise of Cheap Nature." In *Anthropocene or Capitalocene? Nature, History, and the Crisis of Capitalism*, edited by Jason Moore, 78–115. Oakland, CA: PM Press, 2016.

Mooser, William, Jr. *Report on Progress of the Works Program in San Francisco*. San Francisco: Works Progress Administration, 1938.

Moretti, Gerald Richard. "A Communication and Problem-Solving Study of the Jet Airline Noise Conflict at the San Francisco International Airport." MA thesis, San Francisco State University, 1962.

Murch, Donna J. *Living for the City: Migration, Education, and the Rise of the Black Panther Party in Oakland, California*. Chapel Hill: University of North Carolina Press, 2010.

Naber, Nadine C. "So Our History Doesn't Become Your Future: The Local and Global Politics of Coalition Building post September 11th." *Journal of Asian American Studies* 5, no. 3 (October 2002): 217–42.

National Research Council. *Sea-Level Rise for the Coasts of California, Oregon, and Washington: Past, Present, and Future*. Washington, DC: National Academies Press, 2012.

Northrup, Herbert R., Armand J. Thieblot, and William N. Chernish. *The Negro in the Air Transport Industry*. Philadelphia: Wharton School of Finance and Commerce, 1971.

Northrop, Vernon D., and Bernard M. Doolin. *Preliminary Study: Proposed Airport Development for the State of California Showing Past Expenditures and Estimated Future Costs*. Sacramento: Emergency Relief Administration for California, 1934.

Olsen, Gilbert, and Richard Floyd. "The San Jose Railroad and Crocker's Pets." In *Chinese Argonauts: An Anthology of the Chinese Contributions to the Historical Development of Santa Clara County*, edited by Gloria Sun Hom, 132–42. Los Altos Hills, CA: Foothill Community College, 1971.

Orenic, Liesl Miller. *On the Ground: Labor Struggle in the American Airline Industry*. Urbana: University of Illinois Press, 2009.

Ortlepp, Anke. *Jim Crow Terminals: The Desegregation of American Airports*. Athens: University of Georgia Press, 2017.

Patel, Raj, and Jason Moore. *A History of the World in Seven Cheap Things*. Oakland: University of California Press, 2017.

Peterson, Marina. *Atmospheric Noise: The Indefinite Urbanism of Los Angeles*. Durham, NC: Duke University Press, 2021.

———. "Atmospheric Sensibilities: Noise Annoyance, and Indefinite Urbanism." *Social Text* 131 35, no. 2 (June 2017): 69–90.

———. *Sound, Space, and the City: Civic Performance in Downtown Los Angeles*. Philadelphia: University of Pennsylvania Press, 2010.

Pitt, Leonard. *The Decline of the Californios: A Social History of the Spanish-Speaking Californians, 1846–1890*. Berkeley: University of California Press, 1966.

Pitti, Stephen J. *The Devil in Silicon Valley: Northern California, Race, and Mexican Americans*. Princeton, NJ: Princeton University Press, 2003.

Porter, Eric. "Affirming and Disaffirming Actions: Remaking Race in the 1970s." In *America in the 1970s*, edited by Beth Bailey and David Farber, 50–74. Lawrence: University Press of Kansas, 2004.

———. "Jazz and Revival." In *In the Wake of Hurricane Katrina: New Paradigms and Social Visions*, edited by Clyde Woods, 167–87. Baltimore: Johns Hopkins University Press, 2010.

President's Airport Commission. *The Airport and Its Neighbors*. Washington, DC: US Government Printing Office, 1952.

Puar, Jasbir. *Terrorist Assemblages: Homonationalism in Queer Times*. Durham, NC: Duke University Press, 2007.

Public Works Administration. *America Builds: The Record of PWA*. Washington, DC: PWA, Division of Information, 1939.

———. *The First Three Years: PWA*. Washington, DC: US Government Printing Office, 1936.

Ramírez, Catherine S. *Assimilation: An Alternative History*. Oakland: University of California Press, 2020.

Ramírez, Mauricio E. "Visual Solidarity with Central America: An Interview with Maestra Muralista Juana Alicia." *Chiricú Journal: Latino/a Literatures, Arts, and Cultures* 4, no. 1 (Fall 2019): 115–27.

Record, Wilson. *Minority Groups and Intergroup Relations in the San Francisco Bay Area*. University of California Berkeley Institute of Governmental Studies, 1963.

Regnery, Dorothy F. "The Oldest Railroad Station in California." *La Peninsula* 21, no. 3 (May 1984): 4–14.

Reich, Michael, Peter Hall, and Ken Jacobs. *Living Wages and Economic Performance: The San Francisco Airport Model*. Berkeley: University of California Berkeley Institute of Industrial Relations, March 2003.

Reinhardt, Richard. *Treasure Island: San Francisco's Exposition Years*. San Francisco: Scrimshaw Press, 1973.

Rich, Nathaniel. *Losing Earth*. New York: Macmillan, 2019.

Ritchie, Hannah. "Climate Change and Flying: What Share of Global CO_2 Emissions Come from Aviation?" Our World in Data, October 22, 2020. https://ourworldindata.org/co2-emissions-from-aviation.

Robinson, Cedric J. *Black Marxism: The Making of the Black Radical Tradition*. London: Zed Press, 1983.

Rodriguez, Joseph A. *City against Suburb: The Culture Wars in an American Metropolis*. Westport, CT: Praeger, 1999.

Rodríguez, Juana Maria. *Queer Latinidad: Identity Practices, Discursive Spaces*. New York: New York University Press, 2003.

Rodriguez, Robyn, and Nerissa S. Balce, "American Insecurity and Radical Filipino Community Politics." *Peace Review* 16, no. 2 (June 2004): 131–40.

Rome, Adam. *The Bulldozer in the Countryside: Suburban Sprawl and the Rise of American Environmentalism*. New York: Cambridge University Press, 2001.

Roque Ramírez, Horacio Nelson. "Communities of Desire: Queer Latina/Latino History and Memory, San Francisco Bay Area, 1960s–1990s." PhD diss., University of California Berkeley, 2001.

———. "'That's *My* Place!': Negotiating Racial, Sexual, and Gender Politics in San Francisco's Gay Latino Alliance, 1975–1983." *Journal of the History of Sexuality* 12, no. 2 (April 2003): 224–58.

Rosen, John J. "'Work for Me Also Means Work for the Community I Come From': Black Contractors, Black Capitalism, and Affirmative Action in the Bay Area." In *Black Power at Work: Community Control, Affirmative Action, and the Construction Industry*, edited by David Goldberg and Trevor Griffey, 68–89. Ithaca, NY: Cornell University Press, 2010.

Rubens, Lisa. "The 1939 San Francisco World's Fair: The New Deal, the New Frontier and the Pacific Basin." PhD diss., University of California Berkeley, 2004.

Saldaña-Portillo, María Josefina. *Indian Given: Racial Geographies across Mexico and the United States*. Durham, NC: Duke University Press, 2016.

Salter, Mark. "The Global Airport: Managing Space, Speed, and Security." In *Politics at the Airport*. ed. Mark Salter, 1–28. Minneapolis: University of Minnesota Press, 2008.

Sampson, Anthony. *Empires of the Sky: The Politics, Contests and Cartels of World Airlines*. New York: Random House, 1984.

San Francisco Art Commission. *Annual Report*, various years. San Francisco Public Library, Government Information Center.

———. *Minutes*, various years. San Francisco Public Library, Government Information Center.

San Francisco Arts Commission, Airport Art Steering Committee. *Minutes*, various years. San Francisco Public Library, Government Information Center.

San Francisco Arts Commission. Joint Art Enrichment Committee. *Minutes*, various years. San Francisco Public Library, Government Information Center.

San Francisco Bay Conservation and Development Commission. *Living with a Rising Bay: Vulnerability and Adaptation in San Francisco Bay and on Its Shoreline*. San Francisco: SFBCDC, 2011.

———. *San Francisco Bay Plan*. San Francisco: SFBCDC, January 1969, January 1979, as amended.

San Francisco Board of Supervisors, Airport Committee. *San Francisco Airport: A Report*. San Francisco: The Committee, 1931.

San Francisco Department of the Environment and SFPUC (San Francisco Public Utilities Commission). *Climate Action Plan for San Francisco: Local Actions to Reduce Greenhouse Gas Emissions*. San Francisco: City of San Francisco, 2004.

San Francisco Ecology Center. *The San Francisco Airport Expansion Plan: A Critical Study*. San Francisco: San Francisco Ecology Center, 1973.

Saxton, Alexander. *The Indispensable Enemy: Labor and the Anti-Chinese Movement in California*. Berkeley: University of California Press, 1971.

Schaberg, Christopher. *The End of Airports*. New York: Bloomsbury, 2016.

———. "Mini Object Lesson: Why Attack Airports?" *The Atlantic*, July 2, 2016.

———. *The Textual Life of Airports: Reading the Culture of Flight.* New York: Continuum, 2012.

Schafer, R. Murray. *The Soundscape: Our Sonic Environment and the Tuning of the World.* Rochester, VT: Destiny Books, 1994.

Schafran, Alex. *The Road to Resegregation: Northern California and the Failure of Politics.* Oakland: University of California Press, 2018.

Schiller, Reuel. *Forging Rivals: Race, Class, Law, and the Collapse of Postwar Liberalism.* New York: Cambridge University Press, 2015.

Schrenk, Lisa D. "Visions of Progress and Peace: Foreign Architectural Representations at the Century of Progress and Golden Gate International Expositions." In *Urban Reinventions: San Francisco's Treasure Island,* edited by Lynn Horiuchi and Tanu Sankalia, 69–95. Honolulu: University of Hawaii Press, 2017.

Scott, Mel. *The San Francisco Bay Area: A Metropolis in Perspective.* Berkeley: University of California Press, 1959.

Self, Robert. *American Babylon: Race and the Struggle for Postwar Oakland.* Princeton, NJ: Princeton University Press, 2003.

SFEI (San Francisco Estuary Institute) and SPUR (San Francisco Bay Area Planning and Urban Research Association). *San Francisco Bay Shoreline Adaptation Atlas: Working with Nature to Plan for Sea Level Rise Using Operational Landscape Units.* Publication #915. Richmond, CA: San Francisco Estuary Institute, 2019. www.sfei.org/sites/default/files/biblio_files/SFEI%20 SF%20Bay%20Shoreline%20Adaptation%20Atlas%20April%202019_ lowres_0.pdf.

SFHRC (San Francisco Human Rights Commission). *Annual Airport Employment Profile,* various years. San Francisco Public Library, Government Information Center.

———. *Annual Report,* various years. San Francisco Public Library, Government Information Center.

———. *Meeting Minutes,* various years. San Francisco Public Library, Government Information Center.

SFO (San Francisco International Airport) Commission. *Airport Shoreline Protection Project Fiscal Feasibility Study.* San Francisco, 2019. https://sfgov.legistar .com/View.ashx?M=F&ID=7513892&GUID=EC2CED9E-FB3A-4A25-930E-D481824BE6AD.

———. *Facts about San Francisco International Airport.* San Francisco: San Francisco International Airport Public Relations Office, 1967.

———. *Final Environmental Impact Report—San Francisco International Airport Expansion Program.* Vol. 2, *Comments and Responses.* San Francisco: Airport Commission, 1973.

———. *Minutes,* various years. San Francisco Public Library, Government Information Center.

———. *San Francisco International Airport Sustainability and Social Equity Plan: SFO's Green and Blueprint to Achieve a Sustainable Future.* San Francisco, 2019. www.flysfo.com/sites/default/files/media/sfo/community-environment /Sustainability_and_Social_Equity_Plan.pdf.

————. *San Francisco International Airport 2007 Sustainability Report*. By Vanasse Hangen Bruslin Inc. San Francisco, 2007. www.flysfo.com/sites /default/files/default/download/about/reports/pdf/ESReport-2007.pdf.

————. *San Francisco International Airport 2014 Sustainability Report*. By Vanasse Hangen Bruslin Inc. San Francisco, 2014. www.flysfo.com/sites/default /files/media/sfo/community-environment/sfo-2014-sustainability-report.pdf.

————. *SFO Climate Action Plan*, fiscal years 2011–20. www.flysfo.com /environment/sustainability-facts-figures.

SFPUC (San Francisco Public Utilities Commission). *Factual Data on San Francisco (International) Airport*. San Francisco: Airport Department, 1945.

————. *Proposed Expansion Program, San Francisco (International) Airport*. San Francisco: Airport Department, 1945.

————. *Report (Annual Report* as of 1949–50), various years. San Francisco Public Library, Government Information Center.

————. *San Francisco International Airport 1937*. San Francisco: The Commission, 1937.

Shanken, Andrew M. "How to Celebrate a Bridge." In *Urban Reinventions: San Francisco's Treasure Island*, edited by Lynn Horiuchi and Tanu Sankalia, 49–68. Honolulu: University of Hawaii Press, 2017.

————. *Into the Void Pacific: Building the 1939 San Francisco World's Fair*. Oakland: University of California Press, 2014.

Sharpe, Christina. *In the Wake: On Blackness and Being*. Durham, NC: Duke University Press, 2016.

Sheller, Mimi. "Air Mobilities on the U.S.-Caribbean Border: Open Skies and Closed Gates." *Communication Review* 13, no. 4 (2010): 269–88.

Sheller, Mimi, and John Urry. "The New Mobilities Paradigm." *Environment and Planning* 38 (2006): 207–26.

Shirzaei, Manoochehr, and Roland Bürgmann. "Global Climate Change and Local Land Subsidence Exacerbate Inundation Risk to the San Francisco Bay Area." *Science Advances* 4, no. 3 (March 7, 2018). https://advances.sciencemag .org/content/4/3/eaap9234.full.

Short, C. W., and R. Stanley Brown. *Public Buildings: A Survey of Architecture of Projects Constructed by Federal and Other Governmental Bodies between the Years 1933 and 1939 with the Assistance of the Public Works Administration*. Washington, DC: US Government Printing Office, 1939.

Sides, Josh. *Erotic City: Sexual Revolutions and the Making of Modern San Francisco*. New York: Oxford University Press, 2011.

Simard, H. A. "Portion of Bayshore Freeway Expected to Be Completed Early Next Year." *California Highways and Public Works* 26, nos. 7–8 (July–August 1947): 10–13.

Singh, Nikhil Pal. *Black Is a Country: Race and the Unfinished Struggle for Democracy*. Cambridge, MA: Harvard University Press, 2005.

Skowronek, Russell K. "Sifting the Evidence: Perceptions of Life at the Ohlone (Costanoan) Missions of Alta California." *Ethnohistory* 45, no. 4 (Autumn 1998): 675–708.

Smith, Jason Scott. *Building New Deal Liberalism: The Political Economy of Public Works, 1933–56*. New York: Cambridge University Press, 2006.

Smith, Stacey L. *Freedom's Frontier: California and the Struggle of Unfree Labor, Emancipation, and Reconstruction.* Chapel Hill: University of North Carolina Press, 2013.

Snipper, Martin. "Art Commission of the City and County of San Francisco." *Performing Arts Review* 1, no. 2 (January 1, 1969): 365–69.

Snow, John William. "Air Freight Forwarding: A Legal and Economic Analysis." *Journal of Air Law and Commerce* 32, no. 4 (1966): 485–95.

Solnit, Rebecca. *Infinite City: A San Francisco Atlas.* Berkeley: University of California Press, 2010.

Somerville, Siobhan B. "Sexual Aliens and the Racialized State: A Queer Reading of the 1952 U.S. Immigration and Nationality Act." In *Queer Migrations: Sexuality, U.S. Citizenship, and Border Crossings,* edited by Eithne Luibhéid and Lionel Cantú Jr., 75–91. Minneapolis: University of Minnesota Press, 2005.

Stanger, Frank M. "A California Rancho under Three Flags: A History of Rancho Buri Buri in San Mateo County." *California Historical Society Quarterly* 17, no. 3 (September 1938): 245–59.

———. *South from San Francisco: San Mateo County, California, Its History and Heritage.* San Mateo: San Mateo County Historical Association, 1963.

Svanevik, Michael, and Shirley Burgett. *San Mateo County Chronicles.* 3rd ed. Svanevik and Burgett, 1995.

Sze, Julie. *Environmental Justice in a Moment of Danger.* Oakland: University of California Press, 2020.

Tiemeyer, Philip James. *Plane Queer: Labor, Sexuality, and AIDS in the History of Male Flight Attendants.* Berkeley: University of California Press, 2013.

US Federal Aviation Agency. *Sounds of the Twentieth Century.* Washington, DC: US Government Printing Office, 1961.

US Federal Works Agency. *Final Report on the WPA Program, 1935–43.* Washington, DC: US Government Printing Office, 1947.

US House. *Aircraft Noise Problems: Hearings before Subcommittees of the Committee on Interstate and Foreign Commerce.* 86th and 87th Cong. Washington, DC: US Government Printing Office, 1963.

———. *Examining TSA's Management of the Screening Partnership Program: Hearing before the Subcommittee on Transportation Security of the Committee on Homeland Security, House of Representatives.* 113th Cong., July 29, 2014. Washington, DC: US Government Publishing Office, 2015.

———. *Exclusion and Deportation Amendments of 1983: Hearing before the Subcommittee on Immigration, Refugees, and International Law, of the Committee on the Judiciary.* 98th Cong., June 28, 1984. Washington, DC: US Government Printing Office, 1984.

Van Vleck, Jenifer. *Empire of the Air: Aviation and the American Ascendancy.* Cambridge, MA: Harvard University Press, 2013.

Vernon, James. "Heathrow and the Making of Neoliberal Britain." *Past and Present* 252, no. 1 (August 2021): 213–47.

Wachter, Robert M. *The Fragile Coalition: Scientists, Activists, and AIDS.* New York: St. Martin's Press, 1991.

Walker, Richard A. *The Country in the City: The Greening of the San Francisco Bay Area*. Seattle: University of Washington Press, 2008.

Weems, Robert E., Jr. *Desegregating the Dollar: African-American Consumerism in the Twentieth Century*. New York: New York University Press, 1998.

Weheliye, Andrew G. *Habeas Viscus: Racializing Assemblages, Biopolitics, and Black Feminist Theories of the Human*. Durham, NC: Duke University Press, 2014.

Weiss, Robert J. *"We Want Jobs": A History of Affirmative Action*. New York: Garland, 1997.

Wilson, Neill C. *400 California Street: A Century Plus Five*. San Francisco: Bank of California, 1969.

Wurm, Ted, and Harre W. Demoro. *The Silver Short Line: A History of the Virginia & Truckee Railroad*. Glendale, CA: Trans-Anglo Books, 1983.

Index

Note: Illustrations are indicated by *italic* page numbers.

Climate Action Plan for San Francisco
(2004), 205
Climate Action Plans, 209–11, 215
climate change: Bay Area activism on,
219–20; climate justice and social
equity, 203–4, 206–9, 214–20;
decolonial responses to, 220–21; effects
of, in sustainability programs, 211–14;
as existential threat, 214; greenhouse
gas emissions in, 201–2, 204, 205–6,
209–11, 215–16, 218–19; in "holistic
sustainability" programs, 207;
mitigation efforts, 200–202; municipal
and state mandates on, 204–6; resilience
to, 211–14; and sea-level rise, 11–12,
203, 211–14, 218; self-representation
and public relations in, 201–2, 206–8.
See also sustainability
Climate Change Goals and Action Plan (San
Francisco), 205
Clinton, Bill, and administration, 170–71
Coalition for Immigration and Refugee
Rights and Services, 162–63
Coast Guard, US, 61, 70–71, 74–75
collective bargaining, 102, 109, 115–16, 178
colonialism/settler colonialism: and Black
labor, 91; in differing degrees of
inclusion, 150, 151, 155–56, 178; in
early development, 41, 43–44, 54–55; in
Filipinx immigration, 173–74; and the
Flight Festival, 71–72; at the Golden Gate
International Exposition, 61–62; and jet
noise politics, 120–21, 124, 141–42,
145–46; Mexican, 19–22; "railroad
colonialism," 230n39; represented in
public art, 185, 195, 197–99; SFO in
relationships of, 1–6, 9–10, 87; sinking
infrastructure reproducing, 219; Spanish,
15–19; and sustainability, 203, 214–15,
219; in transformation of land and
people, 14, 16–19, 22–23, 25, 27–30, 38,
202, 228n9; US, 22–24. *See also*
imperialism/imperial reach
*Colorado Anti-Discrimination Commission
v. Continental Airlines*, 95
commerce: in early development, 42–43, 47,
50, 60, 62–63; in jet noise politics,
137–38, 142; in postwar expansion,
69–70, 75–76, 77, 79–80, 84; and
sustainability, 215–16; in transformation of wetlands, 20–21, 22, 26
commuter flights, 69–70
commutes, automobile, 86, 94, 194–95,
209–10

competition, regional and interregional,
43–44, 53–54, 66–67, 77–78, 81–82
concessions/concessionaires, 93, 102–3,
110–13, 114–15, 179, 212–13
construction: Black employment opportunities and discrimination in, 92–93, 107,
111–12, 114–15; in early development,
56–59, 65; in jet noise politics, 132–34,
138–39, 141; New Deal programs in
funding, 49–60, 63–64; postwar boom
in, 69–70; projected benefits from, 78,
79; public art budgeted in, 184–86;
racial discrimination in employment in,
72, 92–93, 107, 111–12, 114–15; US
military in, 41–42, 64–65
consumers/consumerism: Black, 97, 108–9;
in jet noise politics, 124, 126–27,
128–29, 145–46; LGBTQ, spending
power of, in inclusion, 159–60; in public
art, 195–96; in sustainability, 215;
white, as beneficiaries of airport
expansion, 72
Coolidge, Calvin, 47
Cooper, Sally, 134–35, 136–37
CORE (Congress of Racial Equality), 94
Cortiñas, Jorge, 164, 171
cosmopolitanism/cosmopolitan image: Bay
Area, 4–5, 72, 155–56, 157–58; in Black
employment, 94, 96, 97–98; of Black
skycaps, 89; in public art and cultural
programs, 187–88, 195–96
cost-benefit analyses: in affirmative action,
98; and climate change impacts,
216–17; in jet noise politics, 120, 125,
126–28, 134–36, 137–39, 147
cost of living, 192–93, 198
Cranston, Alan, 154
Crissy, Myron S., 39–40
Crocker, Charles, 28
Crocker, Edwin Bryant, 28
Cruz Garcia, Arturo Javier, 154–55, 158
culture: Indigenous, revitalization of, 220;
public art in support of, 181–82;
queer-friendly, 155–56, 157–58, 172.
See also multiculturalism/multicultural
display
curatorial practice, 181–82, 188–89
custodial work, 116, 118
CWA (California Civil Works Administration), 51–54

Dannemeyer, William, 167
Davila, Arlene, 184
DC-3s, 54